Reflections
OF A TRIAL JUDGE

A Collection of Lectures by

The Honorable William G. Young

of the United States District Court

for the District of Massachusetts

Massachusetts Continuing Legal Education, Inc.
Boston, MA 02108

ISBN 1-57589-099-2
Library of Congress Card Number 98-87892

INTRODUCTION

As I go through the draft manuscript of what will become this book, I am reminded of words that my father gave me 14 years ago–words that so clearly and accurately captured what he had tried to do as a judge. It is with pride, respect and love that I now give these words back to my father and, in doing so, know that he has thoroughly succeeded, "with heart and soul and mind to do justice."

MARK E. YOUNG, ESQ.
PEABODY & ARNOLD LLP

Boston, Massachusetts

OCTOBER 20, 1998

ABOUT JUDGE YOUNG

The Honorable William G. Young has been an active trial judge for over 20 years, serving on both the Massachusetts Superior Court (1977-1985) and the U.S. District Court (1985-present). Beginning in January 1999, he will succeed The Honorable Joseph L. Tauro as Chief Judge of the U.S. District Court, District of Massachusetts. After receiving his A.B., *magna cum laude*, from Harvard University in 1962, Judge Young served two years as Captain in the United States Army. His legal career began in 1967, when he was admitted to the Massachusetts bar upon graduating from Harvard Law School. He served as law clerk to The Honorable Raymond S. Wilkins, Chief Judge of the Supreme Judicial Court. Following his clerkship, he practiced law as an associate and then as a partner at the Boston law firm of Bingham, Dana & Gould. His legal career has also included stints as a Special Assistant Attorney General and as Chief Counsel for the late Francis W. Sargent, former Governor of Massachusetts.

A longtime teacher of evidence and trial advocacy, who is commonly referred to as "the Education Judge," Judge Young has taught at several law schools, including Harvard, Boston College and Boston University. He is active in judicial education at the Federal Judicial Center, National Judicial College and the Flaschner Judicial Institute. Judge Young volunteers much of his time to educating the bar and has been a staple at continuing legal education programs and institutions, including Massachusetts Continuing Legal Education, Inc. (MCLE), Practising Law Institute (PLI) and Suffolk University Law School. He has won national acclaim for his work on MCLE's award-winning annual lecture series *On Trial with Judge Young*, which offers each fall an intensive 15-week study of trial techniques and trial evidence.

In addition to teaching in the classroom, Judge Young has written extensively. He is the principal author of *Massachusetts Evidentiary Standards* (1992) and co-author of the 1989 and 1991 supplements to Hughes, *Massachusetts Evidence (Massachusetts Practice Series)* and "*Daubert's* Gatekeeper: The Role of the District Judge in Admitting Expert Testimony" (Tulane Law Review).

FOREWORD

Throughout the lectures in this book, you will come across references by Judge Young to the judge as teacher. Although Judge Young has worn and continues to wear many hats, the description of teacher perfectly characterizes him. He is the quintessential teacher. He flourishes in that role, and as a result, the bar—whether sitting in the courtroom or the classroom—benefits greatly.

As only modestly reflected in the biographical abstract included in this book, Judge Young has taught extensively at both law schools and continuing legal education seminars and conferences. It is from the CLE context that the idea for this collection arose: Since 1990, Judge Young has generously donated a Saturday morning each December to teach evidence and trial techniques at MCLE. This book is an attempt to capture and distill several of those lectures from transcript form into a more permanent, textual format. The lectures exist in as much of their original form as possible, in order to give the reader a sense of being there in the classroom during those remarkable Saturday morning events. Judge Young has not had an opportunity to edit these versions of his lectures; in fact, with this first edition, some of the lectures are being printed for the very first time.

Our intent in producing this compilation was to thank and honor Judge Young for his selfless service of educating the bar. MCLE intends to both honor and surprise Judge Young by presenting him with this publication on the occasion of MCLE's Annual Meeting Reception, December 2, 1998. At that presentation, MCLE will dedicate all revenue from sales of ***Reflections of a Trial Judge*** to support The Honorable William G. Young Scholarship Fund, which will be established to provide subsidies to lawyers who wish to attend MCLE programs. MCLE hopes that the beneficial effect of the scholarship initiative will reverberate through generations of lawyers, as a lasting "thank you" to Judge Young for his volunteer spirit and for the intellectual gift he so willingly shares.

We at MCLE hope that this publication will preserve some of the dynamic lessons taught by Judge Young over the years—and may it demonstrate to him the significant value that MCLE places upon his friendship, his professional commitment to continuing legal education and his immense talent as judge and teacher.

***

Some words of acknowledgment must be expressed to all those who were instrumental in this first edition from its inception through to its presentation to Judge Young:

Of course, we thank Judge William G. Young for his gift of teaching and inspiring so many. MCLE is grateful to have, through these lectures, an ongoing archive of

Judge Young's thoughts, his mastery of jurisprudence, his valuable and instructive courtroom advice and his sparkling wit.

We thank MCLE's Board of Trustees for bringing CLE to Massachusetts 30 years ago and for maintaining a standard of excellence ever since. It is through their support of MCLE's efforts that Judge Young's lectures have become accessible to so many lawyers over the years.

Special thanks are in order to Salvatore Ricciardone, Esq., MCLE Publications Attorney, whose energy, sensitivity and remarkable publishing talent were valuable in the compilation of this collection of Judge Young's lectures. Sal's interests lie in the nexus of law, education and publishing: An enthusiastic student of jurisprudence and an admirer of Judge Young's dynamic teaching style, Sal is also familiar with Judge Young's commanding courtroom presence, having practiced in the Judge's motions session while he was an associate at Palmer & Dodge LLP. Sal compiled the lectures, thoughtfully selected the quotations and photographs and skillfully managed the copyediting that transformed the lecture transcripts into the written word. He did so while exercising complete discretion, taking care to keep the project well hidden from Judge Young right up until the surprise presentation at MCLE's Annual Meeting Reception. We congratulate Salvatore Ricciardone on his editorial efforts, and thank him for the significant contribution he makes to MCLE.

Finally, we thank the many persons at MCLE who, along with Sal Ricciardone, worked to make this first edition a reality. Annette Turcotte, Prepress Manager, for her capable hand in guiding this book through production; Sheila Baker, Copyeditor, for her talent for maintaining the freshness of the spoken word while transforming it into text; Leslie Lovett, Marketing Assistant, Sue Theil, Graphic Designer, and Maritza Medina, Layout Artist, for their artistic and technical contributions to the book.

JOHN M. REILLY, ESQ.
MCLE EXECUTIVE DIRECTOR AND PUBLISHER

Boston, Massachusetts

DECEMBER 2, 1998

Reflections of a Trial Judge

CONTENTS

iii Intro

v About Judge Young

vii Foreword

ix Contents

1 CHAPTER 1: Judge Young on Unlocking Evidentiary Mysteries

- 2 Hearsay Defined
- 6 Exceptions to Hearsay
  - *7* Prior Statements
  - *9* Statement of Party Opponent
  - *12* Present Sense Impression
  - *13* Excited Utterance
  - *13* State of Mind Exception
  - *14* Statements of Medical Diagnosis or Treatment
  - *15* Past Recollection Recorded/Refreshing Recollection
  - *16* Business Records
  - *18* Judgment of Previous Conviction
  - *19* Unavailable Witnesses
  - *20* Former Testimony
  - *21* Dying Declaration
  - *21* Statement Against Interest
- *22* Totem Pole Hearsay
- *22* The Law of Confrontation
- *30* Inferences, Presumptions and Prima Facie Evidence
  - *30* Inferences
  - *31* Presumptions

34 Prima Facie Evidence
35 Social Policy
36 Legislative Policy

39 CHAPTER 2: Judge Young on the Practical Arts of Trial Advocacy

40 The Trial Lawyer
41 The Client
43 Teaching the Factfinder: Judge or Jury
45 Strategic, Tactical and Personal Considerations
46 Strategic Considerations
46 Tactical Considerations
49 Personal Considerations
49 Forum Shopping
50 Comparing Jurors
51 Comparing Judges
52 Comparing Court Procedures
52 Other Criteria
53 Comparing Clerks' Offices
53 Comparing Rules of Evidence
53 Analyzing Judes
55 Help From the Courtroom Deputy Clerk, Court Reporter and Court Officer
56 Use of Magistrate Judges
56 Impaneling the Jury
57 Questioning the Venire First
57 Filling the Box First
57 The "Struck" System
58 The Mechanics of Impanelment
62 Motions in Limine
65 Using the Jury List
65 The Pretrial Charge
67 Help From the Court Reporter
67 The Opening Statement
71 The Defense Opening
73 Directed Verdict After Opening

74 Structuring the Presentation of the Prima Facie Case

75 Events Cases and Status Cases

76 Order of Witnesses

78 Direct Examination

80 Putting Exhibits in Evidence

- 81 Show the Exhibit
- 81 Mark for Identification
- 81 Laying the Foundation
- 82 Offering the Exhibit
- 83 Show the Exhibit to the Jury

84 Special Problems with Tape-Recorded Testimony

84 Prior Inconsistent Statements

86 Cross-Examination

- 87 Impeaching a Witness

89 Demonstrative Aids

90 Direct Examination of Experts

91 Cross-Examination of Experts

92 Motions During Trial

92 The Charge Conference

92 Closing Argument

95 CHAPTER 3: Judge Young on Advanced Trial Techniques

98 What Makes a Great Trial Lawyer

- 101 Read
- 102 Participate and Teach

103 Pretrial Management

- 104 Seize Control of Your Case
- 106 Determine Appropriate Mechanism for Dispute Resolution
- 108 The Court's Docket
- 109 The Joint Case Management Schedule and Discovery Issues

113 Judges

117 Trial Management

121 Experts

- 124 Scientific, Technical or Other Specialized Knowledge
- 126 Frye, Daubert and Lanigan

131 Expert Interrogatories and Reports
133 Preliminary Finding Regarding Expert's Qualification to Testify
134 Standard of Proof
136 Juries
139 Empowering Juries
140 Juror Exhibits
141 Jury Questions
141 Getting a Fair Jury
141 Computers in the Courtroom

145 CHAPTER 4: Judge Young on Juries, Judges and Judging

149 Jury Pools
155 Impanelment
155 Questioning the Entire Venire First
155 Filling the Box First
158 The "Struck" System
158 Impaneling the Jury: Practice and Procedure
167 Pretrial Charge and Jury Issues
167 Pretrial Charge
168 Juror Note Taking
168 Juror Questions
168 Other Jury Issues
170 Taking a View
171 Choosing the Foreperson
172 The Jury's Verdict
174 Judges
181 About Judge Young as a Judge
184 Jury-Waived Cases
185 Judicial Practices and Techniques in Jury-Waived Cases
190 Motions
192 Evidentiary Issues
192 Relevance
194 Submitting Evidence de Bene
194 Conspiracies
194 Experts
196 Sentencing

196 Final Thoughts

201 CHAPTER 5: Judge Young on Evidence for the Trial Advocate

203 Players in the Adversary System
204 The Law of Evidence
206 Burdens of Proof
209 How to Prove Things
210 Mathematical Proof
211 Relevance
213 Brief Briefs and Using Precedent
214 Relevance, Rule by Rule
219 Habit
219 Exclusionary Rules
221 Scope of Examining Witnesses
222 Adverse Witnesses
222 Impeachment
224 Prior Inconsistent Statements
226 Hearsay
228 Exceptions to the Hearsay Rule
235 The Confrontation Clause
237 The Law of Experts
242 Privileges and Confidential Data
245 Admitting Evidence

251 CHAPTER 6: A Case Study of a Session in the U.S. District Court

254 Structure of Lecture
256 The People Who Make Up a Session of the U.S. District Court
256 Courtroom Deputy Clerk
258 Court Reporter
262 Docket Clerk
264 Chamber Staff
266 The Judge
268 Resources of the Court
271 The Governing Principles

271 Judges Should Try Cases

272 Judges Should Have a Routine

273 Judge as Law Teacher

275 Judge Young's Biases in Favor of Juries and Fairness

276 Institutional Litigation

283 Pretrial Matters

284 The Initial Case Management Scheduling Conference

290 Handling Discovery Motions

295 Dispositive Motions

303 The Final Pretrial Conference

306 Trial of a Case

306 Impanelment

308 Motion for Directed Verdict at the End of Plaintiff's Case

308 Jury Charge

313 CHAPTER 7: Judge Young on Experts, GHOST and Daubert

314 GHOST

315 Daubert

317 Knowing the Legal Framework

"By its nature, our adversary process is a search for the truth within limits. In a way, it's an archeological expedition into the past and what happened in the past, because rights turn on what happened in the past."

—Hon. William G. Young, December 4, 1993
From *Young on The Practical Arts of Trial Advocacy*

CHAPTER 1

Judge Young on Unlocking Evidentiary Mysteries

DECEMBER 5, 1992

WELL, good morning. First let me say, and I say this most sincerely, how truly honored I am that you would give up a Saturday morning and come out and discuss evidence. I think these matters are important. And I am honored that you're spending the time to do this.

Second, I dedicate these remarks to the memory of Irving Younger, who I think is probably the best evidence teacher I ever saw. He had the remarkable facility both to teach the rules of evidence, the structure of the evidentiary approach to things, and to put it in a most practical context. Though I am but a pale reflection of Younger, I unashamedly imitate him and acknowledge that.

Now, third, what are we going to do? Let me get all the mechanics taken care of. This is not an update of Massachusetts or federal law or recent cases decided in the courts. The goal here is to think of yourselves as though you were back in law school, except here the professor's goal is not to put you down or to teach you to think in some sort of bizarre way that is not familiar to human beings. Here you hired the professor, and the whole idea is for me to explain things that would be useful to you.

Now, hearsay. I do want to go back to Younger to start talking about the law of hearsay, though conceptually the law of hearsay is one of the three most difficult ideas in the law of evidence. Hearsay is conceptually difficult not only because the concept takes some working on, but because we have riddled it with exceptions. There are so many exceptions that some commentators have argued that we ought to do away with the rule against hearsay.

I state my bias very clearly. I am in favor of the rule against hearsay. The rule against hearsay in large measure is a best evidence rule. That's probably not the best way to teach it because I don't want you confusing it with the best evidence rule as it applies to documents, but it's a general social policy that requires us to come up with the live witness who can be cross-examined.

And so, now the Younger bit. Younger of course takes you through 300 years of history. He starts out with Sir Walter Raleigh. You know, Raleigh is there, he's in prison for treason against the king. And what happens is, two fellows get off a ship;

you can see it, you know. It comes into Bristol, they get off a ship, it's there. It's after the Armada. Spain is feared by the English. And these two sailors get up and they say, "You know, we were recently in Corona. We heard these two priests say that Raleigh is a traitor." And Raleigh gets up in his own defense. Here he is, can you imagine, pro se. Gets up in his own defense and he says, "What, am I to be beheaded on the testimony of two papist priests in Spain?" The answer, of course, is "yes, that's right." There was no law against hearsay, you know. After that they say, "Well, maybe we shouldn't have been so hasty."

And then—I can't do all the Younger stuff—but Younger ends this and he gets you through this history and then he does the following. I've seen it. I will not do it. I've already spread my papers out. He gets up on the desk, and he jumps off the desk after, of course, he's primed the audience. And as he's going down, arms outflung, he says this: "Never in three hundred years has any judge ever been reversed for admitting hearsay." ***(Applause)***.

Of course, I've been reversed for admitting hearsay. ***(Laughter)***. That's true. I have a friend who's Chief Justice of the South Carolina version of our Appeals Court, and I've told him this story. He says, "Well don't worry, Bill. We had two cases back to back. In the first we reversed the judge for admitting hearsay; in the second we reversed the judge for excluding hearsay. So pay no attention to it."

And I take comfort in that fact. We all know appellate judges. Appellate judges—them folks that come down out of the hills when all the fightin's over and the dust is all settled and blown away. And then them appellate judges in the cool, clear, reflective light of dawn, they shoot the wounded. ***(Laughter)***.

HEARSAY DEFINED

Simply stated, hearsay is defined as an out-of-court statement offered for the truth of the matter asserted. Let's break that down. Hearsay involves a situation where out of court there is a person. We'll call that person the declarant, whereas the witness is the person at trial. The declarant sees the event. And after seeing it he's going to tell us something about the event. He says what he saw in the hearing of the witness. The witness hears it, and then the witness is going to tell us at trial what the witness heard.

Now, what's the matter with that? That's how life works generally. The risk that we can see is that this witness may have an inability to hear straight. The witness may have some problem in hearing. It may have been too far away. What's more, the witness, even with the little pea brain I have given him, may have some motive to fabricate. The witness may have some idea, some bias, some reason not to tell us the truth.

Are we daunted by that? Clearly not. Why? Because we have the greatest engine of truth and discernment ever discovered by humankind—cross-examination. The witness is on the stand, and we can cross-examine him with respect to his ability to hear, and we can tear him to shreds with respect to his willingness to fabricate and lie.

But you see, we can't do that with respect to the declarant. We don't know whether the declarant saw what the declarant says that he saw. And what's more, we don't know what was going on in the little pea brain of the declarant.

Any out-of-court statement that is offered for the truth of the matter asserted is hearsay. The difficult part comes in trying to figure out what a statement is. We'll start with what's easy. A statement covers any declarative sentence. That's a statement. "It is raining." A declarative statement that states a fact, that's a statement.

Now what about conduct that's not a verbal statement? There is conduct that is obviously of an assertive nature. Let's say, in response to the question, "Who assaulted you?" I point to someone. I don't speak. That pointing is assertive conduct. That's a statement.

What about, though, things that aren't so clearly assertive? Let's get at it this way: The test of whether something is assertive conduct turns on whether the declarant, the out-of-court speaker, intends that it be assertive conduct. The traditional thing is you look out the window and you see someone with an umbrella. You think, well, that's hearsay; these people are intending to assert that it's raining. That's poppycock. They're intending to keep the rain off their heads. The fact that you can infer that it's raining doesn't make it hearsay.

The difficult case, the case that I find difficult, is the borderline case. What about the priest in Operation Rescue? He's indicted for assault and battery outside an abortion clinic, and so they're going to be after him, and he comes in and he wants to wear his clerical collar. And they say—I mean the *Globe* reports it (who knows what the truth is; it's all hearsay)—but I mean from reading the papers they say, "Wait a second, you can't come in here dressed like that. You're making an assertion about a whole variety of things." Well that's not an easy case, it seems to me.

Is that assertive conduct? I think that's hard conceptually. I think the answer is this: So long as the person in the mores of the society is either authorized by the mores of society to dress in that way in that setting, then you're not going to make much of that with the judge. Certainly the priest is entitled to come to court dressed as priests dress. The man is a priest.

I am not entitled to appear before you in a robe. Remember that picture of state Judge Garrity, Paul Garrity, the sludge judge, and there he's standing by the waters of Boston Harbor sort of like Moses? And remember how that struck everybody? I mean what's he doing out there in the robe? Usually if you see judges in robes you know they're in their courtroom. That's okay. I don't have any problem with that, but when they start going out in the streets in their robes it sort of strikes you a little bit, right?

Hearsay, and I think you should think of everything as hearsay, is an out-of-court statement offered for the truth of the matter asserted. Now let's come to that phrase, "the truth of the matter asserted." How often have you been in court and you think,

"Here comes something," and they're going to ask about an out-of-court declaration. You know it's coming and so you're getting ready, and now they ask about it. You leap to your feet, mouth formed in an "O" and you say, "I object." And the judge says, "Sustained." It's quite something to leap to your feet, judge there presiding, and win an objection. Somehow there is an adrenaline crash. I haven't done a study on this, but my own clinical experience leads me to believe it's so. And for 30 seconds that lawyer is semi-comatose, basking in his victory.

And then the other side says, "Judge, I'm not offering it for the truth of the matter asserted." The judge says, "Oh, okay." And then it comes in.

That takes us back to the concept of relevance. I'm not going to spend much time on that this morning except to talk about how you analyze things.

As judges, what should we do when that counter is made to us, "Judge, I'm not offering it for the truth of the matter asserted"? We should ask ourselves, and of course you as lawyers should ask yourselves, why is it relevant that the out-of-court declaration was made, that whatever was said was said? If it's relevant that whatever was said was said, the declaration itself is the evidence that it was made and you're not worried about hearsay.

Let me give you a variety of examples. If I say, "I offer you to buy that pen," and the lady here says, "I will sell it to you for 50 cents," and I say, "I accept," the law gives independent legal significance to the interchange between us. We have just formed an executory contract. The law gives legal significance to our verbal expression. As a matter of fact, the law of contracts gives so much significance to what we say to each other, it's not really concerned with what is going on in our minds. The law really isn't too interested in what she's thinking or what I'm thinking. The law is interested in what we said: offer and acceptance. It's not hearsay, you see, it's not offered for the truth. What's important is that we said the words to which there's legal significance attached.

How about notice in a tort case? Take this case. The area in front of the cabbages was wet and slimy, and a person, not the person injured, said to the cabbage boy, "Hey, you'd better clean that up; it's all wet there." Then, 10 minutes later another shopper in the supermarket slips and breaks his leg. On the issue of notice, the original shopper's statement is admissible. Not to prove that the floor was wet, but to prove that someone said it was wet and that the reasonable cabbage boy or A&P employee should have gone out and looked, and if it was wet, mop it up. This goes to notice.

We haven't done any exceptions yet. We're just talking about the concept of hearsay. Let me go through some problems. You should be able now to get the answers to all of these problems. The question is only: Is this hearsay? Whether it's admissible or not, is this hearsay?

The first problem, and appreciate that in each of these problems you must understand what's relevant because the outcome is determined by what issue is relevant. The issue: Did the defendant strike the plaintiff? The witness testifies that she saw the defendant strike the plaintiff. No hearsay. No problem. The witness is competent. The witness saw it.

Same issue, the witness testifies that Xavier told her that the defendant struck the plaintiff. That's hearsay because what's at issue is whether the defendant struck the plaintiff. The out-of-court statement from Xavier is hearsay.

On the same issue, did the defendant strike the plaintiff, the witness reads an entry that she made in her diary on the day of the alleged fight, and it says, "Today I saw the defendant strike the plaintiff." That is an out-of-court statement. She's reading what's in the diary. She is now on the stand, but that is hearsay. Now I hasten to say that there may be ways to get that in evidence. It may be recorded recollection, but it is hearsay.

The same situation but now the issue is whether the plaintiff was the first aggressor. In other words, it's self-defense and it's the defendant who's offering the witness's testimony. It makes no difference who offers it; what's written in the diary is still hearsay.

Now this, the issue of whether Xavier is a citizen. The witness has attended a naturalization hearing, and she is prepared to testify that she saw Xavier raise his right hand and take the oath of citizenship. That is not hearsay because what the law attributes significance to is precisely that—taking the oath of citizenship. So someone who saw it can testify that they saw it and it's admissible on the issue of whether Xavier is a citizen.

Now, consider a will contest, where the will says, "I leave all my worldly possessions to Zeno, who is the most loving and honest of my seven children." If the issue is who is the sole heir, that's admissible, because, of course, that's what the law has given legal significance to.

If the issue is whether Zeno is more honest than the other six siblings, that's hearsay. Remember, the will says, "I'm leaving it all to Zeno because he's the most honest." The law will admit that for the purpose of leaving all the property to Zeno, but it is no proof that Zeno in fact is the most honest, because the old man may have been confused.

How about on the issue of whether Xavier loved Zeno more than his other children? You admit it for that because one way of proving an intangible like love, hate, and the like is gifts or expressions of love—things like love letters or hate mail. Those things would come in not for the truth, perhaps, of what they assert but as tangible evidence of the state of mind of the person who is making them.

How about if the cat knocks over the goldfish bowl and the witness sees Xavier (who is a child in this example) crying? There is no hearsay if what's at issue is whether the goldfish meant something to Xavier. The fact of crying is not the assertive conduct. He's not asserting anything by crying.

How about the photo of a disabling back injury? It's a tort case and the plaintiff says, "I can't work." The defendant sends out their investigators and they've got their videotape of the plaintiff shoveling snow. That is not a hearsay problem. The plaintiff is not meaning to assert anything by shoveling snow, and they've got it, or not—the plaintiff isn't asserting anything.

How about a criminal case where the issue is burglary, which must take place in the nighttime at common law? The testimony states that the burglary took place one-half hour before the cock crowed. That's not a hearsay problem, but also it's not relevant. Who cares about the cock crowing? We don't think that that's significant.

On the issue of whether a phone is being used for gaming purposes, let's say there is testimony by an undercover agent that they heard one end of a conversation and in that conversation the person was taking bets or laying off the bets that had been taken. That's admissible, not for the truth of the specific bets but for the verbal conduct that takes place over the phone, which of course is an element of the crime that you have to prove.

On the issue of the loyalty of a defendant to the United States of America, let's say there is a claim that after a security check, the FBI granted the defendant a secret clearance. That's a hard one. I would not admit that. That's the position of the FBI. They could be wrong. It neither proves the defendant's loyalty nor disloyalty. It's their views—I'd have to get in the actual agents.

On the issue of someone's domicile—and we'll put it in Hawaii the way I have the problem here—Xavier says, "Hawaii—the tropical breezes, the sun, the sand, the perfume of the plumerias—I know of no place that is nicer." I'd admit that, not that Hawaii is such a nice place, but on the issue of the plaintiff's intent to be a domiciliary of that place. Of course, if that was the only evidence, that wouldn't be good enough, but I would admit it if it came in along with some other evidence.

So hearsay is an out-of-court statement offered for the truth of the matter asserted.

EXCEPTIONS TO HEARSAY

Now the exceptions. Everybody says, and indeed I started, by saying that the rule against hearsay is riddled with exceptions. You can keep your eye on the ball better if you think of all the different exceptions, and I'm going to go through them as being divided into four major types.

The first types are those exceptions that occur when the declarant and the witness are the same person.

The second group of exceptions depends upon the declarant being the party opponent in the trial; they depend upon the position of the declarant in the case on trial. A way that I try to remember is to say that they depend upon the declarant being on the opposite side of the versus, Smith v. Jones. When Smith wants what Jones said, then Jones is the party opponent to Smith, and what Jones said comes in as an admission. Really it's the law of admissions. But when Jones wants what Jones said, it doesn't work because they're on the same side of the versus. So the second types of exceptions are the exceptions for admissions.

The third types of exceptions are those things that are roughly grouped together because we think that, while the stuff is hearsay, we think it's reliable hearsay.

Then the last major group of exceptions is what I call the necessity exceptions. They've grown up because we need them. Logic does not play a great role in the law. There's a nod to it, but it really is a bit player, and because we need these exceptions they exist. We need them because we haven't got a witness.

Prior Statements

So, let's take those exceptions in the time that we have here. We'll go back to the first group of exceptions where the declarant and the witness are the same person. Understand that the precondition is that a witness is on the stand and has testified. You don't get to any of these exceptions unless the witness not only is in court but the witness has taken the witness stand and testified.

Now, if the witness has testified or is testifying, then under state law any statements that the witness has made that are inconsistent with the witness's testimony on the stand are admissible for the limited purpose of impeaching the witness. That is, the jury can hear that on another occasion the witness said another thing, but not for the truth of what was said on the other occasion. The jury hears it simply so it can compare what was said on the other occasion with what the witness is saying now in order to better understand whether they believe the witness.

I once spent two hours with a lonely old man. This fellow figures in my speech because he had the most marvelous collection, and I had to work on him for two hours until he'd give me a statement. Of course, I was very honest. "Who am I? I'm Bill Young. Here's my card. I work for this law firm. Did you work on the ship?" And then we sat around in his little one-room apartment and he showed me his collection of dust balls. He said, "See this little black one? This one I found under the bed. And don't breathe. See the big white one? That one?" And how he ever got this dust ball into this cigar case, I don't know. This man had a collection of dust balls and I remember him. And after two hours he gave me a "know-nothing" statement: "I don't know anything."

And I went back thinking I had done a great job because now he was not going to be a witness for the other side. It has nothing to do with anything under oath. If you give a prior inconsistent statement and you testify, state and federal, they can use it to impeach you.

In federal court, though, if you give an inconsistent prior statement, it comes in substantively, that is, it comes in for the truth of the matter asserted. The federal rules define this as nonhearsay, but I can't understand the theory why, so I teach it that these are all exceptions to hearsay as we've just worked through hearsay.

Now also suppose that you have the testimony of a witness that is consistent with the witness's prior statement. Now, the question is: What color was the light? It's a simple tort case. At trial the witness says that the light was red. In deposition the witness said that the light was green. Now, if the other side argues, in light of the deposition testimony, that the light was green—that your witness's testimony at trial that the light was red is a recent fabrication—then you can surely get in evidence a prior consistent statement. Let's say that at a time previous, say at the time that he gave the accident report, the witness said the light was red. That comes in. In state court you can get it in to rehabilitate the witness. In federal court you can get it in substantively, whether or not it's under oath.

State court has, given the nature of their docket, one other impeachable prior consistent or inconsistent statement, and that's fresh complaint in a rape case or a sexual assault case.

Now, understand the preconditions for that type of testimony. The victim has to testify first. You don't get in the fresh complaint witness until the victim, or alleged victim, testifies. Once the alleged victim testifies, then we will receive evidence from others to whom the victim made fresh complaint. I will tell you that the psychology of the fresh complaint is that if it is a consensual encounter of a sexual nature, then we are discreet and will keep it quiet. If it's a nonconsensual encounter, we will scream bloody murder and we will complain to the first person we see.

Oddly enough, the courts recognize rape trauma syndrome, although it's completely inconsistent with the doctrine of fresh complaint. All of the studies on rape trauma syndrome tell us that someone who has been violated in that most hideous of ways first has to put herself together and the first thing that she will do is keep very quiet about the fact of an assault of that nature. In fact, they may even see the same person who has raped them or be in the presence of that person and still not report it. They may only report it when the healthy anger and belief in self comes out. And that's what's taught as the rape trauma syndrome, which is completely inconsistent with fresh complaint, but fresh complaint we still have. No one wants to get rid of it. It is, after all, politically correct, so we still have it.

Now, Massachusetts has a couple of prior statements by a witness that they will admit substantively. If a witness testifies inconsistently with their testimony on the stand and the prior testimony was given to a grand jury, then you can introduce that inconsistent grand jury testimony substantively. That's as far as Massachusetts is going. You can't just introduce the deposition testimony of a witness, as opposed to the opposing party, substantively.

Also, Massachusetts state courts and the federal courts will admit the prior statement of identification of an assailant after the witness has already identified that person in court. That's admitted substantively. The witness gets on the stand and testifies, "I saw this assault and battery."

"Can you point out the assailant in the courtroom?"

"I can. He's sitting there."

"Let the record reflect that the witness has pointed out the defendant."

Then if you've got a witness who can make both an in-court identification and can testify that this is not the first time that he identified the assailant, then he can testify, "And I identified him right afterwards and I picked his picture out." And not only can we get the witness to say that, but now we get our police officer. Here he is, Adam 12. He sits down with all his heroism things and is asked, "Were you there? What did the witness say when shown this photo array?" —A fair array of course. "The witness said, `He's the man!'"

What about this? It's gang business, and now the witness gets on the stand and is asked, "Can you identify the person?"

"No, no, I can't."

"Oh, now, look now, come on now. Didn't you say before that ...," responds counsel.

"No, no. I must have been mistaken," states the witness.

You know, his fears get to him. He won't identify the defendant. You can't then put on hero police officer to testify contrary to what the witness said and say, "Oh yes, he identified him. He identified him." You can't do that.

Statement of Party Opponent

Now the second one. The second one is the out-of-court declarant who is the party opponent. It's got to be the party opponent. Then both state and federal now admit the admissions. The theory of admissions of the party opponent is simply this: The idea is that if you let the witness testify to what the person who is the party opponent said, if it's not true, the part opponent is necessarily in court. They've got the interest, the standing, the concrete dispute with the other party. They'll get on the stand and deny it. They'll get on the stand and testify themselves. And then of course we like that because we can cross-examine both sides and we believe in that.

Now, we know in the real world, especially in criminal cases, that there may be lots of reasons why a criminal defendant doesn't want to get on the stand. He may have a record as long as his arm, which will come out if he takes the stand but won't if he remains silent. But we say, so what. We still like that theory, and it's a little inducement to get him on the stand. That's just a choice he has to make.

When I talk about the law of admissions, however, and mention criminal cases, don't think an admission has to be a confession. An admission is anything that the other side says that is relevant. It may just contribute to the circumstantial evidence. The fellow says, "Oh, I was at Norumbega Park on such and such a day." Not a big deal. Thousands of people used to go there and dance under the totem pole and the like.

But if that's circumstantial evidence with respect to where the fellow was at the time of the crime, it comes in. He's not confessing to it, he's denying it. But it comes in if he's the one who said it, if the government wants it, because they're on the opposite side of the versus.

So let's go over the exceptions. A is a statement that is the person's own statement, or one that is made in a representative capacity as a trustee or as an officer of a corporation. Fed.R.Evid. 801(d)(2)(A); Mass. Evid. Stand. 801(d)(3)(A). B is a statement of the person who has manifested an adoption or a belief in its truth. These statements fall into two categories—adoptive admissions and judicial admissions. A judicial admission is the statement of your agent, the lawyer. An example of an adoptive admission is where people are standing around after a house is on fire and someone says, "Hey, Jones, I just saw you run out of that house before the fire broke out. You're the arsonist, aren't you?" Now, this isn't the police officer who says this; Jones is not in custody. And Jones says nothing. He doesn't deny it; he just stands there. That, of course, is an adoptive admission, because we believe that someone who's accused like that normally will deny it. If they stand silent, and, not being in custody, they don't have the benefit of the Fifth Amendment privilege against testifying, and a regular person says that to them, then that can come out at trial even though they said nothing. Now, that's a statement in which you have manifested a belief in the truth. Fed.R.Evid. 801(d)(2)(B); Mass. Evid. Stand. 801(d)(3)(B).

C is a statement by a person authorized by a party to make a statement concerning the subject. Fed.R.Evid. 801(d)(2)(C); Mass. Evid. Stand. 801(d)(3)(C). D is a statement by an agent or servant concerning a matter within the scope of the agent's or servant's employment. Fed.R.Evid. 801(d)(2)(D); Mass. Evid. Stand. 801(d)(3)(D).

It used to be that only statements by people who were authorized to make a statement concerning the subject were admissible in Massachusetts. The federal courts would admit the statement of any agent speaking during the agency within the scope of the agent's employment. In other words, the federal courts would admit cabbage boy's statement if cabbage boy was the person on the scene talking for A&P.

It used to be that the state courts would only admit the authorized statement of the agent once A&P pulled itself together and made a statement. No longer. Now the state and federal rules are the same. ***See Rusycyk v. Secretary of Public Safety***, 401 Mass. 418, 421–22, 517 N.E.2d 152, 154–55 (1988). The statement of any agent concerning a matter within the scope of the agency—that's the test. Does what cabbage boy says concern cabbages, something within the scope of the agency? If it does, it not only binds cabbage boy, but it also binds A&P. It's an admission by A&P's agent.

And, finally, a statement by a coconspirator made during the course of and in furtherance of the conspiracy. Fed.R.Evid. 801(d)(2)(E); Mass. Evid. Stand. 801(d)(3)(E). We've got to pause on that because that's used state and federal and it's used civil and criminal. The theory is the law of partnership, that coconspirators are partners of each other and, therefore, the statement of one conspirator is the statement of all.

The question that immediately comes up is: Who decides whether there is a conspiracy, just to decide whether you're going to admit this evidence? And the answer to the question is: Judges decide, but it's done differently whether you're in state court or federal court. *See* Fed.R.Evid. 104(a); Mass. Evid. Stand. 104(a).

What is the fairest way to do it? The fairest way to do it, of course, is to hold a hearing out of the hearing of the jury and put in all the evidence of conspiracy. Then the judge will decide whether there is a conspiracy. And if there is a conspiracy, then the judge will go to the case and allow in all the coconspirator statements. Nobody does that. That's the fairest way, but nobody does it because it's too slow. We don't want to have two trials.

Here's how Massachusetts does it: Massachusetts says you've got to put in your independent evidence of the conspiracy, limited against the conspirators. *Commonwealth v. Beneficial Finance Co.*, 360 Mass. 188, 275 N.E.2d 33 (1971). "The admissions of the lady here are admitted against her. Ladies and gentlemen, pay no attention, this has nothing to do with the case against these folks, just against her. The gentleman here, they're admitted against him and not as to her and not as to these folks."

And then once you've got enough independent evidence, the judge finds, not by reasonable doubt but by a fair preponderance of the evidence, that there's enough. Then, usually toward the end of the trial, the judge says something like this, if you're a defense counsel, "Now, you remember all those limitations that I put on the evidence as you followed it? Forget them all. Everything's in against everybody." And you think, "Geez, what about that? That really sort of croaks them in the end."

The feds avoid that problem by doing it this way: Everything is let in, in a conspiracy case, including all the coconspirator statements, and the judge doesn't make a judgment until the end of the whole case. Only at the end of the whole case does the judge make a judgment, again by a fair preponderance of the evidence, whether there's a conspiracy. *See Earle v. Benoit*, 850 F.2d 836, 840–42 (1988). If the judge thinks there is, he or she doesn't say anything at all. The jury doesn't know about all these limitations, so removing them doesn't hurt, and the case goes to the jury.

What if the judge doesn't think that there is enough? There is an actual case, *United States v. Pitocchelli*, which was my case, 830 F.2d 401 (1st Cir. 1987). This case involved a bar owner and arson of a bar in interstate commerce. It was the first time I ever had a case like that. And I originally thought it meant that the bar had to be somehow moving, but that's not it. It means bars are in interstate commerce because they buy their liquor from different places. And the government puts on, they flip these two—everyone would agree—complete sleazeballs. These sleazeballs are guys that the owner has thrown out of the bar repeatedly, and they're caught burning the bar down. And now the government wants to say that although the owner has thrown the guys out of the bar repeatedly, he hired these guys to burn his bar down because he thought they were the best ones he knew who might do a job like this.

I listened to this. We get all done, and I think to myself that I don't believe these sleazeballs. I don't think that what they have to say about their meetings with this guy is worthy of anything. So I strike out—we're at the end of the trial and I say, "Remember they said they met with Pitocchelli and they planned it? Strike all that out, pay no attention to that." But then I think to myself, you know, there's enough evidence because Pitocchelli did buy some gasoline, he was at various places and he did have a motive. I think it's a pretty thin case, but I think there's enough that it goes to the jury anyway. I've told them to strike out the bad parts. The defense counsel, who's on a roll because he's got the judge (the judge doesn't believe the government's case), doesn't move for a mistrial. They convict Pitocchelli. He gets 10 years. There you are. I didn't believe it, but the jury did, and that's okay, because, you see, the test of whether there's sufficient evidence to the jury is much different than the initial test of whether the coconspirator statements come out.

Now this. Frequently you have cases like this—what if you have a hub-and-a-spoke conspiracy? This happened in the Exam Scam case. *United States v. Doherty*, 867 F.2d 47 (1st Cir. 1989). Suppose you have the conspirators here in the hub and these X folks, their job is to steal civil service exams and sell them. That's what they're involved in, and they're selling them to people who want to be police chiefs. And then suppose out here you've got a series of police captains who want to be police chiefs, as we had in that case, and each one of those folks buys an exam. The same thing would be true in a cocaine conspiracy, the retail purchasers. It would be true in a prostitution ring, the johns. Each one of these people is engaged in a separate conspiracy with the people at the hub. See, F is not the least concerned with E buying an exam unless E buys an exam for the same department. F just wants to buy his exam. E wants to buy his exam. So the testimony of all the Xs is admitted against all the Xs, and it's admitted against F with respect to the exam that F is purchasing but it's not admitted as against E because E is not part of that conspiracy. E is only in it with respect to the spoke. It doesn't work, though, with respect to the chain of, for instance, drug conspiracy, the vertical distribution. All of those people are thought to be in it together from the source in Colombia, or wherever, down onto the street vendor, their role in the deal, the chain to get the contraband drug out. All right. That's the second one.

Present Sense Impression

Now let's go to the third major exception, Federal Rule of Evidence 803. We don't need to spend much time on this, but we'll spend some. And here if you look, if you compare what I've given you as to the state and federal exceptions, I want to point out the differences, and I'll go through it very quickly.

The first exception we don't have in Massachusetts is the present sense impression. That's what I call a reporter's exception or the periscope exception. It has nothing to do with excited utterances, but it's a statement describing a condition as it's happening or immediately thereafter. The time sequence is important. It has to be operating virtually at the same time.

Suppose the lady in the back has just come in, the door is open and she's not in any danger herself, but she's standing at the door looking out at those high doors and she says, "Gee, the office down on Winter Place has just caught fire." She's a lawyer, after all, and she's not excited by that. It's just an occurrence that she thinks we might like to know. In the federal courts that's admitted. Understand how these work. She doesn't have to testify to it. All of you who hear her, you don't see it, but it's admitted that the building across the way is on fire. It's admitted for that purpose. We don't have that in state court.

Excited Utterance

Second, the excited utterance. Both state and federal have that. Feds call it excited utterance. Massachusetts calls it spontaneous exclamation. No reason for that—they're the same things—but that's how federalism works.

Now, the key thing here is the person has to be under the influence of the excitement. And the theory is if you're very excited you aren't going to fabricate. These are the reliable exceptions. There's a case that just came down a week or so ago, *Commonwealth v. Brown*, 413 Mass. 693 (1992), and think of this: This is a situation where the victim of the crime is being inquired of by a doctor five hours after the event and the victim is not exclaiming at all. Instead, the doctor says to the victim, "Who beat you up? Who did this to you?" And the victim tells the doctor. The Massachusetts Supreme Judicial Court says that's a spontaneous exclamation.

Now, don't think that I'm bad-mouthing the case. Let me give you the other facts. The victim is three and a half years old. He's been scalded in his home. He is terrified even five hours later, and he is crying and virtually hysterical.

The case comes on before Judge Irwin, who held a special hearing on this and decides that's still spontaneous on the part of the victim. The SJC just upheld it. This is unlike the present sense impression, the reporter's or periscope exception. The reason I call it the periscope exception is that it's like in the movies—they say, "Oh, there's bearing 356." You can look in the periscope and see. The lady coming in here says, "There's a fire there." We can all run out and see it if we want to. We can check on it. You're not going to say something unreliable.

For the second one, the excited utterance, you have to be excited. So long as you're still under that excitement, even though the event is sometime in the past, it works.

State of Mind Exception

Let's talk about the then-existing mental or emotional condition, the state of mind exception. That's a crucial exception. You want to think with respect to that exception of the seminal case *Mutual Life Ins. Co. v. Hillmon*, 145 U.S. 285 (1892). The way the *Hillmon* case works is that the then-existing mental impression of the witness cannot be retrospective. If I say, "I am having a heart attack," that's admissible as to my mental impression. It's also admissible if I say, "When I leave here I'm going to meet my wife, who's shopping." At least so much of it as states my intention is admissible—my prospective intention. That's evidence, for instance, if I pull a Judge Crater and I leave here and I'm never seen again. It's some evidence that I did not intend to flee that I stated to you that I intend to go and see my wife.

When I said it, I said, "who is shopping." That would be hearsay. If what was relevant was what my wife was doing, that's hearsay. That has nothing to do with my intent. But when I say I'm going to meet my wife, that's admissible. If I say to you, "I am getting hoarse," that's admissible. If I say to you, "I stayed up too late last night and that's why I'm getting hoarse," so much of it that says, "I'm getting hoarse" is admissible. What I did last night is not admissible.

Statements of Medical Diagnosis or Treatment

I want to jump now to Rule 803(4), statements for purpose of medical diagnosis or treatment. The language is important here. In state law it is the statement of a patient made to a physician or physician's agent for the purpose of medical diagnosis and treatment. Compare that to the Federal Rule of Evidence 803(4) where it says statements made for the purpose of diagnosis and treatment.

Now here's why that's a difference. The witness was asked this question: "And when the doctor came in after your operation, what did the doctor say to you?" "Objection, hearsay." The doctor's not there now. The witness is the patient. I routinely let it in. And I let it in of course because what the doctor says to his patient is a statement made for the purpose of treatment. What's the very essence of the doctor-patient relationship are these two people. That's what the patient wants to know more than anything else: "Doc, how am I going to be? Am I going to get better? What's going to happen to me?"

So when the doctor says that you've got a herniated disk and you have to do this and you have to do that, I am perfectly clear that under the federal rules all that comes in. The issue is this: As an exception to the hearsay rule, will the state admit from the patient what the doctor told the patient? Clearly in federal court they will, but not necessarily in state court.

In the state court you can now get in the doctor's written statements, a maneuver, and I don't criticize them for it, by the plaintiff's bar. They got the legislature to agree to that. You won't get those in evidence in federal court unless you can somehow get them in as a business record or the like simply because we don't allow it. We have no exception that allows for those records not made between physician and plaintiff. We don't allow in the doctor's own statement about the treatment.

Past Recollection Recorded/Refreshing Recollection

Past recollection recorded. I want to take a moment to contrast refreshing recollection, which is present recollection refreshed, and compare it to past recollection recorded. Present recollection refreshed simply deals with what you do when the witness testifies that he can't remember. You pick up something, it can be anything at all. You can refresh recollection with a banana. That's true if the banana will refresh recollection. You can refresh recollection with your own notes. It doesn't have to be some evidentiary thing.

The theory is you just say, "Mr. Witness, I show you this. Does this refresh your recollection? In other words, does it jog your memory on the subject?" If the witness says, "Yes," then the idea is he's got a memory, a present memory. It's from his present memory refreshed that he testifies. And you cross-examine him because he's not testifying on the basis of the out-of-court statement. He's testifying from his presently refreshed recollection.

Of course, you know too that if the other side uses the document to refresh the witness's recollection on the stand in Massachusetts, you are entitled to see it when the other side has finished with its direct examination. Don't ask for it in the middle of the direct. That's the great trap for the unwary because there's an old Massachusetts case that hasn't been recently cited, ***Leonard v. Taylor,*** 315 Mass. 580 (1944). It stands for the proposition that if you embarrass a direct examiner by asking for the document on direct, then at the option of the examiner it comes into evidence. So sometimes you have lawyers that are like two scorpions in a bottle and the guy stands up and says, "Gee, I'm not sure I've seen that. Could I see what you're using?" And the fellow whirls around and says, "Are you demanding this document?"

"I'd never think—God forbid I demand it. I just asked if I could—I certainly don't want it now."

"He demanded it, Judge."

"I never demanded it."

What they're doing is playing out the last vestige of a case no longer cited, but we keep it alive in lectures like this so you can all worry about it.

Federal Rule of Evidence 612: I'm sort of off the hearsay topic, but you need to know it. Before you put a witness on the stand, the other side can make a demand to see anything that you used to refresh the witness's recollection at trial or before trial. The other side gets to know how you prep the witness, except in criminal cases under the Jencks Act they don't get to know until after the direct examination by the government is complete. So be careful how you prep the witness.

Now, past recollection recorded is different. The witness doesn't have a present memory but at or about the time the event took place he made a record of the matter and he's willing to testify that the record he made of the matter is true, and he made the record of his own personal knowledge.

Let's say that when I served in Korea during peacetime, I kept a diary so my children and grandchildren can see it. I confess to you it's not scrupulously accurate, but I've remembered now the stuff that I fudged. It was the stuff when I was sort of on leave and the like. ***(Laughter)***.

I have to tell you there's a dispute between Chief Justice Liacos in his book and the way I teach it. I think you have to exhaust the witness's present testimony before you get to his past recollection recorded. Most commentators are with me. In Liacos' book on the Massachusetts law—and this is the bible on Massachusetts law—Chief Justice Liacos takes the opposite position. He says you don't have to exhaust it. I think you do.

The examination would go something like this: "Do you remember?" If I don't have a memory, then they'll try to get the diary into evidence. And the diary, they'll say, "What's this?" I identify it as my diary from the days there. And then they'll ask me, "Are you able to tell whether this is true?" Now, assuming it's my time there with the troops, I say, "Yes, I'll swear now that this is true." And then they'll ask, "And when did you make this entry?"

"I made the entry that night, or at least, let's see, this is in the field and we came back on the Monday. I made it no later than the Monday following the Friday that the event happened."

"And these events that you describe, where were you with respect to them?"

"Oh, I was there. I did all these things."

That's enough for past recollection recorded. I have personal knowledge, although I've now forgotten. I made the diary on my personal knowledge. I made it contemporaneously with the events. It doesn't refresh my recollection. I know it happened, let's say, but I don't know when it happened. The date is there, but it was the diary. I was keeping the dates straight.

So what you do is you read it to the jury, but the diary itself does not get into evidence. And the reason is that it speaks more loudly than my testimony. What you've got to do is read it to the jury and they have to remember it.

Business Records

Let's jump to business records, records of regularly conducted activity. The laws are similar, both state and federal. Fed.R.Evid. 803(6); Mass. Evid. Stand. 803(6). This is how to lay the foundation to put business records into evidence:

The first question is, "Mr. Witness, I show you what has been marked Exhibit A for identification. Do you recognize it?" That's a good question, see, because it makes very clear what the witness has been shown.

The second question is, "Can you please identify it?" And he does and he tells us generally what it is. The first two questions are always the same.

Now, with a business record you have to have the custodian of the record. Remember that the custodian can be anyone whose business duty it is to see to it that the records are regularly maintained. That doesn't mean that it has to be the file clerk or the person in the specific office. It can be the chairman. It can actually be the president of the corporation. I mean imagine Roger Smith at GM as custodian. He isn't anymore, but he was; now he's just getting his million a year—but then he was custodian of all GM's records.

Remember, business records don't have to be the records of a business. They can be the records of a church, the Army, any government agency. They can also be the records of a household—bills, things like that.

Now for the third question, after the first two, which are always the same for whatever you want to put in evidence, you ask the custodian, "Is it the usual course of the business of whatever you are in to maintain records like this?" Now, those of you who have a holistic view of evidence will note immediately that I've asked a grossly leading question. Don't worry if you're following a standard foundation. Judges let you do this so long as you're doing what we're familiar with and you're doing the regular foundation.

Once he says yes to that, then you say, "Is this record, Exhibit A, kept in the usual course of that business?" And that's the order, the third and fourth questions are in that order. The third question is to tell us the practice, the routine business practice. The fourth question asks, "Is this record kept in that practice?" Then under state practice, so long as the judge can infer the other requirements that it was kept in good faith and there was no reason to believe that it was flimflam for the litigation, it would come in.

In federal practice, Rule 803(6) requires that the record be made by someone with knowledge, personal knowledge, and that the record be made roughly contemporaneously with the events that it records.

Sub (7), Fed.R.Evid. 803(7), is important in the federal rules; the state I think would do this but we couldn't find a case on it. The federal rules make clear that the absence of a record is proof that the event didn't happen. In other words, if you've got your records and they say that on such and such a day so many cartons were shipped and then there is no record for a specific day, that's evidence that no cartons were shipped on that day.

State law is a little different on that, but under federal law you can argue that no cartons were shipped because you've got a regular course of records and they show no cartons shipped. I want to stop on 803(8). Now 803(8) has been interpreted, especially 803(8)(C), now, that's just in civil actions unless it's against the government, so that they are allowing in factual findings resulting from an investigation made pursuant to authority granted by law. *See In re: Adoption of Irwin*, 28 Mass.App.Ct. 41, 43–44, 545 N.E.2nd 1193, 1195, *review denied*, 406 Mass. 1103, 548 N.E.2nd 887 (1990).

The key case, *Beech Aircraft Corp. v. Rainey*, 488 U.S. 153 (1988), interprets that very broadly. Under that doctrine, all sorts of government investigations come in evidence substantively. They just come in evidence for proof of the matters asserted. Once you prove you have the authentic record, in it comes.

Think of its application. All this cigarette litigation, there is a lot of government stuff out there on cigarettes. All your Superfund litigation, your CERCLA litigation. How about all the governmental investigations? And you know the investigations can be made with respect to your specific site to investigate similarly when the EPA is doing it.

And let's bring it home. What about the St. Clair report in civil rights actions, the report about the conduct of the Boston Police Department? Does that all get in evidence as proof of what the department knew?

Now, I can say no more because I have that case. I'm not the only one. Lots of judges in our court have that case. How it ultimately gets worked out, how that St. Clair report is going to be used, if it can be at all, I will say nothing other than to raise the issue as framed under 803(8)(C).

I will tell you Judge Keeton has issued an order striking references to the report in various civil rights complaints, and the rest of us are pretty much going along with it, striking the references. No one suggests that that means that that is a determination that the report could not come in as evidence at the trial. No one suggests it cuts either way. In effect, we duck it for the moment. The city, of course, is very alert to this, and they're trying very hard to keep it out. Watch decisions of the district court, and maybe that will get appealed in the future, because how that works out is going to be very important.

Now, the only other thing—I just want to jump ahead here, I'm not going to go through all these—I do want to talk a little bit about learned treatises because very recently the state courts adopted the federal approach to learned treatises. The old state statutory rule, trumped now by a case, I believe it's *Commonwealth v. Sneed,* 413 Mass. 387, 394–96 (1992), has adopted the language of the federal rule in toto. It's Rule 803(18). We're altering the standards for the 1993 edition, so be aware that that's there.

Judgment of Previous Conviction

I want to point out one other thing that's in the federal rules but not in the state rules—Rule 803(22), a judgment of previous conviction. Now, you all know that if a witness takes the stand, you can use a prior conviction to impeach the witness. We're not talking about that. We're talking about using that conviction substantively as evidence of those matters as to which the conviction stands. A good example would be federal criminal RICO (18 U.S.C. §§ 1961–1964), where you have to prove the predicate acts. Suppose the person's been convicted of one of those predicate acts, then whether or not he takes the stand, under 803(22) in federal court, you can put in his conviction that he was convicted of mail fraud. That goes to show the pattern—you have to do two or more—which will support the racketeering conviction. There is no state counterpart. If you begin to get state RICO (the bill is a perennial bill), you want to be alert to see if the law evolves that way.

I want to say a word about the innominate exception. We don't have an innominate exception under state law. We do under federal law at Fed.R.Evid. 803(24). The short of it is, don't depend on it. Don't depend on it, especially in a civil case. You have some hope if you represent the government in a criminal case because the First Circuit has been most amenable to allowing in what otherwise would be hearsay and inadmissible hearsay under the innominate exception. The growth in the common law, has come to favor the government in criminal cases. Other than that, we really don't read in the 803(24) as a very valid exception.

Unavailable Witnesses

The fourth set of exceptions are those where the witness is not present. The first thing you have to consider is whether the witness is unavailable. This only works if the witness is unavailable.

Let me stop here by raising a famous case, ***Commonwealth v. Bohannon***, 376 Mass. 90 (1978), ***appeal after remand***, 385 Mass. 733 (1982), a case that can teach us a lot. The case is an ugly case. Fellows by the names of Bohannon and Stonestreet are alleged to have raped a mildly retarded woman in a sandpit in Brockton. Bohannon is represented by Pat Piscitelli, who died untimely and was a great criminal defense lawyer on the South Shore. The case comes on to be tried before the Honorable Thomas Dwyer, a magnificent judge of the superior court.

The victim testifies. Once the victim testifies, Piscitelli starts asking the victim about prior false complaints of rape. "You've complained that you've been raped before, haven't you?" Dwyer is right on top of that. He calls Piscitelli to the sidebar and says, "What are you doing? What about the rape shield law in Massachusetts?" Piscitelli says, "I believe there are psychiatric records that show that this woman has made repetitive false complaints of rape and I want to cross-examine her about those false complaints because she makes it up, it's not true." Dwyer says, "What is this, Mars?" The transcript is great. "Prior misconduct of a witness is not admissible in Massachusetts. You can't do it."

The trial goes on. Both Bohannon and Stonestreet are convicted. The case goes up to the Supreme Judicial Court, where it is reversed. Reversed not on the confrontation clause, but because the rape shield law doesn't keep it out. They weren't talking about her actual conduct. They were talking about whether she made the complaints or not. The SJC thought Piscitelli should have it. That's when I got the case. I'm sitting then in Brockton. Bohannon has been sentenced to MCI Framingham where they have men and women, though primarily women. He's off in a little cottage by himself or with some other fellow, only he's on work release. And for some reason he drives a red MG. And so here he comes driving back to ...*(Laughter interrupts the judge)*. No, no. This is all true. He's out on work release.

He's being rehabilitated. He drives back in his red MG to Framingham where he's supposed to be at a set time. There's the Plymouth Sheriff's Office. They shackle him up. He asks, "What did I do? What did I do? I'm back on time." They said, "Congratulations, Bohannon, you've won your appeal. Now you're awaiting trial. Back to Plymouth jail." So back he goes. He's not in Framingham at all. He's not terribly happy.

It comes on, and I say, "Great, this case is over, isn't it? You know, let's dismiss it." "Oh no, oh no," says the district attorney. "Remember there was a preliminary hearing and at the preliminary hearing Piscitelli tried to scare this woman off? And so he asked her a lot of questions at the preliminary hearing. He asked them under oath, and that prior testimony is admissible in this trial. And she's not available. She's gone to Florida, and so now we're going to get the prior testimony in and we're going to try the case."

I said, "That's ridiculous. Florida is not Siberia. You get her back here from Florida."

"Oh, judge, you know, we've got this prior testimony."

"No, no. She's not unavailable. You know where she is in Florida. Bring her back."

So they go, or so they say, and then they come back. I'm still sitting there. It's my month in Brockton. They say, "We can't. She won't come back."

"Well, she's your witness, and she's the only witness. Why won't she come back?"

"Well, because her mother—remember this is a mildly retarded young woman we're talking about—says, 'The system in Massachusetts stinks. She's been through this once. I'm not letting her come back. The heck with you. We're happy in Florida.' So, your Honor, now she's unavailable."

I say, "She's not unavailable. Get a court order and bring her back."

"Oh, judge we … da, da, da … but she's not going to be that good of a witness. We've got the prior testimony."

I say, "Do it. That's the only way the prior testimony comes in."

They go down. The Florida judge says, "You people in Massachusetts are crazy. She's been through it once. I'm not ordering her to come back."

Well, then they come back and say, "Well, now, judge, come on, okay. She's unavailable, right?" And I say, "Yes, she's unavailable." That's the thirtieth day. I leave Brockton.

Former Testimony

Let's jump down to the exceptions now. The first one is former testimony. And the reason I use *Bohannon* is notice that the key language is that you have to have an opportunity and similar motive to develop the testimony. In this case Piscitelli took it. He thought he could scare her off from testifying at trial and he asked all sorts of questions. That's sufficient. He's representing the same party.

And so they bring in Bohannon and Stonestreet. Bohannon, by the way, is a great big fat guy. He's huge. It's tried before the Honorable Andrew Meyer, a most distinguished judge. They put the whole thing together. It takes place about seven to nine months later. And I'm long gone and know nothing about this. But the trial comes on, I'm told, and all they do is read her prior testimony. There's no witness. And that's it, since she's the only witness to the event. They just read in her prior testimony.

The jury goes out, convicts them both again. Bohannon faints. He's so heavy that he takes down the rail in front of him. The rail falls over and he's there like a great whale. And back to prison he goes.

Dying Declaration

Let's look at the other exceptions quickly. Statement of belief of impending death, or the dying declaration. Fed.R.Evid. 804(b)(2); Mass. Evid. Stand. 804(b)(2). You don't have to die, but you have to believe that you're going to die. In federal court you don't have to die. In state court, however, dying declarations are inadmissible unless the declarant dies shortly thereafter. *See Commonwealth v. Nolian*, 373 Mass. 45, 50, 364 N.E.2d 1224, 1228 (1977). The psychology of that is if you believe you're going to die, you're getting your affairs in order. I don't know that that's sound scientifically. Maybe you're going to take the last chance you have to shaft someone you don't like. *(Laughter)* No, I say this in all good conscience. The key thing is you have to believe that you're dying and it has to relate to the cause of your dying.

Statement Against Interest

Another exception is a statement against interest, the statements against your pecuniary interest. It's in recent years, not so recent as I get older, but it's within my memory that we've adopted in Massachusetts statements against penal interests as an exception to the hearsay rule. *See Commonwealth v. Carr*, 373 Mass. 617, 369 N.E.2d 970 (1977). And the statement against penal interests must be accompanied by substantial guarantees of trustworthiness.

I did very little criminal work as a lawyer, but I did make myself available to be appointed. In one of those cases, I defended someone who had been in a barroom brawl. It was an assault and battery case. My client told me, "I didn't hit him with the bottle. Smith hit him." I said, "Oh really? Where is this Smith?" My client responded, "I'll get him to come and talk to you."

Even at Bingham, Dana & Gould this was pretty neat. I didn't even have to go out and find Smith. The guy was coming to me. So, Smith comes in. I'm very careful. I say, "Now, remember, I represent Jones here, and you're going to talk to me about this." I give him my card, and I get a stenographer. I ask, "You're not intimidated by the stenographer, right?" He doesn't appear intimidated. Here I am. I think I'm Perry Mason. The guy is going to leap up under my questioning and say, "No, I did it!" and then we will blow the case away.

So, I take his statement. Lo and behold, Smith says, "Yeah, I did it, yeah. He was there and I jabbed him with the bottle." I am thinking I wish Smith had a lawyer; this is just too easy. And, of course, it is too easy. I dig it all out, and it's wonderful, and I think that I am all set for trial.

The case comes for trial. Of course, there's no Smith. That's been known by the people involved except for yours truly from the beginning. My client says, "Well, hey, you know, Smith did it." And I say, "Yea, but where's Smith?" My client says, "I don't know. But Smith did it, and you've got his statement."

No, no, no. It doesn't work that way. I sent out process servers to serve Smith. I was trying to find Smith because I had blown this case. You see, you can't get in Smith's statement that he did it without those particularized guarantees of trustworthiness. You don't get in these statements against penal interest that get the defendant off the hook until it is accompanied by particularized guarantees of trustworthiness, for obvious and good reasons. *See Commonwealth v. Gagnon*, 408 Mass. 185, 557 N.E.2d 728 (1990).

TOTEM POLE HEARSAY

I think that's all I want to say about that, and that's pretty much all I want to say about hearsay other than to say that hearsay within hearsay, or totem pole hearsay, can be admissible. The test is whether each statement satisfies an exception to the hearsay rule. So long as each one satisfies an exception to the hearsay rule, the hearsay comes in.

The fact that it's totem pole hearsay doesn't keep it out. You could have an excited utterance heard by someone who reports it as a present sense impression and it's admissible so long as each part satisfies the hearsay rule. Fed.R.Evid. 805; Mass. Evid. Stand. 805.

THE LAW OF CONFRONTATION

Now, let me talk about the law of confrontation. There are four strains to the law of confrontation. Before I get into the different strains or the different aspects of the law, I want to go over the Supreme Court law.

Before I do, I want to mention the case of *Barber v. Page*, 390 U.S. 719 (1968). That is the Supreme Court case that under the Sixth Amendment right to compulsory process requires or makes real the ability of a criminal defendant to have process to get people in to testify.

To use my ***Bohannon*** case, it's the ***Barber v. Page*** doctrine that makes the judges go to the limits of seeking a court order. If there's any lawful way to compel a witness who may be helpful to the defense, the judge has to bring in witnesses.

Now, there are four aspects to the law of confrontation. I will discuss them and develop them quickly through the various cases. The law of confrontation and compulsory process arises out of the Sixth Amendment and out of Article 12 of the Declaration of Rights of the Massachusetts Constitution. It has application only to criminal cases, not to civil cases. None of these doctrines has anything to do with civil cases.

The four separate applications that we're going to touch on are: What is the relationship of the right of confrontation to the law of hearsay? What does the law of confrontation teach us about multidefendant cases? What is the relationship of the law of confrontation to the state law of privilege? What is the inchoate right of confrontation, how does it play out with respect to the law of evidence generally and the ethical duties of an attorney?

Let's go through them. The first case, the case that applies the right of confrontation spelled out in the Sixth Amendment, to the state under the Fourteenth Amendment, is ***Pointer v. Texas***, 380 U.S. 400, a 1965 case, written, as you might expect, by Mr. Justice Black. It was a deliberate attempt to further articulate the law of confrontation as a constitutional doctrine. Black equates the law of confrontation with the right to cross-examine.

Of course, the interesting thing is if the law of confrontation is equivalent with cross-examination, what happens to what we've talked about earlier? With every single hearsay exception, you can't cross-examine. That's the whole thing. You're letting in evidence, the statements of declarants, that you can't cross-examine except in the first instance where the declarant and the witness are the same. What happens to all that law if in a criminal case you have a right to confront the witness against you?

The next case along that line is ***California v. Green***, 399 U.S. 179, a 1970 case written by Mr. Justice White. The ***Green*** case is frequently used in trial practice courses because it's so short. The ***Green*** case is a simple case. In it, there is a preliminary hearing at which a fellow by the name of Porter testifies and is cross-examined. His testimony inculpates Green, but at trial he's very forgetful. He can't remember what happened.

With Porter being unavailable because he can't remember, the federal rules would work this way—this is under the California state rules—his prior testimony comes in substantively, and Green is convicted. Green says, "I never had a chance to cross-examine Porter before the jury because, of course, before the jury, he couldn't remember anything."

Affirmed, says the Supreme Court. You did have a chance to cross-examine Porter at the prior hearing. So we learn that if the right of confrontation is equivalent to the right of cross-examination, it's sufficient if the right of cross-examination is exercised at any time before the trial as well as at the trial.

In other words, if you take a deposition in a criminal case and examine and the witness is unavailable at trial, the deposition could be read in evidence as prior testimony and would come in. No problem under the law of confrontation.

The next case along these lines, ***Dutton v. Evans***, is a case that's come in for a great deal of criticism, but the Supreme Court has never overruled it or limited it. And the reason we talk about ***Dutton v. Evans***, although everyone says it's a lousy case, is that it sets us up for the most recent explication of the relationship between hearsay and confrontation. In ***Dutton v. Evans***, 400 U.S. 74, again a 1970 case, Mr. Justice Stewart writes a plurality decision.

Evans and two others are charged with the murder of three state troopers, a very serious case. The third guy cuts a deal for immunity. The second guy, Williams, is put to trial. The third guy testifies against Williams, and Williams is convicted and sent to prison.

Now Evans comes on for trial. The third guy testifies against Evans, and then the government comes up with Shaw. Shaw is Williams' cellmate (Williams has gone off to prison for the rest of his life). And Shaw says that Williams said, "If it hadn't been for that dirty son of a bitch Evans, I wouldn't be here now."

Now, under everything we've talked about, how can that possibly be admissible? And, you know, it's simply not admissible. That's no exception to the hearsay rule. The Georgia continuing conspiracy rule is "Once a conspirator, always a conspirator," so Williams is still a conspirator even though he's convicted and in jail for life.

And so Georgia says that what Williams said to Shaw is an exception to the hearsay rule because it is the statement of Evans' coconspirator Williams. So under Georgia law, in it comes.

The Supreme Court affirms. Here's their theory: If ***Dutton*** is good law, there's never an opportunity for Evans to cross-examine Williams. He can't cross-examine him at the time he—he can't call him. He never has an opportunity to cross-examine him either before trial or at trial. The only one he's got is Shaw, who's telling us what Williams says.

And the Supreme Court says, "Well, that's not a problem because it's not harmless error." Today, they might say it's harmless error, but in those days they said it's not harmless error. They said, this hearsay is hearsay, but it's not crucial or devastating hearsay.

And then they say the mission of the confrontation clause is to advance the truth-determining process of the trial. Don't you love it? I mean, it's a get-the-bad-guys rule. And then they say this Shaw hearsay was so reliable that, as Younger would say (and he would proceed to dance around in ways I can't), "it's superduper hearsay!"

Why? What makes Shaw so reliable? Shaw, who's in prison himself, wants out of prison, and has every reason to concoct something to help the government. Shaw, who's the type of witness about whom you would probably get an instruction from a federal judge saying, "Now watch out for Shaw, scrutinize his testimony with care." Well, that's specially reliable hearsay. The Supreme Court of the United States has never disavowed that.

And so that has left us nowhere until we get a case called *Ohio v. Roberts,* 448 U.S. 56 (1980), that sets up the current law, sort of. This is the last general word on the relationship of confrontation and hearsay.

Here's the rule. When a hearsay declarant is not present for cross-examination at trial, the confrontation clause normally requires a showing that he's unavailable. Even then his statement is admissible only if it bears adequate indicia of reliability. Reliability can be inferred without more in a case where the evidence falls within a firmly rooted hearsay exception. In other cases, the evidence must be excluded at least absent a showing of particularized guarantees of trustworthiness.

Now, where does that leave you in a criminal case? In every criminal case, the 803 exceptions that I've just mentioned don't work because they all depend on or turn on the reliability of the person sitting in the front row. So the confrontation clause says in effect, put the person sitting in the front row on the stand, cross-examine him. And that is the logic of *Ohio v. Roberts,* only they haven't followed it.

They have said that in three cases. In *United States v. Owens,* 484 U.S. 554 (1988), the witness who testified had a memory, and he had made a prior identification, but on the stand he didn't remember. Can the prior identification come in consistent with the confrontation clause?

We know it can under the rule against hearsay. "Yes," says the Supreme Court, it can come in under the confrontation clause.

United States v. Inadi, 475 U.S. 387 (1986), demonstrates the coconspirator exception to the rule against hearsay. Must the government show that the coconspirator is unavailable? "No," says the Supreme Court, because the coconspirator exception is one we've had around for a long time and we think it's a pretty good exception to the rule against hearsay.

In *Bourjaily v. United States,* 107 S.Ct. 2775 (1987), under the confrontation clause, they did an interesting thing. They challenged the judge's finding that there was a conspiracy. Remember, I said the judge's finding is made under Rule 104. It's a preliminary finding. And the defense said that under the confrontation clause, the judge can only make that finding on the nonhearsay evidence, the evidence that would get in anyway, the independent evidence. Only if on the independent evidence the judge thinks there's a conspiracy can we admit the coconspirator statement. Some circuits had said no, you can look at the coconspirator statements and the independent evidence, and if that convinces the judge by a fair preponderance that it's a conspiracy, he can base it on that.

The defense said, "How can we adequately confront the witnesses against us? We can't call all these coconspirators. They may be codefendants. They're protected by the Fifth Amendment. We can't call them, and, therefore, that violates the confrontation clause."

No, said the Supreme Court. The judge can properly look at both the independent evidence and at the hearsay evidence itself to decide whether there is a conspiracy.

Bourjaily is significant in another whole area of the law because of the emphasis it places on the judge's powers under Rule 104.

Now, with respect to who can be an expert, judges are making rulings under 104 that they don't think that the expert is qualified and, therefore, they're excluding experts from testifying. You can't get to the jury if you don't have an expert in certain cases. And they're doing it notwithstanding—I've heard this from Jack Weinstein himself, one of the draftpersons of the federal rules. He has said unequivocally that when 104 was drafted, no one ever thought the judges would use 104 to keep experts out. Even so, they're—I mean we're—doing it.

Now, that's the first strain. Second strain on hearsay: What do you do in multidefendant cases? The first decision under multidefendant cases is *Douglas v. Alabama*, 380 U.S. 415 (1965). You'll notice it's decided on the same day as *Pointer v Texas.* And Justice Brennan writes it.

In *Douglas v. Alabama*, two folks by the names of Douglas and Lloyd rob gas stations. Lloyd confesses. He's convicted. Lloyd is called in Douglas' trial. Now we've got Lloyd on the stand. His confession, by the by, inculpates Douglas. So we say, "Mr. Lloyd, you in fact rob gas stations with Douglas, don't you?" Lloyd says, "I refuse to testify on the ground of the Fifth Amendment." And the government says, "I show you this statement. Do you recognize this?" Lloyd says, "I refuse to testify." "That's your signature, isn't it?" "I refuse to testify." "In the first sentence of this statement you say, 'I rob gas stations with Douglas,' don't you?" "I refuse to testify."

"Second sentence you said, 'Douglas went in and I stayed out in the car.'" "I refuse to testify." "Third sentence says, 'Douglas carried the gun.'"

Of course none of it's in evidence, is it? There's no evidence there because the judge would always say, "Now, remember, ladies and gentlemen, the questions aren't evidence. Only what the witness testifies to is evidence."

The Supreme Court, taking a practical view, says, "That's rubbish." They've heard Lloyd's confession. Lloyd's confession croaks Douglas. There's no way Douglas can cross-examine Lloyd, and, therefore, his confrontation rights are violated, *Douglas v. Alabama*.

Then comes *Bruton v. United States,* 391 U.S. 123 (1968). And in *Bruton v. United States,* the rule is laid down that if you have a multidefendant case and the confession or admission of one defendant inculpates another, you've got three choices. You can sever the defendants and give two separate trials; you cannot use the confession, and if you don't use it, no problem; or you can redact the confession. I never heard the word "redact" until I got to be a judge and I learned about this case. And I heard it from a South Carolina lawyer in my first murder case. *See*

Commonwealth v. Best, 381 Mass. 60 (1980). And I knew what *Bruton* was. I was proud of that. The lawyer said, "We've got to redact. We've got to redact this confession." And I thought I couldn't hear him right. I thought it was his accent. And as you do when you have a translation problem, I said, "What?" And he thought I was hard of hearing. He said, "Redact, Judge, we've got to redact this confession." And damned if I understood what he was talking about.

Finally, I understood. We had to edit it. You get into some very dicey questions here. Of course, if you edit it and you've still got the defendant who confessed but he says, "I just drove the get-away car," what are you going to do? Edit it and say X went in with a gun while Douglas is sitting right there? Or are you going to drop that part of the sentence and say that Lloyd said, "I rob gas stations. I sit in the get-away car. I drive away"? You really have this lopover. And of course, the guy didn't say that. He said, "Douglas put me up to all of this." And once you've made the redacted confession, it may be harder on Lloyd than what he actually confessed to.

For instance, in *Big Dan's,* they never used these statements, although it was the reason they split the trial. *See Commonwealth v. Vieira,* 401 Mass. 828 (1988); *Commonwealth v. Cordeiro,* 401 Mass. 843 (1988). These people had a strange view of what constituted rape. One of them had made a statement that "I didn't rape the victim; all I did was hold her arms." And another one said, "I don't know what you're talking about. I didn't rape the victim. All I did was hold her legs." And they had those statements. And then they went on to say who else did what. So you had a *Bruton* problem. You had to give them different trials.

Or how could you redact? You couldn't logically redact that. You'd still have some other actor in the assault. So *Bruton* says that no instructions will cure this; it's either severance, don't use the confession or you redact it. And if you mess up, if something you've redacted out gets in, it's an automatic mistrial. You can't instruct out of it. You can't save the trial.

Now, then comes a case that I need not mention because it's not good law, but what do you do if you have interlocking confessions? Sort of my *Big Dan's* problem could be argued to the interlocking. What do you do then? *Cruz v. New York,* 107 U.S. 714 (1987), was Mr. Justice Scalia's first case.

And he says that where you've got interlocking or overlapping confessions, the government argues, "Look, these confessions interlock, they're all the same. They confessed to the same things, it's just different aspects of the same thing. They've got to be reliable."

Justice Scalia and the Court itself, and I think rightly so, say that's the worst type of confrontation violation because that's when the spillover effect is going to be the greatest. They are going to believe that the confession of A, which croaks B, is the truth if the confession of B agrees with it. That's the time where you've got to follow *Bruton* and give them separate trials.

Now, following that, in *Richardson v. Marsh,* 107 S.Ct. 1702, again Justice Scalia, he says redaction is no good if you just blank out the references to the defendant but the jury can fill in the blanks. And that's fair. He's right. That doesn't get it. So you're sort of pressed to going the whole way and in fact giving them a severance or not using the confession at all.

The third strain to the rule of confrontation is its relation to the law of state privilege. And in *Davis v. Alaska*, 415 U.S. 308, a 1974 case written by Chief Justice Burger, the Supreme Court held that juvenile cases are confidential and secret, and a juvenile record is secret. No one can see it. But the government's chief witness against Davis was a juvenile.

And the defendant wanted to cross-examine Davis about his juvenile record to show that he was under the thumb of the government, that he was biased in favor of the government. Because if Davis didn't testify the way the government wanted, they could recall his probation. And the judge says, "Don't be silly. We're rehabilitating the witness. That's all secret. You can't go into that."

The whole purpose of the juvenile law held in *Davis v. Alaska* was to say, yes, you can; your right to confront the witness overcomes the state policy of protecting the witness. The counterpart Massachusetts case, which was the first Massachusetts case on this point, is *Commonwealth v. A Juvenile*, 384 Mass. 390 (1981). It is from this line of cases that we have *Commonwealth v. Stockhammer*, 409 Mass. 867 (1991), the decision about the rape crisis counselor privilege and it being overcome by the need to confront the witnesses that will be called against the defendant in a case and its progeny.

The problem, as well illustrated in *Bohannon*, is that we can't criticize Mr. Justice Dwyer, because the law he provided was correct at the time. Remember that Piscitelli said, "I believe there are psychiatric records that show that the victim has made false complaints of rape." They tipped it over on that. No one has ever seen those records. We don't know whether Piscitelli ever had such records.

And the real problem under *Commonwealth v. Stockhammer* and its progeny is, what sort of showing do you have to make before the privilege is tipped over in view of the confrontation clause? Is it, as defense counsel say or argue, and who's to fault them, enough to say I'm defending a person on a charge of—you name the charge—but the witness against you has some privilege, a psychiatric privilege, a rape counselor privilege, a domestic abuse counselor privilege? The area of privileges is the big expanding industry in Massachusetts. There are more privileges on the books that the legislature has passed in recent years than any other comparable change in Massachusetts evidentiary law.

Does the confrontation clause trump them? *Davis v. Alaska* says, yes, it does, if you can show by trumping the privilege the bias of the government witness against you. The question is, what sort of showing do you have to make? Is it enough simply to say, "Turn those records over to me," or is there a stopping point? Do you say, "Well, the judge will look at them first?" and then say, "Well, what does the judge know? He's not an advocate. He doesn't know all the ways I, as a skilled attorney, can use these records."

But where do you stop? What is the weight to be given to these social policies? Well, I'll leave you with that.

The last point comes out of ***Chambers v. Mississippi***, 410 U.S. 284 (1973). It's well to understand that case, a very interesting case. In ***Chambers v. Mississippi***, some Mississippi police officers rousted a black bar. They came to a bar frequented by black persons to find someone. And apparently, they were not terribly pleasant. All the lights went out in the bar and shooting erupted.

When the shooting stopped, there was a dead Mississippi policeman on the floor and there was a manhunt on to find the murderer. The person charged with the murder was one Chambers.

Northern civil rights lawyers came down to defend Chambers. There was very severe concern about the racial aspects of this trial, and they found a fellow by the name of McDonald. McDonald admitted to killing the police officer. Can you imagine where this is going? But unlike my incompetence, these lawyers really hung right onto McDonald. And after the state had rested, they called McDonald to the stand.

And now, true Perry Mason style, they're ready. They say, "Mr. McDonald, what's your name?" "My name's McDonald." "Were you in the bar that night?" "Yes, I was." "Who killed the policeman?" He said, "Chambers killed the policeman." This is real trouble for Chambers.

They have his statement. "Well, just a moment. Wait a second," says the Mississippi judge. "We have strict voucher here in Mississippi, gentlemen. You put this witness on the stand, and you called him. You can't impeach your own witness." "Give me a break," say these lawyers. "What are you talking about? You're going to execute this guy. We have a statement that the murderer is sitting on the stand. At a minimum, you're going to let us put that statement, just to impeach him, Judge."

"I'm sorry. The rules of evidence are the rules of evidence and they are just and fair, and you guys shouldn't have called him to the stand. Sit down. No cross-examination of this witness." And McDonald gets off the stand saying Chambers killed the officer.

Chambers, not surprisingly, is convicted. The Supreme Court says the right of confrontation required the judge to allow that cross-examination. And the interesting thing is, though I think I've fairly given you the case, the justification just isn't there. If it is, as many commentators argue, everybody has a right to a defense, and who cares about these rules of evidence? You've got a right to a defense. And it is argued from ***Chambers v. Mississippi***.

There are distinguished members of the defense bar who say that in a criminal case, it is ethically and indeed constitutionally justified to put on a defendant you know is lying to confront the government's case, because if you really believe in the adversary system, that lying defendant should be able to take the stand and tell his story, because the cross-examination that the government gives him will bring out the truth.

And an interesting thing is that in Massachusetts, the rules of ethics take no position on this. And the reason that they take no position is that the justices would have been divided if they took a position. Some justices say it's crystal clear that as officers of the court, you cannot, as the ABA canons say, put on a person who is going to suborn the truth. Massachusetts is silent concerning what happens if the defense lawyer learns that his client has lied on the stand. Under federal law, we can't put on a lying witness, consistent with the canons that govern, or at least that's my understanding.

INFERENCES, PRESUMPTIONS AND PRIMA FACIE EVIDENCE

Let's talk about presumptions. What I'm about to teach you is a theory or an approach to the law of inferences, presumptions and prima facie evidence that is both accurate and harmonizes about 75 to 85 percent of the cases, state and federal.

I have to pompously say that the other quarter of the cases are flat out wrong. So if you find one that helps you, be my guest. But I'm going to teach an approach to this that harmonizes most of them and, so far as I know, is accurate.

All the text writers say the law of presumptions is a morass, it's not understandable. But that's because, as true geniuses, they're trying to figure it all out, and the truth is the judges don't understand it. And since we don't understand it, our major flaw is to call things that are not presumptions presumptions.

Presumptions is only one of five different relationships between a basic fact and a resultant fact. I'm going to detail each one of the five. I want you to think about them in the ascending order of evidentiary impact. I'm going to go from the weakest to the strongest. And in each case except the fifth case, where it's not applicable, I think you can best understand the relationship if you think of what the judge must charge. Now, you get a chance to advise the judge on this, so think of what the judge must charge and you'll have it right.

Remember, what we're doing is talking about the relationship in law between a basic fact and a resultant fact.

Inferences

The first relationship I want to talk about is the inference. *See* Mass. Evid. Stand. 301(b). Inferences are simply the relationship that details the situation in which proof of the basic fact allows, but does not require the jury to infer the resultant fact.

And where a higher court, such as the First Circuit or the Supreme Judicial Court, has specifically spoken to the point, you have a case that details this inference, and you know that if you prove the basic fact, you've made it to the jury, because you've got a case that says they can infer the resultant fact.

An example of an inference is that Massachusetts doctrine of common law that says that violation of a safety statute or an injury to someone covered by the statute allows an inference of negligence. *See Adamian v. Three Sons, Inc.*, 353 Mass. 498 (1968).

For instance, in this beautiful building, I imagine that if the lights all now go off, in the stairwells, emergency lighting will go on. If you prove that someone fell down the stairs and you prove that the emergency lighting was not on, you're to the jury on negligence. Query whether you have to prove some causation. We can analogize the same thing in a public building where they're supposed to have sprinklers or in a landlord/tenant situation where they're supposed to have fire detectors. If there's a fire and there's injury and the smoke detectors don't work, that allows the inference of negligence.

There can be all sorts of evidence to the contrary—evidence that the smoke detectors worked right up until the moment of the fire and the reason that the smoke detectors didn't work then was some bizarre situation as the nadium ray came through and that skewed the diode and they didn't go on and it was completely unforeseeable. That's fine, but the statute says that working smoke detectors shall be there. They didn't work. Someone was injured. The jury can infer from the very fact that they didn't work that there was negligence. That doesn't mean that they can infer causation, but they can infer negligence.

So what is the effect if you prove the basic fact, that the smoke detectors, the lights in the hallway, didn't work? That allows the jury to infer the resultant fact, but it does not require it. Does the judge need to charge on anything? He may, but he doesn't have to charge. You can get judges sometimes to charge on an inference of due care or something like that. You can get them to charge that the violation of a safety statute permits an inference of negligence, but they don't have to, they just have to pay attention to it and allow the case to go forward, because the inference operates.

Presumptions

The second type of relationship, which is somewhat better in some respects, is the true presumption. *See* Mass. Evid. Stand. 301(c). A presumption simply says that if you prove the basic fact, the jury must find the resultant fact unless some rebuttal evidence is offered. Let me put this in context.

The law of inferences just discussed applies both to civil and criminal cases. It must; you can convict someone on entirely circumstantial evidence. That means that there is no direct evidence, no eyewitness, but the circumstances allow the jury to infer beyond a reasonable doubt the guilt of the person involved and, therefore, the case not only goes to the jury but the conviction is upheld.

In criminal cases, only inferences operate against a criminal defendant, nothing else. It is a violation of constitutional magnitude to have a presumption or prima facie evidence or some other thing operate against the defendant. ***Sandstrom v. Montana***, 442 U.S. 510 (1979).

Now, that doesn't mean that various affirmative matters may not be set up by the state to require the defense to produce some evidence that place the matter in issue, but the burden always remains on the state. Once some evidence has been produced, in Massachusetts anyway, the state must carry their burden but beyond a reasonable doubt. *See, e.g.,* ***Commonwealth v. Williams***, 377 Mass. 916 (1979); ***Commonwealth v. Rodriguez***, 370 Mass. 684 (1976).

Now, what am I talking about? The defense may have to come up with some evidence of self-defense, but once he does, the government has to prove that there wasn't any self-defense, and they have to prove it beyond a reasonable doubt.

In the case of someone found with contraband, the defense may have to come up with some evidence of license of a weapon, or some form of firearms identification. Once they do, the government has to prove that they weren't licensed.

Mental capacity doesn't get into a case until the defense raises it in a criminal case, i.e., the fellow isn't mentally competent either to stand trial or mentally competent at the time of the event. Once they raise it, the government has to prove that he was competent beyond a reasonable doubt, and so on.

Only inferences can operate against a criminal defendant. We still have some cases, because the constitutional law is retroactive in this respect, where there used to be state judges who would charge that an evil, killing malice could be presumed. And you know that in the state system for murder, there has to be malice, and then deliberately premeditated malice aforethought for first degree, but second degree is the killing with malice. And they would say, if you find the evil here, you can presume the malice. Well, that violates the constitution. You can't presume or have prima facie evidence or anything against the defendant, only inferences.

So now I'm beyond inferences, and I'm talking just civil cases. In civil cases, proof of a basic fact, if it's a presumption, tells the jury they must find the presumed fact unless there is some evidence to rebut the presumed fact. Then the bubble bursts and the presumption drops out of the case. And that's not glib talking. That's the distinguished Thayer, the bubble-bursting approach to presumptions. It is the approach followed both in Massachusetts and in 301 of the federal rules.

When rebuttal evidence comes in, the bubble bursts, and it no longer is in the case. For example, it is presumed in Massachusetts, contrary probably to the great quantity of personal experience, that a letter that is mailed is in due course received. Therefore, proof of the mailing presumes the receipt in the absence of contrary evidence.

So let's take the two situations. It's a contract case, and in order to make the acceptance, we're trying to prove that the acceptance was mailed within the option period or within the offer period, and then, given the normal delays in the mails, that it would have been received.

So we, plaintiffs, put on a witness, and the witness says, "I mailed it. It was the acceptance, and I mailed it."

Now, you can attack this—if that's all that happens. Let's stop there. If that's all that happens and there is no rebuttal evidence to that at all, this is what the judge will charge:

> Ladies and gentlemen, if you believe that the acceptance was mailed, then under the law you shall presume, that is, you shall find that it was received by the Widget Company. It's up to you whether you believe it was mailed; but if you find it was mailed by a fair preponderance of the evidence, then you shall find that it was received by the Widget Company.

Now, suppose there is rebuttal evidence and the rebuttal evidence can attack both basic facts and it can attack the resultant fact, that is, you can go in with evidence that it was never mailed; some other witness saw it on the secretary's desk weeks later—that's rebuttal evidence. You can go in with evidence that attacks the resultant facts. Your side can get on and say, "I never received it."

If you come up with evidence like that, the bubble bursts, the presumption is gone, and the judge simply will say nothing about it. There will be no charge to the jury. You can argue to the jury, "Now, you remember the secretary, how professional she was, and she said it was mailed. And you know all the motives they have to deny receiving it. You should find that it was received."

And the other side can get up and say, "My man said it wasn't received. These people are kidding themselves." The judge will say nothing. It will be the weight to be accorded to the witness's testimony. The bubble has burst. But if there's no rebuttal evidence, if they believe the basic fact, they must find the presumed fact.

In the language of the rules, which I think is sort of arcane, the operation of a presumption shifts to the party against whom it operates the burden of going forward or the burden of production, but the burden of proof remains always on the party who has to prove the point.

In other words, once you prove the basic facts, once there's evidence sufficient to allow a finding of the basic facts, the other side had better come up with something or the resultant fact is going to be accepted if they believe the basic facts. But if you come up with something, the presumption is gone, and the party that has to prove the fact bears the burden of proving it.

Prima Facie Evidence

Now, that's the only thing that's a true presumption. The next level up is what is called prima facie evidence. It's called prima facie evidence in Massachusetts; in federal courts, it's called presumptions of the middle ground.

Now, prima facie evidence has a better whammy than a presumption, because it doesn't disappear. It works the same way, but it doesn't disappear. It has independent evidentiary weight. Here's a common example of prima facie evidence under our Massachusetts system.

You have a case that's amenable to a jury trial. You want a jury trial, but not much amount is in controversy, so you have to try it first before a state district judge. So you try before the district judge, you win and you get your finding. I find for the plaintiff in the amount of $2,000, but the defendant doesn't want to pay and appeals to the jury of six.

Under Massachusetts law (G.L. c. 231, § 102(c))—and I'm not saying in a trial practice sense that you should do this—I think this would not be wise—but you can do this, you're the plaintiff—I offer a certified copy of the finding of the district judge before whom the case was tried that finds in my favor. It's accepted, received in evidence and read to the jury. You then rest. Then the defense comes on with 10 days of why they're not liable, and you do nothing—you just sit there. Ten days. And they are never liable: "If I was liable, I didn't buy it and, therefore, I'm not liable." Okay. And then you never put on any other evidence. Your case is nevertheless to the jury, and the judge will charge as follows:

> Ladies and gentlemen, you will recall Exhibit Number 1. It's what we call in Massachusetts law prima facie evidence, and, therefore, that means you should give it such weight as it is due. Thank you very much.

They won't explain it any more than that, but they will say this is some special type of evidence. And you evaluate it, you give it some weight because it's prima facie evidence.

Now, remember, the example I've just detailed for you is a situation where you've proved the basic facts, that you've won before the judge alone, but then there's been 10 days of rebuttal of the resultant facts, not liable. You are entitled to attack the basic facts, though in my example, no one ever does. How are you going to attack unless they mess the records up where it's pretty obvious what happened in the district court, but theoretically you can attack the basic facts.

Let's say, though, you put on no rebuttal evidence. If you put on no rebuttal evidence and they put on prima facie evidence, the case will never get to the jury. The judge will say if the basic fact isn't attacked and it's clear that you've won before the judge alone, the defense has just been stalling if they don't put on the evidence, and it will be a directed verdict for the plaintiff because the jury will have to find for the plaintiff because the basic fact is not disputed.

Prima facie evidence is just like a presumption, except the bubble doesn't burst. With prima facie evidence, the evidentiary force resultant from proof of the basic fact, which is prima facie evidence, gets you a judge's charge. Whatever happens, the judge will charge. And if there's no rebuttal evidence, the judge will require from the jury the finding of the resultant facts. And in my example, if that's the whole case, the judge will take it away and decide it himself.

Social Policy

The next relationships I want to talk about are relationships based on social policy. These are sometimes inappropriately named, because they don't work like the conclusive or irrebuttable presumptions.

My example of this is no longer good law. If you want the state of the current law, look at a case called *CC v. AB*, a Supreme Judicial Court case. 406 Mass. 679 (1990). These are the best type of relationships you can have because proof of the basic fact prohibits any proof about the resultant fact. In other words, the social policy is so strong that if you prove the basic fact, the jury has to come out with the resultant fact, and we're not going to let any proof having to do with the resultant fact go before the jury.

The best example is the ancient common law presumption that a child born in wedlock was legitimate. And the reasons come from the property law that stated that illegitimate children couldn't inherit. *Kent v. Barker*, 2 Gray 535, 536 (1854). The goal of the law has been to favor the child so they wouldn't be starving and homeless. The strict common law rule was if the child was born in wedlock, the child was legitimate.

Now, you can imagine a child born only a few days after the wedding. You can imagine a child born to someone whose husband has been at sea in the East Indies. And there are all sorts of cases like this. No matter, proof of the basic fact, the basic fact is the marital status and the timing of the birth, that ended it.

You could, of course, attack the marital status; you could attack the basic fact. You could say they were never validly married. You could attack the timing and say the kid wasn't born then, he was born some other time. But if the kid was born in the marriage, that was it; we just wouldn't accept any evidence of the contrary.

Then the law relaxed a little bit. And the law at the time of Blackstone was—well, it's a presumption (and again they're using the word wrong because it's like superduper prima facie evidence)—it can only be rebutted by clear and convincing evidence, not just some evidence. It has to be clear and convincing evidence, as though we're putting the burden on the side that has to rebut it. And, what's more, husband and wife are incompetent to testify as to nonaccesss. We won't let anyone testify as to who has been sleeping with whom or not. We're just not going to hear that evidence because, of course, we want the kid to be legitimate.

Now, after CC *v. AB*, a fascinating case where the putative father wanted to pay child support and wanted to have his parental rights recognized, the standard in Massachusetts is that it is like a special type of presumption. The kid is presumed to be the child of the married husband but you can testify to nonaccess, and all the blood tests can come in, and the defendant or the putative father who wants the visitation rights has to prove by clear and convincing evidence that he is in fact the father. That's a special case.

But I use the example because I want to give you an example of a relationship based on social policy. Proof of the basic fact does it; we don't get into proof of the resultant fact.

Legislative Policy

And the last relationship is what I call the deference to legislative policy. We'll call it deference to legislative policy. *See* Mass. Evid. Stand. 301(f). Now, this deference does not operate with respect to those statutes that are given a second tier analysis under constitutional principles because they are suspect. It doesn't apply to statutes where race or gender or unequal treatment of some sort is involved. But to your ordinary routine statute, the deference paid to the legislature is so great that another term for it is the presumption of constitutionality. (Again, we are using the term "presumption" improperly.) When I say deference to legislative policy, I'm talking about the presumption of constitutionality.

My example is *Shell Oil Co. v. Revere*, a case I had in the superior court, but the cite I prefer to use is the Supreme Judicial Court. 383 Mass. 682 (1981). Revere passed an ordinance saying there shall be no self-service gas stations in Revere. And since the gas companies make more money from self-service gas stations, they attacked the ordinance as unconstitutional and as denying them equal protection because it's utterly irrational. And they went to town like gangbusters.

There was no dispute that the ordinance of Revere was on the books. But they then came on and put on overwhelming evidence that self-service gas stations were safer, their sprinkler systems more effective, they allowed the gas to be sold more cheaply and they could extend their economic resources further and, therefore, have more gas stations in any location. And Revere never even tried to rebut any of this. The Shell Oil Company had everything its own way, and it would have been a violation of my oath to find contrary to any of those contentions. The company's contentions were clear.

The parties rest. The case is jury-waived, so I go back to think about it. And because of the deference that is owed to the legislature, I get to dream up some reason why the aldermen in Revere possibly could have done that. But you have no evidence from them. They don't bother to come in and say, "Hey, we thought ..." The legislative history of the board of alderman in Revere is a difficult thing to look up—there is none.

So there's no evidence, and I think, well, a lot of people started out pumping gas, and maybe there's the summer jobs program, and maybe the gas pumper might know more about motors or changing tires than those fellows who just take your money and sell you cigarettes. I never think they know anything about mechanics, but somehow the guy who pumps your gas has got to know how to turn it on and how the machine works. I think that he can do stuff for me. And those people—remember the old days—they used to check your oil. I thought they were virtual wizards. And I think that it's a good idea to train people to do that.

So I write this opinion and I say Revere could well understand that their young people have little work and to train them as mechanics is a social good.

Shell Oil says, "We can prove, no, no, no," and I say, "Too late. You had your chance. I've dreamt this up. Sounds pretty good to me." I'm affirmed.

So significant is the deference to legislative policy, if we're on a first-tier analysis, that's why it's outcome determinative. If you get something that impacts a certain protected class wrongly and the judges take strict scrutiny, then the government has to come in and explain it, and it had better be the best way to do it or they're dead.

But for routine laws, because we have a separation of powers, we get to dream up reasons. And even though all the evidence sweeps the other way, so long as we can dream up a reason they haven't figured out, we'll affirm the statute, and we are right.

Well, that's all for today. You've been very faithful. I thank you very much. It's been my privilege. *(Applause)*

"...we have the greatest engine of truth and discernment ever discovered by humankind—cross-examination."

–Hon. William G. Young, December 5, 1992
From *Young on Unlocking Evidentiary Mysteries*

CHAPTER 2

Judge Young on the Practical Arts of Trial Advocacy

DECEMBER 4, 1993

IT'S time for final argument in a civil case. All these stories I actually saw or someone told me, but I saw this one. Final argument, federal court, the defendant is arguing first. The defendant has been somewhat roughly handled during the course of the trial. This is how the transcript reads:

> Judge, ladies and gentlemen of the jury. You may have noticed some awkwardness in the presentation of this case. Well, this is my first time in federal court. It will be my last.

That was the best part. It went downhill from there.

My name is Bill Young. I'm truly honored, I mean this, that you would spend a Saturday morning here. I want very, very much to make this worthwhile for you, so in beginning it, let me explain where we are, where we're going, and how I think you can make this work for you.

This is the third annual presentation in what I propose to be four years of talking about evidence, practice and procedure. The first year I tried in four hours to explain what I knew about evidence, or thought I knew, and that was all right. Last year in a program called *Unlocking Evidentiary Mysteries* we went back and talked about what I think are the most difficult areas of evidence. This year I want to talk about trial practice, not evidence, though we will touch on evidence. Then I think I'm good for about one more Saturday session a year from now—on the differences between state and federal practice. Beyond that, I'm not competent to say anything. And after those four years, we'll take a year off, and then of course the law will change sufficiently that I can start in again on another four-year cycle.

So this morning is trial practice. I want very much to have you ask questions. I propose to fill the four hours we have together by talking through various aspects of trial practice, but I do want this to go where you want it to go. Therefore, there's no formal question-and-answer period. If you have a question about anything, stop me and I'll try to answer it.

I caution you, I guess, that when I talk about trial practice this is different than teaching evidence. It's different in this respect: When I teach evidence I teach it as well as I know how, but I teach it at the trial level, where it seems to me evidence is most pertinent. And with an attempt to at least average competence I can tell you what the rule is, and I try very hard to be candid in telling you how judges interpret the rule—or how I think they interpret the rule—and how they go about it.

With respect to trial practice, though we're going to talk about the rules of procedure and we're going to talk about customs of proceeding in the various courts—state and federal, civil and criminal—all trial practice is significantly formed by your own tactics and techniques. I am quick to say that I have more fingers and toes than I have completed trials to my credit as a lawyer. I was privileged to be appointed to the bench after 10 years of practice, so I was never an accomplished trial lawyer. I don't pretend to be. I wanted to be, but I took the opportunity to serve on the bench.

I am fascinated by the process, and I am eager to talk about it with you. I like nothing better than the privilege of trying cases, that is watching cases be tried, but I don't stand before you this morning as one of the leading trial lawyers in the Commonwealth. I never was.

There are certain things, and I will try to be candid about it, where I don't have a trial lawyer's theory about how to do it. We're going to talk about how it's done. I'm going to share with you everything I know, but I don't pretend to say this is a workable theory or that you should adopt this theory.

THE TRIAL LAWYER

I think it is important in talking trial practice to be very clear about who I think we are, because I think that forms everything that you do as a trial lawyer. I'm talking about trial practice now. I'm not talking about being a litigator. I'm talking about being a trial lawyer, going into court where a factfinder, either a judge or jury, is going to resolve the dispute.

And I submit to you, and I do this with utmost seriousness because to me everything else technical that we talk about this morning depends on this, that we are teachers. That's what it means to be a lawyer. To a less important degree, that's what it means to be a judge.

Those of you who are trial lawyers have a special obligation that the rest of the bar does not have. The words "zealous advocate" are not self-defining. In fact, there are moves afoot to strike the word "zealous" from the ethical considerations because it is thought in some quarters, including by my chief, Joe Tauro, that the word "zealous" has contributed to the demise of civility and the acerbic wrenching you experience as you get cases ready for trial.

Well, I do like the word, properly interpreted. I think the way to interpret it is to consider yourselves teachers. William Christensen said this from the Harvard Business School, but it epitomizes it the best I know how: "Teaching is a very special kind of caring." He's right. It's the great glory of our civilization—I'm not going to preach to you—but it is the great glory of our civilization, at least on the criminal side, for those who cannot afford it and the weight of the state is brought against them, that we will provide a lawyer. And in this state we provide an outstanding caliber of attorney. If we did more on the civil side, the quality of our practice would be considerably better.

When you have a client, you are first and foremost a teacher. The first person you have the obligation to teach is the client. The client may not want to learn necessarily, but it is your obligation to teach that client. The client may have a very inflated idea of the client's rights, what the system will afford the client. But you know, Lincoln was correct, and Lincoln was a great trial lawyer. It is your duty if at all possible to avoid litigation, to avoid the very thing that you are in fact experts at.

We are ambivalent as a bar about what it is that we're going to talk about this morning. On the one hand, we purport to revere those people who protect the downtrodden, the despised of the society; but on the other hand, we do not revere them. In fact, society tends to lump those who represent the disadvantaged, the segregationists, the polluters, with the clients whom they represent.

THE CLIENT

What you are primarily are teachers. Let me test this for just a minute. Think to yourself of the most embarrassing thing that ever happened to you. There's an avoidance of eye contact now. Don't worry, I won't call on you. This is not back in law school. But I will share some stories. When I was about nine years old, I stole a neighbor's sign. I was immediately found out. I was a cub scout denounced, tragically.

When I grew up I once was invited to a dinner party in my honor, for I was doing some alumni work. And I forgot about it. I didn't tell my wife. The party was held. We never showed up. I am embarrassed by that. Once in the 10 years in which I was in active practice I was complained of to the Board of Bar Overseers. I cannot tell you that without immediately adding I was in the right. They never investigated; they did nothing with the complaint. The fact is, though, that someone complained about me.

Now, if you watch me here, you see that when we get to something that hurts, someone questioned my ethics as a practicing lawyer, you see how defensive I am. The important thing is to know that my own sense of self, my own sense of how I must deal with other people, other professionals, impels me to defend my own conduct.

Generalize from that and think to yourself the most embarrassing thing that ever happened to you. You remember, as healthy adult professionals, those things in ways that make you feel as good as you possibly can feel about the errors, mistakes and carelessness that we are all prone to make as human beings. With time, you've learned to sugarcoat them a little. Everybody does that. Your clients do that.

Do you think for one minute that those people in the high towers—those middle managers in the banks, in the real estate divisions, in the loan offices—do you think for one minute that they're not remembering the '80s in a way that is perhaps not exactly the way it happened?

How about the person who goes out and hits a pedestrian? Did the pedestrian dash in front of the car? What about that terribly human need to think of yourself as a competent driver when you've run over the little kid? How are you going to live with yourself unless you think of yourself as someone who was being careful and not inattentive? What if you are a victim of rape, completely blameless, or is it improper for me even to suggest that there could be blame? How can there be blame if it was rape? Don't you think that that person is remembering the situation in such a way that puts the person together as a human? Of course he or she is. We all are. And these people are your clients. By the very nature of the adversary process, your first duty is to teach them, to teach them the limits of the process to which we all have devoted our lives. They're not going to like that. The way you do that is in part formed by how the case develops.

An example. I once, but I was part of a big firm and I was with other people, defended a case on which a bank had not paid on a letter of credit. Now, I need not go into the commercial law to tell you that the whole idea of letters of credit is that they're subject to a bright line rule, and the bank has to pay if the bright line is crossed. The bank didn't pay. They were immediately sued. And this is a lay-down case; the other side wins automatically. They come in for a mandatory injunction. We beat the mandatory injunction. I'm very proud of that. Then I go to our client, the bank officer, and I say, "Now, pay the money. You're dead in the water. I'll try to negotiate no interest and no costs."

And, you know, I misjudged the psychology. He looked at me and says, "But you've won."

"Oh yes," I said, "We've won. But that's the battle. The war is yet to be fought."

And he said, "No, I think they're fraudulent. That's what you argued."

I said, "Yes. That was enough to fend off the mandatory injunction, and we can argue that in good faith, but you are dead in the water."

"I think we'll hold on a little bit. No more than 50 cents on the dollar," my client responded.

"You are dead," I say.

He doesn't say it, but he's thinking, "You are a wimp. I want aggressive lawyers out there."

I remember this because it happened right at the time when, through no credit to me, I am transmogrified into a judge. Not everyone is so lucky. I give him this advice. I tell him that he is dead. He sort of fends me off, and then it is announced that the governor has appointed me to the superior court bench. He does not change his view. The case lasts for six to nine months, a year later. By then I am wearing a robe. He is, in fact, dead.

The point is to try to get them in the right frame of mind. One thing in advising your clients, never—this is absolutely true—never say to a client, "You've got a 100 percent case. This is a sure win. We will beat this case." This works against both plaintiff and defendant, because whatever fates or gods there are, they will strike you down. It happens in every single case.

TEACHING THE FACTFINDER: JUDGE OR JURY

Now, let's get to the subject at hand, but on everything I say, it's going to be formed by this idea that you are teachers. And your obligation as teachers, as trial lawyers, is first to teach your client, and then to teach the other side. Don't be glib; don't hold things back. If there is evidence that makes you win, you be sure you rub the other side's nose in it. If you win because the statute of limitations has been missed here, you let the other side know that as soon as possible to keep the transaction costs down. You emphasize the law. And then you are teachers to the judge, who is herself a teacher of the law in the case. And ultimately if we use jury trials as our paradigm, and here I'm going to do that, you must teach the jury. Teach them; don't slip stuff by. Again, I'm not preaching; I'm talking about what I think is absolutely the best practice—not obfuscating things, but in fact teaching the jury, making them understand what it is that is at issue in this case.

That takes into account two very separate concerns. By its nature, our adversary process is a search for the truth within limits. In a way it's an archeological expedition into the past and what happened in the past, because rights turn on what happened in the past.

So your duty as trial lawyers is to lay what happened in the past out for the jury in a way that they can understand it. Let's consider that for just a moment.

I'm 53, a white man from a middle-class background who has lived, I hope not a sheltered life, but a straight life. I served in the Army in peacetime, married, had kids, went to the public schools. We'll revert to that; this is not a course about me, but you want to know what you can find out about judges.

I have never dealt in drugs—it sounds like I'm running for office—I have never dealt in drugs nor inhaled. I am not an adulterer. My business dealings are few because I'm privileged to have been a judge for 16 years. I am familiar with the usual ailments of a family, and we've been blessed to avoid major catastrophe. So I'm a rather bland and uninteresting person.

It is my duty as a judge to know about all of those things, and I don't know about them firsthand. I don't know what it is to be the victim of a crime of violence. I don't know what it is to be driven by the compulsion of addiction. I don't know what it is to have a multimillion dollar deal on the verge of going down the drain. I don't know where to go to leverage to make the buy-out or figure the point spread on the interest rates to assemble the property to do the deal. I don't know how to repair the disk in the thoracic spine that's causing the pain to radiate down the leg, and I have not experienced that pain. But it is your job to make all of those things vividly real for jurors who ostensibly are as bland and uninteresting as I am.

That is the essence of your teaching job, to make that evidence a matter of concern and interest to those jurors where, by the whole definition of our system, they don't know. If a juror comes to the venire with too much knowledge about the actual matters in issue—the person is a thoracic spine surgeon, for example—that arguably is a reason for challenging that juror for cause because the juror will be thought to dominate the debate in the jury room. So what are we going to get? We're going to get ignoramuses. That's the whole idea. We're going to get people who don't know. Now, I'm glib when I say ignoramuses. That isn't necessarily what you want, but you get people who don't know anything about the case, and it's your job as lawyers to teach them.

I believe this. I absolutely believe this passionately. If you're going to be a trial lawyer, you had better reserve time to spread your net of acquaintances as broadly as you possibly can, to the disadvantaged, to people of other cultures, to people in areas of endeavor that are completely foreign to you—finance, music. You must be interested in all humankind. And because there aren't enough hours in a day, I urge you to go to good movies, the movies that explore the human condition. Read the good books—and it's not for me to define what is good. Read trashy books if you think that they tell you something about how human beings behave.

And don't be elitist in your reading. The popular press serves a remarkable and I think unsung virtue in our society by translating the most complex into something understandable for people of the street.

I give you two examples: A former colleague of mine, he's still an excellent lawyer, has kept that *National Geographic* article on computers. They did a whole issue some years ago. From his point of view it's the best description for a layperson to understand about computers, a complex area of endeavor. Now, he can't put that article into evidence, but he uses it. Why? To get the journalist's phraseology, the manner in which they explain reality, when he has to teach that reality to a jury.

I used to defend some slip and fall cases where I had to know a little bit about the lower back. I have an article out of *Cosmopolitan* that talks about back pain. I don't know that the article was good medicine, but I was fairly well-satisfied after talking with the doctors that we used that it wasn't bad medicine. The great advantage of that article was how the journalist explained in simple layperson's terms what it was that I had to explain.

Don't think that the knowledge you need is found only in *Scientific American.* It's not. It's found in the daily newspapers; it's found in the popular magazines. And when you get articles that pertain to the things that you are concerned with, you want to retain them, put them in the file.

Strategic, Tactical and Personal Considerations

I think that you can consider each step in a trial at three different levels, and I'll give them names, and they are in this order of importance: the strategic level, the tactical level and the personal level.

Don't get fooled by the military analogies. The military analogies came to me, but I must be a dissident. This is not combat. Those people who analogize it to combat miss the great glory of the law—the limits and the common shared responsibility to the rule of law that has nothing to do with combat. With that aside, I think military analogies will help us to understand, and that is why I use them.

I should tell you that the idea that it's combat once got translated in the 1980s by that famous Chicago firm Kirkland & Ellis. Lawyers in that firm thought that the problem with trial lawyers was that they were trying to do two different things. On the one hand, they were trying to fight in court. On the other hand, they were trying to negotiate and settle cases—trying to "get to yes." So what they did was divide up their litigation department into negotiators and trial lawyers.

It was a disaster, organizationally and institutionally. It was a disaster and properly so. The trial lawyers immediately became macho caricatures of themselves. They became unthinking bullets going for the throat of the opposition. The negotiators, whose goal was to get to yes, were immediately dismissed as wimps. No one would talk to them. You did not have to talk to them. There was nothing that they could do to you—their goal was to settle, not fight. So get rid of them, and instead deal with the trial lawyers. The firm abandoned the bifurcation very quickly, unfortunately after ruining the careers of some people. There is a profound moral that stands behind this.

My experience as a judge—I was never a great trial lawyer, maybe a passively okay trial lawyer, but never a great one—now convinces me that it is the best trial lawyers who are the best settlers, the best private resolvers of cases. Most cases should be settled, but you never want a reputation as someone who will always settle a case. I had a case against a fellow years ago when I was practicing, and I argued a motion. In those days, there were motion sessions. We were close to final pretrial, and I argued this motion for summary judgment and lost. So I had to go to trial. As I was leaving the courthouse, a very respected lawyer said to me, "What was all that about?" As we walked down the courthouse steps, I explained to him that it involves a commercial case and I explained the case to him. He told me this about the lawyer on the other side: "He will settle the case on the first day of trial." The lawyer on the other side had just won this big motion. I thought I had a good motion for summary judgment, and I had just lost it. Why would he settle the case? In my inexperience, I did not believe this veteran lawyer who was talking to me. Also, I remember thinking that my respected friend on the courthouse steps had just insulted my opposite number. You see, my opposite number had a reputation for caving at the last moment. As events proved, that's exactly what happened. My client ended up winning 100 cents on the dollar, plus interest.

The point is that you don't want that reputation. You've got to be a good trial lawyer. You've got to know how to try the case if trial is what is required. At the same time, because you are a good trial lawyer and you are aware of the many uncertainties and you know the risks and the limits—and there are limits to our adversary system and what it can do for your client—you are in the best position to settle if you have to. So you also have to know how to resolve the case without going to trial. It is never a disgrace to settle a case adequately. It is never a reflection on you to adequately settle a case. And adequately doesn't mean that your client is going to be happy; it means, all things considered, the settlement in effect will make both sides happy.

Strategic Considerations

Now, with all that in mind, let's talk strategic considerations. By strategic, I mean the overarching legal principles that concern you in a case, that drive the case. It is, after all, not combat, not how many lawyers you have in your firm or word processors or how many witnesses you can line up. It, instead, consists of those things that the law requires. We have an adherence to legal principles. I am not going to spend much time on this except what I have to to explain the tactical—why we are doing what we are doing in a case. Just remember that everything is governed by those strategic considerations. Everything is governed by what you have to prove in the legal sense to make out a prima facie case. It is all governed by what you have to prove to get the case to the jury, and, because you are teachers, what you have to do to carry your burden of persuasion to convince the jury.

Tactical Considerations

The place that we're going to spend our time here is on the second, the tactical. And by tactical what I mean is how you do it, what you do in court. That's what I think will be most helpful to you. How to actually convey the information or teach the information.

And my paradigm is going to be a jury trial. I use jury trials recognizing that many cases are jury-waived. In fact, most of your practice may well be before a judge alone, but we're going to talk jury trials, and the reason is simply this: If you hold yourselves to the standard of a jury trial you'll do fine jury-waived, only the reverse doesn't work. So prepare every case as though it were a jury trial.

I'm here to tell you a jury trial goes better than a trial before a judge and it goes better because it goes every day. You're not under the cruel and unusual punishment of a judge saying, "Well, a couple of afternoons here, and then we'll do another couple of afternoons there," and then waiting a year and a half to get the decision. Jurors give you a decision. They decide the case. The rules of evidence are strictly adhered to in a jury case. Jury-waived, you may be up against this: You remember Judge Wyzanski, a famous judge, and I was privileged to be his colleague. He had the first of the antitrust cases—a big one—***United States v. United Shoe Machinery Corp.*** In *United Shoe,* he wrote the really basic law on the attorney-client privilege. You can find it at 89 F. Supp. 357 (D.Mass. 1950). Well, they get in before the judge. They're doing pretrial now. The judge had half-glasses. And they've got lawyers from New York. I'm not against lawyers from New York, but you'll understand when I tell you this story.

And the judge said, "There, there, there seems to be"—he had a high-pitched voice—"There seems to be a lot of documents here. How long is it going to take to work through the issues with respect to these documents?" This is jury-waived now so that Wyzanski's going to decide everything.

The New York lawyer said, "Well, if your Honor pleases, it's going to take us a year, probably a year. There are hundreds of thousands of documents, and it will probably take us a year sitting, you know, if you take a few weeks off in the summer."

So Wyzanski looked at him, and he says, "No, no, no. Everything is admitted. It will have such weight as it is due." ***(Laughter).***

What does that mean? It means nothing. It means mush. It means unless the judge is good to you, the judge can do anything he or she wants and let it all in. Then the judge writes whatever he wants or finds whatever he wants. You don't know what they're basing it on. And it's a lousy way to proceed. Oh, Wyzanski was a brilliant judge, and he had the whip hand, but that's a lousy way to proceed. You don't want to get caught in that circumstance. If you are trying jury-waived, I will tell you, you want to guard against that; you want to try to make clear what it is the judge is relying on because you may need it on appeal. *See* Fed.R.Evid. 103.

We're going to take jury trials as a paradigm. What are the reasons for doing that? Don't for a moment think that judges, because they are judges and are familiar to you, are free from prejudice. Now here is where I skirt close to the critical legal studies people. I don't go for their politics, and I think they're wrong when they say that judges are just the fascist implements of the ruling society. I didn't take the job that I revere with all my heart to do that, though I have had a fellow call me a fascist on the bench. And we tried to give him a fair trial. In fact, he prevailed.

But I do say this: Holmes was right in his 1897 speech on legal realism. You see, the critical legal studies people have just taken that one step further. If you want to know what the law is, watch what judges do. And, remember, judges are the people that they are.

I will talk about great judges I've known. I don't presume to be at that level, but I certainly try. Judges try so hard to look beyond their prejudices, to look beyond their backgrounds. Sometimes you want to watch out for a judge who's looking so beyond his background and bending over backwards that he's bending too far. You want to watch out for a judge that you know, that you've been before, that you've seen on bar association work. Maybe the judge is guarding against you. You want to watch out for that because the judge is trying to do the ethical job.

Don't think for a minute that you try a jury-waived case to a judge any differently than a jury case. I'll give you this example: We're in the Ninth Circuit, and we're talking appellate judges here. What do they know? In the west horses that run free are a danger to the grazing lands, and so every now and again there are horse roundups to get these mustangs off the grazing lands. And you're authorized to do a horse hunt, horse roundup, and the way they do it is they send in helicopters that drive the horses into a canyon. The horses are wild, after all. So when they're in the canyon you can go in and round them up. The horses are running from the helicopter because they're scared, and because they're running some of them fall and are injured and have to be, as they say in equine circles, put down.

The normal value for a horse that is put down is $50 if you're doing an authorized roundup—you have to pay the government for that because that's part of the common good. A top-flight environmental lawyer, however, gets $250 per horse. And everyone is astounded in Idaho, where this horse hunt occurred. He gets $250 per horse for the government. And the rancher who did the hunt immediately appeals to the Ninth Circuit because that's five times as much as anyone has ever gotten. The going rate for horses is $50 a head. So he goes up to the Ninth Circuit, and the environmental lawyer wins. People ask him afterwards, "How did you win that case? No one's ever gotten $250 per horse. It's always been $50 as long as we can remember. You got $250."

He said, "It really wasn't too difficult. You just tell them what happened. They drove the horses into the canyon, some fell and broke their legs. Then they came in and they shot the horses, and then they had the power saws and began to cut them up." Which, of course, is what they did with their chain saws. The judges were pretty squeamish at that. I don't mean to drag it out. If that's how you try that case to a jury, that's how you try it to a judge.

So our paradigm here this morning is trying cases to juries because they will work the same with judges. And that's what we'll focus on.

Personal Considerations

Lastly, it will be necessary, I think, if I'm going to be helpful to you, to make some personal comments. I think in the hierarchy of values, the personal comments are the least important. I know there are these trial practice courses where they even teach you how to dress. I went to a NITA course once. I got in the elevator. I had come in the middle of the course. There were men and women, and they all had blue suits and white shirts, and they looked like clones. We rode down in the elevator together, and I wondered what company they all worked for. And I found out they were all in this NITA course, and someone had said that's how you dress. I don't go for that.

I know there are these people who talk about your body language, and I'm not saying that there isn't some value to that. In the hierarchy of things I think that value is minimal compared to the things that need to be talked about.

But I want you to critique me. Decide for yourself whether what I say makes sense, and decide it in the strategic sense; the sense of what it is that has to be proved in a case. What we're going to emphasize is the tactical—what you do in court and how you do it.

And lastly, ask yourself if you could do it, if personally you could do it. And to say something personal for a minute, I really think that your personal style is absolutely your own, and there is no right personal style. I am committed to the belief, and not just because I am privileged to be a judge, that whatever we may say, jurors look beyond you to the facts of the case. Judges try to get them to do that. That's what they do. You do not have to have a strong and confident voice. You do not have to talk with your hands. It is just as effective if your voice is a softer voice. You can always emphasize things by dropping your voice so that they have to sit forward and listen to you. That's how you can make something important. You don't have to be any "thing" as a trial lawyer. You don't have to be a certain way. Sixteen years on the bench, and I believe that that is true.

Most of the work is in the strategic preparation. Most of the work is done before you get to the courthouse, but anyone can present a case. The model is the model of a teacher. You stand up before a jury or a judge, and you're a teacher.

All right. Now we'll start. You come to the courthouse. You're ready. You've got whatever papers you bring. You have a couple of witnesses to start. You're going to pick the jury and give your openings. You've got the witnesses under subpoena and you think they will come. Let's start.

Forum Shopping

Forum shopping is something that you should do and we all should try to prevent. The law permits forum shopping as between certain of the trial courts within

Massachusetts. For instance, in a civil case that starts in district court, you want to decide if you will ever want to get to the jury session in district court. The probate and family court has certain overlapping jurisdiction with the superior court, and you want to decide, on the bases that we're going to discuss, which of those courts you like the most. I'm going to discuss making the choice between the Massachusetts Superior Court and the United States District Court, and I will presume for purposes of this discussion that the case could be started in the federal court.

Comparing Jurors

If you can choose your forum, what forum do you choose? If you are the plaintiff, especially in a personal injury case, you would probably prefer the state court. In the state court, you don't have to have a unanimous verdict. G.L. c. 234, §§ 34A and B. (Of course in criminal cases the verdict must be unanimous pursuant to Mass.R.Crim.P. 27(a).) In federal court, civil or criminal, you have to have a unanimous verdict. Fed.R.Civ.P. 48(1); Fed.R.Crim.P. 31(a). People whom I respect tell me that you want state court for five-sixths because if you can cabin the jurors who are at odds in to two out of twelve jurors so that ten agree upon a verdict, you get a verdict. You have fewer to convince.

There are other considerations. Think for a moment about where your juries are going to come from. If you're in state court and you have different venue requirements but you could pick your county, which county do you pick to try your case? Again, taking the personal injury case as the paradigm, you want an affluent suburban county. The best is Norfolk, and the second best is Middlesex, if you have a choice. Why? Because in Norfolk, they are pretty much all bedroom communities except for Quincy. Middlesex is such a big county that while you have communities that are clearly not affluent, you do have a fair number of affluent suburban communities to leaven the jury.

If you choose Suffolk and you're a plaintiff, the best analysis is that you'll win but you won't get big money. The reason you want an affluent suburb, especially if you're a plaintiff, is that if you have a good liability case, and you are going to win on the merits, the people in the community are more used to dealing in big sums of money. If you win in Suffolk and they give you $50,000 because that's more money than they've ever seen in their lives, that may not be a win for a permanent injury. The same case in Norfolk may give you a higher price tag.

What about the number of jurors? Let's consider the absolute number of jurors. In state court, in the superior court, the number is 12. G.L. c. 234, §§ 34A and B. In federal court, by local rule, the number is six; more precisely, the number is a minimum of six. Local Rule 48.1. Therefore, maybe you think you'd like federal court because, even though it's unanimous, you only have to convince six. In fact, today six usually means eight, because now we can impanel more than we need, and under the federal rules, there are no alternates. The jurors left at the end of the trial deliberate.

Fed.R.Civ.P. 48. Most of my colleagues and I will pick eight; and if someone gets sick, you're down to seven; and if two people get sick, you've got six; but still the jury goes forward.

Judge Woodlock and I believe, and the sociological studies show, that the optimal number of jurors is between 10 and 14 to have very good small group dynamics. Despite the fact that the rule says you shall have at least six (the idea is that we will have six to save money), Judge Woodlock and I usually impanel 10. As a matter of fact, Judge Woodlock may impanel 12. I usually impanel 10 and I keep 10. So if you're before us and you're a plaintiff, you've got more people to convince.

Comparing Judges

There are other things to think about. Suppose it's an equity case. It is still true that injunctions are easier to come by in the state court than they are in the federal court as a general rule of thumb. So if you want a quick injunction or temporary restraining order (TRO), a superior court justice probably is the person you want.

Let's discuss getting an injunction. First of all, you want to be very well prepared. This is true in both state and federal courts. You want to be sure your complaint is verified. Fed.R.Civ.P. 65(b); Mass.R.Civ.P. 65(b). At a minimum, most state judges want at least telephone notice to the other side that you're coming over to get that injunction. If you are in any doubt about the procedure to submit the injunction to the state judge (this is true in federal court, too), go to the judge's deputy clerk and ask him or her how it's done. He or she is not talking out of turn when he or she tells you. If it's one of those where the papers are taken in to the judge—on a temporary restraining order, for instance—you may not see the judge, and you may not have a chance to make an argument. Who takes the papers in to the judge in that case? It's the courtroom deputy clerk. If it's presented to the judge in a form where the matters seem to be in order, the judge may more likely allow what you want. But if you miss anything—if it's not a verified complaint, if it's not signed by the client, if there are no supporting affidavits made on personal knowledge, and if you have not given at least notice to the other side—the judge may not allow what you want. I'm sure there are superior court justices who are as strict as I would be, but my sense is that you've got a better chance of getting an injunction or TRO in the superior court than you do in the federal district court.

One other reason to go state is that they are less likely—keep in mind that this is changing—to impose a high bond requirement. The rules are the same state to federal, but federal judges are more likely to impose a higher bond requirement in order to keep the injunction, or really to get the injunction. And federal judges perhaps are somewhat more formal in how you get before them.

There were times when I was at the bar that the quality of judges court to court was significantly different. That's not true today. The quality of judges on the Massachusetts Superior Court is comparable to those on the United States District

Court, and we are comparable to the superior court. The variation is necessarily greater on the superior court, where you have 72 egos, backgrounds and levels of experience, than it is on the federal court, where you have 13. Person for person, we're as good as they are; they're as good as we are. You might be unlucky with some judges. Your risks are greater on a 72-person court than they are on a 13-person court.

Comparing Court Procedures

Remember that in the state court, while they have gone to room lists and the like, the judges still in the superior court ride a limited circuit. It's a much more limited circuit than it was when I was privileged to be a superior court justice. That's probably for the better, because you're dealing with the same judge; you can persuade the same judge and you can teach the same judge. While the superior court has settled their judges down, the state district court, which is understaffed, as all the state courts are, is overwhelmed by the criminal business that it has to adjudicate, and has now taken to popping judges into courts day by day. You're very uncertain what judge you will get in a specific state district court. You're much more certain of what judge you can get in the superior court once you're assigned. In federal court, you get the judge you get from the outset, and that judge takes the case through to conclusion. The judges, as I say, are of equal competence.

Other Criteria

Another criterion to consider in choosing a forum is that discovery is virtually the same state and federal. Actually, that's not true anymore. Now in federal court, we have the local Expense and Delay Reduction Plan—where we require voluntary discovery. *See* Local Rule 26.1. As of December, the Federal Rules of Civil Procedure were amended and they permit voluntary discovery. The state doesn't require voluntary discovery yet. Most lawyers are more comfortable with state practice than they are with the new Expense and Delay Reduction Plan on the federal side. Candidly, I'm saddened by that, because I think we have a good plan. But the fact is that most lawyers are more comfortable with the state, because they think they can control a case more on the state side than on the federal, and that's desirable if you have a choice. I encourage you to review the Expense and Delay Reduction Plan of the United States District Court, District of Massachusetts, which was adopted November 18, 1991 and has been integrated into our Local Rules effective October 1, 1992.

What about the state of the docket? The state of the docket is better on the federal side. And once we get the five new judges—three will be sworn in on the 5th of January—it won't be rocket docket. None of us likes the concept of rocket docket, but we will have enough judges in Massachusetts to do the federal district court's work, and you can expect trials very rapidly. Maybe you don't want that, but that's what you can expect. I imagine that the judges will put to trial any case within a year.

On the state side, they've done a magnificent job in boiling down the backlog that they have, but there is still an enormous number of cases in any state court. Skilled lawyers think that they have a better chance of controlling when the case comes on for trial in state court.

Federal judges tend to be more peremptory in requiring you to appear for trial. As an aside, what is the difference between a federal judge and a terrorist? You can negotiate with a terrorist.

(Laughter).

Comparing Clerks' Offices

It's a good idea to check the organization of the different county clerks' offices. The degree of organization of the office can have a significant effect on whether you will face delays, such as delays in getting your execution. It seems to me that Middlesex is still pretty good, Norfolk is good and Suffolk is not. When you go further out, there's less of a burden and probably, they're more up to date.

Comparing Rules of Evidence

There's one other criterion in forum shopping—the rules of evidence as they pertain to experts. The Federal Rules of Evidence are more liberal as to who can testify as an expert than are the state rules. That doesn't mean the judges will be any less liberal in letting your expert testify in the state court. But if you are following the rules of evidence strictly, experts and the things that experts can base their testimony on are more restricted in the state courts than they are in the federal courts. It is fair to say that in the federal courts, they've become so liberal that it's created a backlash of judges who construe the rules strictly on experts in the federal courts. Judge Keeton is strict. I am strict. To a somewhat lesser extent, I think Judge Woodlock is strict. Judge Mazzone's taken senior status now, but he's strict. You may want to have that in mind.

ANALYZING JUDGES

Once you're in court, what judge are you before? What judge have you drawn? The particular judge that you're before makes a big difference. You want to know everything you can about that judge. Let me point out some of the things that you can do to get ready to deal with that judge.

In big cases, if your litigation budget can stand it, run the judge's decisions on LEXIS or Westlaw. I'm really talking federal now, because you can't run the state judges' decisions on LEXIS or Westlaw. I suggest that if you practice in a specific area, such as employment discrimination, you want to get the lawyers' newspaper. You want to get those cases that are in your area even if they are in the lowest trial court, and you want to file them away or at least keep a record. And then when you come before that superior court justice, or that judge in the district court, you want to know what cases that judge has decided about your problem. Institutional litigants, like the Massachusetts Teachers Association and the law firm that represents GM, keep records. As a matter of fact, the big car companies share all the legal documents that pertain to their issues, as do the tobacco companies. So if you have a products liability case, you will see briefs that cite not only the Supreme Court of California, but also the-umpth Superior Court in California, Maricopa County. They can give you the whole decision. If you look at those decisions, you'll find that many of them are in haec verba—the same. Why is that? Because the tobacco company wrote them, and the overworked trial judge in some other state simply signed his or her name to the findings of fact that the well-heeled litigant wanted. And, you know, that's law. Of course, it may not be that persuasive, but suddenly the brief that you're faced with in the superior court or district court has every citation that ever was on the point. You could never find that stuff yourself. Who's going to go to Maricopa? Who would think to do it?

I'll come back to the Massachusetts Teachers Association. They have every injunction, every denial of injunction, everything about teachers' strikes that exists. And when a superior court justice gets one of those—that's public area labor litigation, which is done in the state court—they have every blessed order that's ever been issued. And among the orders that have been issued are orders that have been issued by the judge's own colleagues, and don't think that doesn't make a difference.

Trial judges have to work alone, and we rise or fall on what we do ourselves. We tend, all of us, to respect our colleagues. The institution is designed to foster that respect because we at the trial level can't be tearing each other down—it would never work. We have to pass cases off to each other, and we have to back each other up; and, if anything, we can be faulted for backing each other up.

If you give me a decision, published or unpublished, by federal court Judge Zobel, I'm going to pay very close attention to it. She is a wonderful judge. The same thing would happen with any of my colleagues. And when I was a superior court justice, if you gave me a Jim Lynch, a John McNaught, and I could name dozens of them who I thought were the best judges that ever were, you give me a superior court decision, why should I reinvent the wheel? So you want to get out there and get it.

On the federal side, though, with big cases, run LEXIS or Westlaw. Find out what that judge has written. You can tell all sorts of things about the judge. One of the things you can tell, if you just read the decision, is that if their style and technique vary vastly from year to year, the law clerks are writing the decisions; the judge isn't writing them. The judge is signing off on stuff that the law clerks are writing. In the federal court, we get two law clerks, and they're outstanding young people. You want to consider your audience, who you're going to be persuading.

Also, many judges tend to follow the same constructs; they cite the same courts or the same series of cases. That's what tells you what judges think works. I don't just mean the court for whom the judge himself or herself works, such as the First Circuit in the federal system, or the Appeals Court and Supreme Judicial Court in the state system. You will find that judges go back to the same constructs. They think those are good law.

Help From the Courtroom Deputy Clerk, Court Reporter and Court Officer

In every case, talk to the courtroom deputy clerk, and ask him or her: "What is this judge like?" "What does this judge expect?" "How does this judge do it?" We're going to go through each of the things that happen during a trial. How does the judge do the things the judge does? The clerks are not ethically bound to keep that information from you; they will share it with you. It is their ethical, professional duty to do so. However, don't ask, "What's he going to do with my motion?" They won't tell you that. They have no right to. They should be fired if they do, because they talk privately to the judge. They may know how the judge is slanting, and they won't discuss that; but they will tell you whether the judge hears evidence on a motion for preliminary injunction, whether the judge gives a pretrial charge or how the judge rules on objections. They'll give you their views on the judge's position on sentencing, and other information like that.

Now that the superior court moves around less, you might also want to go to the judge's court reporter, because the court reporter has all the things the judge has done while the court reporter has been working with the judge. And in the federal system, where they tend to work year-in, year-out with one judge, they've got it all over time.

Also, you may wish, if the judge has been in place for some time, to talk to the court officers in the state system. Don't think the court officers are just ciphers. The court officers are excellent observers of the trial process. So you should find out what they can tell you. The other people who are active in the session will be too busy, and their view of what goes on may be affected by the fact that they are filling out papers or marking documents or doing whatever they do. This is not so with court officers. Talk to the court officer. He or she knows, and they know in the sense that jurors know, what's working in the courtroom. They are good people to talk to as the trial progresses.

But you have to talk to them face-to-face. If you depend on the telephone, you're never going to get anywhere. They just don't have the time to answer their calls, state and federal. Of course, it's your time too, but this is a determination you have to make; go over to the courthouse. For one thing, you may want to be over in the courthouse because it's helpful to bring your witnesses in a key case or your client. Let the client see the courtroom in which he's going to be testifying. Walk around. Wait until after the trial session. Then see if you can talk to the clerk. If you invest the time to go over there and to make it worthwhile, go over there as you're preparing your witnesses and talk to the clerks. The clerks will like that investment of time.

USE OF MAGISTRATE JUDGES

Here's a word on federal court judges sending cases to magistrate judges. We have magistrate judges who, if you consent, are authorized to try civil cases. Whether you consent or not, federal court judges can send all discovery matters and the like to magistrates for mediation. The court varies on that. Judges are paired with the magistrate judges, and you can find out what the pairings are. Judge Zobel and I are paired with Magistrate Judge Collings. Judge Keeton and Judge Wolf are paired with Magistrate Judge Karol. I forget the others, but you can find that out.

Some of us don't send things to magistrates; we want to use the magistrates as judges. Judge Zobel and I are two examples; we use Collings as a judge. He wants to be used as a judge. I have various ways of trying to convince you that it would be wise to go before Magistrate Judge Collings. The way I do it is simply to say he gives you a day certain; I never will. Other judges—Judge Wolf, I believe Judge Harrington and Judge Woodlock—send all discovery matters to the magistrate judge and you're stuck with the magistrate judge until after you get out from under discovery.

How will we do it when we get the new judges? We're still going to pair them, and we will do it however the judges want to do it. I am responsible for teaching the new judges. I'm going to teach using the magistrate judges as judges.

Legally, the decision of a magistrate judge on a particular matter in a case, pretrial or otherwise, is not binding on anything, but there's a formal procedure you have to go through. Practically, it depends. How many district judges are going to second-guess a magistrate on a discovery issue? If it's summary judgment on which they can't decide, they can only make a report and recommendation. *See* Mag.R. 3(a)(A)(5). If the report and recommendation go against you, the side that won clearly has a leg up, but the judge will do an independent job. But as to everything, magistrate judges are not final; the judge is, unless you consent to proceed before a magistrate judge. If you consent to go before a magistrate judge, which is what I try to talk you into, then that judge is the judicial officer; you stick with that judge to the end.

IMPANELING THE JURY

I want to go through impanelment. You've gotten to your judge, and you're ready to start the case. The case is a jury case, and therefore the people most important to you, the people whom you're going to teach, are the jurors. You know how many you're going to get or you know what the principles of the judge are. How are they in fact chosen? This is the first thing that happens in trial, and it's one that people know the least about in terms of just the little intricacies, such as where you stand and what happens and the like. So let me talk us through it.

There are three major methods by which judges, state and federal, pick juries. Every judge does it slightly different, and that's something to ask the courtroom deputy clerk about so you're not blind-sided ahead of time. But here are the three major variations: Some judges bring the venire in, sit them in the back of the courtroom, and ask them the questions. You have in mind now that in state and federal, it's the judges who ask the questions, though some judges will allow you a limited voir dire, but most of us won't. And we oppose those bills that would require or would permit it to be done as a matter of right because it would slow things down. So usually it's the judge asking the questions.

Questioning the Venire First

But let's get to the mechanics. The venire sits out there in the courtroom. They're sworn to answer the judge's questions honestly. The judge asks them a bunch of questions. You take care of the challenges for cause by those who answer the questions affirmatively. Then the box is filled. Then the peremptory challenges are handled at the sidebar. And once you've got the jury picked, the trial goes on. This is the first method.

Filling the Box First

The second principal variation is as follows: the venire is in the back of the room. The very first thing that the judge does is pick at random from the venire the jurors that are going to sit in the box. The judge puts the specific questions to the jurors who sit in the box. Some of them, let's say, answer yes, and they are excused for cause. Then at random other jurors are brought up and put in the box, and the judge says to them, "Would you answer yes to any of the questions I've just been asking of the ones who have been sitting in the box?" And if the new juror raises her hand and says yes, then she's inquired of further. That's the second principal variation.

The "Struck" System

The third principal variation is what's known as the struck system. This system is usually used in "capital cases" on the state side, and cases where life imprisonment is a possibility on the criminal side, but it can be used in any case. And some judges favor it. Judge Wolf, I think, follows the struck system in our court. What is done is an inquiry of the venire, sometimes individually. The goal is to pick a jury of indifferent jurors, that is, jurors who are beyond challenge for cause, until you have as many as you are going to sit plus as many peremptory challenges as both sides have. That gives us a finite number of jurors.

And then the struck system works like this: Let us say in my court, civil, I'll pick 10 jurors, and under the rules each side has five peremptory challenges. Under the struck system I would pick 20 jurors that I knew were indifferent. Then we would strike down to the 10 by turning to the plaintiff and asking, "Who do you strike?" She'll strike off one of the list of the known 20. Then I'll turn to defense counsel. "Who do you strike?" This will be out of the presence of the jury. We'll be at sidebar. You strike off the one that you like least. Back to her, back to him, and when we're done, they've both exercised all their peremptories. The advantage to you of doing this is you've got a known pool of jurors. You won't get the jurors out of that pool you like the best, but you can get rid of the jurors you like the least.

Now those are the three methods: inquire of the venire first, randomly pick the jury first and the struck system.

Now I want to take you through the actual impanelment of the jury, and we will use the way I do it is as the paradigm simply because I'm familiar with it.

The Mechanics of Impanelment

You're ready to try the case. You are at counsel table. Get to the right counsel table. I mean, be familiar with the jury. Do you want your client there? Probably. If you represent an institutional client, you'd better have someone from that institutional client there. Will the judge let those clients sit at counsel table? Find that out. Do you want the client to sit at counsel table? Probably, if the judge will allow you, unless the client's a fussbudget and is going to be getting in your way passing notes and the like. You want human beings there.

You will have given the judge a list of your witnesses. It's nice to have addresses, folks, as well as their names. You will have already given your name and address because the judge is going to ask about that.

You will have gotten a jury list. The jury lists on the state side are much better than the federal. They give much more information, and they have one feature that the feds don't have: they have already been randomized. That is, the list of jurors in the panel that you get is the order that the judge is going to put those jurors in the box. The reason that's significant to you is if you know that and you don't like this juror, but you dislike the next juror even more, then you might not exercise a challenge. And the reverse is true. If you're really trying to work down to get to a juror below, then you would exercise.

In the federal court it's all random, and all you get is the general jury list. It's harder for you. The state system is much better for you as litigants in this respect.

The jurors come into the court. The judge is on the bench. You're not asked anything yet. The judge introduces you—some judges are much more cryptic than this.

For instance, some judges simply introduce who they are and they expect then, without any prompting, that you will stand up and introduce who you are. Unless you know that, the other side will smoothly stand up and introduce herself, and you'll look like a donkey, not even knowing what you're supposed to do. Do I get up now? Is it an objection? You know, your breath begins to become short, and you're off on the wrong foot right away.

All of this stuff can be spared if you've checked with the courtroom deputy clerk. She knows how it's supposed to work, and she's happy to tell you because she wants it to go smoothly. The way I do it is I introduce myself. I say this is important. The clerk then swears the venire, and I start asking questions.

I want to give you the standard questions, because if these don't fit, you're going to want to have already asked the judge to ask more questions. Some judges will, some won't, and some will ask some of them. But here are the standard questions:

> Here are the parties to this suit. They are represented by these lawyers. Counsel, would you please stand? Thank you very much. These are their names. This is who they work for. Do you know or are you acquainted with any of these people? Have you ever been employed by any of these people? Have you or a member of your family ever been involved in any litigation, either as a witness or as a litigant, whether or not the case ever came to trial, which involved any of these people? Have you heard, read, or seen anything about this case? Have you discussed this case with anyone right up to today? Have you formed an opinion about this case? Do you have any interest in the outcome of this case? By interest in the outcome of this case, I don't mean a natural curiosity about what the evidence may show. I mean do you stand to gain or lose anything depending upon how this case comes out? Are you sensible of any bias or prejudice in the case about to be tried? When I say "are you sensible of it," I mean are you aware of any. Do you know any reason why you do not stand indifferent in this case? When I say "stand indifferent," I'm trying to search out any feelings you have about this case, about these people, about this type of case. For example, I'll say for a case that the lawyers call a products liability case, anything I should know? Then I go into a little bit about the schedule of the case. I'm one who sticks to time limits that we've agreed upon ahead of time, so I can tell the jury exactly, in a civil case, how long the case is going to take to try. I say, is there any reason why you ought not to be called to sit as jurors in this case?

Now, there's one prime variation on that, and most judges will do this for you. If it's a criminal case, most judges will ask the jurors about law enforcement relatives, so you'll know if they are police or state troopers. If it's the type of case where there's a lot of evidence from a particular industry, many judges will ask, "Do any of you work for…" Let's say it's a suit directly against an insurance company. You wouldn't bring the issue of insurance to the fore, but they will ask if the juror or any member of the juror's family works for an insurance company. If a corporation is involved, another question that should be asked is "Do you own any stock in the corporation, or debentures or the like?"

Now, the jurors then answer. If they answer in the affirmative, most judges will then take them one by one at the sidebar. You come up, and you make sure that the court reporter is making a record of it. If they're in those courtrooms where they've got these tiny little mikes out and you've got a voice-writer, you want to be very sure that those mikes are working. And it is not improper for you to ask the judge on the record, "Is this on the record, Judge? Respectfully, I'd like all aspects of the trial on the record." This makes the judge pull up his socks; it shows how professional you are.

Let's get the jury picked so that we can take a break. Now, once we've got an indifferent jury, the box is filled. Once I get them in the box, I will have each person speak and tell us what he or she does, where they work, and what his or her spouse does. I think that's very helpful to you. I do it for you. One, you hear them speak, and that shows you they can speak, and they're not deaf. And you can tell a lot about a person by hearing how confidently that person speaks. And also, it's just wonderful. They tell you a little bit about their jobs and the like. And then I invite you over to the sidebar.

Now, how peremptory challenges are exercised varies again from session to session. In the session where I preside we do it this way: Plaintiff exercises her peremptories first, but I will not fill the box. I then go to defense and say, "Now, of the ones that are left, who don't you like?" And you should know how many peremptories you have. If you don't know, ask the judge, ask the clerk. Don't fly blind thinking you can challenge all if really you only get three peremptories because how you spend them is terribly important. Then the clerk will excuse the whole bunch that you've challenged without saying who challenged them. That's the only fair way, after the huddle at the sidebar. And we will then refill the box.

Unlike many states, in Massachusetts, state and federal, you don't get back-strikes. In other words, you can't go back, after having passed once, and say, "Oh, I really don't like him. He's now looking squint-eyed, and I'm going to knock him off." If you've passed him by in a certain round, you've passed him by. He stays on the jury.

For the second round over at the sidebar I'm going to start with the defense because I think that's fair. She got to start on the first round, so he gets to start on the second round. He goes first, challenging who he doesn't like. We're only working with replacements now. Then I go back to the plaintiff. She challenges who she doesn't like.

Some people will object to the way I do it. Defense counsel say, "I'm entitled to see the whole 12. And so what you should do is excuse the plaintiff's challenged jurors." Plaintiff, let's say, has knocked off four. "I'm entitled to see 12 and shoo off whom I want. And then that's my round, and then the next round we'll go back to the plaintiff."

I know of no law, state or federal, that requires that, though I am sometimes told that with great firmness. And if that's what you want, tell the judge with great firmness.

Once we have the jury, don't think that if you run out of peremptories you are dead. Ask for more. The judge can deny it and usually will; but ask for it, and explain on the record why.

Beware of striking on the basis of racial, ethnic or gender factors. It's pretty clear that the judge has discretion to sit such a juror if you have a pattern of striking that juror or that type of juror. I know I'm going a little further than the actual cases go, but most trial judges think those are the rules now, and that's how we'll follow it.

A pattern can be one. Don't think that you get to knock off the one ethnic minority and say, "Judge, I just knocked off one. I mean, where's the pattern?" If the judge thinks you're doing it because of that person's ethnicity, race or gender, the judge can sit that person. That's the remedy. He can do this over your objection. *See Batson v. Kentucky*, 476 U.S. 79, 96 (1986). Age so far is not a basis for judicial questioning. You can knock off all the young people—you can knock off all the old people—if that's your reason for exercising peremptory challenges. *See United States v. Kresta*, 825 F.2d 538 (1st Cir. 1987); *United States v. Lynch*, 792 F.2d 269 (1st Cir. 1985).

Now, how do you do it? I don't have a theory on this. I'm going to recount for you some theories that I have heard. Chief Justice Steadman, who was a top trial lawyer before he ascended to the bench, always said that he would take the first 12 in the box unless he had a specific articulable reason for knocking the person off, something he could really tie to his case. That's who he'd take, and he had an outstanding record.

I know that there are these psychological studies that are done. I've tried cases where people have used those studies. That was done in the *William Kennedy Smith* case. I know that nationally famous trial lawyers like Gerry Spence, who defended Weaver who allegedly shot the marshal out west and got an acquittal, absolutely refuse to go with any of this psychological stuff. Spence says it's his duty to look the jurors in the eye and size them up.

Candidly, I never had enough trials to have a theory. I sit there as you do it, and I wonder what you're thinking. *(Laughter)*.

I live the process. I have no idea what you're doing. I don't know why you're striking him or her. The patterns that I see are that some people don't want an educated jury. Some people appear to want an educated jury. In my mind it seems to have no effect on the outcome, though I try to keep notes on this.

Here are some of the things that I have heard. A fellow by the name of James Jeans wrote a wonderful book on trial advocacy. I think it's one of the very best. No one uses it in the law schools today because it's not politically correct. So I tread on dangerous ground because any advice I give you here necessarily stereotypes people, and we don't want to stereotype people, and we should not do that. But if you're going to think about this as a process, you're going to think about stereotypes. Here are some that Jeans has in his book. He says if you are going against the government and you represent the defendant, never allow people employed by the postal service on the jury. And the reason is that they have the best retirements of any federal employee. There is no heavy lifting in the postal service, so they still think the government is good. It pays them. Don't get a postal person on your jury.

He also said, and you can see how I'm on dangerous ground, if you want anti-authoritarian types because your client can be typified as standing up against authority, then you don't want Lutherans. I think Jeans comes from the Midwest where there are more Lutherans. And you can see why everyone is afraid to use his book, but it's a very good book. He says why? Because the Lutheran Church is a very authoritarian church. I don't know. I'm not saying that it is, but he gives you those sort of ideas. I have no ideas. I don't know why people pick whom they pick.

Last point on this: Who will be the foreperson? That may make a difference. Some judges pick the first seat in the first row closest to the bench. If for one reason or another you don't want that person leading the discussion, that's a seat you want to watch carefully for a challenge. Not because you're really against that person, but just because you wouldn't want that person leading the discussion.

State Judge Zobel lets the jury elect the foreperson. I disagree with that because you have more hung juries. Sometimes they never get beyond who's going to be the foreperson—they can't agree. ***(Laughter)***.

I'll tell you candidly that I pick a person that I think is going to be a good discussion leader, and that has nothing to do with education, though that might be a factor. A shop foreman would be good. A receptionist would be good. A teacher would be good. I'm just looking for someone who I think is going to be a good discussion leader.

Because the foreperson's seat is known to the jury, obviously I will never cause a minority to leave that seat in favor of someone else. Now, in terms of gender, if a woman is in that seat, I would never replace a woman with a man. I'll look at my group of women and pick whom I think will best lead the discussion. In other words, it's the judge's responsibility. I'm telling you how I do it. Many judges just pick the person that's in the seat without thinking. If you've got a judge like that, you want to think about it.

MOTIONS IN LIMINE

Next, I want to discuss motions in limine—the motions that govern the actual trial of the case. How effective are they? How do you raise them? Motions in limine are the motions that start the case off—"in limine" means "threshold." What are the subjects of motions in limine? Primarily, they are things that you are afraid will happen. Unless you get the judge to control them early on in the case, the case may go askew. That's really the reason for filing motions in limine.

Here are two of the best examples of when to file motions in limine. If you have a client who has a prior criminal record, you'd like to know if that criminal record will be introduced in evidence. Likewise, you'd like to know, if you have some problem with the qualifications or the supplementation to answers to interrogatories or the like, whether your experts or the other side's experts will testify, because if they will not or if you can nick them sufficiently pretrial, that may be outcome-determinative, and it will change the settlement posture significantly. Likewise, if there are charts or diagrams or mentions of something that you think would be particularly prejudicial, you want to know that before the trial starts. You want to get the judge to rule on that. And you frame those things as motions in limine.

When are motions in limine heard? They are ripe at the time of the final pretrial conference. In my federal court session, however, that conference comes a month or two or three weeks ahead of the trial. That really is the optimum time, but unfortunately, with some judges, the conference comes months before the trial, which makes it of less value. So motions in limine should not be renewed if you've lost them, but bring them up again on the first day of trial. Bring the motions in limine with you, or have them at least sent in to the judge. She may not give you a hearing. She may be ready to call the jury. On the other hand, she may talk to you.

What will happen on motions in limine? Here, I'm going to start off with a personal comment, but I think my practice is not dissimilar from most judges, and I do so with that apology. I think you are entitled to know whether a prior criminal conviction will be used in a trial or not. In a criminal case, of course, that's going to affect whether you're going to have your client take the stand. And I especially think in that circumstance that a criminal defense lawyer is entitled to know whether the prior conviction that the government has relative to his client will be introduced in evidence. And so I think I'm in a position to rule, and I do. If it's a witness, I think judges should rule.

I favor getting the bugs worked out with respect to expert testimony prior to the trial, and more and more judges do. Expert testimony is crucial at a trial, and it's something that should be worked out ahead of time. And I will rule on those motions in limine if they go to the qualification of the experts to speak to the subject matter that the expert purports to speak to.

I suggest that you push those types of motions as early in the proceeding as possible if you oppose the expert. The reason I say that is as follows: Suppose you finally get the expert interrogatories supplemented and you learn who the other side's expert is? You think the other side's expert is a hack and has no business testifying to those things that he purports to testify to. I have heard it said by my colleagues on the federal bench that you should bring a motion for summary judgment, especially if it's the type of case that you're not even going to get to the jury unless the plaintiff's expert gets you there, such as a medical malpractice or products case. If the judge doesn't think the expert is qualified, you win on summary judgment, and the case is over.

I don't think that's the best motion you can bring, because the rule on summary judgment is that all inferences have to be taken in favor of the side that opposes summary judgment. Therefore, all breaks have to be given to the expert in the hypothetical that I have given.

Here's the motion I think you should bring. Under Rule 104(a) of the Federal Rules of Evidence (the state practice is the same as the federal practice), there are certain things on which a judge has to make a preliminary finding. Let me give you some examples.

In a criminal case, the government can't get a confession before the jury unless the judge finds in the state court beyond a reasonable doubt, in the federal court by a fair preponderance of the evidence, that it was voluntary. (For the state standard, *see Commonwealth v. Fernette*, 398 Mass. 658 (1986). For the federal standard, *see United States v. White*, 847 F. Supp. 219 (D.Mass. 1994).

In conspiracy cases, civil or criminal, the evidence of the statements of a coconspirator do not come in evidence against the other partners in the enterprise until the judge finds, state and federal, by a fair preponderance of the evidence that there is in fact a conspiracy. *See United States v. Petrozziello*, 548 F.2d 20 (1st Cir. 1977); *Commonwealth v. Beckett*, 373 Mass. 329 (1977). The judge in this case is acting as a factfinder.

Judge Keeton calls this finding "premise facts" and has written a whole law review article on it in the *Minnesota Law Review.* I think the reason it's significant is that you make a motion under Rule 104(a) to seek to have the judge find, not rule, that the expert is not qualified. And you see with the findings that we judges don't have to give all intendments in favor of the expert; instead, we look at the expert and say, "The guy's a hack. It's ridiculous. He has nothing to say about this." Now, of course we are bound, because it is more liberal in the federal court, to follow the rules.

I just want to point out that motion under 104(a). I teach this in law schools. I have been permitted to make a presentation that teaches exactly this to the judges of the First Circuit. I want to give you a caution. I did it on a panel with Jack Weinstein, former Chief Judge of the Eastern District of New York, but better known if you practice in federal court from *Weinstein On Evidence*. He was one of the drafters of the Federal Rules of Evidence, and he has said there is nothing in the legislative history or the drafts of the Federal Rules of Evidence that permits what Judge Young is talking about. We never thought the rule could be used that way. To Judge Weinstein, I say, "The rule says what it says. It's statutory, and it gives the judge that discretion."

I've now given you both sides of the argument. The issue is important.

Back to motions in limine. Other than the stuff I've just been talking about, I and most judges tend to duck motions in limine. "Duck" is perhaps a little too pejorative.

The more principled statement I would make to you is that it's hard for us to rule on a motion in limine until we've heard some evidence. We're not going to make the choice as to whether to cut out a whole part of the case until we know whether witnesses are really going to testify in that fashion.

I follow the rule of thumb that other than what I've just discussed, regarding experts and prior convictions, I'll rule on a motion in limine only to the extent that I have to, to control the trial. If it affects what's going to be said on opening, I'll work out what has to be said on opening. If it affects what diagrams are going to be shown on opening, I'll work that out. But if it's not going to come until the third day of trial, I'll wait until the third day of trial to rule on the motion.

Using The Jury List

State and federal courts will give the lawyer the jury list and the data as early as possible on the day of trial. We are forbidden to give it to you the day before trial. Why? We're afraid that litigants may be out there influencing potential jurors.

So how do you combat the problem of not having enough time to read the descriptions of the jurors before being asked to make decisions about challenges? Get there early in the morning when the doors to the clerk's office open.

Once the jurors have checked in, the state courts may give you a list that's not quite accurate, and they'll say, "Well, it's not accurate." But as soon as you can get it, you get it, because they have them randomized by computer. Their only flaws will be the no-shows.

So, recognizing that you may not get everybody, if you can talk them into it, there's no legal bar to the court giving you the list on the day of trial.

The federal list is lousy, let's face it. You don't get any more time. I don't criticize our jury commissioner; we're just not set up as well as the state, even though we choose from the same pool as the state. And then the one thing I give you, and you might argue it to another judge, is this business of letting each juror state what he or she does and what his or her spouse does. That buys you a little more time, and you can see the juror in the box.

The Pretrial Charge

We've impaneled the jury. What happens next varies significantly from judge to judge. Some judges, once the jury is sworn, turn to the plaintiff or prosecution and say, "Ms. Smith, do you wish to make an opening?" And then you're on. Other judges give a pretrial charge, more or less complete. On the most complete end are judges like myself. I'm not going to spend too much time on this, but I want you to know what goes into it.

Once the jury is impaneled, the next person to speak in the courtroom is the judge, who proceeds to do a variety of things, including exhorting the jury about fairness and impartiality and the like.

I pass out notebooks to all the jurors in every case. I tell them they can take notes, and that they can ask questions in writing. I explain how a trial works. Many judges will just say a few words about how trials are going to work and who bears the burden of proof and so forth. They'll put everyone to their ease.

The judges who talk more completely may go on and give, in effect, a pretrial charge. I'll say, "Mr. Jones here brings this products liability action. He's got two theories. One is negligence and here's what he's got to prove for negligence." Then I tick off duty, negligence, proximate causation. I don't explain damages, but I say, "and then, if you get to that part, damages." Then I explain that the other theory is products liability, and I focus on the product itself. And I have my little charge, and I explain it, not in the detail that I will explain it when the evidence closes, but I explain who has to prove what.

Now, how are you going to know if you get a judge like that? You're going to know because you've asked the courtroom deputy clerk and the court reporter. I do this in every case. It doesn't change case to case. Obviously, you want to influence that.

So right at the outset of the case you have your proposed pretrial charge. Submit it as early as the final pretrial conference if possible but certainly on the day of the trial so the judge can look at it. If you don't, suddenly you may have the judge getting up and saying something that's wrong—you don't think you have to prove this or this is stipulated—or something like that. It's not really an issue in your case.

So if the judge is going to do that—I think it's fair; I think it helps—guide it. Make that a part of the pretrial conference. And if the judge has said something wrong, don't let it sit. It's just like the judge is charging the jury. There he is up there, still wearing the robe. He is, after all, the authority figure. He's the first person to speak, and he has just told them something that's legally wrong. Don't sit there and take that. Ask to go to the sidebar and explain that you know in this criminal case, the burden of proof really is on the government, not on the defense—the defense has nothing to explain. Don't sit mum. Sitting mum usually happens because you're perplexed when something happens in the trial that you never expected. You never saw a judge do it before, and you haven't got tactics to deal with it. So we go back to what I mentioned earlier—before you ever get to trial, find out how the judge works. Ask the clerk, the court reporter and the court officers what the judge usually does.

Help From The Court Reporter

A court reporter who has worked with the judge has all this boilerplate forever. They're part of the records of the case. So if you want to know what Judge Young says or what Justice McHugh says, or what a judge who gives a pretrial charge or even standard boilerplate says at the beginning of the trial, go to the court reporter and get it or, more specifically, buy it. It's a public record. You have a right to it. And it doesn't have to be your case. You can get a products case, if yours is a products case, and find out what the judge had to say in the case. You can also get the charges in the same manner. And why is that important? Because that's what the judge thinks the law is.

Oh, yes, we're bound by the Supreme Judicial Court, by the First Circuit, by the Appeals Court—make no doubt about it. That's our oath. We desperately try to follow the law as they teach it to us. But if you want to know what the judge thinks the law is at any one moment in time, go to the court reporter and find out what the judge is teaching about your subject. And then find the errors in it, and correct them early on, as early as the pretrial conference. That's what will help you.

Now, not all judges do that. Some do everything I've just talked about, and I'm an example of that. Some only do the introduction, which says "Good morning. This is a civil case. The plaintiff bears the burden of proof." They explain that the plaintiff will put on the evidence first, and that the lawyers aren't the source of evidence, the witnesses are. They also explain that there may be sidebar conferences if there are objections, and that they shouldn't hold it against the lawyers. And then the judge will turn to the plaintiff or prosecution and say, "Do you wish to make an opening statement?"

Other judges are at the silent end of the spectrum. Once the jury is impaneled, in a criminal case, they read "Harken unto the evidence" and the like from the ancient common law. In a civil case, the very next words may be, "Mr. Jones, do you want to make an opening?" And what you then say makes a difference.

The Opening Statement

So, let's come to openings, and we'll take the plaintiff's opening first. The best thing that I've ever been taught on openings I was taught by Bill Schwarzer, who's a judge in California and is now the head of the Federal Judicial Center. He said this: You want to ask yourself on openings three questions. The first question is, "Are you going to win this case?" Honestly ask yourself whether you're going to win the case. If your answer to that first question is no, what are you doing there? In other words, you should have settled it. Your problem is not with the trial; your problem is with your client. You should have pleaded. If you're a prosecutor, it should be nol prossed, or you clearly have instructions from your client to go ahead, and you do the best you can.

You've got to search your soul and ask, "Have I worked things out properly with my client?" Because if you're standing up to make an opening statement and you don't honestly think you're going to win your case, you shouldn't be there.

But let's say you think you're going to win. Oh sure, there are butterflies in your stomach. If there aren't, it's time to hang up your hat. There ought to be an adrenaline rush.

Janice Berry, who's clearly one of the best lawyers I've ever seen, tells me that she always avoids taking a drink of water during the course of examining a witness while the jury is there. She tries to wait to have her drink after she has sat down and the other side is cross-examining because she knows if she needs a drink her hand is going to shake. And it's not because she's scared. She prosecuted the longest trial we ever had in the federal district court. She's a magnificent lawyer. It's because the adrenaline's there, and she's got it pulsing through her as she's doing the job that you all do.

So, of course you're scared when you get up to open, but do you think you're going to win? The answer should be yes.

If you think you're going to win, then you come to the next question: "What facts—forget strategy now—what facts have you developed that convince you that you're going to win this case?"

And then the third point is: Tell those facts to the jury like you were talking to a social acquaintance. Explain things in those same terms that you would use talking to your husband or wife. Actually, that's a bit misleading because that sort of communication assumes so much common experience. You don't have common experience with jurors, and so you're talking as you would talk to a social acquaintance. This means you may have to explain a little bit about the setting in which the people found themselves. But simply speak the facts as you are going to establish them.

How about the actual technique of doing this? I have a position on this, and think this is the best way to do it. I watched Tom Connolly, now Justice Connolly, do this. I watched him long before I was a judge. I was sitting there. They called him, "Mr. Connolly, do you wish to open?" And he stood up and said:

"This is a plastic Y valve ***(indicating)***. It costs 27 cents. If the Goddard Memorial Hospital had purchased this Y valve, my client, Sally Smith, would be a happy, healthy seven-year-old girl instead of the hopelessly confined quadriplegic that she is and always will be. My name is Tom Connolly," and so on and so forth.

Now the point I want to make with you is it's easy if you're a plaintiff and you have that type of case. Of course, you probably have a patent case or something. ***(Laughter)***. Well, don't laugh. Distinguished patent counsel are here in the hall today. How are you going to make this strange complex computer intersection leap for the jury? I don't know, but I know you have to.

The point I want to make, I saw Joan Lukey, another magnificent trial lawyer, do this in the case of emotional damages for a child. She had these few sentences first before she said one word about herself or about the setting or anything else. ***See Lareau v. Page***, 840 F. Supp. 920 (D.Mass. 1993). The point I'm trying to make here is figure out those first couple of sentences, and put it before your introduction. Captivate them, because until now, I've been talking all judge stuff and lawyer tactical stuff. Now for the first time we're talking about something that's being said to the jury.

All right. Those very first words if you're a plaintiff or if you're a defendant, those first words where you stand up as a teacher on behalf of your client and you address that direct democracy which is the jury, that's electric. You want to make it electric. And therefore, I think it's a mistake to start in by introducing yourself again and by introducing your client. Certainly don't tell them what I've already told them or what the judge has told them. It's a big waste. Instead, get to something new. Get to the facts.

Now, if you have a silent judge, put up first why you're going to win the case. You see, in those first few sentences in my Tom Connolly example, that's why he should win the case. If that's proven, plus a couple of other things, he ought to win if that is what the reality is. Then he comes back with who he is, to humanize himself. His client, if he's in the courtroom, may be introduced and asked to stand. Then you go on and you make the opening.

When I say you talk the way you talk to a social acquaintance, we all know that we tell each other stories. I chair the Security Committee of the district court, and the other day as we were talking about security in the courthouse, we learned that there is a secret elevator in the courthouse. Would you believe? This is in our courthouse. I won't tell you where it is, but none of us knew about it. Now, I think that's sort of amusing. None of us ever knew about the secret elevator.

So of course, that's a funny story. I tell my secretary. "At the Security Committee meeting yesterday afternoon, we learned that there's a secret elevator!" Now, how do I tell her the story? I tell her what people said about it. I tell her where it is. I tell her where it runs to. I tell her how it's shut down and the like. I don't tell her, "Let me tell you about this thing that happened yesterday at the security committee meeting. Mr. Small, the building manager was there, and he said…; and Bob Smith, the clerk of courts, said…; and Grace Carey, representing the circuit executive, she said, expressing amazement about the secret elevator…; and when those three people had spoken, I thought it was necessary to say a few words, but the marshal then immediately said… " Who would care? No one ever tells a story like that. Don't you ever do that in an opening.

The witnesses will be there. Now it may be necessary, depending upon what the judge said, to allude to that fact, after you get in the punch lines. Say, "Ladies and gentlemen, we all here are devoted to the law. And as Judge Young has told you, we will be presenting this to you witness by witness in accordance with the legal requirements. And not every witness saw every aspect of what I've told you, but keep that in mind as we go through this."

If you just lay it out the way it's going to come into evidence, what you're not telling them is the law. They're not interested in the law. They came here to deal with the facts.

Moving down here, not so much in the technique, the tactics, but into the personal, I submit to you a couple of things. I think openings should be delivered without notes. Under the superior court rules you get 15 minutes for openings; the federal court will give you somewhat longer. I think you make a real impact if you deliver an opening without notes.

Be comfortable in the courtroom. One of the things that's good about state practice is that if you've passed the bar, then you are entitled to work within the bar enclosure and you're entitled to move. You don't have to stand at a table or behind a podium in order to speak.

Federal courts tend, though I'm just as liberal on moving around, to be more strict. Some judges require you to stand behind a podium. Now, I am quick to say, being a short and unprepossessing fellow, that if I have to speak from back here (indicating), I am not the person I am if I can stand right out there and step up on the lip of the stage, and I just want to do that. If I have something to say to you and I'm pretty pleased and proud to be here to talk these important things over with you, I don't want to be back there. I want to be out here talking to you except when I have to refer to the notes.

Now, you can go too far of course. Don't invade the jurors' privacy space. By leaning over into the jury box, you will have done something that socially is inappropriate.

You must remember what authority figures you are. Now, you say you don't feel like an authority figure. You come into the court, and the judge is very scary, and you don't know who any of the jurors are. You've got a vicious curmudgeon on the other side, and this is pretty wrenching. I recognize that it is, but compare this to the jurors who've been processed through the jury commissioner's office, walked into a courtroom, sworn to tell the truth, sees some fellow wearing a robe looking very strange, flags, books, is told to sit in this chair. Now someone stands up and speaks. As compared to you, they are really feeling put upon. They are not feeling empowered. The person that they will ally with most closely in the courtroom is not the judge, it's the witness, because they know that the witnesses are people like them. So when you go to beat on a witness, I'm jumping ahead here, be very careful because their natural instincts are not to be skeptical of the witnesses but to be skeptical of you. You people are lawyers. They've never seen a judge before, so they sort of take the judge as an authority figure. Maybe they won't like the judge if the judge is too overbearing. Maybe they will like the judge, but they know the judge is supposed to be neutral. They're automatically skeptical of you. Lawyers don't stand in very high regard in this society. I don't say that in any way to get a laugh. I think that's very wrong, and I think if we only could show the public the contributions that lawyers make as teachers to really hold the whole heterogeneous society together, the profession would be much better. The fact is, you don't stand that high, and they're sympathizing with the witness. Therefore, don't do anything socially incorrect.

In fact, your demeanor I think throughout must be one of complete professionalism. Never talk down to juries. They are collectively smarter than you are. Use street talk. By street talk, I don't mean vulgar. I had a fellow who tried a whole case, and he won, but he didn't know the difference between "see" and "seen." "Now, when you seen him, what was he doing?" I think you can do better than that, and I expect better than that from you, though I wouldn't correct it. And I think that the jurors don't think very much of that. Obviously you don't use vulgarities in language or cheap talk to the jurors.

But while we're on that, you don't shy away from or be squeamish about vulgarities that are used in the actual street parlance. If that's what a witness says, don't make much of it. Don't say, "I know this is difficult for you to say, but what did he shout out?" That's malarkey. These people have heard these words before.

Professionally you say, "And what did he say then?" The witness then should answer truthfully, not dance around.

"Well, he swore."

"Well, what did he say?" *(Laughter)*.

There's something more profound behind this. I'll make it a little more serious. Suppose it's a sexual assault case and we are actually looking at undergarments and those undergarments are stained and torn, bloody, and have semen on them. You can't be squeamish about that. On the other hand, you don't hold them up and wave them or something like that. A sexual assault case is a good example to talk about because that's such a taboo and yet an interest in our society that you will have skewed the jury away from your teaching job, which is to evaluate the evidence. And I suggest to you that you have simply to teach, simply to tell the truth, but don't dramatize. The drama comes in from the events themselves. Don't dramatize and don't be squeamish, and that's how you talk in your opening. So, to summarize, try not to use notes, stand in front of the jury—but not so close as to disturb the jury—and don't be squeamish.

The Defense Opening

Defense opening. My view, and again I don't apologize when I talk trial practice for speaking personally because that's all you're getting here. If your tactics are different and your tactics work, then your tactics are just as good. But my duty is to tell you what, as I perceive it, my best judgment is.

I think that defense counsel should always open after the plaintiff's opening. You have the right under the rules to reserve your opening until the beginning of your case, but never do that. The only time I would ever think you would be justified in waiting on your opening is if you have what I call a ships-passing-in-the-night defense. You don't care what evidence the plaintiff is putting in, for whatever evidence the plaintiff puts in, even if it's believed, you will still win because they were beyond the statute of limitations and the statute of limitations defense is going to save you. Even then I don't know that I would wait.

I would suggest to you that you make your opening, if you're going to make one, right after the plaintiff's opening. And how you do it in a civil and a criminal case is different. Just the technique is exactly the same. You want to be just as forthcoming. I think you should be able to do it without notes. I think 15 or less minutes is about right, except in the most complex cases.

The principle is the same. Why do you think you're going to win the case? Why should it be a defendant's verdict? You get up, and you tell the jury why. You tell them the facts. You tell them the facts as they go your way.

I have a personal dislike, though it's frequently used, for saying, "He didn't tell you the other side of the story," a la that famous radio commentator. The reason I personally don't like that is this isn't a story. This is all reality. The jurors get too much storybook stuff on TV. The "other side of the story" suggests that there are two versions and their job is simply to choose between versions.

As a trial lawyer you want to convey by every statement, by your entire attitude, that there's only one truth, and you're telling the truth. Not the other side, but you're telling them what the truth is. Now, you can't just come out and say that. You can't argue it, but you have to by your demeanor set out the facts that you intend to prove.

If you're a criminal defense lawyer, your job is especially hard. You don't want to lay out your defense in your opening because your defense may not work out that way. You don't necessarily want to commit to have your client testify unless you absolutely have gone over it with him before the trial. You have to have his permission to mention it in the opening, and you are convinced in your own mind that he is in fact going to testify. Then you may want to say he's going to testify. You may want to say, "And he was there, and he knows, and he will get on the stand to tell you thus and so, and he looks forward to this opportunity to deal with the truth." In other words, you may want to be affirmative in those cases, but many cases aren't that way. In many cases, your fellow is not going to testify. In many cases the question is only can the government prove it.

So what are you going to say? Most judges will allow you to mention the concept of reasonable doubt and rub the jurors' noses in it and ask the jurors to question whether this or that is shown beyond a reasonable doubt.

In fact, I think it's fair to say that most judges will allow defense counsel, but not prosecutors, to do a little arguing in the opening statement if the argument is only to suggest that the jurors should be careful about accepting the government's evidence.

In any event, it is my view that you should open. You should not forgo your chance. You should, even as a criminal defense attorney who has nothing to say, stand up and make an opening, emphasizing the difficult burden of proof that the government has.

All right. The openings are done.

Directed Verdict After Opening

I think the risks of the directed verdict after opening are minimal. I know of only one or two cases where it has been done, and I know of no judge who will not, when the other side comes to the sidebar and says, "He made an opening; he didn't mention proximate cause; I'm entitled to a directed verdict," say, "Well, do you have anything on proximate cause? Go back and mention it."

I've been doing this for 16 years. I directed one case on the opening, and it was a pro se. The pro se got up, and he huffed and puffed, and then the other side said, "He hasn't said anything about negligence, Judge."

And so I said, "Mr. Smith, do you want to say anything…"

The pro se party said, "I do not. I've made my opening."

I said, "I'm going to be very serious. You've said nothing about negligence and it's my duty…"

He said, "I'll say nothing more. Now I'm going to testify."

I said, "I don't think so."

(Laughter).

He said, "You can't tell me how to operate my case."

And I said, "Respectfully, I think I can. I think I am going to tell you how."

And he said, "This is an outrage. I'm appealing."

And I said, "That's correct, judgment for the defendant. Now appeal it."

(Laughter).

I was down in Fall River. So life goes on. I become a federal judge. Eight years later I get a motion against Justice such and such, not me, but some other one he sued, and I look up, and there's my friend. And now he has gone against this judge who allegedly denied him his civil rights. And he remembered me, and I remembered him. But that's the only time in 16 years I've ever directed on an opening, and I gave him his chance.

STRUCTURING THE PRESENTATION OF THE PRIMA FACIE CASE

Now I'm going to discuss how to put on the case. We're plaintiffs. We're prosecution. Before we put on the case, what are we going to think about? I want to tell you something about strategy here.

What you're going to do depends upon what you have to do legally in order to make out a prima facie case. What you're going to present to the jury depends upon what the law requires you to come up with in order to satisfy your burden of production—that's what beats the directed verdict. With the jurors, your burden of persuasion is to convince them in a civil case by a fair preponderance of the evidence, or beyond a reasonable doubt, that your version is correct. So that dictates the different types of witnesses you're going to have to call. You're going to be concerned with the direct evidence, circumstantial evidence and the like.

You're also going to have, in most cases, various finite things, like exhibits. When you come to your planning, I suggest to you that the following principles apply: You want to start strong, and you want to end strong. And I'll give you some examples of those. Those principles are good principles for the trial of any case.

You want your first witness to be one who will tell a lot of the detail; one with whom the jury can empathize. In a personal injury case, that is frequently, but not always, the victim of the accident—the plaintiff himself.

You want to end strong. Frequently, that means ending with the expert, but not necessarily. And you want to do the other work in between.

Now, whether you can do the other work depends in part upon the law of evidence. And that is nowhere more significant than in deciding what exhibits you are going to put in evidence, because exhibits must have a foundation, and the foundation must be laid by a live witness. And if you want a witness to comment on an exhibit, the exhibit has to be in evidence. And, of course, this is immeasurably complicated by the need to try to accommodate your witnesses' schedules, especially your experts' schedules, because they often don't want to come to court when the judge wants them to, but want to come to court when they want to.

Now, you deal with that by trying to let the judge know early on that the expert will be in on such and such a day. You deal with it with the other side by trying to secure his or her courteous agreement to your taking a witness out of order. You shouldn't hesitate to concede to or ask for those agreements, and you should cooperate among yourselves. But if all else fails, you're going to be asking the judge to take the evidence, and they'll say "de bene" or take it subject to linking it up. Judges vary on that. Some are very strict in refusing it. I'm on that end. Others are very liberal and say, "That's fine, it makes good sense." The strict ones are strict because they're not sure you can link it up and they want to see what the foundation is first.

The order necessarily is start strong, end strong, but have your exhibits in there at the time you want them in evidence so that they will have the most powerful effect with the jury. How you do that depends upon the type of case. Now, I am talking strategy—I'm talking the legalities of cases.

EVENTS CASES AND STATUS CASES

I suggest that cases tend to fall into two different types: first is what I call the events case. Most tort cases are events cases, even if they're discrimination or some land damage and certain personal injury torts.

Some cases are status cases. The most common status case is a contract case. What's significant in this type of case is the status of the parties—do they have a private law, which is the contract between them, and how do they perform under the private law?

An antitrust case is frequently a status case because it turns on whether there was a monopolization in the market. A Robinson-Patman Act case would be a status case. Some Superfund pollution cases are status cases, as are Chapter 21E cases on the state side, because the question is simply "What is the status of the landholder?" In these cases, it's really not disputed that the land in question is their land.

How you prove one of those cases varies. If it's an events case, the easiest analytic tool is chronology, because that's how we tend to think about events. The best jury studies show that juries try to make a coherent story out of everything they hear in court. Even though there are different versions, they try hard to reconcile those versions and make it into a coherent story so that they can do justice with respect to that story. We all know how to tell stories. We all know how to listen to stories. You can teach the jury by giving them the chronology.

But with a status case, that won't work. Here's a simple example: In a contracts case, if you start with the beginning, when the two parties met and entered into negotiations, you're in no end of evidentiary difficulty because of the parole evidence rule, because we don't know whether they fully integrated their deal into a writing. The place to start in a status case is with whatever creates the status. And usually, in a land sale case, it's the deed; in a contract, it's the final version of the contract that was signed. Get the contract in evidence. Put that in first.

If it's a case where your performance is obvious or it's easy to show, many people think the way to try a contracts case is to put the contract in, put in your evidence, rest, and then let the other side try to get off. Let them try to show the exemption if it's an insurance case, so they bear the burden of proof on that, to show that they were exempt under the insurance contract. Let them come in with all their evidence of exemptions. Why? That's the perfect type of case for rebuttal evidence. If they've raised all this stuff for exemptions, and they bear the burden of proof on exemption, you come back with all your nonexemption evidence. So, you've gone first, you've proved the contract. The insurance company tries to get off, and shows all its exemptions. You come back and put on all your nonexemption evidence.

Simply because you start out, don't think you have to put all your evidence in first. But you've got to watch out that the insurance company doesn't try a very tight case, or that they've got something for nonpayment of premium, in which case, they don't worry about the exemption at all. They say, "There's a contract. He never paid the premiums. We rest."

And then you say, "Wait a second. I thought this case was about pollution and the pollution exclusion, and I'm ready to put on." And the judge says, "It's too late. You rested."

So I'm not asking you to act blindly, but I am saying, with a status case, start with the status.

ORDER OF WITNESSES

Now, here are some examples that show that there are some inventive variations to the rules. In the Big Dan's rape case—that was the barroom pool table rape—you would think that the victim would be the logical place to start. *See Commonwealth v. Cordeiro*, 401 Mass. 843 (1988) and *Commonwealth v. Vieira*, 401 Mass. 828 (1988). She was, after all, the key witness. They didn't start with the victim, and they didn't start at the beginning. The first witness was a fellow driving a pickup truck through the streets of New Bedford. He had nothing to do with the Big Dan's Bar. He was driving along with some buddies, and they were going from bar to bar, but they weren't going to Big Dan's. They see a woman who's unclothed from the waist down, and she's trying to flag them down. She's in the street. They stop the truck. The driver gets out. This is the first witness. The woman, unknown to them, runs up, throws her arms around his neck, clenches him, and is sobbing and screaming, "I've been raped. I've been raped. They all raped me." And he's sort of a short witness because these really were Good Samaritans, and all they did was get a blanket out of the truck, put the blanket around the woman, go to a phone, call the police, and keep her in the cab of the truck until the police car arrived. That was it. That's all they had to contribute. They didn't know who she was. They didn't really interrogate her and the like.

And so now I'm going from the general principle: start strong and end strong. This is how they ended the examination of that witness. They took us through that story that I've just told you.

But then Bob Kane, the Assistant District Attorney in the case, said, "Going back to when she had her arms around your neck—how did you get her off your neck?"

"Well, my friend had to pry her fingers off, she was clenching them so tight."

"Your witness."

You see, you want to save something. You want to save that little vignette about the hysteria of the woman. And, you see, we start at the end; by then, the event was over. But how are you going to cross-examine that witness? That witness has no bias. That witness wasn't at the bar. There was no suggestion of any cheering crowd. This witness is the Good Samaritan. So they have him testify, they have his two buddies testify and only then do we get into the bar. And then we've got a woman who, after it was over, showed every evidence of being terribly, terribly brutalized, and we are setting ourselves up for her testimony. I think that's brilliant.

So you use the same skills that the novelist uses; determine how you're going to present this evidence, even in an events case, when your analysis is chronological.

How about closing strong? I saw Newt Esdaile try a case of a fellow who was at Children's Hospital—again, this is before I was a judge. The fellow, who was a resident, dove into a pool and broke his neck. The last witness was his mother. And you would think that the mother would be easily impeached, because she's obviously biased for him and the like. Would you end with the mother? This is how Newt Esdaile ended his direct examination of the last witness that he had called. We know about the broken neck and how it always would be broken and his rehabilitation. And so we get the mother's testimony, which is as follows:

"What did you do?"

"I was called, and there was this accident. And I came, and I was in the hospital."

"And what did you do?"

"Well, I came to the hospital."

"Well, how often did you come to the hospital?"

"I came every day."

"And what would you do?"

"I would turn the pages."

"Could you explain?"

"I would turn the pages in my son's books."

"Well, what was he reading?"

"He was reading psychiatry texts because he had decided to become a psychiatrist."

"Your witness."

This is just a stunning example of the human spirit. How are you going to cross-examine that witness? She wasn't asking for any pity. She wasn't asking for anything. The guy is quadriplegic and will be forever, and he decides to become a psychiatrist. Pretty good guy. And of course that's what Esdaile wanted to show. And he stops.

I'll go back to another sexual assault case tried by Senator Kerry when he was first assistant in Middlesex. This is a rape of a BC student. Senator Kerry has used in a very professional way the garments and the like, but he's never introduced them in evidence. They've been marked for identification. The last witness was—I think it was in Newton—a Newton Police officer. The officer gets on the stand. And who is the officer? He is nothing more than the evidence technician. He knows nothing about the events. He just checked them in and checked them out to court. So now, of course, they all have letters. They're marked for identification. "And now, Sergeant Owens, I show you this," and he went through each garment.

"I show you this parka. I show you this item that's been marked Exhibit A for identification. Do you recognize it?"

"Yes, I do."

"What is it?"

"This is the parka that was brought in on the night of November 6th."

"What did you do with it?"

"I checked it in."

"Later on, what did you do with it?"

"I checked it out for court."

"I offer…" Now, any other witness could have gotten it in, but, you see, it's admitted as an exhibit. Then through the outer garments, through the undergarments, 2, 3, 4, 5 and so on.

"Your witness."

The defense has no cross-examination for that witness. And yet you see that the dynamics of the courtroom put those things now in evidence. They're going to go to the jury room. They could be put in evidence, if we went back to talk about evidence, by the victim herself, by the doctor or by anyone who recognized them. Patches were cut out and sent for forensic purposes. No. He had one witness that they couldn't touch, and he put him in at the end of the case.

I'm not saying you always do it that way. I'm just saying those are the points of starting strong and ending strong.

DIRECT EXAMINATION

Let's get to specific witnesses now. We'll talk direct examination. Direct examination is how cases are won. Everyone knows you shouldn't lead on direct examination. Everyone does lead on direct examination. Judges permit it, more or less. You should not lead on direct examination because it's not effective examination. Here's the problem:

There's so much intensity when you are examining a witness and you are so much in need of controlling the witness—this is when it's on direct examination your own witness—you want the witness to say what the witness has said on deposition, what you've prepared the witness to testify, that you are cabining in the witness with the questions that you ask. And you say, "Well, did you go to the store?" "And did you buy oranges?" "And once you bought the oranges, where did you go?" That's not leading. "And then on the way home, did you see the light at the intersection?" You know these things are all significant. And the witnesses say, "Yes, sir," "Yes," or "Yes, I did see it." And every now and again, you'll give them a little latitude, and every now and again, the other side objects that it's leading. And if the judge is strict, he'll say "Sustained." And that's how trials go.

If you're going to use the word "did," put the word "what" in front of it. The way to do direct examination is to use the words that begin with "W"—who, what, when, and where. There are others also—how, describe, explain. If state of mind is at issue in a mugging case and when the witness is put in fear, why did it happen? Who, what, when, where, how, describe, explain. That's not to teach you evidence. That's to teach you effective examination.

If you're up there saying, "Did this happen? Did that happen? Did the other thing happen?" you're doing your lawyer's tricks, and you're demeaning your witness. Your witness is more persuasive to the jury if you let the witness testify to her version of what went on. She is more credible. She is more valid in the eyes of the jury if you let her testify. Ah, but you have to control her because you have to control every witness.

How do you control? The best way I can explain it is to think of your examination much like the freeze frame on an old movie—each question you put is a frame of reality, and so you want to cut the action down to the shortest possible steps so the witness gets the chance to give her entire testimony in a way that is most persuasive.

Now, clearly you can't do that throughout the whole witness's testimony, because you have to get the witness to the place where the event took place if we're trying an events case, or where the really relevant testimony is. And do that with a few general questions like this, "Directing your attention to September 23rd of last year, where were you on that date?" And then pick up from there.

I like to think of the construct of the Christmas tree—you're putting ornaments on the branches, and the ornaments are the who, what, when, where, how, describe, explain. But the difficulty is going from branch to branch. I suggest for the examination of a witness that you want notes before you start. You don't necessarily want to hold them. Obviously, you don't want to hold them up in front of you as you examine the witness, but it's not wrong. But you want to have eye contact with the witness. You want to have the witness answer your question. And by your pacing, you want to be ready to ask the next question—a short question. If you keep the questions short, you'll both have more control. It will be obvious to the witness and to the jury—which, after all, is the audience you're concerned about—what it is that you're asking, and the witness will be given a chance to give her testimony.

Let's take a particular example, because people generally foul this up. Suppose you want to get a conversation in evidence—and I'm going to take two subsets of putting a conversation in evidence. In the first, what is said during the conversation is admissible, or you think it's going to be admissible as an exception to the hearsay rule or it's not hearsay. Here's how you put the conversation in evidence:

"Ms. Smith, when next did you hear from Mr. Jones?" "Well, a couple of days later." "How did you communicate with him?" "Well, I saw him in the store." "Now, who was present?" "Where were you?" "What did he say to you and what did you say to him on that occasion?"

Now, that's where you've got an exception, because that's asking for hearsay, if it is hearsay. But do you see the questions? "What did you say" and "what did he say," not "describe the conversation." That's secondary. Even though that's not leading, that's secondary.

That tends to elicit from the witness the best memory. Now, she may just give it generally. "Well, we talked about our pets. And I told him that Fido was eating that herbal-flavored dog food." That may be the only thing you get from the witness by asking the questions, but that's the way to ask them.

Let me jump back out of the trial a minute. If it's on deposition, always ask, "Was anything else said by either of you during that conversation?" You've got to ask that closure question on depositions, because at trial, you're going to get a longer conversation and if you haven't asked it, she'll say, "Well, you didn't ask me." "I told you one thing, yeah, you never asked me." But if you ask her, "Was anything else said?" and she says, "No," that's what you're going to impeach her with at trial.

Now, let's say that the conversation is hearsay. You're never going to get the conversation in evidence. "When you saw the fire, what did you do?" This might be an excited utterance, but let's say, "On the day after the fire, what did you do?" "I called the fire department." "And with whom did you speak?" "I spoke with the receptionist there." "As a result of that conversation, what did you do?" "I went to confront my neighbor." Let's say that's her answer.

Now, we don't need the conversation. She talked to somebody—maybe she said, "I called the fire department. I asked to speak to the arson investigator."

(Laughter).

"With whom did you speak?" "I spoke with a guy who said his name was Lieutenant Jones." "As a result of that conversation, what did you do?" "I went next door right away." We don't need the conversation, but do you see the key? You set up the conversation, and then the question is: "As a result of that conversation, what did you do?"

With someone across the street, you do it the same way. If it's important enough, then do it the same way. You say, "Where were you?" "Where were you looking?" "What did you see?" And if all else fails, "What next happened?" The "next" is to prevent a narrative answer, just going on. Some go in and they say, "Now, tell us everything that you know."

PUTTING EXHIBITS IN EVIDENCE

Now, how to get exhibits in evidence? I touched on it in my example of the clothes in Senator Kerry's case. Let's go over getting exhibits in evidence, not to dwell upon the evidentiary foundation, but just on the technique. Most exhibits are not self-authenticating. Some are self-authenticating. I want to go over the steps, though. If they're self-authenticating, like a certified copy of a birth certificate, you simply show it to the other side and offer it in evidence, because you've got the certified copy of the certificate, you've got the certified copy of the zoning ordinances of the town, and the like.

Show the Exhibit

Here's how you put anything in evidence. Here are the steps. You don't always have to use all these steps, but it's worthwhile going over all these steps, because if you have them in mind, you'll never go wrong. The first thing you do if you want to put something in evidence is show it to the other side. The law doesn't require you to do that, practicality requires you to do that, because if you don't do that and you're examining the witness, laying the foundation before the witness with the document, the other side may say, "Judge, I'm not so sure I've seen that. Do you think I might see that?" How does that make you look? To the jury, it makes you look like you're trying to slip one past them. You don't ever want to do that.

And so the first thing you want to do is show it to the other side. You don't have to say, "Let the record show that I am showing her the document." You just go over and show it to her, but then say to her sotto voce, "Do you object to this?" And if she says no, you turn around and say, "This is without objection, your Honor. May it be entered in evidence as the next number?" And you don't lay any foundation at all, because that's a waste of time. You get it in evidence, and then you work with it. But if she's going to object to it, and you should know this from pretrial conferences, she should know what you're showing. And if it's a deposition, you should have the courtesy to say, "And now page 3, line 7." That's a courtesy, but it also protects you against her saying, "What page, Judge?", so that it looks like you're not being small.

Mark for Identification

So the first thing is to show. The next thing, if it hasn't been done already, is to mark it for identification. Now, under the federal, with very complex pretrial orders, we'll have everything marked for identification and the like. Most times in the superior court you will, but if you don't, that's the time to mark it for identification.

Laying the Foundation

Now we're going to use it with the witness that we have. And the first two questions are always the same. If you master these two questions, you're well on your way. "Mr. Witness, I show you what has been marked as Exhibit A for Identification. Do you recognize it?" That question is absolutely fair. It's not pejorative. It doesn't characterize the thing that you showed. It makes reference to it by its identification letter, so on appeal we know exactly what's going to go on. And you say, "Do you recognize it?" Answer: "Yes." That's the first question that you must ask.

The second question is: "What is it?" That's what the jury is thinking. Ask that question, because every time you can ask the question the way the jury is thinking, you are closer to the jury. The question is technically objectionable under the best evidence rule, because if the witness purports then to characterize what it says, the best evidence of a writing is the writing. The best evidence of a photograph is what the photograph shows. If you get a really strict judge and a really strict opponent and it's objected, just back off and say, "Just identify it generally."

But you don't want to start off by saying "Identify it generally." It's too weak. You want to ask the question the jury's asking. Question one: "I show you what's been marked as Exhibit A for Identification. Do you recognize it?" Question two: "What is it?"

Offering the Exhibit

Now, where you go from there depends upon which exception to the rule against hearsay you're relying on. And I'm not going to go into that. But once you've laid the foundation, you offer it in evidence. And that's the step where the other side gets to come to the sidebar and argue against it if they're going to. Frequently, they don't object. It is then marked in evidence.

What if you've got a tape recording on an incident that is the complaining witness who spoke and actually recanted all of her allegations in a criminal case? Here's how you get that tape recording in evidence. What witness are we going to use is the first question. One certainly would be someone who recognizes that person's voice because the tape recording came in at the defendant's residence. All right. We're going to need more than one witness, though. Who's going to testify it hasn't been tampered with? How do we know that this is the same tape recording? Have we got any witness to say that? Is there anyone in the house that can show that it hasn't been tampered with? If not, you've got a problem. You argue that it hasn't been tampered with. You see if you can't stipulate that it is authentic. The prosecution is going to say it's not authentic, that they sandwiched the words in. "Lots of technology, Judge. They could do that." And you're going to have to put on some evidence that it is authentic, but here's how you do it if you can get over that evidentiary hurdle. With a knowledgeable witness, you do the following:

Show the tape. Take the tape as an example. You've marked it in some way. You've actually physically got the plastic tape with the tape in there. You mark it. Before it gets in Exhibit A, you mark it when you first take custody of it or you have the defendant mark it so he puts his handwriting on it. "I show you what has been marked Exhibit C for Identification. Do you recognize it?" "Yes." "What is it?" "This is the tape out of my answering machine in the month of October '99."

With this type of tangible evidence, the next thing is, "How do you know?" He says how he knows. He says, "When I took it out, I put this stamp on it and I wrote the date that I took it out and I wrote my name. I recognize my handwriting." Then you have to have a witness for authentication to say, "Is it in the same circumstances now?"—Well, see, I make it easy on me. I put the defendant on, and you can't, but recognizing that so we go through it: "Is it in the same shape now as it was when you took it out of the phone answering service?" You can sort of presume the thing is working right, that it hasn't been tampered with, just like we presume a camera is going to work. "Is it the same shape now as when you took it out?" "Yes." "How do you know?" "I listened to it last night," or some other way he does know.

Then we still haven't shown its relevance. Notice that I'm leading a little bit. Not to worry. They'll let you lead when you're laying a foundation rather than substance. "Whose voice is on this tape?" The lady's voice in your hypothetical, by name. "How do you know?" "Because I speak to her frequently and I spoke to her on the phone and I've listened to her on the phone."

Now, we still don't know that it's relevant because we won't know that until we hear it, but I would then offer it in evidence. At the sidebar if they say it's not relevant, you say, "Judge, you have to listen to it, but it's relevant." And it would be nice to have a transcript of it, give it to the judge and say, "Here's what it's going to say." Then you have to have it set up so that you can key right into it.

Two nights ago, I sat for an hour and a half looking at—I admit I was reading, as well—a surveillance tape in a so-called drug bust, only I thought it was my duty to look at it all. And finally, I kept trying to find where the so-called conspirators spoke, and I couldn't find it. That was like three minutes out of a two-hour tape, the guys come into the room and mumble.

(Laughter).

Show the Exhibit to the Jury

But I listened to the whole doggone tape, you know. You don't want a jury to do that. They'll never do that. So you have to have it keyed in to whatever it says, and probably you want the little mechanical thing. Our answering machine says, "...beep, nine o'clock p.m...." or whatever, because, you see, that's a record of when the call was made. So what you want to do is have your tape all keyed in, which helps the judge move on to the next stage. It's never enough to get stuff in evidence. If it's enough to fight to get it in evidence, it's enough to play it to the jury or show it to the jury.

Special Problems With Tape-Recorded Testimony

Some special problems crop up with tape-recorded testimony. Following is an example. Say that in state court, a previous trial was on a tape rather than transcribed by a stenographer. You want the witness to come up on a next trial, and you have to get the tapes somehow. You want to impeach him with the tapes. You get it into a transcript somehow.

You now have to send the other side a transcript because query who you have transcribe it. If they only have a tape system, you don't have an official court reporter. It's one of the real tragedies on the state side that we're getting away from an official record. The tape is what's going to impeach him, but you may only want his voice on the tape for a few seconds.

You get a transcript made from the official tape. You try to get the other side to agree that the transcript is an official transcript. Of course, it's much more complex if the people are talking in a foreign language, but if they're not, maybe he will agree if the tape is at all adequate that the transcript is accurate. Then you use the transcript just like you would use a deposition. It is a prior statement under oath.

Let's say you now have the transcript but the tape has on it two questions and answers that are real killers. You're the defendant—let's say this witness testifies for the plaintiff. You are now in a position to impeach the witness by the deposition, the police report, or, in this case, by the tape. I would want a transcript of the tape. You may not get this, but let's see where we want to go.

I'd like to get the other side to agree that the transcript is accurate. When I was ready to impeach, having gotten the agreement from the other side, I would mark the transcript and the tape for identification. I'm only going to use it to impeach now, but I want a record. Say, "May the tape be marked as Exhibit D and the transcript be marked as Exhibit E for Identification, your Honor?" And then say, "It is stipulated"—don't ever position the other side. Say that it is stipulated between you and your opposite number that this is an accurate transcript of the proceeding before Judge Fallon on such and such a day in such and such a court. And then the judge probably will look at the other side and say, "Do you so stipulate?" And, of course, you do stipulate.

Sometimes you want to have the judge read the stipulations. You may think they'll have more power, but in any event, you get the stipulation.

Prior Inconsistent Statements

The way to impeach with a prior inconsistent statement is to employ the three Cs—confirm, compare and confront.

First, confirm. The witness on the witness stand has said the light was red. In the prior trial the witness said the light was green. In confirming, you don't want to necessarily take the witness back over his direct, because then he gets to say it twice. This is cross-examination, so I am trying to demonstrate the control in each of my questions. I'm not asking open-ended questions. You want to say something like this, "Mr. Witness, you say you were at that intersection, standing on the corner there that we've marked on the diagram?" "Yes." "And you say you saw the color of that light?" "Yes." "And this morning you seemed quite sure of that." "Yes." That's the confirm.

In other words, you just want to box the witness in. Give the witness a chance to say, "Really, I'm not so sure," because the best situation for you is if the witness will change his mind and say the light was green. Then you don't have to impeach the witness. You've got the witness affirmatively testifying. The witness says, "No. You know, there was a big fog bank that came over," or something like that. You want to build on that. The witness says, "Yeah, I saw it."

Then you want to compare. "This isn't the first time you've testified about these matters, is it? In fact, there was another proceeding." Of course, to compare is to make the other proceeding more impressive than this proceeding. "It was closer in time to the accident," "You were under oath then," "You wanted to tell the truth then."

You haven't shown the transcript at all, but you may hold it in your hand. "And you were asked questions about the color of the light, weren't you?" "Well, I don't remember." Maybe that's the time to confront, but first you want to do all your comparison. "And your counsel agrees that this is an accurate transcript of what was said." Maybe it's a third-party witness; then, you just want to remind the witness of the stipulation. "And counsel here, we agree this is an accurate transcript of what was testified to at the trial."

And now the confront. "Mr. Witness, I show you page 7, line 5." And then you want to show him. "I show you what you said. I show you the transcript."

And then I would go for more than the impeaching if you can, and you then take it away and say, "And that's the truth, isn't it?" "I don't think it says—no, no. The light was red." Why do you think the witness flipped his testimony? What are you going to impeach him on? "And you are the brother of the defendant?" "Yes, I am." Then you leave it, but that's how you impeach.

Now, since you also have the transcript, once you've done the whole thing with the transcript and you've got it all set up, you say, "And now let me play the question and answer as they were heard by you at that trial." Click. And these things have to work perfectly. Question: "What color was the light?" "The light was green." "That's what you testified." Then they hear his own voice. You don't want to go on too long. And, of course, the tapes are not of good quality, so sometimes you have more control if you get the transcript. That's how you impeach a witness.

CROSS-EXAMINATION

Let's jump to cross-examination because it's important to talk about it, though much less so than direct examination. As in all of these things, especially on cross-examination, I cite you to the tapes by Professor Irving Younger, which are clearly the best. He has a whole lecture, an hour and a half long, on the arts of cross-examination, and I am but a pale reflection, except that I agree with everything he has said. I have some observations on cross-examination. They depend in large measure on his analysis, and so I cite him to you, but these are points I would make on cross-examination first.

Ask yourself whether you want to cross-examine the witness. Younger makes a big point about how powerful it is when you don't cross-examine. My experience is not as strong as Younger. In other words, you stand up and say, "I have no questions." In effect, you blindside that witness, say this witness is not important. If the witness is truly not important, Younger is correct, but today jurors expect cross-examination. They expect objections, and I want to talk about objections as well.

If you don't cross-examine—and I differ from Younger on this—far from discounting the witness's testimony, the jury thinks, "Well, that witness is testifying to the truth, and the other things are disputed."

Let's go back to the first witness in the Big Dan's case. How would you cross-examine that witness? First, we'll discuss theory and then some practical things about how to examine that witness. Theoretically, every witness who's up there can do something affirmative for you. Maybe that witness has some testimony that will help you. If the witness does not have testimony that will help you, it may be clear that the witness is not capable of testifying to various things that would hurt you. And if the witness has testified to such things and has hurt you, there are a variety of ways of impeaching that witness. Let's go over each of them.

Suppose the witness has things that will help you. I suggest that if there are things that support your theory of the case—this is during the defense now, or at least when you're opposed to the witness that's on the stand—that's where you want to start in your cross, unless it's very important for you to hit the witness right between the eyes first to gain control over him or her.

If the witness has stuff to help you, get right up and get the help. Do that with every witness. It reminds the jury that there's another version of events. It reminds the jury that there's more coming to the case, that you'll be there. Even if the witness has nothing to help you, maybe the witness can't hurt you as much as another eyewitness or another witness. You want to point out what the witness doesn't know—that the witness wasn't there, the witness was outside, the witness has nothing to say about this, it was a long time ago, and the like.

Impeaching a Witness

The major grounds of impeaching a witness are that first, you want to think about impeaching the witness's perceptions of the events that the witness testified to.

Now, the witness heard something. The witness heard the event or saw the event and is now going to speak about it. You want to impeach; you want to cross-examine both prongs. I don't necessarily say you have to do it in this order, but you want to think about it in both prongs.

What is the witness's opportunity to observe the event? Does the witness wear thick glasses like I do? Were those glasses on? Were they the right prescription? Could the witness hear? Was it too far away?

In the movie *Twelve Angry Men*, the subway comes through at the time that the witness says that the witness saw the murder. But the witness didn't really see the murder—the witness is simply recounting what makes him think he is telling the truth. The witness is now the center of attention in this big murder case, and Henry Fonda turns the jury all around. That all turns on the witness's perception of the events. The witness couldn't have seen it; not that the witness was lying.

Once you've gone over the perception of the event, then you want to cross-examine on the witness's bias. What motive does the witness have for falsifying? Relationship to the party? Stands to gain or lose something depending upon how the case comes out? Has made prior inconsistent statements? We've talked about that. Those are the things you want to cross-examine on.

Now, how much cross-examination? By and large, you want to cross-examine, but the choice of what to cross-examine on is crucial. If you simply get up and whack away at the witness, like Younger so skillfully points out, you will fail because the witness will get the chance to tell the same story twice. So you want to pick your targets. And I suggest that in picking your targets, if the witness has stuff to help you, that stuff comes first.

Next comes what the witness doesn't know. If the witness has nothing to help you, start with what the witness doesn't know.

And last, because that's what you want to have stick in the witness's mind, that the witness is impeachable by bias—bias out of some motive to help the government, to hostility toward your client, and the like.

It is the general rule that you do not call a witness a liar. And that goes back to what we were talking about before, that the jury is going to identify with the witnesses and not with you. If you call a witness a liar, you are going to hurt your case. There's an exception to that.

The exception is a good example. It is *Lakian v. Globe Newspaper Co.*, 399 Mass. 379 (1987). Back when Lakian first ran for governor, the *Globe* did a hatchet job on him and he sued them for libel. The *Globe* was represented by my former partner, Fran Fox, a captain in the Navy. And one of the things that Lakian had remembered inventively was that he had a battlefield commission, and he didn't. And there were about six things there, and when Fran examined Lakian, he would say, "Now, when you said you had a battlefield commission, Mr. Lakian, that was not true, was it?" "No, I guess it wasn't." "That was false?" "Well, it was not true." "Mr. Lakian, that was a lie when you said that, wasn't it?" And he would say, "Well, I don't know if I'd characterize it as a lie." Fran went through six different things, and on each one he said, "And that was a lie, wasn't it?" He didn't point at him, but he said, "The *Globe* wins, no libel." "That was a lie?"

So what we are talking about here is tactics. I stand by the general rule for the reason I gave you. If you think you have a case that's an exception, then your judgment on behalf of your client must govern.

I suggest that you end with bias because if you really want to attack the witness, that's what you want to leave in the jury's mind. And I believe, and I am with Younger on this, that the shorter cross-examination is the best.

Let's go back to Newt Esdaile's case, where the last witness is the mother of the victim. Compare these two cross-examinations. In the first, the defense counsel says, "Mrs. Berhoven, you are the mother of the plaintiff, correct?" "Yes, I am." "I have no other questions."

Compare that with this cross-examination: "Mrs. Berhoven, you are the mother of the plaintiff in this case, are you not?" "Yes, I am." "You love your son very much, don't you?" "Yes, yes, I do." "And you'd do anything to help him in this case, wouldn't you?" "I will tell the truth." "And you think that the truth will help him?" "I do indeed."

Well, of course it's easy when you play both sides. What do you think is the best cross-examination? The short one, because if you have to argue it or even leave it hanging out there, what are you going to do with this lady? If you don't have anything to do, it is still a fact that she is the mother, even if she is an utterly truthful, selfless mother who wants truth above all. Don't take her over those facts, just emphasize the fact that she's the mother.

And then on closing, you might say "And who could the plaintiff get to testify on his behalf? No one, only his mother. I rest." Whereas if you'd really cross-examined her, you'd give her the chance to say that she will tell the truth and she wouldn't lie for her son, she's here to tell the truth, and she believes that what she's saying is the truth.

Now, we've talked over direct and cross, and there are three other things I want to go through. First, you fail in your job as lawyers if you limit yourself simply to what the law of evidence will allow you to do at a trial.

DEMONSTRATIVE AIDS

I want to mention demonstrative aids. You really want to put demonstrative aids before the jury. If you have a witness who can draw something, such as an intersection, that is powerful evidence.

Here's an example. This is Jimmy Meehan trying a case on behalf of the families of 94 people who came in on a Delta Electra back in 1970, in pea soup fog. The Electra crashes at the end of the runway. And he's prepared the case. One survived about four days, hideously burned. And his theory is that Delta has merged with Northeast, that's true, and that the Electras in Northeast's fleet set their altimeters counterclockwise and the Delta altimeters were set clockwise. There was a Delta pilot on a Northeast plane after the merger, and he set the altimeter wrong and flew the plane into the ground.

Meehan got a very large wallboard and he got an artist to draw the City of Boston, all to scale. The drawing showed the harbor and Bird Island Flats; that's where the runway is. Then he plotted a point in the sky as accurately as can be shown, showing the course of the plane as detailed by the altimeter. And it's much too steep a rate of descent. The plane gets about a couple hundred yards onto the runway; it really should be a quarter of a mile.

Then Meehan takes the actual radar plot in the tower. No one could believe they were going to fly the plane into the ground, so they never even radioed to the plane. The parallax is very, very, very slight until you get down close to the ground, when the plane hits the berm and doesn't land. And, of course, most fly this by about five. Then he takes strobe lights on his two lines so that when you start it, it blinks and gives the illusion of movement.

On the top of this huge thing he's created, he has a digital clock that says that the point in the sky is a minute and 49 seconds before landing. And the digital clock reads backwards—a minute 49, a minute 48, a minute 47, and so on. And then synchronized with all of that, he has the black box, which had been recovered.

And then he plays it, and it plays out like this: "Flight 317, cleared for landing, cleared for landing, runway 3, cleared for landing. Commence landing check." "Landing check commenced." "Wheels down." "Wheels down, check." "Starboard." "Starboard check." "Port." "Port check." "Ailerons." "Ailerons steady." "Very well. Flaps down." "Flaps down." "Eight degrees, 15 degrees." "Give her 17." "17 degrees." "Air speed." "210, 170, 160, 145." "Hold it there." "Sure is foggy." "Just fly the plane." "I got . . ." "CHRIST!"

He really had this. He's got this down in his office. At the trial advocacy programs that MCLE does in the summer, they've had him come and do it, and I've been privileged to watch. He gives a whole lecture on demonstrative aids. I watched the people in the audience cry, because that's the last minute and 49 seconds of 94 human lives.

And the question is: Would the judge let him do that? We don't know, because the case came on before the Honorable David Nelson in the court where I now sit, and it was played in the lobby and the case settled. So we don't know whether Nelson would let the jury see it, but Meehan has the idea so far as I'm concerned of what it is to be a teacher. That's not evidence. And you can imagine all the gyrations that you'd have to go through to be allowed to show that to the jury. But that is what I'm talking about as teaching.

Direct Examination of Experts

I want to say a word about experts. I've touched on how to knock experts out, but I want to explain the law as it relates to direct and cross-examination of experts.

We'll begin with the expert's opinion. In every case, there are two building blocks—one is noncase-specific and the other is case-specific. Noncase-specific means the general knowledge of the expert. That's not enough. The expert needs case-specific knowledge. Even if you have a generally qualified expert, how does that expert know anything about your case? There are four ways the expert can learn about the case. The expert can be given a hypothetical question that tells him or her about the case. The expert can also observe an event. For example, if the case involves a hand surgeon and the expert is the person who observed the surgery, the expert is an observing, percipient witness. The expert can sit throughout the trial, hear the testimony that the jury's heard and then give his or her expertise about it. The expert can also be told about the case outside of court, which would be considered hearsay. The federal and state rules on this differ. Under the federal rule, what you tell the expert about the case outside of court must be the type of hearsay that the expert relies upon in the practice of his or her profession. This is an objective test. The state rule is stricter. Under it, what you tell the expert outside of court must be information that would be admissible if it was in court. It doesn't have to have been admitted, but it has to be evidentially admissible.

With every expert, if you are the proponent of that expert, the first thing you do is to qualify the expert generally. The technique is not to ask the expert, "Give us your qualifications, Madam Expert," because if she talks for half an hour, she's going to sound pompous even if she is the best expert in the world. You want to break down everything about her expertise, such as where she went to school, what subjects she studied, whether she is board certified; all the bells and whistles of professional attainment.

If you're wondering what motivates the judge on whether the expert is an expert, here's my rule of thumb, which I think most judges follow: Does this expert, in the practice of her profession outside of court, give this type of opinion in the free marketplace of ideas? It doesn't mean that she has to be paid for it, but is she out there teaching this knowledge to students? Is she out there treating patients? Is she out there building roads or performing these accounting services? If she isn't, and if all she's doing is testifying in court, judges who are strict on experts are going to have some problem with her.

You don't have to ask the judge to qualify an expert. In the southern districts, when they're done, they always say, "Judge, may this Doctor Smith be qualified as a qualified orthopedic surgeon?" We don't do that in New England. The judge will say, "Just ask the questions."

Then you go on to ask the case-specific questions. You can use a hypothetical, but hypotheticals are tricky. The three case-specific points you want to make, which make up the second building block, are the following three questions. Do you have an opinion, to a reasonable degree of certainty, in whatever the profession is, about whatever it is? If the expert were a doctor, the buzzwords would be "a reasonable degree of medical certainty." The reasonable degree of certainty is significant because unless it's an FELA case or an admiralty case, where any connection will do, the opinion has to be by a fair preponderance of the evidence. The profession has to have advanced to a degree where the person isn't just speculating; the person has an opinion as to whatever it is, causation or the like. The next question is: What is your opinion? The third question is: What is the basis of your opinion? Always get the expert to teach the bases of the opinion.

Cross-Examination of Experts

In the cross-examination of experts, it is more vital than anywhere else to get the expert's help first, and then go after the expert as to bias. If you reverse it, the expert won't give you the help that you probably would get if you treated the expert well at first and then went after him or her. Be aware that if the expert is testifying as to certain premises and you factually don't agree with those premises, you should change the premises in your question to the facts as you believe you can bring them out. Judges will let you do this. Here's an example. You might say, "If the facts were not what you testified to, Doctor, if the facts were this, your opinion would be different, wouldn't it?" If the doctor says no, he sounds like he's a hired gun and he won't differ. If he says yes, you may make him your expert, because then the question is not the degree of difference between experts; the question is what the facts are going to show. You're going to prove the facts your way.

MOTIONS DURING TRIAL

It is key that you make a motion for directed verdict, if you are the defendant, at the close of the plaintiff's case, because that's the only time you have a chance of winning. Technically, it is also key that you make a directed verdict at the close of your case. If you don't, you waive the right to make one for judgment NOV.

But, once the whole case is over and all that remains is for the jury to decide the case, the judge is going to deny the motion. The judge will let the jury do what it wants, and then will take the case away from the jury, judgment NOV. Why? Because the judge is hoping the jury will save him. And if the judge thinks it's not a good case anyway, who needs it? The judge can go on to another case. He can get a jury verdict. There won't be an appeal. The judge has done everything right. You're not going to win that motion for directed verdict at the close of the case, but you may win it at the close of the plaintiff's case, so that's the time to make it. Be absolutely certain that you make it at the close of all the evidence.

THE CHARGE CONFERENCE

Be aware that more judges are offering, in a civil case, to charge the jury first—before closing arguments. This actually makes for a more understandable closing. "First" really means first and last, but the judge will charge and explain the law to the jury. Then you get to argue. I think that's good. I think it helps you because you're then arguing based upon what you know the judge has said about the substantive law. You save your rights as to the charge, following argument.

CLOSING ARGUMENT

Very few words, just mechanically, about closing argument. You know that the order of closing on the state side is defendant and then plaintiff. It's unclear what the rationale is for that. Some people say that's just the way it is. Some people say that's because the plaintiff generally bears the burden of proof. If you've got a judge who thinks the latter and you as defense bear the major burden of proof in this case, argue to the judge that you'd like to argue last if you could, because you bear the burden of proof. Let the plaintiff go first. I don't know how it will work out, but some judges will do that because some of them think that the order of argument turns on the burden of proof.

Because most judges in the federal courts were state practitioners first, we generally on the civil side follow the state procedures, except for Judge Keeton. Keeton, who was a Texas practitioner before he went to the Harvard Law School, will let you, if you can agree, decide whether the argument is going to be defendant then plaintiff, which is our normal argument in Massachusetts, or plaintiff then defendant, and then plaintiff rebuttal, which is how it is in many other places.

On the criminal side in the federal court the order of argument is defined by law. It's prosecution, then defense, and then prosecution rebuttal. There is no defense rebuttal.

Once a jury goes out, stay there. Don't leave. Don't have your client leave. The jury may come in with a question. They may come in to go home for the day. If they've been working all afternoon and at 4:00 or 5:00 they come in to an empty courtroom and you're not there, jurors know you've gone off to make money somewhere else. I don't know whether that affects them. I don't think it should, but you'd better be there. And every time the jury comes in or out, you're standing. Look at the jurors. Look at them throughout the trial. Meet their eyes. As that jury is filing into the box, I suggest to you it's a good technique to be standing and always to be looking at them. Don't smile or wink or do anything unprofessional, but just look at them. That charges them with the need to be responsive to you.

And lastly, I want to tell one more story, and it has nothing to do with the law, but I think to me this story tells you how you ought to behave in court. You remember in *The Music Man*, the famous musical, the Robert Preston character who's the con man, who promises that there's going to be a band? And then he gets soft on the librarian, and the librarian has a club-footed son, and the club-footed son wants to play in the band. And the son believes the con man, the Preston character, is going to create the band. But there's never a band, and but for the love interest, he's going to escape to another town.

And in the show there's this one confrontation where the kid is the first one to realize that the Preston character is a con man and there isn't going to be a band and it's all a sham. And he's crying, and he's hanging onto Preston's leg, and Preston's saying, "There is no band." And of course the son says, "No, no. I always thought that there would be a band."

To me that's very important. I always believed that when I went into court, whatever court, that it was the Supreme Court of the United States. If you believe that, if you always think that there's going to be a band when you go out for your client—even if the courtroom is vacant, even if the judge seems to have some difficulty staying awake, even if you don't have that much—if you think you're going out there because you think there's a band, in the eyes of a little kid—and I don't mean to denigrate your client—but in the faith that that client has for you, you'll do really what's required of you as teachers and as trial lawyers.

And I thank you for bearing with me.

(Applause).

"[A lawyer's] happiness is not the touchstone of admissibility."

—Hon. William G. Young, December 7, 1996
From *Young on Evidence for the Trial Advocate*

CHAPTER 3

Judge Young on Advanced Trial Techniques

DECEMBER 3, 1994

I WANT to start with a story. How many of you have heard the airplane crash story? Raise your hands. Okay, you are a minority. You are going to have to hear it again. This is a true story. Boston lawyers were involved in this actual case. It sets the theme to unify the different things I'll be discussing.

In 1979, Northeast Airlines merges with Delta, both of whom fly Electra jets. It is foggy at Logan Airport, and a Delta Electra jet, the survivor in the merger, is flying in with 94 people aboard. There's no particular wind, wind shear or anything like that. The plane comes in on a normal wide path, but instead of hitting the runway, it crashes into the berm at the end of the runway, and the debris and bodies and everything are spilled out across the runway. One fellow lives for four days, hideously burned, and then dies. Everyone is dead.

The estates of the passengers bring a lawsuit. Jimmy Meehan represents them. And they do an investigation. And they think that the error, the negligence, if you're going to put it in legal terms, is that in Northeast planes, the altimeter is set counterclockwise and in Delta planes they set it clockwise. And after the merger you have a Northeast pilot on a Delta plane. The theory is they set the altimeter wrong and simply flew the plane into the ground.

Back in 1979, this was before they had transponders in the runways and in the bottom of the plane that would say, "pull up, pull up" if you're getting too close to the ground. There is no warning to the pilot. So that's their theory.

So, they're getting ready for trial and they get these huge pieces of wallboard and they get an artist, you know, because they've recovered the black box, so they can do computer simulation. And they do them. They crunch the numbers. They take the radar bearings from the tower, and they try to figure out, as of course the FAA has tried to figure out, why this plane went down. They think in an evidential sense they can pinpoint the plane a minute and 49 seconds before impact.

So first of all, they take these wallboards and they draw to scale on the bottom a horizontal view. To the left is a little outline of the City of Boston. Back in '79, the Customs House Tower stood out more. Then it's flat for a long way. Then it rises just a little bit because that's Bird Island Flats, where Logan Airport is, and that's where the runway is.

Then—and I am, of course, foreshortening this—you figure out where the plane is, how high the plane is in the air a minute and 49 seconds before it hits. And they plot that. And then they take the black box altimeter reading and they plot that, given the wind speed, given the air speed that the plane was going through the air, and they plot what the altimeter reading was telling the pilot.

And the plane, after all, was trying to land, so it's in a descending line. It's not a very good landing, but the plane makes it to the runway. Usually they'll land about over a quarter of a mile beyond the end of the runway. Here it's a couple of hundred yards, but the wheels of the plane would have touched the berm of the runway, not the rocky area that builds up there at the end of the runway. And so the plane would have made it, and it would have landed in the fog.

So that line that the altimeter was reading to the pilot they draw there in a black arc. Then they take the radar plot, and the radar plot from the tower works out to exactly the same point in the sky a minute and 49 seconds earlier, but then they plot the radar down. And at some stage, because of the ground interference, of course, the tower loses the plane. When it gets too close to the ground, you just don't see the plane anymore, but they extend the line because it was just in an avenue that the plane was going down, in the proper glide path slightly below. The parallax is a little different, but if you extend the line, it extends right down to the point of impact. The point of impact is not on the runway, but it's right at the end where it hits where they build up there. And that's in red. They have that, and it shows the difference.

Then, they take strobe lights and put them on the two lines so when you start this, it lights up and it gives the impression of movement toward the landing. And then on the top they put a digital clock, but not any digital clock, one that reads in reverse: a minute 49, a minute 48, a minute 47, and so on.

Then they take the black box, because, of course, they have the voice recorders, and they make it work exactly with what's depicted on the screen, and they turn it on. I've seen this in the trial practice course that MCLE runs in the summer. Sometimes they have Jimmy Meehan out, and he'll play this for you, and you hear it. And so they turn it on, and there it is:

"Flight 317 cleared for landing, Runway 3."

"Cleared for landing, Runway 3, aye."

"Commence landing check."

"Aye. Check commenced."

"Wheels down."

"Wheels down."

"Starboard."

"Starboard locked."
"Port."
"Locked."
"Flaps down."
"Flaps down."
"Give me 8 degrees."
"8 degrees flaps."
"Air speed."
"240, 220, 200. Foggy, isn't it?"
"15 degrees flaps."
"15 degrees flaps, aye."
"Aileron steady."
"Aye."
"Counting: 175, 165, 140. Hold it."
"Sure is foggy."
"Just fly the plane."
"I've got a" ?
KRUSSHTTTTT!

Now, in an evidence course we would ask whether we would ever let that be shown to the jury. I'm going to come back to that. It's a remarkable depiction, and my voiceover is a pale reflection because I've sat off to the side, not in this great hall but where we have done this summer course, and I've watched people who have taken that course, and while Jim Meehan plays that, people will cry, because, of course, that's the last minute and 49 seconds of 94 human lives.

That, I think, is as good an introduction to what I'm going to try to do this morning as I know. Let me step back and be very clear about what I'm going to try to do and how I'm going to do it or how I'm going to try to do it.

We billed this as Advanced Trial Techniques, and I have done a fair amount of thinking about it. We'll see whether it's any good or not, but the secret is, and the confession is, that there is no such thing as advanced trial techniques, there is only trial techniques. As cases get more complicated, some people seem to be able to handle the demands of trial practice better than others.

What I thought would be helpful is to try to identify those things about the best trial lawyers (I've been privileged to watch them for 17 years), and also to talk about what I think are some cutting-edge issues in complex cases.

Now, there are two caveats right at the outset: I will as candidly as I know how tell you what I think are the hallmarks of trial lawyers. I don't want you thinking, because I aspire to do some of these same things as a judge, that this syllogism works: Well, he tries to do this, and, therefore, he is or was a great trial lawyer. It's very clear that I was not. And I want to say that right out front. The best I ever was, though I'm fascinated by the process, was a journeyman trial lawyer. But I've seen great ones, and

I still see them, and I've tried very hard to think about what it is that sets them apart, and I want to talk to you about that.

The other risk of trying this is because we billed it as Advanced Trial Techniques, people will be hesitant to ask questions because the questions won't seem advanced enough. Big mistake. I'm here for four hours to serve you. I don't want to repeat what I did last year, but I will engage any question. I'll see to it that we cover the material that we have to cover here. Any question is an appropriate question because there is no such thing as advanced trial techniques. There are skilled trial attorneys, and there are complex cases, and I want to talk to you about both. And I want to talk about a number—I've got ten, I guess—of disparate things that I think are right on the cutting edge and are worth kicking around.

One other mechanical thing. The book that we have passed out is an MCLE book, which I asked be given as part of this course, and it's entitled *The United States District Court Speaks*. It will be a good book for you to have, and I'll tell you why—it is a very thorough questionnaire and the answers of all the judges and magistrate judges of the United States District Court in the District of Massachusetts as to how they handled a variety of things. And then, in the back, are all our standing orders and how we manage cases, and the like.

The reason this book is valuable to you in this course is it is absolutely the best outline that I know of. And I can say this because I had nothing to do with preparing the outline. It's the best outline of which I am aware of those things that you want to ask yourself about the judge and about the forum in which you find yourself. That is, if you are in the land court, the superior court, you want to ask how the judges in those courts handle these matters. So it's the outline that's key to you.

If you are before us in the federal court, well, then we'll give you the answers, too. We'll tell you how the judges do it in our court. But that's not what makes this valuable to you, and that's not really the value of the book and why it ties in with this course. The value of it is it tells you those things you want to know, those questions you want to ask every time you go to court, any court.

WHAT MAKES A GREAT TRIAL LAWYER

Now, I want to share with you what makes a great trial lawyer, recognizing that I am not one, with some practical hints as to what you can do to be a great trial lawyer. And this is a little general, but I won't take too much time. I think this works. Part of it is repetitive for other courses that I've given, but it bears repeating.

The first thing all lawyers need to know is who you are, really, in society. If you are a trial lawyer, the words "zealous advocacy" leap out, and you know you're supposed to be a zealous advocate. I'm here to tell you that those words are not self-defining, and there's a lot of confusion in the profession about what that means.

These committees on civility say we even ought strike the word "zealous" because that has too much machismo.

I want to share with you this vision of what a trial lawyer is, what all lawyers are, but more specifically trial lawyers: What you are, really what we all are, are teachers. That's what I am as a judge, but you're much more important than the judicial officer in the actual operation of society. Bear with me for just a little bit on this, because this will explain everything else we do. This will explain in a very real sense why Jimmy Meehan conceptualized the terrible airplane accident in the fashion that he did.

What you are are teachers. That's what being an advocate means. That's what the whole adversary system is about. It's about teaching in a very special sense. It's about a hands-on type of teaching, first of your client. We live in a rights-oriented society; that's what "liberty and freedom" means. If you do mortgage foreclosures, you know that's an impression of the property rights in our society.

What you have to do first, and throughout a lawsuit is teach your client what their rights are. And that's what you're doing. That's what you're doing if you don't come to court. If you do mergers and tax work, wills and estates, what you're doing, what lawyers do in our society, is make the whole heterogeneous. It really has this enormous centrifugal force as we all follow our own ideas and do our own thing and pursue happiness. What you do is hold the whole thing together.

I am really keen on this. Oh, they all say, kill the lawyers first, but, you know, that's what you do in society. That's why we need lawyers. They only have five percent of the lawyers that we have in the United States in Japan. They don't begin to have the society that we have here in the United States. The culture is vastly different. And if we really care about rights, if we care about individuality, then we're going to have lawyers.

Now, enough preaching. You have a special job because your job is not only the job of teaching the law, whatever it is. Teach it to the clients. Teach it to the other side. That's what negotiation is, after all. That's the idea of expressing it to the other side in a way that convinces them. And, ultimately, teach it to judges and juries.

And those of us who are trial lawyers, unlike the rest of the bar, have this enormous additional responsibility of teaching the facts, teaching something that happened in the past in a way that a factfinder, be they judge or jury, can figure out.

The best thing I can throw out to you is that if that's what you think of yourselves as, if you think of yourselves as teachers, everything falls into place. What you have to do to prepare for trial falls into place, what you have to do on trial falls into place, and you ought not be ashamed of being a zealous advocate if you truly see yourself as a teacher. There's no glibness. There's no shallowness. There's no mouthpiece in teaching, because, you see, you are trying to get at the existential facts—you're not the judge of your client—in a way that some third party can understand them. That's what we all do.

What makes the great trial lawyer? Proust, the philosopher, said that the mark of an intellectual is the ability to hold two contradictory ideas in the mind at the same time. And I really think that's it. That's what separates the good, the well prepared, and that's what separates the litigators from the great trial lawyers.

The great trial lawyer can see not only what their client's position is, can crystallize it, can see it in the fashion that will best present it, but he or she can see the other side. He or she can see the force of the other side's arguments, can see how the other side will present their arguments, and can prioritize and evaluate them.

An example that brings this home: Ernie Babcock, a lawyer from Maine, taught for us in the summer an MCLE course on trial practice. It was one of these labor-intensive courses. You get a lot of lawyers in, and they demonstrate things, and then the students, the younger lawyers, do their things.

We were doing closing arguments. Ernie was scheduled to do the defense argument, and he was primarily a defense lawyer. The person we had for the plaintiff's lawyer was gone. The teachers were Judge Hallisey and me, Judge Young. Hallisey would have been great. He was a member of the American College of Trial Lawyers. But I couldn't do the closing. And to be very candid with you, I couldn't get up and do the closing. Babcock said, "Well, I think I can help you out," so he got up and he delivered the defense closing in the mock case that we had and it was a very good closing. We'll talk about techniques of closing. And then he got up and, as the plaintiff, delivered the plaintiff's closing.

Now, that was just a show on a mock case that he prepared, but his plaintiff's closing was as good as his defense closing. And he's a great trial lawyer for that skill, that ability to understand that the other side has a case that you have to deal with (if it was all that easy, we'd never have trials). You know, if we knew what the law was and we were clear on the facts, surely most cases should and do settle. Trials are about those ones on the margin. And if they're not about that, if you haven't taught your client right, if your client is just poorly advised and is slogging ahead for no good purpose, of course you fail.

That's the mark of a great trial lawyer. I want to share with you three ways to be a great trial lawyer. These are different than things I think you've heard elsewhere. They're at a level of generality, but I think they work. And, again, I advance them to you with some diffidence because I'm not able to do this stuff, though I try.

I think you should read, you should participate, and if you get a chance, you should teach, and you should look for chances to teach.

Now, you say, "Well, fine, that's all very well for him to say because he doesn't have to bill out 2,200 hours a year." And I understand. Well, now they laugh at that. What, it's up to 2,500 hours they're looking for each year? Well, even though that's a fact, and even though it's very hard to take your eyes off the printed page or the case that you're preparing for, take just a moment to reflect on this: What do I mean by "reading"? I'll be very specific. We're going to talk computers here, not that I know anything about computers, but I have some ideas about how they can be used to prepare and be used at trial.

You people are all—I know it because my law clerks are whizzes on this—you're all expert on CALR, computer-assisted legal research; LEXIS/NEXIS; and Westlaw. We have fewer books now because we have more computers. Of course, you should use this technology. There is an insidious problem with it, and the problem is this: garbage in, garbage out. You ask the computer to run certain things for you. The computer can do it. It saves you a lot of time. It does your research, and it gives you all the cases about a specific issue. It's discrete. Of course it should be used, and we'll talk about some techniques about how to use it.

The flaw in that type of reasoning is it does not synthesize. And the best teachers, of course, synthesize. I could start it this way: I could say get a life, in other words, do stuff other than the law, but we'll talk about the law here because you want to know how people live. You want to do more than just go to the office each day and get ready for trial, because you want to understand how society actually interacts.

Read

I suggest that you do the following: Pick out the court in which you practice the most, and then read all the decisions—I don't do this, but I try—of the appellate court for which that court works. Now, of course, read the decisions in your area, but the important thing is to read decisions out of your area.

For instance, I started out as a law clerk for the Supreme Judicial Court (SJC), and I knew them all. I got into doing this. And when I was in practice—and I was sort of 50 percent federal and state—I'd read all the SJC decisions. Well, of course then they create the Appeals Court, and I couldn't keep up, but I tried to read them all. I was never a probate lawyer or workers' compensation lawyer, but I would read those decisions.

You would be surprised—and this is my whole point—how often there'll be something that Westlaw will never pick up; those little gnomes that write the headnotes. Can you imagine graduating from law school and doing that? That's what you do for the rest of your life? They don't see that in this probate case a judge has thought that this type of evidence, which doesn't meet the rule against hearsay at all, is probative. And in your murder case you need it, and you need some authority. So that's one thing to read, although it's virtually impossible to keep up.

Pick a court and read their appellate court stuff. It makes sense to pick a court that governs the court in which you work. Of course, that is one of the real risks of when we went to law school and had Ames or Grimes, the great moot court. There is an insidious misapprehension in moot court. It teaches you that all law is equal, because, of course, they make them up, and a fake jurisdiction, so that in that jurisdiction, with these visiting pretend judges, all law is equal. It isn't.

Courts work for other courts. If you are in the Woburn District Court, it works for the appellate division, the Appeals Court, the SJC, and, remotely, the Supreme Court of the United States. You can find great stuff out of the District of Rhode Island, but that is persuasive, not controlling. Judges of my acquaintance have said, "Ha-hah, the 9th Circuit." Presumptively wrong.*(Laughter)*.

Now, in addition, you all went to law school. With the exception of Northeastern, all law schools have law reviews. Subscribe to your school's law review. Read it. There's all sorts of bizarre, frequently stupid stuff in them, but you'd be surprised how these people who want to get tenure and stuff put together the world. It's different than the way that those of us who have to appear before judges or try to judge put together the world. You read some of this stuff on Bayesian theorems of whether or not to admit evidence. I can't understand the math. People make a living on this; I'm not trashing it. You'll never even know those ideas are out there unless you do some reading.

The last thing you should subscribe to is those things in your area, and we have a bunch of them in Massachusetts. We have the *Massachusetts Law Review* and the *Boston Bar Journal*. Now the Massachusetts Academy of Trial Attorneys is putting out a journal. There is a defense bar and a civil defense bar. There is a criminal defense bar. There is ATLA, the plaintiffs' bar journal. There is all sorts of stuff out there. I say subscribe or get it in your firm. This is money well spent. You can't possibly read all these things, but you ought to skim the stuff. Rip the stuff right out, and have a file system of stuff you may need, because, you have to broaden yourself about ideas about the law. That's what the common law is. It's not a static target.

It goes back to Bornell (phonetic), that somehow you could go to law school and there were those nice books, they all looked the same, and you could go and find the law. And, of course, the whole idea of law school was to teach you it didn't work that way at all. So you have to keep up.

Participate and Teach

First, read. Second, participate. And by "participate" I mean take an active role. Participate–it doesn't have to be in the teacher/student continuing legal education role. Participate in a bar association, that's the way to shop your ideas. The best trial lawyers, the best that we have, do not think that the ideas that we all depend on are trade secrets. They'll tell you.

When you get a case, shop your ideas. Ask someone, "What about this?. . . Have you ever had a case where. . .? What if I argued. . .? How do you think this would work?" This is still a profession.

Trial judges will tell you, in the superior and federal district court, that the trial lawyers in the Commonwealth are somewhere between 2,000 and 5,000 lawyers, but we know most of the trial lawyers.

The last thing is, and I'm not here shilling for MCLE, but MCLE is the premier education body here. But they are not the only one. The bar associations have functions that they intend to put on of their own. If you are in firms of a size where they have litigation lunches, or the like, don't hesitate to volunteer to put something together.

If you teach, it brings home to you in a way that you cannot get any other way the discipline of trying to hold two contradictory ideas in the mind at the same time. It is because your obligation, of course, is not simply to put together something coherent, but to test it against the other ideas that are out there. So read, participate and teach.

Now, of course, you can't do that stuff because you have to bill out 2,200 to 2,500 hours a year, but you should try. Try to get your eyes off the page and think about that. The best as I know, and we're going to talk about how it works in actual practice, that's what the best trial lawyers do. It has nothing to do with seniority. It has nothing to do with age, though there is something to be said for experience. However, experience only teaches you the most simplistic things. It teaches you where to stand. It teaches you what happens mechanically next in a trial. Those are important. Basic trial practice courses cover that. We've got a number of things that will give you the experience of the courtroom in a situation where people more experienced can comment on what you do or comment about the courtroom. And those are all good things, but that's not what we're here for this morning. I'm trying to think about what makes a great trial lawyer. And you've got to go further than just how the mechanics of the trial work to be a great trial lawyer. That's the unifying theme. We're all teachers.

I have suggested to you the techniques of how you can be a great trial lawyer/teacher, and now I want to turn to the disparate items. They are disparate; we're not just starting with how you prepare for trial and go through a trial. I want to go through the disparate items, and they're generally in order, but I'm going to talk about pretrial management issues and trial management issues. Then we're going to talk about jury selection and jurors, what's hot in that area, computers in the court and experts. Then we'll talk about multiparty cases, which are terribly important. Then we'll talk about demonstrative aids. That's when I'll get back to the original story. I want to talk about jury instructions, what's new in that area, and I want to talk about opening and closing argument, really the theme of how you directly teach the jury.

Pretrial Management

Now, my paradigm, what you need to think about to have my teaching comments make sense is to think of this type of case: a jury case. It can be civil or criminal. It can be superior court or federal district court, but that's the model that I have in mind. We're thinking the complex case with many parties that will be tried to a jury. I want to talk about, in some detail, how you interact with the judge, but we will take as our model for this morning's discussion the jury case. And that's a good model, even if your primary practice is jury-waived. The reason it is a good model is that if you prepare every case so that you could try it to a jury, you will be most persuasive to the judge.

Judges get jaded too often in the state district courts and in the probate courts because they don't sit with juries. I know the district courts do in some sessions, but if your practice is jury-waived, too often the judge, because of the extraordinary press of business, will cut corners by saying, "I've read the papers, we'll dispense with openings, put on your first witness." You don't want that. If you think of yourself as the teacher, your case cries out for individual treatment. And that's whether you're a plaintiff or defendant, because if the judge addresses your case like every routine case, you're going to get the routine answer. And you should know going in what the routine answer before that judge in that court is, and so you try every technique to make the case unique. Now, I'm talking about "the big case."

Now, let's talk about pretrial management. This will work for plaintiff and defendant. I want to make some general comments, and then we'll make some specific comments. A case comes into the office. It's a big case, with sprawling parties, issues that you haven't yet researched, and can't research, at least immediately.

The initial technique of the real trial lawyer—and you will see this dichotomy of keeping two separate things in mind at the same time throughout my remarks this morning—is to seize control of the case.

Seize Control of Your Case

Whether you are in a system like the federal system is now, which in effect mandates that you seize control of the case early, or whether you are in the state system, which will put you on their time standards but will allow you to string out your preparation, you've got to seize control of the case immediately. That means you are going to, as soon as you get the case, invest a lot of time in it. You want to start either billing out that time or, if you have taken the case on a contingent fee, you have to be prepared to invest that time early, immediately.

Now, you say that's preachy, he's a judge, he hasn't done it for 17 years. You have to find out stuff first. How are you going to invest the time? You do research, and then you figure out depositions and stuff. That's not what I'm talking about, though it's a secondary concern. What I mean about investing the time early is this: Most important as a trial lawyer is, as soon as you get the case, to closet yourself with the client if it's an individual client or, if it's a corporate client, the liaison you're going to have. Find out from the person with whom you are going to be interacting what they think the theory is, what they think went on, and what their expectations, ideas and goals in bringing the litigation are.

Don't be seduced by it. You're not going to accept that necessarily. You've got to apply your independent judgment as you are the teacher of that fact/law interface, but you've got to listen. You have to figure out what is going on here. And immediately, you've got to have some idea, some theory, some approach to the case. If you're taking the case, if you're not going to reject the case, what is your theory as to why, if you're plaintiff, the plaintiff prevails, or what's your defense? You've got to have that early on.

That's one prong of the two inconsistent things you have to have in mind at any one time. Start immediately figuring out your theory of the case. But then, contrary to that, you have to think of all the other possible theories, perhaps less important, but you have to think of them. You have to. Before you bring that complaint, that complaint had better have every theory that will work under Rule 11, and you've got to then take the time.

If you are in a large office, you have to shop your ideas about the case with your colleagues. If you are in a small office, you've got to shop your ideas about the case—you don't have to reveal confidences, you may not reveal confidences, but you should shop your ideas about the case with others in your bar association or other lawyers you are dealing with. Go back to your file of articles and commentators. Review what you read.

What is there about this case, what new causes of action, what wrinkles on old causes of action? But while that's completely inconsistent with what I just said, your primary goal is to have a theory of the case, and have it just as soon as you can formulate it. At the same time, you've got to be ready to abandon it, change it, refine it as discovery goes forward—but you have to have it.

Judges will tell you how appalled they are, especially in jury-waived cases, if there hasn't been a strong pretrial conference and the case starts and it becomes apparent to the judge, who of course has a different take on the case and is seeing the case for the first time, that neither lawyer knows what their case is about. There are literally cases brought as contract cases that are tort cases for interference with advantageous contractual relations.

The story told of Judge Wyzanski—this is a rather mean thing—of a lawyer who got up before a jury and made an argument and said, "This is a contract case and this is how I will prove it." Wyzanski looked at him and said, "Actually, this is a tort case for interference with advantageous contractual relations. Proceed."

Oh, of course he's dead. That croaked him before the jury because they thought he didn't know what was going on. But jury-waived lawyers bring in witnesses, and they testify, and you don't know what the theory of the case is. You've got to have a theory early on, and by "early on," I mean at the first or second interview. You've got some response. You think something about the case.

Because now you're going to have some interaction with the other side, what pretrial management things need be done? Here we can come to some specifics because state and federal are different. I'll talk federal because federal is where the state is going, I predict. This is going to happen to you on the state side whether you like it or not.

The feds, in their so-called Expense and Delay Reduction Plan, require that within 90 to 120 days of the response of the first defendant, there be an initial case management scheduling conference. The feds require by law that that conference be presided over by the judge who is going to try the case, not a magistrate judge. The scheduling orders are in the book that you've been given, so we didn't focus on them specifically other than to say that's how the scheme is because I want to talk about how you negotiate that. They require that you meet with the other side, and that you negotiate out the joint case management schedule.

Now, the state doesn't do that. The state allows you to ease into the case within the time standards that are applicable to the case and allows you, with greater flexibility, to schedule your discovery events. It's very clear that the state system is preferred by the bar. You're more familiar with it.

It's also clear to me, and informs our discussion this morning, that the federal techniques are, more and more, going to be imported into the state. More and more, we're going to have the judge trying to have an initial conference early in the proceedings. I'm going to take that as my model, and we want to talk a little bit about how you prepare for that and what considerations you want.

Determine Appropriate Mechanism for Dispute Resolution

One of the early things you have to decide in your mind is whether you're going to go for trial or whether you want alternative dispute resolution (ADR) early on. How do you make that choice? Now, it's not a one-time choice. That is to say, if you don't go for alternative dispute resolution early on, you can ask for alternative dispute resolution later in the case, but you must recognize that both you and the other side will have invested more money in the case later on. The settlement value of the case by definition is going to change after a year. Plaintiffs take cases on a contingency. Plaintiffs are going to have, and the lawyers are going to have, an investment in the case that's going to color their willingness to compromise the case a year into the case. Defense have, if they're billing on an hourly basis, the insurance company that has sunk a lot of legal time and money into the case. Their willingness to compromise is going to be different after a year, not gone but different.

I recognize that all of these things I say are probably too finite because there's going to be specific cases where this is different, but I want to argue to you that you must early on make that alternative dispute resolution choice. Make it wisely.

On the federal side we still strongly believe in a jurisprudential sense in voluntary ADR. No one is going to force you to go to ADR. On the state side we are more and more pushing mandatory ADR. In other words, it's ADR for the small case but not for the big case, not for the bet-the-ranch case. My view of it is (and you'll see I'm biased on this), that it is a form of special pleading. You see, in the small case where the small guy is up against the institutional litigants, the institutional litigant in a small case will always want ADR. Here is why: ADR is not justice. Now, I'm not preaching. It's a form of dispute resolution, but it's not rights-oriented justice.

All the ADR systems—whether they be mediation, early neutral evaluation, summary jury trial or arbitration—have a nod to our system of justice. You still have to know the law in ADR, but all of them have as the goal the resolution of the dispute.

Those of you who practice before arbitrators know that in the main, you will much more likely get half a loaf than a zero sum gain. You're not likely to get nothing if you're playing it, but you're not likely to get everything. You're likely to get half. And of course the same is true for the defense. So an institutional defendant will tend to want arbitration. That's of course why they want it in the securities industry. They want arbitration because these tend to be small claims that get resolved. And there's no doubt that any form of arbitration and any form of ADR is cheaper—there are some doubts whether it's faster, and I'll come to that in a minute—than trial. It's your duty to your client to explore those things.

Some firms—I learned the other day that Hill & Barlow is one –set up an ADR practice group, and they propose to deal with cases where you're going to have a trial practice group, and you'll hire your trial lawyer (if you can stand the tariff), but they'll also engage someone from the ADR group because they think that those are different disciplines.

Respectfully, I differ with that, but maybe it works. Again, I'm out of practice. I'm just watching it. Kirkland & Ellis, the huge Chicago firm, tried this some years ago. They had trial lawyers, and then they had a settlement group. It was a disaster because no one paid any attention to the settlement group. They were—and I know I'm using the machismo imagery here, but it works—they were wimps. They wouldn't try cases. They were all talk. Why return their phone calls? There's nothing they would do to you.

The trial lawyers, on the other hand, became machismo caricatures of that because they were freed from the need of teaching anybody. It was just scorched earth from round one: "There you go. That's what I was hired for. Okay. We're going to warm up those word processors. Day one this, day two that. Want a seventeenth deposition? Why not? We'll start asking questions. I take two days to warm up. Then we'll ask for more questions. I know how to take depositions. Of course. Come in here. We'll have coffee, yes. And where did you go in the 8th grade, and so on." Absolute disaster.

That might have been in the 80's, but people won't pay for that. Also, it violates the theme that I started with. It separates what we're really talking about here: that ability to hold two contrary thoughts in mind at the same time, which is the hallmark of the trial lawyer. The trial lawyer can at one and the same time prepare for trial and, because the trial lawyer sees the weaknesses of the other side, can be the best mediator around.

It's no secret, for instance, that Endispute—and I'm not shilling for Endispute; there are others—has as its mediators judges of the stature of Chief Justice Lynch or Sam Hoar, a senior partner at Goodwin, Procter & Hoar. Sam Hoar is a wonderful trial lawyer. The reason of course is they can see both sides. But the point to remember with respect to ADR is that the goal is not ride Tory into justice. The goal is the end of the dispute. Get the dispute concluded. Take economic power, for instance. The whole idea of all the procedural niceties of the trial is to even the playing field; that's why the rules of evidence and so forth are there. They're just not in ADR.

Now let's say you're making that choice, you're holding the ADR card in your mind, but also you think you'd better prepare for trial. You're going to prepare for trial. Here again, my advice is unorthodox. Well, I think it works, and I think the great trial lawyers do it. If you're going down the trial aspect, what you want to do is drive for trial. If trial is what you want, if that's how you've evaluated your client's interests will best be served, plaintiff or defendant, go for trial, exude, and it doesn't have to be machismo, because of course you're talking settlement all the time, but get out of your head that you have any particular advantage in the motions. Remember how it used to go: first file the motion for more definite statements, when you lose that, file a motion to dismiss; when you lose that, file a motion for summary judgment; when you lose that, file a motion for partial summary judgment; when you lose that, say, well, now, I guess I'll have to go to trial. It's not a cost/benefit thing. It's a trial tactics thing. Drive for trial, whether you are a plaintiff or defendant.

All of these things that we're talking about, these counts that should drop out, the summary judgment, you can handle them most effectively at about the time of the final pretrial conference because if they don't have it, plaintiff or defendant, the judge is going to be at her most eager to get rid of the case. That's the time when those things are going to have the most weight. What is the countervailing weight to that? You will have invested a lot of money to get to that point. The parties will be less eager to settle. So of course, the counterweight is there are a few motions to dismiss and a few motions for summary judgment that ought be brought, but only a few.

The Court's Docket

Federal court has individual docketing, and in the state court they have these room lists now, but still more than one judge is probably going to deal with your case. In federal court—judges don't admit to this, and in the main we struggle against this, but I want to share it with you— if the judge decides a motion for summary judgment, the case is gone, and the appellate court, First Circuit, is more likely to back up a grant of summary judgment. In state court, it's not that the case is gone. The judge may be gone, and even though they've liberalized the standards for summary judgment, they're still hostile to summary judgment, so the judge knows he can never get reversed if he'll deny it, and he may not have to try it because you may be in another county. Now, I was a superior court justice, and I think it's the best common law court in the nation. I love them, but just be aware of that dichotomy.

Something else on timing: Thanks to Senator Kennedy pushing President Clinton, the federal court is at strength, and the five new judges are terrific. The individual case load of a judge of the United States District Court as we speak ranges from a low of 150 cases (Judge Zobel) to a high of 350 cases. I've been at the bar 27 years. There has never been a court, if it was the part-time district court of Ware, that had so low a case load, ever, in over a quarter-century. The counterpart figures for the superior court as I speak are about 1,200 to 1,500 civil cases per judge and in Essex, 2,200 cases. And that's with all magnificent efforts they've done to burn them out.

What's the secret? Or what's the result here? If you want a trial in the United States District Court, there's no reason why the judge won't give you one, and they may give you a trial fast. No one goes to the rocket docket in the federal court because we think it's unfair to, as they do in the Eastern District of Virginia, force every case to trial in six months. Every case goes to trial in six months. They're ruthless about it, and they're nationally known for it. It's just not just. That's not our court. There are a lot of other good judges down there, but you can get a trial fast.

Here now is a personal technique. You move for a preliminary injunction in the session in which I sit. That gives the judge the power to combine the case with the trial on the merits. I always do it. My first question, if you're in for a preliminary injunction, is, "Well, you really want this? Western civilization will come to an end if you don't get this injunction? When would you like to try it?" I first say, "Does anyone want a jury trial?"

Now, a jury trial will earn you until the next Monday, because that's when we impanel, on Monday. So they say yes or no. And of course no one is prepared to answer that question. That comes as a stunning question to them because everyone is prepared for the motion for a preliminary injunction. And I say, "Okay, you want a jury trial? We'll start next Monday." And you get them whining as though discovery were a constitutional right. I point them to Rule 65(b), and I say, "No, no, no. We're going to trial, and I will see that no one is ambushed."

Now, of course I'm playing a game too, because in most cases people will then settle, but some will go to trial. Since I sit 9:00 to 1:00, I can fit people in in the afternoon. And we actually start; we impanel and we start. I think that's just. Also, I argue that other judges should do it. That's what I tell other judges.

The Joint Case Management Schedule and Discovery Issues

Now, let's come to the negotiation of the actual joint case management schedule, if you have one. What do you put in it? What do you want? They don't require this in the superior courts. Why do we take time on this? I take time on it because even though it's not required, you want to be thinking of these issues early on. You're a trial lawyer now. What's your budget for the litigation? You've got to work this out with the client. We require that it be certified, but that's simply a forcing mechanism so lawyers will think about it.

What do you want in the way of discovery? What order do you want to pursue your discovery options? Now, let's talk just a moment about that. Again, stepping back to a level of generality, the great trial lawyer knows that most cases turn, or are decided, on a few ultimately disputed facts.

Irving Younger, whose tapes I'm sure you watched in law school and bear revisiting, was in my mind, brilliant beyond what people gave him credit for because he was such a great entertainer. We watch his tapes, and they're so entertaining. We think we know something of them, but remember in his 10 commandments of cross-examination he uses the image of a cup and he says a cup will take only so much water. Once you continue pouring water into that cup, the cup will simply tip over and the water will pour out. And his point on cross-examination was you've got to select your target—you've got to make some points on cross-examination and sit down.

That concept is appropriate for trials in general. That is to say, early on and as you go through the discovery process, you are trying to figure out what really is going to drive this judge, this jury to find in your favor, prosecution or defense counsel.

Now, again, you have to keep in mind everything else that may make a difference, which you're also trying to discover and you're also trying to deal with, but you recognize, and you're not afraid of. The litigator is afraid of the fact that the whole pleading system, the whole way that people get to a trial, is by narrowing the issues for trial. That's what Rule 16 of the Federal Rules of Civil Procedure (and Local Rule 16.1) is about. It's about being afraid to give up the issues, afraid to say this one is not worth it.

Tactics are important. Pursue success, something that's working. Arguments that seem to be going nowhere—don't give up on them. Make a record for appeals. The case may look different. The law may change. But don't waste your time on them. Drive for trial, and focus on those things you want. You had to in the federal court, and you should in the state courts, pick those depositions early on. They are your most expensive investment. Figure out the interrogatories that are going to be most crucial for you, and focus on those things. If things change, if things look different, you have a reason to go back to the court and say, "I need to discover this," and the like.

Now, of course you should act in a timely fashion, but I'm saying you've got to be able to make those judgments early on, and those are scary judgments. If you throw something away that you wanted to hang onto later, you may have a hard time getting it back. That's why it's scary. I say you have to make them early because it's a forcing mechanism. It forces you to think about the case.

Now, we're going to take the federal joint pretrial document first. Try very hard to work out an agreement with the other side. That doesn't mean you have to accede to what the other side wants, but be reasonable yourself. Try to work out agreements. Give yourself enough time. Build in enough time to do things, recognizing that you have a lot to do.

On the receiving end, go through this type of analysis: If the other side wants more time or if the other side wants something else, your presumption should be to give into the other side unless you have a specific articulable ground as to why it hurts your client. That's how you should practice. If the other side wants more time or wants something rescheduled, give it, unless you can specifically identify a cross to your client that in good conscious you can't give up.

What should the order be? Let me give you the typical order and then give you some variations on that order. The typical order of discovery in a complex case is first your interrogatories, maybe even your document requests to identify the sources of knowledge and identify the location of the documents. The documents should be out there before you take the depositions.

Get the documents first—it's just basic trial practice—then the depositions, then the expert depositions if you are going to have expert depositions, and last, to pin down those things that you may have trouble proving but which really aren't disputed, the requests for admission.

A variation on that—again, these are all case-specific, so this variation may not suit your case—that we see tried frequently now is requests for admission early on. And remember, unlike depositions (I'm talking federal practice now), requests for admission are not limited in number. They are limited in the amount of times you may ask, but they're not limited in number.

Remember that under the Rules of Civil Procedure requests for admission go not only to facts but also to opinions or contentions of law. Get your requests for admission out there early, perhaps because it may force the other side. The other side knows that if they don't respond to the requests for admission, the things you've requested be admitted will be taken as facts. It may force them into choosing their experts too early. If they need experts to answer your requests for admission, they will have to consult with those experts. Then, if those are the experts they are going to go with at trial—they're entitled to consult with experts without revealing that to you—then you get to know that.

Now, just anticipating our discussion of experts, be sure in your interrogatories you ask about the other side's experts. Always ask who they are. Always ask what their expected testimony is going to be. And always ask what the bases for that testimony are going to be.

A recent revision in the Federal Rules of Criminal Procedure, which has allowed the Justice Department to play things much closer to the vest than the state DAs, changed the rule so when the feds use an expert, they must disclose to you the expert's report, and that report must state the bases of the expert's opinion.

Now, one change on the federal side has been the requirement of voluntary disclosure. *See* Local Rule 26.2. We don't have it on the state side. It's not saving anybody any money. We were doing a study on it, and that's our preliminary take, but we're sticking to it on the federal side. So what do you have to disclose, and what level do you have to disclose?

Well, the federal standard is that before any discovery can be taken by you, you yourself, plaintiff or defendant, must disclose all documents relevant to facts pleaded with particularity in the complaint. Now, of course, that puts a high burden—we're getting away from notice pleading now—in federal court to plead facts. Make your complaints longer. Make your complaints more fact-specific, because the other side then will have to disclose more documents.

When you are deciding what documents to disclose, what's the best rule of thumb? The best rule of thumb is to go to your client, talk early on about what this case is all about, and then honestly disclose documents that you, the lawyer, think make a difference in the case, including the ones that help you and the ones that hurt you.

Lawyers don't like this because they think it makes you do the other side's case, to dream up things for the other side. If you are practicing in the fashion that I've been discussing, it won't be so hard, because you are thinking of what the other side's case is, and you may have to advise your client about settlement. You do want to advise your client about settlement. The universe of documents that must be disclosed are the documents that you, as a trial lawyer, think make a difference for you or against you. Now that does not necessarily mean carloads of documents, though we may get into carloads of documents for the requests for production of documents.

Just a word on the initial case management scheduling conferences themselves, and we'll pass from that into actually managing the trial, and how you can advance it yourself. The idea is (in federal court) that the judge will sit down with you early on to talk about what the case is about. If you are practicing in the fashion that I'm talking about, and this idea takes hold in the superior court and they are able to do with it, you've got to send a lead person to that conference. Sending the young associate won't get it. It will tick off the judge, and it won't work because the judge will want to go over what the case is about.

You've got to be ready to give up claims and narrow the issues. You take it really as a pretrial conference at the outset of the case. And if you're not going to narrow it, you've got to be able to tell the judge what discovery you want in order to flesh out that claim. The whole idea is to get you to think about the case early, which is, of course, what you are supposed to do.

A couple of judges—I got this from Judge Keeton, and I do it, so the couple is Keeton and me—*(Laughter)* try to share these things. For one thing, I don't give extensive initial case management conferences, but I'm idiosyncratic on that. The book talks about it, but this is important: When you negotiate in federal court the joint case management schedule—now, if you have a big case in the state court, they still have that rule about special assignment, and you can get a specially assigned superior court judge—you very much want that. You write to the regional administrative justice, you ask the chief justice for the special assignment of a superior court justice to your case. You've got a big case; you want one judge.

The reason? You only have to proselytize the judge once. Get her thinking your way. You don't have to go through a learning curve with several separate judges. And if you have a big case and you sit down with that superior court judge, again, the models that are in this federal court book will serve you in good stead.

Now, here is the Keeton/Young dichotomy. Just be aware of it if other judges follow it. We require that the parties set forth their separate positions in the joint case management scheduling document, and then we pick one position or the other. We don't middle it. We don't do justice. We just pick one or the other on each point. Why? Keeton explains that it's an incentive program. It's an incentive program to make you reasonable, because if you say two depositions and you say 40, the difference is either going to be two or 40. It's not going to be 10 in our sessions. So that drives the two up to the most that the judge thinks are reasonable and drives the 40 down. At least that's our theory.

It works in 92 or 95 out of 100—because I rarely get a joint proposed case management schedule where there are any disputes. So the bar is coming together. My carrot is that we have discovery limitations in the federal court, 30 interrogatories, five depositions—we may expand that. There is quite a press to expand it. We have these discovery limitations. You can have more if you agree. So that's the carrot: to agree. Over 90 percent of the people agree.

There is a judge's decision—he wrote it when he was a magistrate judge—Magistrate Judge Ponsor's decision where this happened [the parties disagreed over discovery]. Since in federal court you don't get any discovery until you make the disclosure, one side made disclosure and initiated discovery; the other side said, you can't have discovery because obviously there is more stuff to disclose and you didn't disclose it. And they started fighting over that.

Ponsor said, "a plague on both your houses, go ahead and take your traditional discovery because we are not going to waste time on sorting out whether the voluntary discovery has been made." He has spoken in groups like this in support of that position. He's also spoken privately in support of that position among the judges. My sense is that a number of my colleagues buy that.

The problem with that is it eviscerates voluntary disclosure. Why have it unless there is some benefit to having it? Because what will happen is when you say, "I won't make disclosure because you haven't," the judge will duck it and won't decide it. The judge will simply say, "Well, forget that, go ahead and ask your traditional discovery."

JUDGES

I have some comments about judges. And we can take them very quickly. Then we'll get into trial. I again want to start with the general.

The great trial lawyer knows that Holmes was right, that the realist theory of the law is the most accurate for his or her work, and it is this: If you want to know what the law is, watch what judges do. That's the realist theory of the law. And it's important to understand Holmes wrote that long before he was a judge. He wrote it when he was a law professor. He wasn't a justice of the Supreme Judicial Court or on the Supreme Court of the United States. That's not too general to be very important to you. If you want to know what the law is, watch what judges do.

I'm here to tell you that no judge gets on the bench wanting to be anything other than the best judge that he or she knows how to be. And most judges feel that way for as long as they are judges. Some burn out, but most feel that way. Therefore, every judge, contrary to the critical legal studies movement, is desperately trying to uphold the oath they took by reaching out for some legal norm to apply in your specific case. Every judge does that. That's where the critical legal studies folks go wrong. But where they are right, and where Holmes was right and is right, as opposed to the natural law theorists, is that you as a trial lawyer have got to deal with your specific judge. You want to know everything about her.

Here in the big case are some of the things you're going to want to know. You want to know these things in the small case too, except you can't invest the money.

First of all, it's very important to know what resources that judge has. You can find those resources out usually if you were a law clerk or know law clerks. They won't tell you what's secret about their interaction with their own judge, but they will tell you what the dynamics of the specific court are.

You see, it's naked self-interest. I suggest that you support the resolution of the problems that the justices of the superior court and the state district court or the state courts have. That's in your self-interest. But past that, you want to know what they have. You want to know what law reviews they have access to. You want to know what books they have.

For instance, in the superior court, when you write a brief, you be sure that you cite the official reporter (Mass. or Mass.App.). Don't cite Northeastern. They don't have it. And when they ask for it—they have lots of court officers, of course—they wake the court officer up, and they say, "Get me 72 Northeastern 2nd." And out he runs, and back he comes with the New England Law Review. It doesn't work. So cite the official reporter, because that's what's given to them. If you have Northeast, make a cross-cite.

Federal judges, of course, have a lot more resources. Know what resources they have; know what computer resources they have. Now, to get into that a little bit, federal courts' opinions are published. If you get a case big enough, you want to run LEXIS and Westlaw for every written decision of that judge. You've got patent cases. Don't just run the judge's patent cases. Run all of them. And here is what you can tell from that: You can tell what body of law the judge looks to, what the judge respects.

Well, in this court it would be primarily the First Circuit, so that doesn't tell you very much. But maybe the judge, for instance, puts in a little parenthetical. We see it in some of our great state judges. You've got a judge that does that. That judge thinks the other judge, the historic judge, is terrific. That's a sign of respect. You want to know that. Look at what law reviews that judge cites. Get a frequency check on the time he cites those. It may show what law reviews he has in the office. That may be it, but if those are what he's looking to, look at them. Also, read the big opinions for consistency—and I don't mean consistency of the law, I mean consistency in quality. If the quality varies from year to year, you know that judge is not doing her own work, she's letting the law clerks do the work. Some years they're good, and some years they're not that good. The judge is just signing off, so you've got to pitch it that way.

If you have any questions that that is what you are in fact doing, come to evidence a moment. Come to evidence in working with that specific judge. I give you this evidentiary problem. It came up, and my source here is *Commonwealth v. Best*, when I was a state judge.

Mrs. Best is alleged to have murdered her husband. Her husband was a Pinkerton guard. And a witness, Bill Bennet—I'm making up the name—is put on the stand.

"And who are you?"

He was very shifty-eyed. "My name is Bill Bennet."

"And, yes, and do you know Mrs. Best?"

"Yes, I know Mrs. Best."

And it turns out that he had had an affair with Mrs. Best. The affair is one month prior to the murder. Actually, this comes up out of the hearing of the jury, because that's the issue. And so I put it to you—now, that's it. This guy Bennet has an absolute alibi. He didn't murder Mr. Best.

The affair, if that's what you want to call it, was a one-night stand where they were intimate when her husband was on duty one month prior to the murder. The government's theory of the motive of the murder is she upped his insurance policy, then did away with him to get the money.

How many of you would admit that? No one. How many of you would exclude it? Some of you—getting ready now to be judges. Some of you will be judges. You can't pass. You can't just say, "you know, okay, we'll go on, call another witness." *(Laughter)*. "I'll think about that." You've got to rule. Okay. I'll change it then. It's a flaming romance that follows until one week prior to the murder. How many of you would admit that? Oh, now, of course if this was a seminar, I would say, Why? What's the difference there? What did it tell you about humankind? What about motive? And the important thing is: How are you making up your minds?

I stand before you, and I'm willing to run this risk. Gary Hart didn't. I mean I am not an adulterer. I am a fairly straight middle-aged white guy. I don't know what got into Bennet's mind or Mrs. Best's mind. I don't know what's going on. That's his testimony.

How do I decide whether to admit that or not? Westlaw is not going to tell me. But that's what judges do every day. They make those determinations. The point I want to make is this: When the judge makes that kind of determination, when a judge says to you, "Have you got any case that's like this?", the judge is asking the most pedestrian type question. The judge is saying, "Have you got any cases that factually are like this?"

Now, that's where computer-assisted research can give you a lot of stuff that Westlaw can't. You can find cases. In this case, I found a 1927 case where the affair was nine months before, and I admitted it. Affirmed on appeal. I'm not saying whether I was right or wrong. I'm not saying whether that's good law or not. All I'm saying is: I didn't know the answer. I found an SJC case. It was an old case, but it gave me some comfort, and I let it in. Or, a judge did what was fair. So much of what you're going to have to deal with, of course, is that individual judge.

I want to tout to you the doctrine of the brief-brief. Yes, the rules now require that you prepare joint pretrial memoranda. You are going to want to file a trial brief with your judge. I suggest to you the idea of the brief-brief. It is this: The brief-brief is no more than three pages long. You law review types are going to have trouble with this, but it's no more than three pages long. It has no more than three citations, and all the citations come from the court for whom your judge works. If you are in the superior court, they're Appeals Court or SJC opinions. If you are in the district court, federal, they are First Circuit opinions. They are quotes only. Make the quotes work for you. Insert with brackets. Follow strict *Bluebook* policy. Insert in the brackets the names of your parties and then the language of the high court, because that takes the wind out of the trial judge's sail, and the judge is reaching out for that law.

Make copies for the other side. If these matters come up in the final pretrial conference or if the judge smokes them out, if the judge says to you, "Okay, what neat evidentiary issues have we here?", don't sandbag the judge. She'll never forget it or forgive it.

Then, you come up with your briefs and you say there is going to be this issue, and I want to handle it this way. But don't think you're doing necessarily great things by working everything out in limine. You may tip your hand too much. Judges duck the in limine motions because they haven't heard the evidence. They're going to wait to see how the trial develops. So if it really is something, if the judge puts the burden on you, honesty is always the best policy. You come up with it.

Let's say it's a truncated pretrial conference and the judge hasn't put it to you. You are in the middle of trial and you get to that evidentiary issue and you say, "May I approach the bench? I have briefed this issue." That takes the judge's breath away to begin with. And when you get to the sidebar, give a copy to the other side and a copy to the judge. In the superior court, you'd better have Xerox copies of the cases themselves. Give them right then to that judge. Remember the pressure that's on the judge at that time. The case has to go on. You're likely to win that evidentiary point. Good trial lawyers may go into trial with nine, 15 of these and use only two. So what? It's still a good invention.

The second point in dealing with judges is, don't think that because you found a case on point, you're home free, even if it's a case on point in the jurisdiction where your judge practices. Here's why: Trial judges are human; they vary from judge to judge; but all of them are reaching out to the very best justice they can possibly do in the specific case that is before them. That's not what appellate courts do. And I'm not trashing appellate courts. One thing you find out when you are a federal judge, appellate courts have got a neat thing: They invite you to sit with them.

And now that Breyer is going to the Supreme Court, they take a district judge, and they take them from Rhode Island and New Hampshire and Massachusetts and Puerto Rico, then Maine for the sessions that Breyer was going to sit on. You get to sit as a circuit judge. And when you have that experience you realize that they ask themselves a different question. And this is the question that an appellate court asks themselves: "Is this good enough for government work? And are we going to let this pass?" Because it may not be the way that the appellate judge may have done it, but it's simply that he or she is not going to reverse the trial judge.

So you get a case that's four square in your favor. Don't think that that means the trial judge is going to follow that opinion, because if the trial judge looks at it and says, "Oh, yes, they were just affirming X because he does it this way, I do it a much better way, and my way is this way," your case doesn't count for much because they set the minimum standards. So, you have to take that case and you've got to see how you're going to make it persuasive to your trial judge.

TRIAL MANAGEMENT

Now then, management of the trial. What are the new things in the management of trials? The biggest issue you're going to face in the future for big trials, state and federal, is something that I call polyfurcation.

You know what bifurcation is. Bifurcation is the big case where the judge splits off damages from liability. We'll try liability first. Sometimes you could conceive of trying damages first. We all know that's a defendant's move, and the sociology proves that that's right. A judge who splits the damages from the liability has done something that favors the defense. The sociological studies show that it's harder to get a plaintiff's verdict on a weak liability case if the jury never hears the damages. It's easier, of course, if they hear the damages on the normal sympathy ground. But if you do that, if you get over that hurdle, there is a payback, and this you can consider in settlement.

If you get to the damages case and it's given that the plaintiff was liable and all that is to be tried is the damages case, the studies show the damages are going to be higher than if they have to deal with damages and liability, because they blend the two. The weaker liability case is going to get weaker damages even if they get over the rail. So the splitting tends to be a defendant move. But there is a payback, and judges will do it if you're taking up too much trial time. After all, the judge has to handle all the cases. Polyfurcation is something else.

Polyfurcation has some constitutional limits, but they have not been explored either by the First Circuit or the SJC. Polyfurcation is breaking the case up into issues and letting different juries try different issues. I can best explain it in an antitrust case.

You let one jury, for instance, try monopoly power. In other words, in an antitrust case the defendant has to be capable of exercising monopoly power. And that's a complex economic thing. If the jury answers no, the whole case is over because if you don't have monopoly power, you can't violate the antitrust laws. But if you have monopoly power, the next jury tries: "Did they exercise it? Did they violate the Sherman Act?" Answer yes to that, and the third jury tries: "And what were the damages?"

Now, those cases are few and far between, but that is the direction we are going in. And here are some of the litmus tests: There is case law now that says if a case is supposed to go over four months—this is Second Circuit case law—judges should think about breaking it up.

Personally—and this has been talked about among the jury—my rule of thumb is a month, 20 trial days. If you are going to take more than a month, the case ought to be broken up because the jurors ought not have to sit there and listen to you blather away for more than a month, both sides. And I'm one who favors polyfurcation.

The other thing that we are seeing on the federal side, and it affects the trial on the state side, is time limits. Lawyers should, but do not, welcome time limits because you think we are taking away your power to try the case, we're caverning you in, we're being unfair. And, of course, time limits can be applied unfairly.

When I talk about time limits I'm not talking about what Justice John Paul Sullivan did in the case that the Appeals Court reversed him on where he said you get 45 minutes for this expert. That's unfair. And the Appeals Court said you can't do it state side. I'm talking about something else. I'm talking about a negotiated time limit that calculates how many hours in the trial day and divides those hours up, perhaps not equally, though we start out equal. The plaintiff has the burden of proof, so maybe the plaintiff should get more time if it's a case where there is going to be a primary plaintiff's case and the defendant only has a shorter case. The time limits are set at the outset of the trial.

I tend to be the authority figure in the court. I try it with the court clerk because I go along with the court clerk. The court clerk has other jobs and may be in and out of the court, and it won't work. And I simply keep time. Every time you are on your feet, that's time against you. So, cross-examination counts for the side that's cross-examining, direct counts for the side that's on direct, and you just agree to the time limits.

You get before a judge like that, and the federal Local Rules encourage that, buy yourself enough time. Don't figure it short. The judges don't start out wanting to gouge you in terms of time, so buy yourself enough time, but don't get in the habit of vastly overestimating the time, because case to case, you will be less credible with the judge, and the judge will be more likely to cut you down.

Now, the reason you should welcome this is as follows: It's virtually the same reason that you should welcome negotiated time limits on the amount of the closings. You know what the other side is going to do. You know how much time the other side has. You are almost guaranteed a happy jury because the judge announces at the outset: Ladies and gentlemen, we're going to pick this case. The case is going to take six trial days and, therefore, we're picking today. I tend not to count the day we pick because I stack juries up. This is Monday, so you are going to have this case Tuesday a week. On that day be prepared to stay late because we are giving you the case. Juries love that. They plan their lives. And, of course, since I am controlling the time, they will get the case on that day because when your time is used up, you sit down, and it's over.

Now, you say you worry about that. But if you have negotiated the time, and it's fair, the advantage to you is—and I've tried big cases this way—boy, people pay attention, they focus, the doctrine of primacy comes out. Don't be against the doctrine of primacy. It was the first thing I said that the great trial lawyer has to have. What's the key thing? Get to the key. Bill Young can't keep 27 different issues in mind at one time. I can't do it. I take notes. I work at night. I can't do it.

I learned somewhere in grade school that you can septatize, that is, you keep seven things in your head at once. I can't do that, but the average person can do that. The studies show that you can't keep more than seven in your head. You've forgotten 8, 9, and 10. The 27 different theories of recovery won't get it. About three are what people grapple with. That's how juries work, and therefore, that doctrine of primacy. The time limits bring it out.

Can the time limit be extended? Keeton does and says that you should. I say that I won't in sort of an in terrorem thing so that people will believe me. The one time I was asked to by a great trial lawyer, Joan Lukey, I didn't. It was an appeal point, and I was waiting for the opinion. In the opinion I was affirmed, but it didn't deal with that point, so she must have dropped it. She must have thought he was not a good case to test it. I think she's great. She is in my first rank. She was acting in complete good faith. She wanted to put on an expert. It was a products liability case and a medical malpractice case against the doctor. She put one doctor on, but she had another doctor expert. She was out of time, and I said, "I won't take the second expert." She said, "Will you extend the time?" She did everything right. I said, "No, I won't." I was worried, so I wrote justifying myself. And she—I know it was an appeal point—apparently never pressed it.

You can't be that dogmatic. I have given you an honest answer. I've never done it, but that's because I've only been asked really the once. And I say I won't do it for the in terrorem effect because if justice required it, of course I would. Don't bet that it would be your case—because I want that in terrorem effect. ***(Laughter)***

A couple of things, and then on to experts. I know I've jumped over juries. I'm going to get back to them, but this discussion about discovery fits nicely into some important law on experts, so I want to jump to experts.

First, the concept that I cite Proust for, and it's very helpful, you know, Bill Moyers does this, The Intellectual Thought, The Western World, and there's a phrase there, "the ability to think in many camps." I suggest that that would be a good thing. I'm going to see if I can't get that and take a look at it because the thought that's behind that is the thought I'm trying to convey.

Second, there was a question about discovery. Here is the question: Discovery is always difficult. You can timely send out all your requests for discovery. By definition, the requests will not be responded to within the time period, even assuming good faith on the other side. We're all busy. Things just don't work out that way. How sympathetic are judges to that problem? Less sympathetic than you would wish. And there are two reasons for it. The state courts are inundated and therefore institutionally and structurally simply shunt discovery disputes to the end or to one side. I don't condemn them. They're just inundated. They tend to get to the merits at a bright line test, which perhaps does not satisfy you, but that tends to be the way they go.

In the federal court there is a more insidious problem that we brought on ourselves, and it's this: With this voluntary disclosure, we in effect—it's a little bit like Vietnam—have declared the war over and gone home. That is, I've heard Chief Judge Tauro say that now we will have mandatory disclosure, and we're not going to be bothered by these disputes; these disputes are not going to come up because now everything is discoverable except—and I don't hear him say this, but he must mean it—except attorney-client and work product, and there will be no disputes. And he has gone so far as to say the adversary system is over with respect to discovery disputes.

And the rest of us—he is a magnificent chief judge—we all sort of nod when he says that even though intellectually I'm not sure what he means. What it seems he means is we don't want to hear them. And the bar is generally afraid because you are not clear how it's going to come out—these things tend to be compromised. It's harder to get a hearing in the federal court. And that has the result—when we talk to ourselves, and we do—no court could be more forthcoming than the Federal District Court in trying to teach, not me, Bill Young, but we were all here in *The District Court Speaks*. We all filled out that God-awful questionnaire , but the truth is among ourselves we don't think there are many discovery problems. I feel that we are missing the boat there. There are, but there isn't a body of law yet to address it. So the answer is that judges are not too sympathetic to discovery disputes.

So how do you deal with it? You deal with it by getting an agreement to extend. And to get the agreement to extend, there must be some pressure points you can put on the other side to get the agreement to extend it. If they won't extend, then you make that one of your points.

The second thing you do is you can't let it lie. A judge is more likely to favor you if the discovery has been sought, not produced within the 30, 60, 45, whatever it is, and then within the week, two weeks, months thereafter you move to compel, you move to do something. If the discovery hasn't been produced, and then nine months have gone by, tough, because you should have been quick off the dime to press them.

We're less satisfactory than we should be, and unfortunately we've got some supposedly intellectual rationalizations for being less satisfactory. It's a perennial problem. I feel—again, now that the district court is up to strength and we have magnificent magistrate judges—at least in our court it's something to press. Maybe they'll bring back the motion session in the superior court. That's something the bar is pushing for. Then you might have a chance directly to address a judge about such an issue, but they've got a million institutional ways of keeping discovery to the end, of shunting it to the side.

Now, someone gave me some law, and I give it to you. Apparently there is some law in favor of requests for admissions not being paper discovery. There is a decision. I was unaware of it. I disagree with it, but it's out there. Magistrate Judge Willie Davis, when he was a magistrate judge, so it's some time ago, apparently wrote a decision saying that requests for admission are not paper discovery and discovery deadlines don't apply to it.

EXPERTS

Now let's jump to experts. I'll come back to jurors, but experts, I think, will follow better. Quickly, I want to give you the law on experts. This is not advanced. This is basic. You should think this works both state and federal, and there have been recent changes you ought to be familiar with.

Think of an expert as giving you an opinion. That's what you want from an expert. And the first thing you have to figure out by definition, the factfinder, the way I think of it, has a body of knowledge. I have it; jurors have it. You all have it. It's your average knowledge. Let's say that's the diameter of average knowledge. Now, we have average knowledge in lots of different areas. This is our knowledge about medicine, about engineering, about chemistry and the like.

An expert opinion should not be received unless by definition it's beyond the fact point, the frontiers of average knowledge. In other words, it's beyond what we all know, in the words of the Federal Rules, and also in the words of the *Massachusetts Evidentiary Standards*. Now it's a little tacky to pump your own book, but I will do it because I think it's helpful.

As you know, we don't have the rules of evidence in Massachusetts codified, though everyone in law school now is taught the Federal Rules of Evidence. To fill that gap, two former law clerks and I have put together something called the *Massachusetts Evidentiary Standards*. West puts it out. It's a supplement to

Hughes' *Mass. Practice* Volume, and the three of us are revising Hughes, but the treatise isn't out.

What we've done is taken the Massachusetts common and statutory law and simply reorganized it in the same order as the Federal Rules of Evidence, so the same numbers work. 801 sub 1 in the Massachusetts standards is the same thing as it is in the Federal Rules except where Massachusetts differs, and then you can get the Massachusetts rule.

This is not an advocacy document. It's not a law review article. It's not what the law should be. It's simply an attempt to codify what the law is, and we're trying to keep it up to date. For what it's worth, we hope it's helpful. It's a thing to take to court. It has the Proposed Massachusetts Rules of Evidence and the Federal Rules of Evidence, and you can just grab it and take it to court. All the superior court justices, by the way, have this. Whether they use it or not is up to them.

Now, by definition under Federal Rule of Evidence 702, in order for there to be the necessity of an opinion from an expert, the opinion has got to be somewhere beyond the frontiers of average knowledge. It's got to be something that the judge and jury don't know. If the judge and jury do know it, then, in the words of the Federal Rules, it's not a body of knowledge that will assist the finder of fact because they know it.

How does this work out in practice? Obviously, I'm not a thoracic surgeon. I don't imagine the jurors are. I'm not an engineer. What was this, physics or chemistry? I'm neither a physicist nor a chemist. I'm pretty hostile, as judges that I know are, on accident reconstruction experts. I don't think they know anything that the rest of us don't know. They can tell us how long the skid marks measure. I wasn't there. I don't know, but I've seen a bunch of accidents, and I think anyone old enough to be on a jury has seen them. There's a lot of it on TV, and I don't know as we need these experts.

I also don't think, on the federal side, we need the experts on secondary impact of trade dress. And the reason is that once I had a fancy expert on that, and it was jury-waived, and finally I said to him, "Well, what you're saying is this is just common sense?" He said, "That's right, judge." I said, "You're excluded." ***(Laughter)***.

It's not beyond the frontiers of average knowledge. And therein, of course, lies much of the problem. By definition, of the experts we will hear from, we don't know whether they're telling the truth or not because if we knew, if we were really sure, we wouldn't need them. We would know of our own knowledge. So what you're going for is an opinion.

The opinion rests on two building blocks. One of them is noncase-specific. It has nothing to do with the specific case. Instead, and obviously, it's general. Therefore, I give you a "G."

Even though you get the best hand surgeon from Mass. General, if your case involves reconstructive surgery to a hand, and this expert knows all about hand surgery and has done all sorts of hand surgery, the expert still will not testify unless the expert has some case-specific data. That is, unless the expert knows something about your specific case.

How does the expert get the knowledge about your specific case? There are four ways under the law, state and federal, that the expert can get the information about the specific case. This is all basic, but I need the framework for the discussion.

You can ask the expert a hypothetical question. I now add an "H." As a matter of trial practice, I don't suggest to you that this is perhaps the best way to do it, but sometimes hypothetical questions work. The legal theory, of course, of a hypothetical question is the expert comes in from outside, and doesn't know anything about the case. For example:

"Who are you?"

"I'm Edward Expert. I have a body of knowledge that will help the jury."

"Now, Mr. Expert, assume"—and then you key into the stuff that's already in the case, assume A, assume B, assume C, assume that all of this stuff is evidence. And it has to be evidence. It has to be in the case, which is a problem. Assume all that stuff. "Can you add something that we don't yet have in the case? Can you add your opinion?"

"Yes, I can."

"What's your opinion?"

That's one way to do it. Another way is the expert can be an observing witness, a percipient witness. Here, I use an "O." It can be the hand surgeon that did the hand surgery. That expert knows a great deal, so that expert can be a witness about how this operation went. It's not enough that the expert just has expertise. The person who did the surgery can testify because she knows how she did the surgery, and ostensibly she knows how to do that surgery.

Another way is that the witness can sit there throughout the trial. That way, the expert witness knows what the jury knows. And the expert has an expert data to add. The expert witness can sit there. Here is our "S."

But that's extraordinarily expensive. There's only one body of experts that's conned us into doing that, and that's real estate appraisers. Somehow in land damage cases the real estate appraisers think they can't give their testimony unless they sit there listening to all the other experts, and of course they charge you for it. It's the only type of expert I know for which we fall for that, but that is a way to get the data.

The other thing is the expert can be told about the case. This is our "T." My acronym is GHOST. G is for general; H is for the use of a hypothetical; O is for the expert as observing witness; S is for the expert who sits in the courtroom; and T is for the expert who has been told about the case. These are the types of things you can remember when the adrenaline is rushing and the trial is actually going on. This (the "T") is where the state and the federal law differ. Quickly, to sketch out the difference.

You can see, if the expert is told about the case outside of court, if what the expert is basing her opinion on is hearsay, or out-of-court declarations. With both state and federal that's okay, but the hearsay basis varies. The more restrictive is the state. Under the Commonwealth of Massachusetts, the hearsay has to be hearsay that if offered in evidence–it doesn't have to be offered–but if offered in evidence, it would be admitted. For instance, hospital reports is an exception, doctors' reports and learned treatises, a business record, something that is admissible.

The feds are somewhat more liberal, as the Federal Rules of Evidence are more liberal, and they say this: So long as the hearsay is the type of hearsay that an expert in this field of knowledge would rely on, then the expert can rely on it in court. And so long as that's properly construed, I have no problem with that.

In other words, if an expert would take off the arm based upon reading a biopsy report and looking at an X-ray, an expert who has read the biopsy report and looked at the X-ray can testify what she thinks about it without taking off the arm. This is permissible because she put her professional career on the line, she hacked that arm off, based on those things. They may be hearsay, but if the expert would act in the real world based upon that hearsay data, we ought to let the expert testify. That's the federal rules. But the standard works, and the standard is GHOST. That's basic. That's background for what the action is with respect to experts.

"Scientific, Technical or Other Specialized Knowledge"

I want to discuss legal action. Then we'll come back to things like the expert's report and how it works. The hot issue in this area has been with respect to the general knowledge of the expert. What general knowledge of the expert qualifies? And the dichotomy has been primarily between the plaintiffs' bar and the defense bar.

The Federal Rule of Evidence says this, and this is going to apply in Massachusetts, so follow the language. It's very important. If scientific, technical or other specialized knowledge will assist the trier of fact to understand the evidence or determine a fact in issue, a witness qualified as an expert by knowledge, skill, or experience, training or education, may testify in the form of an opinion or otherwise. You can find that in Federal Rule of Evidence 702. And we'll start with the feds and then bring the state into line.

Now, the Federal Rules of Evidence are a form of statute, and we all have to follow them. It's all very well to talk about the common law, but it's important to know what we mean by "scientific, technical or other," and "will assist the finder of fact."

Scientific knowledge, both state and federal, is that type of knowledge that we think of as scientific knowledge. My examples are all examples of scientific knowledge–medicine, physics, chemistry, engineering, economics, psychiatry. Although it's a squishy type of knowledge, these are all bodies of knowledge that we think of as scientific. They proceed by way of the scientific method.

Technical knowledge tends to be the mechanical parts. Again, to give you a source on it, there is an article in *Tulane Law Review* called "Daubert's Gatekeeper: The Role of the District Judge in Admitting Expert Testimony," where what I'm telling you is spelled out in more detail. Technical knowledge is computer software, the mechanical arts, the mechanics' testimony about whether the headlights were going on in a car before the accident—that type of thing.

There are a couple of examples of other specialized knowledge. We're going to see why one of them is difficult. In a certain Superfund case, we were prepared to receive the testimony of lobsterers about where they could catch lobsters in New Bedford Harbor. Now, those people didn't go to college, but they know where the lobsters can be caught. That's other specialized knowledge, and they can give an opinion about that if they have the necessary background.

How about this, I won't speak to this, but just to give it some immediacy: Tuesday of next week I have this so-called code-of-silence case, three alleged murders and four attempted murders and a drug ring, and now the government is going to put on the following experts. The first expert is going to be a forensic chemist. Now, that's sort of neat. No problem with that, I don't think. That's scientific knowledge, I expect. And he is going to tell us how the documents that they seized from the defense have trace elements of cocaine on them. I read an article the other day that most of the money in Los Angeles has trace elements of cocaine on it. ***(Laughter)***. I await the cross-examination, but we'll see. But in terms of this law, that's okay.

The second expert is going to be Herman Handwriting Expert, and that's fine, but what's that? A handwriting expert, that's not scientific, is it? But that's really other specialized knowledge, and it's important that we think of the concept of what's knowledge here. We have handwriting experts. We've had them in the court a long time. They can tell you how they do it—they tell you they do it by comparing the angles and how heavy your hand is and the like, so that's okay.

And then they've got Randolph Records Analyst. Who is he?

"And who are you, Mr. Records Analyst?"

"I work in the racketeering section of the Federal Bureau of Investigation."

"What do you do?"

"I analyze drug records."

I guess they want him to testify these are drug records of clandestine business operations. When someone says, "Look at this protocol, judge, the guy has written a law review article, I'm not so sure who published it, but I've got his article," he has got a lot of stuff about what this guy does. Is that knowledge? Is it beyond the frontiers of average knowledge? Because, after all, whatever they are, in evidence, the jury is going to see the records. I won't speak to these. I'm just raising the issue. We'll see Tuesday how this stuff works out.

How about putting lie detector tests in? Well, lots of courts have rejected lie detectors. These people are out there. Lots of industry people use lie detector tests. So given the language that I have quoted to you, which is the language of the Federal Rules of Evidence, the plaintiffs' bar primarily has been pressing for an ever-expanding group of people who will be qualified as experts and then can give their expert opinion.

Sociological studies show, and I read everything I can about how juries decide things, that we as a society are very impressed by experts, so you want an expert in your case. That's not terribly advanced. If your case will in any way lend itself to an expert, plaintiff or defendant, you want an expert.

Since World War II, we really have been impressed by science and experts. Clearly, under the rule, lie detectors, records analysts and clinical ecologists, are not really scientific experts. Maybe a clinical ecologist is. I don't know, but they may fit the rule technically under other specialized knowledge.

Frye, Daubert and *Lanigan*

So the fight has been as to what is the test of the general knowledge that the expert should have, plaintiffs for expanding, defendants for contracting. The old rule was a so-called *Frye* test, that if the expert's knowledge was generally accepted by experts in that field, then that was fine. *Frye v. United States*, 293 F. 1013 (D.C. Cir. 1923).

And, of course, the argument against that was, that Galileo would not have been accepted. He would be out. His knowledge was not generally accepted by his contemporaries. So now, in this expanding knowledge that's going in every direction, the courts are too conservative. That was the knock on the *Frye* test. You're going to cite this case over and over again, *Daubert v. Merrill Dow Pharmaceuticals, Inc.*, 509 U.S. 579 (1993). In *Daubert*, which came up in the District Court in California and then went to the 9th Circuit, Judge Kozinski wrote a strident opinion on whether a certain fertility drug that Merrill Dow put out could cause this birth defect that the child had, and it's a products liability test. And Kozinski wrote flat out that Rule 702 that I quoted to you adopts the *Frye* test, but if you listen to what I said, there were no words in there about "generally accepted scientific, technical or other knowledge." The rule reads "if scientific, technical or other specialized knowledge."

He really wrote it so the Supreme Court would review it. Both the plaintiffs' bar and defense bar knew this was a hot case. The Supreme Court took it. And instead of being affirmed, Kozinski was reversed in an opinion written by Mr. Justice Blackmun, one of his last opinions. It's important to distinguish the holding from the dicta. The holding in *Daubert* is that the rule, which has the force of a statute, does not adopt the *Frye* test. The common law, because *Frye* is sort of in the evidentiary common law in the several circuits, and *Frye* was until last week the law in Massachusetts, under the Federal Rules of Evidence (since the rule doesn't say "generally accepted scientific, technical or other specialized knowledge"), is not the rule. "Yay," says the plaintiffs' bar, wonderful, wonderful, big win. And to a certain extent they're right. But, of course, if *Frye* isn't the rule, what is the rule?

Blackmun proceeds to give us the rule over the dissent of Rehnquist and Scalia, who say, "Oh, don't tell them anything, just, reverse it is enough and we'll let it develop on a case-by-case basis." But Blackmun and the majority don't listen. They tell us the rule. And the rule is very conservative, extraordinarily conservative. "Yay," says the defense bar, here it is.

Even though *Frye* is not the rule, there is a litany of things that you can consider. You can consider general acceptance. After all, the rule speaks of scientific, technical or other specialized knowledge. Blackmun puts a lot into that word "knowledge." He says knowledge imports a received body of data, in other words, data that can be taught. I think he is absolutely right on this. In other words, knowledge is something that sort of works in the existential world. My father could teach me to lobster in New Bedford Harbor. Okay. That's knowledge. Even though he is a much better fisherman than I will ever be, he tried to teach me to fish. He can tell me things. He can express it.

The way I try to teach this myself is that, if you are the best cook that can ever be in making a soufflé, you are the premier chef in making that soufflé to the extent you can teach me how to do it, then that's a body of knowledge if your soufflés come out virtually as good as mine. But if mine are somehow very special, that's not a body of knowledge, because I can't tell you how to do it. I just sort of do it. I know how it's done, but I can't tell you.

That's so important, because if you think of what's significant, and Blackmun does, that's how you get rid of the dowsing rod folks. You know, in Kentucky you spend good money, someone comes around with a willow rod, the willow rod goes down, some man will say, "Dig your well here." You spend a lot of money for that. You dig the well, and you find water, or at least it beats the statistical average. Dowsing rod experts are out there. Would we let them testify in court? Say it cannot be so. Why? Because when you get, you know, Donald Dowsing Rod, he can't tell you how he does it. He may say, "Well, willows have got water in them and it attracts the water." Well, what does that mean? That makes no sense. We're going to come back to that.

Here is Blackmun's list: Is it generally accepted? Though that's not determinative, you consider it. Remember, *Daubert v. Merrill Dow* is talking all about *scientific knowledge*. So query whether this whole list applies to technical and other specialized knowledge. It applies, according to Blackmun, to scientific knowledge.

Consider whether there are peer review articles out there, consider whether the scientific method has been followed, the method of hypothesis tested by control groups and the like. Consider whether the method is publicized so people can criticize it, whether it's been subjected to that free marketplace of ideas. Those are conservative. They're only dicta, but they're conservative. And then Blackmun says something else that all the majority agrees on. He says, "We really have to depend on the district court judges to be the gatekeepers of expert knowledge." In other words, the district court judge has got to make a preliminary finding whether this general knowledge is admissible. Now, that's *Daubert*.

We'll talk about what happens after *Daubert* in a moment, but now I come to the state. And just last week, November 18, 1994, Mr. Justice Wilkins wrote for the

Supreme Judicial Court in a case called *Commonwealth v. Lanigan.* It's the Massachusetts DNA case; but really *Lanigan* is going to be much more important than just DNA because what he says is under the Massachusetts common law, the *Frye* test, which was the test for scientific evidence in Massachusetts, is no longer the test. And we look to the *Daubert* holding, but that's where it stops. They don't adopt the conservative Blackmun dicta. They don't reject it, but they just don't adopt it.

The reason this is so terribly important to you is, after *Lanigan* in the state courts, as well as the federal, you want to look to all these law reviews. You want to look to the federal decisions that cite *Daubert,* because they work in the state court, or at least they are persuasive in the state court because the state's high court says "look to *Daubert.*" General acceptance is not the standard.

So let's recap. *Daubert* talks about scientific evidence, not technical or other specialized evidence. So does *Lanigan.* DNA, after all, is a scientific protocol. So how far does it reach to technical and other specialized knowledge? Reading the dicta of Blackmun in *Daubert,* it should reach to the others as well because the word "knowledge" modifies "scientific, technical and other specialized."

What's the result? So far, not too much, because the law is so slow. But the result probably is going to be more conservative than heretofore. I must reveal a bias on this. I am quite conservative on admitting experts, and I want to teach you straight out, but personally I'm conservative, so be aware of my bias. I think the rule is generally conservative given the Blackmun dicta, even though Massachusetts does not expressly adopt it, and here's why: They expressly give the trial judge the gatekeeper role.

As soon as you tell a judge to do something, she'll try to do it. And as soon as we all get in there being gatekeepers, we'll give you our view of what the gate should be. And, our view necessarily—we've been over that—is going to be different. It's going to be more law, and some of you are going to have experts that you've always thought you could get in and a judge is going to say, "Ohhhh, not here; it doesn't meet *Daubert*; doesn't meet *Lanigan.*" "Why doesn't it, Judge?" "Oh, I don't think it does, there's no peer review."

An example, I was told—I haven't checked the case, au courant, but I was told—Keeton refused to allow a psychologist to testify the other day. I don't know the circumstances so don't take too much on this, but it was a psychologist. Psychologists have to fight all sorts of different things. After *Daubert,* Keeton says "That's too squishy, I don't understand it, it won't work," and the like.

Now, before I leave that thought, this is really the purpose of the Tulane law review article that I cited. Professor Simard at Suffolk, who used to be a clerk of mine, wrote it, and I got to put my name on it with her. I'm not taxing her with it. I believe all this, but she had the laboring oar, and she's brilliant. How does the judge decide? What's a fair way for the judge to decide after *Daubert*?

I suggest to you that this is the way the judge decides: Since we are by definition beyond the frontiers of average knowledge, you look at the epistemology—forgive the big words—the epistemology of knowledge in that area of endeavor. In simple words, how do those people who claim to have that knowledge come by that knowledge? That is to say, a medical doctor claims to have her knowledge after a rigorous training, which includes a great deal of hands-on work and a state licensing system and the like. How does a physicist come to have her knowledge? By different types of training, but really immuring herself in a mathematical model of how the atomic system works. How does a lobsterer come to know how to fish for lobsters? By doing it. How does the cook know how to make soufflés? He can be trained, but by doing it. You look to the epistemology of knowledge, how they think they get the knowledge that they get. And then you ask yourself, you, the judge, ask yourself, is that logical?

If it is, after *Daubert*, the judge is expected to admit it. Don't ascribe it to just an anti-conservative view. The judge is expected to admit it. It's not for the judge—and these are words you can use after *Daubert*: "Judge, it's not for you to pass on the opinion as a gatekeeper—but that would have kept, under general acceptance, Galileo out. Your focus is on the process, Judge, the process of forming the opinion. If that process meets the way people who get opinions in this area of knowledge, even though this physicist, this doctor's opinion is different than the other doctor's, then that's tough, let the jury decide. "I think that's the fair reading of *Daubert*. That's what we espouse in our article, but be aware that the applications, both state and federal, are going to tend to be more conservative.

There is another trend out there on experts that you have got to be aware of. Again, it's a defendant's trend. It's a trend that helps defendants primarily, and it also focuses on the general knowledge here. It's this: There are some of us who believe—I am one of these conservatives—and teach other judges the following criteria. It goes to sort of a second part of the rule, and this works state as well as federal.

You have to be qualified by skill, experience, knowledge, training and education. Those are the words they use. I have a big thing against hired-gun experts who make their living testifying. I think the process of law would be much easier if we went to experts who made their living experting in their areas and people who just went around testifying were out of the system. Now, that may be a bias. It's my view of justice.

If you think that, and some judges do—Keeton is one, but there is a dispute on this, obviously—then in order to be qualified, it's not enough that you go to school, it's not enough that you be an engineer. I'll take engineers as an example. You have to be an engineer—and this is the test—to whom society turns for this type of opinion outside of the courts.

Take the engineering example. Let's say you've got a case where the glass front of a stove blew out and injured someone. And so an engineer is prepared to testify the stove is defectively designed. This engineer has never designed stoves, never designed anything that has a heating element in it. Oh, he's a real engineer, and he really has designed some stuff, but they haven't been stoves. I, at least, have refused to allow that person to testify because that person has never made the judgment in the real world.

Here's the risk with that. I recognize the risk, and I'm going to try to stay away from it, but I tell you this is a defendant-oriented rule. Of course, I can't espouse any rule that is oriented one way or another, so I try to play it right down the middle. But I notice the danger of it being defendant-oriented, because if you limit the experts to the people who designed these specific stoves, the only people who are going to be experts are people from the company, and they're going to say we designed them wonderfully. So, of course, it's got to be broad enough to include the people who teach people who design stoves, the people who consult with OSHA and are on their committees about the safety standards for heating elements and the like. While I would want someone who outside of court deals with stoves, how do judges line up on this?

There is only a minority of us who are espousing this view, but it's coming. I think the tide is against experts. How do they break down? Keeton and I are conservatives on this. Woodlock, interestingly, is not, for prudential reasons. He says, to me specifically, "You know, no one is more than you on saying how great the jury is, and that's true, but you think you're going to put yourself between the jury. Let the jury decide. If you believe in the jury so much, let them decide." Well, I think the law requires me to do that. How is it going to work out on appeal? I think people like Bownes and Torruella, pretty much think, "Let's let the jury decide."

You see how I make book on the people for whom I work. Boudin, who teaches Evidence at Harvard, might go for this. We have no law on it yet. Be aware that it's coming. The risk or the test is the following: Does the expert render this opinion in the society at large?

Here's the last point on experts, except for the production point that I want to talk about. This is a point that has to do with the opinions that the expert renders. I'm not in any way signaling how I'm going to do the records analyst expert that I expect to see next week, but he will be a good example.

The reason we have records analysts, the reason we receive data about the rape trauma syndrome, are to enforce rights in our society. These are rights-based bodies of knowledge. That's why this guy has a job, because we need to analyze these things, and he helps the FBI in investigating cases, and he gets paid. Why do we have rape trauma specialists, battered child syndrome specialists? We need that because we are trying to enforce the law.

There are judges who believe that when you are dealing with a rights-based theory of knowledge such as rape trauma syndrome as opposed to a free-standing body of knowledge such as medicine, the most the expert should be permitted to say is that the symptoms described are consistent with the rape trauma syndrome, not that this victim suffers from the rape trauma syndrome.

The reasons in part are that the second example I've given you is caught up with a legal analysis. I know under the Federal Rules, witnesses can testify to the ultimate question, and in products liability of course they do, that the thing was defectively designed. I know that doctors can testify that another doctor's practice is less than adequate under the standards of care to be expected at the time in question. I'm not undercutting that.

You're going to have judges who will only let these rights-based experts testify that they are records analysts, they've looked at dozens of records, they've been working in this area for years and years, they've participated in all these big cases, and they've looked at what appear to be clandestine drug records, and here is what they look for. And, of course, the jury will be able to see whether those things are in this record. And the records analyst will then say, "my opinion is that these are consistent with clandestine drug records."

I think that's somewhat more desirable and fairer and less involved in the legal determination than to look and say, "Yeah, these are drug records and this means this and this means that." I don't just give you that as a personal view. There are judges out there, though I can't give you decided cases on this, who take that view. Be aware of it.

Expert Interrogatories and Reports

That's what I want to say about experts. Now let's come back to another issue. In the state rules, the supplementation to answers to interrogatories require that you always in your interrogatories say what trial experts you're using, what are their opinions and what are the bases of their opinions.

I was asked how detailed the reports have to be. And I think this: I'll use the words that I use, but then I'll generalize and try to speak for judges, state and federal. There is nowhere that judges are taught to become more strict with respect to experts' reports and the supplementation of answers with respect to experts. Judges have the spine, state and federal, if you spring an expert at the last minute, not to let you put the expert on the stand, even if your case goes down the drain, and is an otherwise meritorious case. Why? Because you sprung the expert late. Remember your duty to supplement the answers to interrogatories, because interrogatories may go out early in the case. If you don't have an expert then, you answer properly, "I haven't selected a trial expert," or you better supplement within a month, and less than that if you're close to trial. Supplement once you hire that expert, lest the judge may say you've been sitting on that expert and you've sprung the expert on the other side. This is not a question of being liberal and conservative. This is a question where judges are taught to be strict. Some are less strict than others, but we're taught to be strict. It's taught to be a game to spring experts at the last minute.

Now, how does that reflect? We know, in the federal system, you have to now give your experts' reports. What are judges looking for in the experts' reports, and how detailed do they have to be?

First, my rubric—it's only personal to me, but it will give you an idea. I say to counsel, and I try to say in my pretrial conference, the reports must be expressed to the level of detail of a patent claim. What do I mean by that? Now I'll generalize and try as fairly as I can to characterize the views of other judges. The reports have to say the why. If the expert gives this opinion, why does he give it? What's it based on? It's not enough to have an opinion that says he will opine that the product was defective because it showed inadequate engineering and failure to consider the safety implications of a buzz saw of this type. Probably that expert in many courts will not even be allowed to get on the stand. And in some courts they'll let him get on the stand and leave him dangling because he can say exactly that and only that.

"What's your opinion, Mr. Engineer?"

"My opinion is that it's defective."

"Why?"

"Well, it's defective because they inadequately paid attention, and let me tell you all the things they did."

"Object."

"Sustained."

It's sustained because it wasn't in the report. In essence, the test is you get that report, you sit on the bench with the report and you listen to what the expert says. When the expert goes beyond the report, cut him off. Now, that's what we're teaching each other. And that's the best guidance I can give you. The report had better say what that expert is going to say on the stand. And if he changes, if she's got a new angle on it, you'd better supplement to deal with that new angle.

And the business about the sequential—it's like a dance. If the plaintiff's experts change and, therefore, the defense experts change, the defense have to supplement too because the judge at trial has got to know what that expert is going to say. That's the theory of the rules, state and federal.

What I just said generally is accurate, I think, and speaks state and federal to the preferred practice. Now let's come down to real cases. In real cases, things may not be that perfect, and they may not be that perfect in large measure because the parties have agreed to something else. In other words, they've agreed instead of doing all this, we'll just take each other's deposition, or no objection is raised to the answers to interrogatories. The answers are made, and they are sort of general, but my answers are general too, and nothing is really raised there.

The point that has been spoken to before, when I said, well, if it's in the interrogatories, and is asked for, even though it's sort of that you sandbag at trial, the rule is the rule, and the rule has to be followed, and it has to be in the interrogatories. I won't let it go on.

And Judge Zobel said, very forcefully, "That's an absurd rule; it's got to be fair; if I think that, I will follow a fair result." I think most of them nodded their heads with Zobel rather than with me because, in part, we like to appear that we're being fair and it's hard for me to adopt a position that she is saying is flat out unfair. I just try to follow the rules. Here I think it's a teaching point.

If the other side gives you formal discovery, get the modification in writing to back off it. If you're faced with formal discovery and then the fallout comes at trial, so long as the lawyers are saying, "Oh, Judge, we agreed," it would be very hard for me to say, "I don't care what you agreed, the rule says this." No judge will do that.

But see, it's not going to work that way at trial. At trial you're going to have a different view of what went on. You've got to get it in writing how you step back. Especially if they give you the formal requirement, they've got to back off it in writing. Don't depend on their agreement to back off. Make sure it is in writing.

Once we get our new rules in place (they'll be in place the middle of this month), we're going to have a report. I think everyone is going to find the reports are what we're looking to, not the answers to interrogatories or the depositions, because, except for a treating physician, the observant witness (in federal court), it has to be a report. And my guess is the state within a couple of years will adopt that. That will be the litmus test. If it's in the report, because they have to be exchanged, it comes in. Short of that, I can't give you a better answer other than making the paper trail. Make a paper trail that we've agreed thus and so.

Preliminary Finding Regarding Expert's Qualification to Testify

One of the techniques on experts, if it's going to be increasingly problematic about whether your expert can testify, is to try and knock out the other side's expert prior to trial. We've seen that. We've had the technique. People bring motions for summary judgment to knock out the other side's expert. I really do not favor this unless you've got some really good grounds; otherwise, it just wastes time and it teaches the other side about your case.

But let's say you've got an expert who is really off in a new field. You've got one of these electromagnetic cancer cases and you are trying to cut the case off at the pass. Don't bring a motion for summary judgment. Instead, bring a motion, under the federal rule now, (and the *Massachusetts Evidentiary Standard* will give you the same cases,) bring a motion that the judge make a preliminary finding under Federal Rule of Evidence 104(a), and the cognate state common law, that the expert is not qualified to testify.

Now, this focus on preliminary findings is very important. We most frequently see it—to jump to another topic, but the analogy works—when a judge is asked whether to allow a co-conspirator's statement in evidence, civil or criminal. If you are at all familiar with that area, you know that the statements of all the conspirators are admitted against all the other conspirators because they're agents of each other. They are partners in the conspiracy, civil or criminal. But, of course, it's conditional. That only works if there is a conspiracy.

How do we know whether there is a conspiracy? The judge decides first. The judge decides first because if the judge decides there isn't a conspiracy, then the statement of each alleged conspirator is admissible only against that conspirator as an admission. The judge has to make a preliminary finding of whether or not there is a conspiracy.

That same theory deals with experts. If the *Daubert* gatekeeper function, which does apply both state and federal, means anything, it means that the judge is making a preliminary finding (not ruling) that, if the expert is qualified because both the body of knowledge is good enough and the expert is sufficiently trained in that body of knowledge to testify, then the case-specific data is as well. Ask for a hearing. Have the hearing. Maybe it's an evidentiary hearing.

Here is the great advantage to you: Win on that hearing and get the expert kicked out. Since that's a finding, it cannot be overturned on appeal unless clearly erroneous. If you go at it by summary judgment, summary judgments are heard de novo by the appellate court. The only question is whether there a genuine dispute. It's a legal question, and all intendments have to be made against the moving party.

So we don't see many of these motions, but we should. We should only have a few of them, really. But when you do make such a motion, you should do it under Rule 104. In New Jersey we see that coming up. Indeed, Justice Blackmun's opinion mentions Rule 104(a). That's the way to do it.

I suggest that a motion in limine would not be the best vehicle for raising the issue of whether the expert is qualified to testify. It's the timing. If you make your motion as soon as you know the expert—now, of course, if you don't know the expert until the trial, then you make the motion as soon as you do. But suppose they timely give you their expert, and that's four, six months ahead of trial, within days after knowing who the expert is, if you think the expert is a crock, you'd better make the motion.

The reason is this: If you don't make the motion, you can be accused of sandbagging, and at trial the judge is really up against it. He knows if he kicks the expert out, the case is over. Whereas it will commend itself to the judge's fairness, if you make that motion six months down the pike, the judge is more likely to allow it because he knows the other side maybe can get another expert. If the flaw is in the general knowledge, we're just not going to accept clinical ecology, well, then no clinical ecologist can testify.

But suppose the flaw is in the training? I'm much more comfortable kicking out his engineer—I have no trouble with engineers generally, but I'm a lot easier at kicking out his engineer who knows nothing about stoves six months ahead of trial because it gives him six months to get an engineer who knows about stoves. If you've waited the six months and we're at trial, now she's whining to me, "Judge, my case is over if you do this." Well, it's all very well to say you're tough, but do you see my problem? Make the motion earlier, and you're more likely to have the judge with you.

Standard of Proof

In deciding whether any evidence is relevant, you have two different components. Is it material, that is, does it help you bear your burden of going forward? I always think of that as a pontoon bridge getting across a river. And is it on some issue that will get you from what your start of trial is to getting to the jury.

The other vector is how much evidence you need; in other words, what's the standard of proof. In a criminal case, it's beyond a reasonable doubt. In a civil case, it's by a fair preponderance of the evidence.

In most cases that require experts, just basic, "Doctor, do you have an opinion to a reasonable medical certainty," equate with "by a fair preponderance of the evidence." In other words, these are more likely to be true than not true. So one of the problems in the cancer cases is that we all know that there are certain very accepted risk factors that put you at a much greater risk for cancer. However, the standard for tort law, at least in Massachusetts, is "by a fair preponderance of the evidence"—more likely to be true than not true.

There is a site licensing system that that is an expression of the state's exercise of its police power within the executive. And that power has some limitations, but they are very, very rare. And of course, to use the cigarette example or the cancer example, the government has every right to require warnings to be put on cigarettes and the like, though the litigation is now beating at the doors. That doesn't mean that the cigarettes are defective. That means that you get a warning.

The government under its police power has every right to do that. And the government, when they recalled the whole cranberry crop, didn't have to have scientists testifying more likely true than not true. They say, "Hey, there may be some problem with the cranberry crop—we're not going to let people get sick. Under our police powers, to avoid multi-million dollar damages, the cranberry crop can't go out." Or "You can't get the swordfish because they may have mercury contamination." So the biologists, in exercise of the police power, simply have to perhaps see a connection.

Well, who cares; I don't mean to make it personal. Legally, I would argue that there is a distinction between what that biologist does for the executive, which implements the police power of the state, and the lawsuit. But you have to look at the case. You have to look at the common law, the lawsuit that up till now has required a fair preponderance of the evidence and, therefore, requires, when the experts testify, that the expert testify by a fair preponderance before we move money from one side to another. It's a different thing, a different animal.

I admit that judges frequently fuzz it, but that's the best argument. The reason that we don't simply say when people die of lung cancer and smoke a pack a day that Reynolds should pay them is that we warned those people. I know we've got other preemption problems, but we don't have the guts as a society to ban it as contraband, so under the police power we warn them. And if they die, at least in Massachusetts, you would have to prove that it was more likely than not that they died from the smokes rather than dying from something else, and we really don't know that much about cancer.

Many states—such as West Virginia, and more to the south and west—that are more liberal in tort law have this enhanced risk. That's another statistical thing, because then, if you can recover only for the enhanced risk, even though we don't know what did it, then you can see how you could get such evidence. But you see the difference? That's a big problem. The issue is primarily an issue of tort law rather than what experts we'll let in. There is no problem with biology. That's a science. The question is the level of certainty. The biologists recite things; there doesn't have to have much certainty at all. That's an executive function. So long as you're under a tort law, fair preponderance of the evidence, the biologist has to say at least more likely than not, A caused B.

JURIES

I want to go back now to juries and the selection of juries and some of the things I've set out here about juries. I'm going to start federal, but we'll get to state because Freddie Halstrom is working there. The Standing Committee on Civil Rules of the Committee on Rules of the Judicial Conference of the United States has just voted within the month unanimously to allow attorney voir dire in civil cases, unanimously, to my horror, because I am with Chief Justice Steadman on this. They voted it. Now, it has a tortuous process. The full committee would have to vote it. It would have to go to the Supreme Court of the United States. And, under the Rules Enabling Act, Congress would have to go for it. But it looks to me like we're going down the California path here.

You know that the plaintiffs' bar primarily is perennially putting bills before the Massachusetts legislature to have lawyer voir dire. I really think that this chink in the armor of the feds is going to bring us voir dire, state if not federal, and so we'd better get ready for it, because we are not familiar with it. I don't know that I'm a terribly good teacher on it, because, of course, I've never done any. I've never seen any. But it's appropriate to raise it now because we've got to be thinking about who you want.

Be aware that this is being played out against a background that continually is restricting the peremptory challenge. In some states, some courts, if they think they can do it by rule, may try to get away from it simply by saying there are no peremptory challenges, there are just challenges for cause.

The peremptory challenge almost by its very nature requires you to stereotype. You're striking people because they are women, old or young, because you have certain stereotypes about these people. What do you know about the people? You just know their addresses. You look at them. You sort of think that the person ought not be on your jury. "I suggest to you, it's very risky to base your decision on race, gender, ethnic background or religious background." Now, state or federal, civil or criminal, a charge on that basis the judge should not allow.

I'll give you an example of how it works. How, though, do you know a pattern is coming up? I had an employment discrimination case, and we were seating the jury.

A juror was seated. We were at the sidebar, where, of course, challenges should be done. The lawyer says, "I challenge the juror who is in the foreperson seat." The other lawyer says, "Well, I object to that." I look over and I say, "Well, I notice that the person in the foreperson seat is black." I look out, I'll make the record, in this venire there is only one other black person, so that's good enough for me at least to ask you—because that's what happens next—"tell me why you are challenging that juror." Now, really any believable answer will do. And this is the answer I get: "Judge, he's black? I didn't know he was black." *(Laughter)*.

I managed to keep a straight face. He says, "That's not the reason. This is a sex discrimination case. I want women on this jury. That juror is a man." I said, "That's not a good reason." He's seated, because, of course, the reason was gender-based. He was knocking him off because he was a man, and that's not good enough. He's seated. They went defendant. I don't know if by him. They had to be unanimous in the federal court. Be aware that these things come up.

But now, of course, we've got to look ahead to a situation where, although the grounds of challenge are going to be largely limited in the sense that they cannot be stereotypical grounds, properly so, you can fashion an argument, "Judge, let's get beyond the stereotypes. Let me ask questions, and I'll tell you why I want them off. Let me exercise my peremptory challenges not in a stereotypical way but because I don't like this specific juror because he thus and so." Today, state and federal, you can get that a bit. The book talks about the willingness of judges in the federal court to allow it. We have the discretion to allow it. So do judges in the state court.

How do you get them to allow it? First of all, raise it early with the judge. The morning of the trial is probably too late. If you have the questions you want asked—many lawyers are good enough to give you the questions in advance—raise those at the pretrial conference. Don't wait until the morning of trial. The judge is too rushed. She's decided what she's going to ask by that time because, of course, she has to ask then. She has to go on the bench and ask the jurors. And if that's when you get the list, your list is going to get short shrift.

Raise the list of questions you want the judge to ask. If you get problems, or even if you don't, if you want to ask a few questions, ask the judge if when she's done asking her questions if you can ask some questions, just a few. I would say just a few now because, of course, you're negotiating against a background where judges are hostile to doing this.

Another thing to think about is jury questionnaires. I'm talking the techniques. And I haven't given you a theory. What are you looking for or what are you looking to avoid? And the reason is a candid one. I haven't got a theory. And though I read fairly broadly on this, the theories that I read are rather shallow. There is a fellow, James Jeans, a distinguished trial advocacy professor. *Jeans On Trial Advocacy*—no one uses his book because it's sexist. In this politically correct era no one will buy his book, but one good thing about it is that he has a section in there on jury selection.

He comes from the Midwest, where they are allowed voir dire, and he gives you some ideas.

Now, this is Jeans speaking, not me, but I at least pass his ideas along, and while they are a little shallow, maybe they're better than nothing. He says, in a criminal case, you do not want postal workers. Postal workers are not only government employees, they have the best retirement and benefits of any government employees, and they are by definition authoritarian. Authoritarian personnel think the government is pretty good. You don't want them. Also, he says, you don't want Lutherans. Well, of course, you can't challenge on the basis that a person is Lutheran, so I can't stand up here and say there's any wisdom to that, but his theory is that's a very authoritarian religion. I don't know that, but he at least makes statements like that.

There's been some discussion as these things come up among judges. Chief Justice Steadman, who was a great trial lawyer before he was a judge, told me this. He said, "I always used to take the first out of the box unless I had an articulable reason for knocking someone off."

Among top trial lawyers that I know, or know of, or have read their writings, opinions are split. Gerry Spence, who represented Imelda Marcos and represented the fellow who at least was indicted for shooting the marshal out in Idaho, and got him off, believes that using focus groups and all this sort of stuff is foolishness. He believes you look at the people yourself—you're in effect presenting your case to these people.

In the William Kennedy Smith trial, they had a whole focus group. And, indeed, based upon what I've read, that's the reason they didn't move for a change of venue—not that people knew either Smith or the alleged victim, but they just figured in that community, their focus groups told them that that was the place to try it.

I don't have a theory, but in terms of technique, in terms of practice, I can say a few things. Negotiate with your judge, respectfully, because for now the judges have the power and at least in this neck of the woods are hostile to doing this, so be reasonable. Get your questions in early. If you want a questionnaire, because that requires a different means, both state and federal, of selecting the jurors, and you have to make sure they answer the questionnaire first if the judge goes for it, and that will cost some more money, apprise the judge of that early on. If you want to ask questions yourself, ask to ask a few questions after the judge asks the questions.

If you are given the opportunity to ask questions, ask questions that are ostensibly neutral. This question is not ostensibly neutral: "If you came to believe that the police officers in this case were lying thugs, would you have any problem finding a reasonable doubt?" That raises the hackles of any New England judge. We may be forced to let you do that in the California style some day, but we're not going for it easy. That's not what you want to know.

But at the same time, don't ask simple-minded questions. I've watched this—I really am strict on this, but other judges tell me that lawyers don't know how to do it. They ask the same questions the judge asked; they just ask them directly. "Well, do you have any bias?" Search your mind. The judge has asked that question. You know, maybe you can ask it better, but if the judge does a halfway decent job, you're wasting your time.

Here is stuff you want to know. I have always liked the question for a questionnaire, "Do you have bumper stickers?" I mean a person who is putting a bumper sticker is making a statement. "What newspapers do you read?" Do people buy the *Globe*, the *Herald*, the *Phoenix*? Find that stuff out. What they read or what TV shows they watch, at least from my observations as a judge in cases where this has been allowed, sometimes do yield remarkably helpful things. Beyond that, I have little to say simply because I don't have a theory with respect to that.

Empowering Juries

I think other things to empower the jury are coming. Jurors are coming! Here are some: Frequently now more judges are doing pretrial charges. And studies show that the pretrial charge really does prep the jury for the trial. The state judges and federal judges are authorized to do it. In a court such as where I sit, where you not only can give the pretrial charge but because you can get daily copy in every case due to our computerization, we give it to the jurors. There is a pretrial charge, and the jury gets it so they know what to look for. They can pass it around in the jury lounge. More judges are going to be doing that.

Note taking. More judges are allowing jurors to take notes. It's within the discretion of the judge, both state and federal.

Juror questions is a practice criticized by the First Circuit but not prohibited, and I think I'm the only one who allows it—some state judges allow it as well. I really think you should empower the jury, and I'm trying to comply with what the First Circuit says. And I think that's the direction we're going with, letting them ask questions, of course always in writing. They can't just say, "There, by the way." The real risk is in a criminal case if they get in an inquisitorial mode with the defendant, but the questions are so rare, I still think it's worthwhile, and I allow it in every important case. We're doing it now in this big criminal case, though it's opposed both by defense counsel and the government, so maybe I've made a mistake, but again, the idea is to empower jurors.

There are other things to make the trial more understandable to jurors in terms of the mechanics of the trial. I am told that a judge who now sits on the 9th Circuit (she was a top district judge) was trying a commercial but complex case about computers. It was about whether computers performed in a certain environment where specs required them to perform, and she allowed an expert to make a joint presentation about computers before the trial began, with her present, and everything on the record. They had for every juror a computer to learn on, and only after that four-day orientation in computers did the trial start. I think judges are authorized to do that. I think that would be rare, but if you think that would be fair and would help in this teaching mode, that's fine.

Judge Zobel, following on Judge LeVal, now in the 2nd Circuit, District Court, who tried the *CBS/Westmoreland* case, has experimented with letting the lawyers make interim summations. That is, she gives them an allotted amount of time, but they could spend it as they see fit. That is, when they got done with a phase of the case, they could stand up and they could say, "Ladies and gentlemen, now, what you've just seen, has been, as I told you in my opening, this is on the monopoly power part of the case. And it's like a closing and an opening. And the next part I'm going to get into now is the business how did they use their monopoly power," etc. and then each time that happened she would turn to the defense and say, "Anything to say about that?"

She liked it, but she admitted that that tended to be a plaintiff-oriented rule because trials have to be linear. We can't think of a way of trying both plaintiff's and defendant's cases together; plaintiff will put on witnesses in the morning, defense in the afternoon. I mean no one has gone for that yet. Maybe that's an idea. It's plaintiff first, then defendant, given the burden of proof.

So the defense didn't have much to say when the plaintiff started spending its talk-to-the-jury time because the defense would sort of knock what you've seen, but they didn't have terribly much affirmative to say. I guess in her case, she's done it once or twice. Now, LeVal did it in the *CBS v. Westmoreland* case. I think we may see more of it.

Juror Exhibits

I'm very strong on passing exhibits to the jury. I think you should do that even if it's the most boring thing. It's a deed and note. If you've taken enough time to get it in evidence, take the time to pass it to the jurors.

Do you ask questions while you're passing it to the jury? Many judges will require you to ask questions while you're passing it to the jury. Others will not, but they soon will start if you pass every exhibit to the jury. And on balance—this is a tactical choice—on balance I would pass the stuff to the jury because it gives an air of verisimilitude. It's the real stuff we're seeing. Now, I don't allow weapons to be passed to the jury. I'll let drugs be passed to the jury but not taken to the jury room. *(Laughter)*.

That's the rule. I mean judges are taught this, don't let the drugs in the jury room. And if you've got a weapons case, though they may be evidence, don't let the weapons and the ammunition in to the jurors. *(Laughter)*. One or the other.

In the *World Airways* case that Keeton tried, though they accepted the verdict, the marshals had to go in twice and separate the jurors because they were throwing chairs against the wall, they were getting into fights. So, you don't send that stuff. I would not let the bloody clothing and the like in an assault or a rape case go to the jury. You treat that as evidence, but I wouldn't let it go in.

Jury Questions

Let's take a step back to juror questions, which I addressed as one way to empower the jury. I ask the jury's questions. I let the lawyers see them first in case they want to approach the bench, but it hasn't happened. Then I ask them, and I always ask them open-ended. They don't frequently ask leading questions, because they don't know how to do it, but they'll ask questions. I always say what or why or when or where, but I'll identify it as a juror question because I want to empower them.

I won't ask the ones that are unfair, such as "How much insurance does this guy have?" Well, that I will pass out to the lawyers so they can see it's on the jurors' mind. And, of course, I have a little charge saying, "If I don't ask your question, it's for a good legal reason. Don't speculate as to why. Pay attention to the witnesses. Don't sit there miffed that I haven't asked your question." I really think it helps for a fairer trial. I wouldn't do it otherwise.

Getting a Fair Jury

As an advocate your duty is to select the jury most favorable to your side. And as a judge I'm not interested in your getting a jury that's most favorable to your side; I'm interested in getting a fair jury. I think the two are different.

Computers in the Courtroom

Now, let me go to computers because I have some things to say about computers. And, again, we're talking cutting-edge stuff. And here the best I can do is say, really, I act like a shill for my court reporter, but I invite you to come down and see the court where I am privileged to sit. It's Courtroom Number 9 on the second floor of the federal courthouse in Post Office Square here in Boston. It is what's called a computer-integrated courtroom because my court reporter has invested in the equipment.

When you come in you see there are four PCs. Really, there's a laptop where the court reporter sits. Each counsel table has a PC. It's on. As anyone speaks, the testimony scrolls up on the screen, as it happens, in every case, not just the big cases. Of course, he is sort of an entrepreneur. He wants you to use it. He wants you to buy the transcript.

Well, I'm suggesting things you can do. Also, there's one on my bench. I'm watching it. This is the tip of the iceberg. In New Hampshire, where they've got a bunch of new federal judges who all came on the bench at the same time, they all got new court reporters at the same time, and they are ahead of us because they network theirs. That is, you can see the transcript in another judge's courtroom.

Let me heighten your consciousness with respect to where the practice of law is going if you really want to use this. It should go toward networking, but let's just take a single court that has this capacity. Of the 13 judges in Massachusetts, 11 of the judges have court reporters who have computer-assisted transcription. Only one has the good fortune of having a computer-integrated courtroom.

And in the state courts, it's lucky if you get a court reporter, but about five of them have computer-assisted transcription. It's not enough just to have computer-assisted transcription. You have to put the data into an electronic database.

To come back to the book MCLE's *The U.S. District Court Speaks,* I submit to you that in your firms, if your firm is big enough, you should have this questionnaire in a database, and you should be making reports about every judge in every room. You should include how you think they answer these questions, and you should put it in a database so you can get it out.

I have the privilege of having a brilliant court reporter, and I've been in federal court 10 years. Let's say you come in to try a case before me. Though I am a Holmes's realist, I swear to you I try to reach out for justice and I try to do it straight. You want to know what I think about the law in a products liability case, in a fraud case, in any sort of case? Where have I taught the law? I mean they may be videotaping this, but I reserve my right to do something else in court.

Where have I taught the jury? You can get 10 years of jury charges. They're right there. You want to know what I think about products—you've got a products case? I've done products cases. You think I'm going to do my products' charge much different? No, because I've got it. I prepare it with the court reporter. But of course does it make it right? No. Maybe I've been doing it wrong for five years. Want to change me? Get into my database because, of course, it's all public. It's in court. The guy wants to sell it. That's why I think I'm like a shill here.

But the real strength of it, you see, is not what Bill Young is saying, because he probably has it wrong, but it may be what Judge Keeton, Judge Zobel or Judge Tauro are saying. And if we network these, we'd have them. I use products liability as a case for a reason. Suppose we could network with the district courts and I could find out what Judge McHugh was saying, what Judge Sweeney was saying, or what Judge White was saying, who do it every day, who do it more than I, because I have to do the other federal thing.

All the good stuff is a year and a half ahead of the Appeals Court, SJC, Court of Appeals and the First Circuit. It's all down in the trial courts. That's where the hot issues are all being decided. How do we know about them today?

I've taught the best I know how. I've shared the time. It's marginal. I think you should go shop your ideas with other lawyers, but it's only anecdotal. We should network what is going on in the courts—for instance, when we have a sidebar conference about the law of evidence, in federal court, where I've got a code, I say 702, 104(a). I try to remember the number.

I know of a judge in Alabama who used to say the numbers without knowing what it was. He was very intimidating. He'd say, "Oh, no, no, no." And the lawyer would collapse. And the judge was just making up the numbers. I try not to make up the numbers. I try to know, but, you see, the reason I say the numbers, because I know now I can get back every time I've said 702 or 104(a) in 10 years. That's a balancing test. I can see everything I thought was more prejudicial, substantially more prejudicial than probative. And I can see it in context, because that's in a database. And I'm not grinding my court reporter down. He can press buttons. Indeed, he's teaching me how to press buttons. I can pull up those cases. If I can, you should.

And who cares about me. I'm only one, and far from the best one. Suppose you could get it all? I will tell you, judges are more impressed–unless you've got a case clearly on point that governs–by what other trial judges do in their own courts, or we're impressed by the superior court if we're trying the same thing. Those are the judges who walk in our shoes. This really is the wave of the future.

I invite to you come to court for any reason. I thank you for sticking with me all morning. We stand adjourned. *(Applause)*

"[An] expert has to be possessed of some body of knowledge. . . that the average lay jurors don't have. Because if jurors and judges know the stuff, we don't need the experts."

—Hon. William G. Young, April 28, 1998
From *Multiple Chemical Sensitivity and Daubert*

CHAPTER 4

Judge Young on Juries, Judges and Judging

DECEMBER 2, 1995

THANK you. Well, good morning. I'm honored that you would take the time to spend a Saturday morning with me, and I mean that sincerely.

I start with a story, and this story has a moral. I was first appointed judge of the superior court on November 27, 1977. The Governor's Council had called me the Friday after Thanksgiving and told me that the governor was of a mind to appoint me to the superior court.

My wife and I stayed up all night, literally all night, discussing it. It was a cut in pay. Well, we were worried whether we could send the kids to college, but that's all worked out. One thing she said has stuck in my mind. She said, I'm worried that you won't like this; it's too passive. As events proved, I do like it, and it's not too passive.

I first sat as a judge on February 24, 1978, and we'll pick up there. I'm not going to go day by day, but the first two days are important. They don't trust you with jury trials when you start out. So all the hoopla is over; you've got your robe; you report to work.

My first assignment was in Room 227, in what we affectionately call the Old Courthouse, as opposed to the New Courthouse, of which they can't use three floors because you'll be asphyxiated. So I report to the room in the Old Courthouse, and I'm going to sit jury-waived, but they haven't really gotten used to the fact that I'm there, and there's no work. Of course, there's an enormous amount of work, but no one has any for me.

So I send word over to the Suffolk motion session; "Here I am, Judge Young, send me some motions." And they do. I go out on the bench for the first time, and it should not be too surprising really, in all candor. Motions are what I've been doing as a lawyer, except I'm now on the other side of the bench.

Well, there are a few surprises. In that courtroom there is a big bookshelf behind you. Many of the state courtrooms and the federal courtrooms have a set of books, and those books make a difference. The Massachusetts Reports are there.

Someone made mention of a case, and I thought that I wanted that case. So, I stood up to reach for the book. Eddie Kelly was my court reporter. He goes, "All rise." And I snapped to attention, thinking a judge is coming in. And then I realized, no, it's me; he thinks I want a recess. But, you know, to humor him I take one then.

Later in the morning, about the time I do want a recess, a real judge comes in, Justice Kaplan. He is planning to use a room behind the lobby to which I've been assigned to do an attorney disciplinary hearing. Seriously, he comes through with some court officer carrying all this tape recording equipment. They don't have court reporters in the Supreme Judicial Court.

So they carry it all through my lobby. I take a recess. I go into the lobby. They're in the next room. They plug this stuff in. Of course it's direct current in those days in that part of the building. It all blows up, and I mean it literally blows up, with sparks and smoke. And, actually, he cursed. That was it for that hearing.

Second day. Now comes the moral of the story. On that second day, they've realized I'm on the payroll, and I have my first case to judge, a jury-waived trial. The issue in this jury-waived trial is whether a woman forged her husband's name to a deed.

You know a little bit about how trials work. So we get under way, and I'm sitting there in the throne chair of Room 227. It has one of these long benches. And the first witness that the plaintiff calls as an adverse witness is the wife. He hopes to cross-examine her and break her down and show that she forged the name on this deed.

She takes the stand. She's sworn in, and I'm ready to take notes. She starts testifying. And the frightening realization comes over me that it is my responsibility to decide whether this woman is telling the truth.

Nothing in my years of practice, nothing as a lawyer, has prepared me to decide whether this human being, under oath, is in fact actually telling the truth; but it's my job to figure that out. As much as I thought I knew what judging involved, it's very clear to me that I had no background in this. And, respectfully, I suggest to you as lawyers we don't either, because as lawyers we are not the judges of our clients.

So I look at the lady, and I think: "How am I going to know?" And in my puerile naive beginnings as a judge I thought I'd better watch her very closely. Maybe she'll sweat. I really thought this. Maybe she'll wring her hands. Maybe if I get over there on that edge of the bench and I look at her, she won't meet my eye; she'll be shifty-eyed.

Well, I'm in the center of this long bench. You can put the whole Supreme Judicial Court on this bench. I'll just get the throne chair over there by the witness box. You see, I don't dare stand up. I've done that on the first day, and the result there was a recess. I don't want a recess. I want to do the job to which I've been appointed.

So I take the throne chair, and I plan to slide it over there. No big thing. And I start, only it's on one of these plastic mats, and when it gets to the edge of the mat, it stops. I go full length behind the bench (indicating). I'm not kidding. I am absolutely out of sight behind the bench. I fall off the chair.

Of course what goes through my mind is that the governor has appointed a buffoon as a judge. This is terrible. And I come up. Let me tell you, I am terribly embarrassed. My face is crimson, and I pull myself up.

And you know, none of them laughed. And that was also a lesson to me. I thought, "Why aren't they laughing?" I don't try to be funny. Some judges do, and in my judgment that's a mistake. Don't try to be funny. But this was idiotic. And then I realize they're not laughing because I'm the judge.

So I take the throne chair and I yank it over here (indicating), and then I sit in it because that's where I want to be. And for about 20 minutes I sulk. I don't pay attention to her. I just sit there thinking of this idiot thing that I have done and what a fool I am and how embarrassed I am. And after about 20 minutes I say to myself, "Gee, I d better pay attention to this lady. I've got some work to do here."

Now, I tell that story for a couple of reasons: One, it's true, and it's a good story; and two, it breaks the ice.

Do we have any real judges here? *(No response)*.

Okay. Well, then I'm on my own. I was hoping for some real judges because if they come, of course, I'm going to pull them up here as faculty members, and they can keep me honest.

JUDGE KILMARTIN: Judge, I'll help you.

JUDGE YOUNG: Oh, okay. Here we are. You're free to go at any time. Would you introduce yourself and the court on which you sit?

JUDGE KILMARTIN: My name is Peter Kilmartin, from the Ayer District Court.

JUDGE YOUNG: Judge Kilmartin, I am very much beholden to you, and let me spell it out. I ask you to stay for as long as you want to stay this morning to correct anything that I say and to offer your own views. I'm going to say a few things about state district court practice and the like, and I just want you to jump in at any time. Please do that. Don't feel you're a prisoner here for the full four hours. Feel free to leave. I do appreciate your helping out.

Here's what I have in mind to do here, and I got the idea for this particular lecture from Justice Lenk of the Appeals Court. She served briefly on the superior court, and she said, "If I knew then when I was a lawyer what I know now as a judge, I would have been a much better lawyer." And that resonated with me.

And I got to thinking: "What is she talking about?" What is it that she knows now as a judge that would be helpful to the bar to know about judging? What is she talking about?

I went to see what's written that would be helpful. I found a book, and I want to tout it to you. My colleague, Judge Keeton, has written a text for law students. West has published it. It's called ***Judging***. And in typical Keeton style, it is a careful and scholarly exposition of what it means to be a judge in today's society.

I will make some references to it. I think if you want an intellectual underpinning to the things that I am going to talk about, you can do no better than Keeton's book. Judge Keeton explains what we all think we're doing if ever we think about it. But these four hours are not going to be a rehash of Judge Keeton's book because it's too theoretical.

Here's what I have in mind: I want to talk practically about those things that I think would be helpful for you to know about how judges approach their work and, inferentially, everything I know about juries, which isn't much. The jury part of it is more procedural.

In doing so, and this is why it's so vital really that Judge Kilmartin has given up his morning to be here, I will tell you candidly I'm walking a fine line. I don't want to talk to you about "This is the way Bill Young judges; this is the way Bill Young does it," because there's only a very small minority of you who appear before me or have ever appeared before me or will appear before me. There's nothing special about the way I do it. So I'm going to try very hard to share with you what I can observe about what other trial judges and justices are doing. My information, what I'm going to share with you, comes from other judges. This is what they say they do.

At the same time it seems to me that anytime you try this you have an obligation to be scrupulously honest. And while I reserve the right myself to do exactly the opposite of what I explain to you, I will be as honest as I know how. I will name all the names I know when I say judges do this; I will tell you what judges, and the like.

I will give you the boilerplate—the standard approach to this and that problem as it has been taught to me. In giving you the boilerplate, I am saying that these are the questions I ask juries, this is how you do it, this is what a structure of a charge looks like, this is how you can affect it, this is what you probably won't be able to affect, and the like.

And candidly, of course, when I'm doing that, I'm telling you what I do. What I do is not important, except as an example to test your own practice and the judges before whom you practice, to test that against that norm. I'm the first one to try this, and I want your criticism. I don't know if I'll do this again. I think there's some value to it. I want you to tell me what was valuable and what was not.

There is no text here—when you teach Trial Practice you know what you want to cover; you want to go from impanelment to verdict. That gives it some structure. When you teach Evidence—those are the subjects I teach—you know what subjects the Federal Rules of Evidence govern.

Although I'm not going to skip over any topic here, I'm eager to go where you want to go this morning. So if I'm not addressing your concerns, this is a chance to ask judges any question that, up until this moment, you were afraid to ask. That's another reason I started with my buffoon story. Ask me anything. I will give you the best answer I know how to the extent that I can.

I want to talk now about lawyer and judicial interaction with respect to juries. We'll start, as the course outline starts, with the impanelment, the picking of juries, but actually your analysis starts well before that.

JURY POOLS

Who are the jurors that are going to try your cases? In all respects we'll cover both state and federal. Massachusetts has one of the best jury selection systems in the nation. I would be prepared to say it is the best. The one-trial, one-day approach to jury selection, with no exceptions, everyone 18 years of age up until age 70. After age 70 you're still summonsed, but you get an automatic bye if you don't want to come. That is an extraordinarily just, it seems to me, approach to making our citizens part of the judicial process.

There is a downside to any system. Juries viscerally understand that it's one day or one trial, but what they hear is it's one day. And of course the state statistics on the superior court show that most trials are three to four days. So you have to get over that hurdle with any jury. It's not that high of a hurdle, but I will say candidly that we have been seriously hurt by the O.J. Simpson trial. Jurors believe they're going to be abused when they come in to the system. They believe they're going to be locked up. They believe their time is going to be wasted.

And we don't start with jurors by placing them in the best areas. In the state system, and to a certain extent in the federal system, we place them in areas that are not as stately as this lovely hall. We put them down in the cellar in Norfolk. We squeeze them into places that have bad heating, and they immediately get the idea that they are not central to the process, that they're sort of an excrescence on the process.

While I'm talking institutionally, those are things that you have to overcome with juries because the model of the jury, of course, is a vital expression of direct democracy, probably the most vital expression of direct democracy in existence in America today: The people themselves ruling.

Now, again, state system: where do your jurors come from? If they are, by and large, an appropriate array of our public, they are summonsed county by county because our state judicial system is set up county by county. That has significant implications, especially for Suffolk County, where a large portion of the minority population of the Commonwealth resides.

Suffolk does a bad job of summonsing its jurors. We require that all jurors be taken from the census or the police list, not from the voting list. Your jurors come from the census or police list, the city lists, which should include everyone in an area. That's the most just way. Suffolk does a lousy job. They don't count everybody. They significantly undercount.

And whom do they undercount? They tend to undercount those who are hard to find, those who are not property owners, on the city tax rolls, people who do not vote, who haven't been involved in that civic aspect of our government. And the result is they undercount minorities.

Something that is going to cut against this now, and something that you are going to be concerned about with the composition of the venires that come in to your court, is the Motor Voter Registration Law. For perfectly good government reason we now have federal legislation that requires that those who register a motor vehicle, because everybody has access to a motor vehicle in this nation, must be registered to vote. Perfectly good. Perfectly logical. We want people on the voter role.

What's the result in Massachusetts? Massachusetts says, "Hey, you've got them on the voter rolls. Why do the census? Let's forget the census. It costs a lot of money. And, after all, what do we really use the census for? We only use it to summons jurors. Who cares about that?"

Well, if we stop taking the annual census in the cities and towns, we are again going to cut out from the group of people who will be summonsed as jurors those who are too poor ever to get a driver's license or are too alienated from the system to go and apply for one.

And I suggest to you that we are going to continue to be underrepresented in terms of minorities. So much so that it causes a constitutional problem? It is not really for me to say. But be aware of the issue.

Other things that you want to take into account, knowing that we summons from counties in the state: Plaintiffs' lawyers tell me that because the jurors are taken from a specific county, the venue in which you place your case is important. They say to me that if you have a good liability case and some damages, you are most likely to get the highest verdict if your jurors are people who are used to dealing in large sums of money.

And where are they to be found? Primarily, so I am told, Norfolk County. Not that it's the most affluent county, but it only has one city, Quincy. The rest of it is bedroom suburbs. Almost equally as good, Middlesex, because while it has a variety of cities, it arches out through many of our affluent bedroom suburbs. So your mix of jurors from Middlesex and Norfolk are supposed to be, so plaintiffs' personal injury lawyers say, an attractive mix, if you have a choice of venue.

What about Suffolk? Suffolk is a good place, they say, to win a case: it's blue collar, and despite the gentrification, jurors feel for the downtrodden. The trouble is that $100,000 is big money, and in today's world a plaintiff is going to be asking, with permanent personal injuries, for considerably more than $100,000. So the common wisdom is, and the common wisdom has more than a grain of truth, you'll win in Suffolk, but you won't get much.

It also is thought that in the outlying counties, the less urban counties, it is both harder to win and you don't get that much. Those counties are thought to be, by and large, more conservative. That's the view. We see, once in a blue moon, very high verdicts with specific cases.

What am I really talking about? I'm talking about forum-shopping. But let's talk about it because these are things that you need to think about with respect, at least, to juries. In the state system, in civil cases, you're going to get 12 jurors. In the district court system, civil and criminal, you're going to get six.

I wanted to ask Judge Kilmartin a question. If we are summonsing jurors to state district court, civil session, is it skewed at all so that the people in the venire that's sent up to Lowell, for instance, won't have to travel so far, or is it just straight Middlesex?

JUDGE KILMARTIN: On both sides, civil and criminal, it's my experience that they come from the entire county, but on the district court level everyone may find it interesting that there's a conscious effort to draw the jurors from the entire county. So, for instance, if we do a jury session in Ayer, many individuals will come from Everett, Cambridge, and Medford, and so forth, and drive past four or five other courthouses in getting to Ayer. Other individuals from that end of the county will go into Cambridge, Woburn and so forth.

JUDGE YOUNG: What is your experience? Are the jurors sophisticated enough that their noses are out of joint because of that?

JUDGE KILMARTIN: Occasionally, yes. But, for instance, I think a lot of the judges, and we spend a lot of time talking with each other there on these issues, meet with the jurors first thing each morning. A judge usually gets in at 8:25, 8:30 in the morning to explain some of the issues that you touched upon: that they're going home that evening; the time they're going to get out of the courthouse; that although they've been put on notice to be there for one day or one trial, the trial possibly will take longer than the one day if they're selected. We try to put them at ease and answer many of the issues that they come in with.

So I think by the time the jurors leave the jury panel room and leave the court officer to go for an impanelment procedure, many of the concerns that you have made reference to have been addressed. They're calm, they're at ease, and they've been told that the judge is going to lead them and help them through the entire process. They've been told that the court officers and the clerks will help them with concerns and questions and issues that may arise during the course of the day, so they're in a frame of mind to do the job.

JUDGE YOUNG: Thank you very much, that's helpful. That's what you hope is being done system-wide. In state district court it's six, right, civil and criminal?

JUDGE KILMARTIN: Yes, but they have civil trials only in two district courts throughout the state at this point. There's legislation pending to have some pilot projects.

JUDGE YOUNG: Right. And in civil it's five-sixths, so it would be five out of six would give the verdict. And, of course, in the superior court it's five-sixths, 10 out of 12 will return the verdict. (In other words, a unanimous verdict is not needed.) So in superior court, drawn from the county, you're going to have a jury of 12, 10 of whom can return the verdict.

Studies show that it is easier to get a verdict, as opposed to a hung jury, if you go ten to two. One need only make reference to that ***Koch/de Castelbajac*** case in the housing court that's been front-page news in the ***Herald*** and ***Globe*** where, apparently, over the possession of the tenancy in the Four Seasons, the jury divided ten to two. Ten went for Koch, but two went for de Castelbajac.

Again, plaintiffs' lawyers will tell you that they favor such a system because it is easier to get a verdict, ten to two, in a civil case. In criminal, of course, the verdict must be unanimous. But plaintiffs' lawyers think that it is easier to get a favorable verdict out of a ten-to-two split.

Now, after the O.J. Simpson case some states are considering ten-to-two with respect to criminal juries. Query the constitutionality of that, and that's not important for our purposes here this morning, but be aware that that's what you're going to get.

Now, with respect to federal courts in Massachusetts, because Massachusetts has the best system nationwide, we draw directly from the state jury pool. We have contracts with the state, and there they've expended the capital resources to put everybody into their computers. We draw from their computers and share the same jury pool. And, therefore, people are drawn to service in the federal court, without exception, 18 years old on up as long as people are alive, without any exception.

However, the jurors we draw are not limited to a specific county. Eleven of us sit in Boston, and we draw from Worcester east, which means all the way up to Salisbury and out to Provincetown and the borders of Middlesex and Worcester Counties.

In Worcester, we have one judge, and we draw from Worcester. In Springfield, we have one judge and a senior judge and we draw from Worcester west, which means Hampden, Hampshire, Berkshire and Franklin. So we have three sections in the federal court, and we make the jurors come from that distance.

We don't have one day, one trial. We have potentially one month's service; but we, as the state court, try to use our jurors efficiently. We impanel only on Mondays. That's important to know, because that means that every jury case is going to start on a Monday in federal court. You may not get to trial on that day because the judges may impanel two or three cases on a day and then stack the jurors up. But in doing your scheduling, in worrying about whether a judge can call you to trial, you've got to know we can't start except on Mondays because that's the day we get the jurors.

Now, we don't, and perhaps we should, as Judge Kilmartin said, go to see the jury at the outset of their service every morning. That's how the state system does it. We don't do that in the federal system. We bring them all together. We have a wonderful jury commissioner, Judy Cook, who tries to do what the state judges do but, candidly, cannot because she does not have the authority of a judicial officer. Then we play them a nice film. The feds tend to have money, and we have a nice film from the Administrative Office of the Courts, and we play it for the jurors, and that's supposed to orient them as to their jury service.

This business of orienting the jury before you ever see the jury may be important to you. I'll give one example from my service. When I went to see the jury and tried to do what Judge Kilmartin has so properly and aptly characterized, both to instruct them as to the importance of their service and to put them at ease, I made reference to it being in the Constitution and a civic duty. I like this line I've already shared with you—that the jury is the most vital expression of direct democracy in America today. But I also made reference to the draft and to service in the nation's armed forces, which seemed to me an appropriate and affirmative good-feeling topic that we would all share about the defense of the nation as a policy.

I ran into a case where the defendants were alleged terrorists, and I had to throw out 500 jurors to whom I had given that speech before the defendants ever heard about it. Defendants are not present, you see, when I instruct the jury. I don't think I was trying to stack the deck against them, but they had wonderful lawyers. We keep a record of the judicial interaction with the jury, and, as is their right, the defendants got my exposition to these 500 jurors. And they said, "Judge, that was completely unfair. My people are against the military. That's what motivated them, allegedly, to do the things that they did. That analogy is lousy."

They're right. I've never used it again. But the point is that something has gone on between a judge and the jurors that you as lawyers are seeing before you've ever dealt with them. It may behoove you to know what went on because the judge may slide into similes, in good faith I would submit to you, but that may happen, so you've got to be alert to it.

So there, we've got our jury. We know where they come from. What do we know about them? Now, again the state takes the lead, at least in our state, as compared to the federal system. You know quite a bit about them in the state system because there is a standardized form that the jurors fill out that gives you their name, their address and their spouse. It tells you where they work and they have to answer whether they have ever been convicted of any crime.

And then, you see, and this is important in exercising your peremptory challenges, the computer has randomized the jury in a fair way, so that the jury list is in the order in which the panels are going to be sent to the courtrooms. It is all established before they ever come in. Then they are sent out by panels to the courtroom, where they will be impaneled in a particular case. They are sent out in the order that they are going to be put in the jury box.

That's vital to know for this reason: If for any reason you don't like juror number 6, it's terribly helpful to know that the next juror that you're going to get is juror number 7. I won't go back to ancient history, but it didn't used to be that way.

It's also helpful to know that since the federal court now takes from the state list, we are confident that the names are randomized before the group of jurors ever comes into the federal courtroom. So those of you who practice in federal court get a jury list, but you won't get it until the day of trial.

Now, in big cases, there have been efforts to draw special venires. If you have a monster case that's been in the newspapers, the judge may adopt special procedures to see that it is fairly tried. For instance, they may send out questionnaires to the venire that will come in. The special venires will be randomized as well, and although you would like to do your best to get a list of the jurors prior to the day of trial, we won't give it to you, and we shouldn't, because we don't want anyone going out and writing books on those jurors.

So you're not going to see the specific jurors until the day of the trial, and in federal you won't know as much. You'll get a jury list, and the list will provide the name, the address and the occupation of each juror.

Mr. Krasnoo, you're frequently there. I don't even know: It doesn't say the spouse's occupation, does it?

MR. JAMES KRASNOO: No.

JUDGE YOUNG: Okay. So you don't know the spouse's occupation.

> And the list is not always accurate. The address may have only the city or town. For a number of jurors there may not be an occupation. That may happen in the state system too. But in the federal system, despite the vaunted extra perks that we have, we prepare the lists that very day as we check the jurors in.

So your list of jurors does not tell you as much in federal court. But what it does tell you, and lawyers don't understand this, is the order that the people are going to be called. They are called in the same order that appears on that list. So if you don't like juror 17, juror number 18 is the next one called. The lists are not alphabetical. It makes it a little harder to work through them, but if you know they're going to be called into the jury box in the order that they're summonsed, that's helpful when you are trying to make a decision regarding whether or not to use a peremptory challenge.

IMPANELMENT

Now, let's talk about impanelment, state and federal, in a jury case. There are three major approaches to impanelment. You all will have variations on these approaches. I attended a federal session in which there were 30 judges, and they asked each of us how we impaneled juries, and there were 29 different approaches. After the 29 came out, one judge, Judge Rosenbaum from Minnesota, said, "And the trouble is we all think we got our approach directly from God." And there's a lot of truth to that.

So although it's vital to know what your particular judge's approach to impanelment is, there are three major ones. The other variations are slight.

Questioning the Entire Venire First

Let me go through the three approaches generally and then with some specifics. The first approach, the one that I submit to you is the most common, is the following: The jurors come into the back of the courtroom. The judge puts certain questions to the jury venire generally and finds out if there are any problems, such as whether the jurors know anyone in the case. These jurors are then challenged for cause. When the judge has a venire that is free of challenges for cause, he fills the box. That's the time when the peremptory challenges are made. The box is then refilled until the peremptory challenges are exhausted or the parties are satisfied. The remaining jurors are excused. You now have your jury ready to be sworn. That's the first approach.

Filling the Box First

The second approach is to take the larger venire of juries and put them in the back of the courtroom, at random—except you know it's not at random. They'll be reading right from the list of the panel they're given or from, in the federal court, the federal jury list. They'll just pick as many jurors as they want, put them in the box, and the jurors that are put in the box are asked the questions. Some at that stage are excused for cause. And then those vacancies are filled by other jurors who are asked a general question:

> Now, ladies and gentlemen, those of you who have just joined us, you heard my questions to the jurors who were first placed here in the jury box. Would any of you answer 'Yes' to any of those questions? Do you think your answer would be 'Yes'? Might it be 'Yes'?

And then if a juror answers, "Yes," again they come down from the box. You handle the interrogation for cause, and then they are excused. Eventually you get a jury in the box that is indifferent, ready to be impaneled. Then you exercise your peremptory challenges against that full jury. Then you have your jury, and that's it.

The third major approach to jury selection is what is known as the struck system, used by some judges in every case. And, again, I invite you all both to interrupt me at any time and correct me when I start telling you Judge X does this. If you don't think so, let's share that. That's why we're all here.

AUDIENCE MEMBER: What do you think of the practice that some judges have of shuffling the selection deck so that you don't have the order that you can follow when you're exercising your peremptory challenges and you have no idea where the next juror is going to come from?

JUDGE YOUNG: Direct answer: I think it's wrong. The whole genius of randomization is that there is no need, constitutionally or practically, to shuffle it, state or federal. If you get a judge who does shuffle it, what he or she is doing is making it harder on the lawyers for no corresponding benefit. I think it's wrong. You'll have a transcript that says so.

Can they do it? Is it a violation of the power that every judge is given to control his or her courtroom? I know of no case that says it is a violation, but they shouldn't do it because the reason for randomizing it in the first place is that we get a fair jury selection. I'm going to get into the tensions between what you want on a jury and what judges may think is fair, but the short answer is they shouldn't do it.

JUDGE KILMARTIN: Can I just offer an observation?

JUDGE YOUNG: Please, at any time.

JUDGE KILMARTIN: If you have a relatively large jury pool and from that jury pool you're selecting one or two juries for a particular morning, the juror who is on a later panel who spent the bulk of the day or the bulk of the morning there has never been called. That individual's number is not even close to being reached, and the juror approaches you or approaches the court officer complaining about why on earth did he have to sit there all day when you knew what order you were going in. He's upset that he wasted four hours, and he's been inconvenienced, and so forth. What's your response?

JUDGE YOUNG: My response is that that inconvenience doesn't justify randomizing the list, which takes away some advantage to the lawyers that is built into a good system. What you should do is keep statistics on the overage, and as judges you should agree on how many you can expect to use.

Now, one of the things that the feds do very well is keep statistics on everything, and one of the things we are becoming more and more frightened of is that more and more you can find out the statistics on us. Oh, my God. You can find out how many motions have been under advisement over six months. That's frightening stuff. We don't care that you know that, but the law tells us now we have to tell you.

At least locally, the direct answer to your question is that our judges have adopted rules on how many jurors can be taken into court to yield a certain number of jurors for a panel. And our rule is this: Federal court, civil, we sit in juries of six. Our rule is you get 18 jurors to get a jury of six. You're not allowed to ask the Jury Commissioner for more than 18 jurors.

Criminal we sit 12; and we take 36 jurors to get 12. That's a judge rule. I submit to you that the proper administrative answer is for the judges to pay attention to how many jurors they need to run the expected number of cases. Because we set the cases for trial, we know however many cases we have on a specific Monday.

Of course, you pick every day in the superior court and in the district court jury session, because you're picking jurors for every day that a judge is going to be available to try the case. This makes it harder, I admit. But in the federal system we are now running jury utilization—that's what we call it—to see how many jurors are called who are either seated or at least summonsed and challenged. We run over 80 percent, which is one of the best in the country. Therefore, 80 percent of all jurors we call are either seated on a jury or at least summonsed and challenged. We used to run at 45 percent, which was one of the worst in the country. Chief Judge Tauro and Judge Zobel, now head of the Federal Judicial Center, get the credit for that. They've done it by talking it through with judges, because we're a pretty collegial group.

If you have a special case, a big case such as a Mafia case, you can get hundreds. When I had the *Big Dan's* case in the superior court, we were literally summonsing jurors by the hundreds, but that's a special circumstance. Your point's a good one. It also costs money. You shouldn't be summonsing more than you're going to use. That's the taxpayers' money.

Judge Kilmartin's point brings out something else. I said that in the federal system we seat six. Now, some people wonder about that. We went to that to save money; no better reason. We think six is enough. Personally, I disagree with that. In a six-person jury a strong juror can dominate the other five. That is less likely in a 12-person jury.

I don't think six persons is a plaintiff/defendant issue, like plaintiffs are more likely to win with six, and so on and so forth. Read Jonathan Harr, *A Civil Action,* which is a really extraordinarily good book about Judge Skinner's case involving the Woburn well. Now, that was a long case, a big case, but only six human beings decided that case.

Talking federal now, a number of us feel that six is too little. I now routinely impanel 12. The rule only tells me I have to impanel at least six. I'll impanel 12 for a civil case. Judge Woodlock will impanel eight to 10. We are telling our new colleagues that you have every right to do that.

In federal court, our rules are explicit that the alternates in a civil case can deliberate with the deliberating jury. So if we have a long case and we've impaneled 12, there'll never be any alternates; we'll put all of them in. If somebody gets sick and we have 11, we'll put in 11. So long as we've got six in a civil case, when it goes to the jury we can go right on.

How the six new federal judges are going to work out is unclear to me now, but the trend is to impanel larger juries. And you would be interested to know that the Judicial Conference of the United States now agrees with that view and is recommending that we go back to 12-person juries in civil cases.

The "Struck" System

I haven't quite finished explaining the struck system. In the struck system you bring them into the back of the courtroom. The judge asks the general questions. The challenges for cause are handled. When the challenges for cause are exhausted, the judge then declares the panel indifferent. And then you have however many you have left. Then, much as you do in arbitration, you take as many peremptory challenges as you are authorized by law to get down to a jury of 12. For example, if you have a panel of 36, you give each side 12 challenges. Your challenges are not to strike out someone in the box. You look at the whole 36. And you say, "Out of these 36 whom do I like the least? I challenge that person." Then the other side challenges. The other side asks itself, "Whom do I like the least? I challenge that one." Back to the proponents, challenge, challenge, until you've each exhausted your 12. And the ones that are the blandest, the ones that no one dislikes, are the remaining 12. They are the jury.

Now, that process takes a little longer because you have to, by definition, have enough jurors both to fill the box and to exhaust both sides' peremptory challenges.

There's one other wrinkle to that system that I want to tell you about. Who uses that system routinely? Judge Keeton uses that routinely. Judge Wolf uses that routinely. Many people think that is the fairest system. You are more likely to get that system if you have a "big case."

Judge Keeton has a variation on it. He doesn't let one side challenge and then the other side challenge. You have to write out all your challenges in writing, and then the lists are compared. If you both dislike the same person, that person sort of goes off without it counting, and you both get another challenge, so that you can challenge someone whom you dislike but the other side likes. All right. Those are the three general approaches.

Impaneling the Jury: Practice and Procedure

Now, I want to go through very specifically how a jury is impaneled using the first approach just as a paradigm. And this, of course, is how I do it, for whatever worth that is. But I want to give you the example so that we can then generalize from that example because there are some issues in that.

Here's what you want to be looking for: There is a big fight now. It's been going on in the state for some time, and it's going to go on in the federal courts now with a vengeance. Should lawyers be part of the voir dire process? Should lawyers get to ask questions of jurors?

I can tell you what the rule is. At present, no. The rule says you don't get to ask the questions. And so you have to propose questions for the judges to ask. I think it will be most understandable if I go through the boilerplate and, in effect, talk you through the impanelment of a jury.

I'm going to impanel a jury in a criminal case, in which a man by the name of Fred Cardozo is a charged felon in possession of a firearm. There are other charges, but I want to tell you just how we're going to do it on a Monday morning. It's all boilerplate, and you see I can do it from memory, for whatever that's worth.

At about 20 minutes after 9:00 the jurors will come into the courtroom. They'll fill up. This has to be a 12-person jury, and the case is only going to take two or three days, so I'll probably impanel 14. The government, under the federal rules, has fewer peremptories than the defense, and they're set by rule. In state criminal cases, the government and the defense have exactly the same number of peremptory challenges.

The jurors are all there in the background. I'm either on the bench or not. And now we start:

> Good morning, ladies and gentlemen, my name is Bill Young. I'm the judge who is charged with presiding over this session of the United States District Court. What we're going to do here this morning is something that is absolutely vital in the trial of the case for which you have been called as prospective jurors. We're going to pick from among your larger number the particular jurors who will sit on this particular case.
>
> Now, ladies and gentlemen, let me ask you this question: How many of you come from cities and towns where you have a direct town meeting? Everybody goes, usually it's to the middle school, and you vote on whether to buy another fire engine, close the town dump, raise the teachers' salaries. I see a number of you.
>
> Well, ladies and gentlemen, you people have experience in direct democracy. In my town we elect people; we elect the members of the town meeting. That's called representative democracy. And in the United States we use representative democracy more than any other country in the history of the world. Representative democracy occurs when we pick the people who will do the governing, but they govern.

> And you and I all do that. We vote for members of the town council. We vote for state representative, for governor, members of Congress, President of the United States. We pick them, but they do the governing.
>
> Not in the judicial branch of government. In the judicial branch of government the people still rule directly. Not all of the people. That's how the ancient Greeks used to do it on market day, but we can't have you all in here every day. You all have lives beyond this courtroom. But we pick from among this larger number of the people in our community the 12 persons who are going to be the jury in this specific case.
>
> And now in a moment Ms. Smith is going to put you on your oath as jurors. And we need to pick from among your number people who are just as fair and impartial as is humanly possible to be. And to do that I'm going to ask you some questions. And they won't be personal questions; but if you think your answer to these questions would be "Yes," could be "Yes," might be "Yes," I want you to raise your hand.
>
> Now, if you raise your hand, we'll make note of who raises their hand, and then when I'm done asking all the questions we'll have you all line up there at the end of the jury rail, and one by one we'll have you up here privately over here at the sidebar. The lawyers will come up, and I will ask some other questions to see whether it's appropriate that you sit as a juror in this specific case.
>
> Now, don't hesitate to raise your hand. If you are not chosen as a juror in this case, it does not mean that you're not fair or you're not fit to be a juror. It simply means that for one or another proper legal reason you will not be picked as a juror on this particular case, and we'll ask you to go back to the jury lounge, and we'll pick you on another case. We have plenty of cases.
>
> So, Ms. Smith, would you swear the venire?

"All rise." And they're all sworn.

Now, here are the questions. These were taught to me by Roger Donahue, Justice of the Superior Court. And I'm still using them on the federal court. At least as a norm these are the questions you generally get:

> Now, ladies and gentlemen, you've been called for possible jury service on a so-called criminal case. This is a case that's brought by the gov-

> ernment, and the government has made an accusation against a particular individual. The government in this case is represented by Assistant United States Attorney Richard Richardson.
>
> Mr. Richardson, would you stand? Thank you.
>
> And the government has made this accusation against a man by the name of Freddy Cardozo.
>
> Mr. Cardozo, would you please stand with your lawyers, Mr. Moscardelli and Mr. Smith? Thank you, gentlemen.

Sometimes they stand up and say, "Good morning" to the jury, but they're usually hesitant to say anything other than that, and it would be improper.

> Ladies and gentlemen, the government accuses Mr. Cardozo of being what is called in the law a felon in possession of a firearm. Mr. Cardozo has pleaded not guilty to that charge. Mr. Cardozo is innocent of that charge. He is, as he sits there before you, innocent of the charge that the government has made against him. And the factual issues that are raised by the government's charge are what we're going to try out in this case.
>
> Now, ladies and gentlemen, are any of you or is any member of your family so far as you are aware, related to or acquainted with Mr. Richardson, Mr. Moscardelli, Mr. Smith or Mr. Cardozo?
>
> Are you or is any member of your family so far as you are aware, now or ever been employed in any capacity by Mr. Richardson, by the Office of the United States Attorney, by Mr. Moscardelli, by Mr. Smith, as they are attorneys or personally, or by Mr. Cardozo?
>
> Are any of you or has any member of your family so far as you are aware ever been involved in any litigation, whether it came to trial or not, any litigation, either as a witness or as a participant, that involved any of these people who are lawyers, in their capacity as lawyers or personally, or that involved Mr. Richardson, the Office of the United States Attorney, Mr. Moscardelli, Mr. Smith or Mr. Cardozo?
>
> Let me read to you the people who may be called as witnesses in this case. I don't say they will all be called, but the people who may be called, I wanted a list from everyone of everyone who may be called.

And I then read the list. I like addresses, but they don't always give them to you. You don't divide between prosecution and defense, plaintiff and defendant. It's improper to do so. You just read the whole list.

> Do you know any of those people? Are you related or acquainted with them? In this case it may be that a number of people who will testify are police officers. Are you or is any member of your immediate family, by "immediate family," I mean mother, father, brothers, sisters, son or daughter, are you now or have you ever been employed by any law enforcement agency, local or state, state troopers, Department of Corrections, federal, FBI, the Drug Enforcement Administration, the Office of the United States Attorney? Thank you.
>
> Have any of you heard, read or seen anything at all concerning this case? I don't suggest that you would, but maybe you have. Thank you.
>
> Though you may not have read, heard or seen anything about this case, do any of you have any opinion about this case, any opinion at all based upon what I've told you so far, concerning whether Mr. Cardozo is either not guilty or guilty of the charge against him?
>
> Have any of you discussed this case with anyone? Has there been any discussion in the jury pool as you waited to come down here this morning about this case or anyone involved in this case?
>
> Do any of you have any interest in the outcome of this case? By "interest in the outcome of this case," I don't mean a natural curiosity about what the evidence may show. I mean do you stand to gain or lose anything depending upon how this case comes out?
>
> Are any of you sensible of any bias or prejudice with respect to the case about to be tried? When I say "are you sensible of any," I mean are you aware of any.
>
> Do any of you know any reason why you do not stand indifferent in this case? By "stand indifferent," I'm trying to search out any feelings that you have about this case, about anyone I introduced to you, about the criminal justice system. Is there anything I should know going in here? Thank you.
>
> Ladies and gentlemen, this case is going to take about two or three days to try. I'm not going to sit on Wednesday, so if we get going today, and

> we will, this case will probably be in your hands Thursday or Friday of this week. We sit in this session of the court from 9:00 to 1:00. I'll let you out each day at 1 o'clock. When the case comes to you, no one is going to be kept in the evening, but I expect you to be ready to sit here until 5 o'clock in the afternoon. We will not sit in the evening. We will not sit on weekends.
>
> Is there any reason why any of you ought not sit as jurors in this case? Now, be thinking of the comments you have on that because I'm going to ask you for your comments, but I want to talk through the whole procedure first.

Then I take the ones that have raised their hands. They line up at the jury rail. One by one they come up, and the lawyers gather round, and I ask other questions. Let's take that police question in the criminal cases because that happens frequently. I follow up in this fashion:

"You answered yes. And who?"

"My uncle."

"Though I didn't ask for uncles; I asked mother, father."

"My uncle is an officer in the Taunton Police."

"Well, let me ask you this: From that background, does that mean that you tend to favor law enforcement testimony just because it comes from a police witness? Does it make you skeptical or hostile to law enforcement testimony just because it comes from a law enforcement witness? Do you truly"—looking them in the eye—"do you truly think that you can be fair and impartial, fair both to the government and to Mr. Cardozo? Thank you. You may stay."

Now, let's say I've gotten appropriate answers to that. When does the lawyer exercise the challenge for cause? We have to think through the practicalities here. You don't want to make a challenge for cause in the hearing of the juror you want to knock off because you may lose and the juror will sit there. So what you have to do with a judge who is operating the way I am explaining it, is you have to wait for that juror to step back. Because we're rolling right along in the courtroom, the next juror is on her way up, but you have to say, "Judge, can I be heard?"

So the next juror has to hold. "Yes. What's the matter with this juror?" And then you have to make your challenge for cause. There's no magic in the procedure as I use it, but you must know what the procedure is so you'll know when to do what you have to do.

With me that's the time. When the juror that I have already said, "You may stay" has started back to go sit down, you want to challenge that juror. You have a right to challenge that juror. So get it on the record, your challenge to the juror. And then, at least the way I work it, I can excuse the juror without any embarrassment to the juror, because my clerk, who is also listening, just takes that card out; we just never call that juror. The juror doesn't know, but he's never going to be called on the jury.

"Okay. I find this panel indifferent. Proceed, Madam Clerk."

The clerk puts 12 people in the box. Now, you ought to be prepared for this. You should diagram that jury box.

"Juror number 16—though with us the numbers don't matter that much because we randomize them—Theresa McDonald, seat number 6 in the second row, six seats in, ma'am." And so on and so on and so on until the box is filled.

Then you've got 12 people. You know who's coming, and you have X number of challenges. Again, just taking it step by step, I immediately say, "Counsel"—well, you may not have enough time then. You have to then say, and I make you do it in front of the jury:

"Could I have a minute, your Honor?"

"Of course you may."

I go over and stand at the sidebar. The clerk comes over, court reporter comes over, and we're all ready. We're waiting for you. One side or another, they may get ready, and they may jump right up and come over. Now, if they do that, I don't want it to appear that I'm engaging in anything ex parte, so I'll then step back and wait. Sometimes I've waited too long and I'll say, "Counsel"—and then, "Another moment."

Now, you may want to consult with your client. And an issue not resolved, state or federal, is whether the client has the right to be there. In lots of places in the country they say it's a violation of the client's rights to do the sidebar conference on impanelment without the client; but, of course, the client may be, theoretically, very dangerous, and the judge thinks that he's bent over backwards even letting the client sit at the counsel table. Does he want the client right up there at the sidebar? Think about that. There are cases on this, though not in Massachusetts, state or federal.

The lawyers come up, and I start with the government. "How many challenges?" The government then makes their peremptory challenges. Again, we are just following the way I do it; you can see some variations. One variation is once the government has challenged, without saying that the people have been challenged by the government, you let the jurors off and you fill the box again. Then the defense gets to challenge the whole 12. There are no appellate decisions on this. I had Tom Burns once tell me that I couldn't do it my way. I do it my way. No one has ever taken me up on it.

I make the defense challenge right then, and so they may only be looking at nine. There are no back-strikes; in other words, you can't go back and challenge someone else who has already been passed over. Let's say the government challenges three and the defense challenges one, and that means out of my 12 I already have eight because four challenges have been made. Then Ms. Smith, my courtroom deputy, just lets the four people step down. The eight remain and you can't go back and challenge them.

I've forgotten one other thing that I do, which I submit is helpful. At the time I have filled the box but before any challenges, I say, "I have one more question for you folks: Would you tell us—you don't have to stand up or introduce yourself—just tell us where you work, what you do, and if you are married where your spouse works and what he or she does." And the people do. I like it. I think you should like it because it lets you hear the jury. It lets you hear their accent, it lets you hear if they can even talk, and it lets you hear if they are listening to what I do. They also are sometimes much more specific about what they do. If they just say, "I work for Digital," I will say, "Doing what?" Or if they say, "I'm a computer programmer," I say, "For whom?" If they say, "Unemployed," I say, "When did you last work?" So that's a little more information for you.

Now we've already had the first round. We fill the four seats that are vacant. I ask the same question. Back to the sidebar. And on the second round, in order to be fair, I ask the defense lawyer to go first. Once the peremptories are exhausted, then I have my jury, and we're ready to go.

And it's a place to stop. I want comments on that. Does that seem unfair to you? Would you rather ask those questions yourself? What other questions do you want to ask? Is that slanted for the prosecution or for the defense? If you want to talk about that, we should.

Here are the issues, and here is the breakdown: There are strong voices on the bar that say that lawyers should be asking the questions; that lawyers should have, at least after we've asked the questions, an opportunity to ask questions. The plaintiffs' bar in Massachusetts, Fred Halstrom is leading the charge on this, had bills before the legislature to require that the judges in the state allow counsel some time to talk to the jury directly.

The judges on the superior court unanimously opposed it, especially Chief Justice Steadman. The argument against it was that the system is already overburdened, and it would take too much time.

Now in the federal court again the Judicial Conference is now holding hearings on a rule change that would allow, subject to our discretion, lawyers, both civil and criminal, to conduct the voir dire because that's how it's done in the south and in the west.

How does our court break down on it? Those who speak to the issue are almost, but not entirely, unanimously against it. The best proponent against it is Judge Woodlock, who makes not the time argument—the rest of us make the time argument, and that may be shallow—but Woodlock makes a brilliant argument that jury service is a community event and lawyers' divisive questioning will diminish the community nature of that event. The lawyers' questions have an agenda, and of course they should, but I'm giving you the judge's point of view now, and the agenda is you wouldn't be a good juror because you think this or you couldn't be fair or you wouldn't award enough money or you lean toward the government or toward the defense. And that's divisive. It challenges the people.

The dissent in our court is led by Judge Gertner, and Judge Gertner is equally brilliant, and is writing law review articles on it. She argues that we are moving in the direction of cutting off peremptory challenges. Peremptory challenges are, by their very nature, made on stereotypes, aren't they? You don't know much about these people, so you're knocking them off based upon your stereotypical view of what the person is like.

And let me face right up to that and tell you what the commentators say about this. I really have two commentators to share with you. One is Professor Jeans, who writes one of the best books on trial advocacy and is a frequent contributor to the ABA journal, *Litigation*. Sadly, not too many people use Jeans' book. And the reason we don't use it is it's not politically correct; it's sexist. But Jeans, for whatever reason, is honest. Here are some of the things that Jeans, who has a chapter on jury selection, says: He says if you represent a defendant in a criminal case, you do not want postal workers on your jury because they have the best retirement system of any government worker; and, by the fact that they've been employed by the postal service, they have died and gone to heaven; and the government is the source of all their beneficence; so they favor the government.

He also says—and notice the thin ground I'm on, but I'll tell you what he says—he says if you represent a defendant, you don't want Lutherans. I don't say that, I am quick to say. How do I know? He writes out there where Garrison Keillor writes *(Lake Wobegon Days)*, and I guess it's more Lutheran. And why does he say that? He says Lutherans are part of an authoritarian church. Well, I would say, and I say it with utmost respect, that I thought that the Roman Catholic church was authoritarian, you know, from the top down and ex cathedra and things like that, but I guess there are a lot of back-sliders, and he's not so worried; but Lutherans, he says, they're authoritarian.

Well, okay. If I know you're challenging someone because they're Lutheran or Catholic, you can't do it. If I think you're challenging them because of their religion, make no doubt about it, they're authorized to sit regardless of their religion.

Now something that Gerry Spence said—we all know Spence; he's a commentator. He has written on jury selection in the Imelda Marcos case. And, now, remember he defended Imelda Marcos, who had 5,000 pairs of shoes and the like, for defrauding the Philippine government, and he won. He's very good. He said, "I wanted people who were obese." Why? Because they don't have self-control and they might be sympathetic to someone who just bought lots of shoes. I don't know, but that's not a protected category. *(Laughter)*. And if that's how they're struck, that's okay.

Now, here's what you can't do: I mean this is where the law is; let's be clear. You can't strike people because of gender, race, ethnic background, heritage or religion. If there's any doubt about that, civil or criminal, let me put it to rest. Judges think you can't do that.

Of course, the big rub is how do we know? How do we know that's what you're doing? Except for race and gender, which we can observe, the truth is we don't know. If you're striking someone because the last letter in their name begins with a vowel, and, therefore, they must be Italian and it's a Mafia case or something—well, that's pretty silly in today's world, where people take the names of their husbands or they don't take the names of their husbands and where that really doesn't mean anything.

Does there have to be a pattern? With respect to minorities, not much of one. If there is only one black person in the jury and you want to strike that person, I want to know why. I won't wait. I want to know why. That's enough of a pattern. I've got support for that. ***Batson v. Kentucky***, 476 U.S. 79 (1986). So I come over to the sidebar, and I say, "Why did you strike that person?"

I'll give you an actual case. This is a sex discrimination case. We picked the jury, just as we've talked about. And there is one black person on the jury. Plaintiff's lawyer, representing the woman who claims sex discrimination, strikes that black man. We come to the sidebar.

"Counselor, I observed that the juror that you've just struck is black and there are no other black jurors in the venire. Why did you strike him?"

"Oh, judge, judge, I didn't know—oh, is he black? I didn't know that he was black. No, no, look, judge, honest. This is a sex discrimination case. I struck him because he was a man. I want women on this jury."

"That's not a proper reason. He is seated."

So think of what you're doing. You know, he's out of the frying pan, into the fire. He can't strike him because he's a man. That's improper.

Okay. We have our jury. Now, the case starts. Interaction is now with the jury. Again, I'm slopping over on judge stuff, but we might take care of this. What's the next thing that happens in the case? We're going to focus now on the jury, the factfinders in your case. What's the next thing that happens in the case?

Pretrial Charge and Jury Issues

Now, for a majority of judges the next thing that happens is in the state system the indictment may be read and the historic words uttered. The judge may say a few words, and then we move to the opening.

Pretrial Charge

But in a minority of cases judges give a pretrial charge. In other words, the next thing they do is stand up and explain the case to the jury, at least legally. And they do that before you've had a chance to make your opening.

Now that, of course, all the studies show is a powerful moment in the case. You don't want to lose your case in the judge's pretrial charge. That charge is, if anything, more important than the charge that the judge gives at the end of the case.

If you've got a judge who works that way, you want to influence that pretrial charge. How do you influence it? You influence it by getting to the final pretrial conference, and you submit your requests to instruct. Now, remember, the pretrial charge won't be as detailed, it only reviews the key elements—what the plaintiff's got to prove, what the affirmative defenses are. You want to get that judge to give your language because that's the first thing out of the box.

Juror Note Taking

Second point: A minority of judges, but an increasing minority of judges, now let jurors take notes. There's not much you can do to influence that or have that help you, but I think it's a good practice, and more judges are doing it. Be aware that you may be dealing with jurors who are taking notes on your presentation.

Juror Questions

A very small minority of judges allows the jurors to ask questions. That is a practice that is frowned on, both federal and state. The federal cases are ***United States v. Sutton***, 970 F.2d 1001 (1st Cir. 1992), and ***United States v. Cassiere***, 4 F.3d 1006 (1st Cir. 1993). The state cite is ***Commonwealth v. Urena***, 417 Mass. 692, 632 N.E.2d 1200 (1994). But it is not impermissible, and some judges do it.

If you have a judge who will let the jury ask questions, at a minimum you want the following safeguards: First, questions should be in writing. Second, you ought to get to see them before the judge asks them. Third, you ought to make sure that, in a criminal case, the judge is going to have a policy about a juror asking a question of a defendant who chooses to testify. That question is going to be very important to that juror, and if a question gets asked of a defendant and the juror doesn't particularly like that defendant's answer, one can imagine that that will be difficult for that defendant.

I know about this because I am one of the judges who do it despite the frowning on it. I think it empowers the jury and it's a good idea, but I will tell you I think it's much too risky to let anyone ask a defendant a question. Though I don't tell the jury this, I just never let them question the defendant. I just put the questions, if there are questions, out on the clerk's bench, and the lawyers can see them.

Other Jury Issues

Some other things that are done: I learned this from Judge Bailey Aldrich. In the session where I sit, and other judges do this, we rise for the jury coming in and out. I love that. It demonstrates respect for the jury. That's how it should be for jurors, not for a judge. Fine, you can rise when I come in and out, but always, as we say to each other, "Remember that they're not rising for you, they're rising for the system of which you, Judge X, happen to be a part." It's just nice to have them "all rise for the jury." That's what my clerk says.

Judges have a variety of ways of dealing with the jury. I'll give you an example. I think it is a good one. Many judges remind the jury not to discuss the case among themselves nor with anyone else. That's a good thing. Many judges, even when they're deliberating, will bring the jury back at the end of the day and give them specific instructions not to talk about the case and the like. That's important to you and you want to be there.

Don't ever leave the courthouse when the jury is deliberating because if they bring the jury back to have a question answered, one, if you're not there, the judge need not consult you about the answer to the question. Two, you are not serving your client if you don't wait around for when the jury comes back. Don't wait just to come back when they give their verdict. If they are brought back into the courtroom for any reason, you want to be there.

Now, what about interaction with juries? Some vital points on your interaction: I submit to you that when you rise, whether you're rising for the jury or not, whether the judge does that or not, you might stand and face the jury. That's direct democracy. They're the ones who are going to decide your case. Make eye contact with them as frequently as you can. And you stand out of respect for their position in the system. You're not going to be disrespecting the judge if you're at an angle to the judge, but look at that jury come into the box. They are the ones who are going to decide.

When you put exhibits in evidence never, ever put an exhibit in evidence unless in some fashion you display it to the jury. You may make a copy and throw it up on an overhead projector, if it's, for instance, a weapon or something. I'll share with you some rules we have. In Massachusetts all the exhibits go to the jury room. If you have a national practice, don't think that that's general. In Chicago they only send the exhibits to the jury room that you agree upon. That boggles the mind. Why are they in evidence? Of course they should be sent. In Brooklyn they don't send them to the jury room, whatever you agree, unless the jury asks for them. What are we doing?

But in Massachusetts, state and federal, all the exhibits go to the jury room with these exceptions: Never send a gun and the ammunition to the jury room. Remember that plane crash case, where the nose of the plane broke off at the end of the runway and two people drowned? They were in the front seat, and they fell into the water and drowned. That case was ***World Airways***, tried before Judge Keeton. It was a difficult case. The lawyers didn't like each other. We were hearing stories about that case.

Twice—whether the lawyers know this or not; I guess they do; it was a big story in the courtroom—twice the marshals had to go into the jury room because the jurors were in fisticuffs. Once they were throwing chairs against the wall. The marshals went in and separated them, "oh, calm down, calm down." And then they went on with their deliberations.

So never send a gun and a bullet. Never send drugs to the jury room. If they want to see the drugs, they can sit in the box and you can watch them pass the drugs.

Now, I'm talking about throwing it up on overhead projectors, holding it in front of the jury or asking that it be published, passed to the jury. My position, after 18 years of doing this, is that you let the jurors touch the stuff, the verisimilitude of the actual case. Let them be part of it. Empower the jury. They are, after all, the ones that are going to decide your case.

Time for the break. After the break, judges; we're going to start with questions or comments from you after the break, and then we'll do judges until 1 o'clock. We'll recess for one half hour. *(Recess taken)*.

Let's start up again. I want to start with the questions I got during the break and throw them out for comments because we are covering everything. Two comments; one about jury selection and another about interactions with juries, and I think I should have mentioned them, and I want your comments.

First, what is the better practice with respect to exercising peremptory challenges? Someone asked me to speak to that directly, and I'm happy to. The better practice has got to be that peremptories should be exercised out of the hearing of the juror who is being challenged. If you're running a risk that that peremptory will be refused, for whatever reason or other, you would be very hesitant to exercise it in the hearing of the jury. How fair would it be to have the defendant exercising all of his peremptories and the Commonwealth saying, "We're content, oh, we're content," like the defendant is so guilty that it must be clear and so they will take any juror. But the poor defendant always has to say, "I challenge juror 3, I challenge juror 5."

Also, you'd be surprised at how quickly people make friends. They may not have talked about your case, but they've waited since 8 o'clock in the morning, as we've been kicking around here, and they're meeting new people and making friends. And if the person you think is the nicest person you've met all morning is suddenly knocked off the jury, you may look askance at the person who knocked him off.

So the absolute best practice is to do the peremptory challenges at the sidebar or in some fashion out of the hearing of the jury.

Taking a View

The other observation is that taking a view is something that is done frequently in state practice and less frequently in federal. In Harr's book, *A Civil Action*, they did it, of course, in the Woburn case. I am very much in favor of taking views. You get the jury out of the courtroom. You take them somewhere where something happened. We won't in this session go over the specific practice of taking a view, but that's a way to interact with the jury and show that you're forthcoming.

AUDIENCE MEMBER: Is a view evidence or is it more like a chalk? I've heard that debated a few times.

JUDGE YOUNG: Very good point. In my opinion, the views, the perceptions of the jury, are evidence. A chalk or a diagram is to help you understand the testimony of the witnesses. A view partakes of that

> same characteristic. For example, a witness says that he stood here and saw this, but the juror who has been actually out on that street cannot believe that the witness could have distinguished a facial expression at that distance. That's evidence, and the juror can rely on it.

The appropriate procedure, of course, is not for the litigants to say that during a view but only to say things like this: "Now, ladies and gentlemen, would you stand here, and I ask you to look at this intersection. Please look at the curb cut here. Look down the street there to about that third telephone pole. Note that distance, would you just note that distance." And you're marking things, and the jurors will just look. No one makes arguments at a view.

The judge should always go. I know some judges don't, but the judge should always go. A stenographer should go, though frequently that doesn't happen, and a record should be made of everything said at the view. That's the better practice.

Choosing the Foreperson

I want to say something about choosing the foreperson. I can do it very quickly, but I think this makes a difference because the foreperson has something to do with the deliberations, and then I want to talk about how a jury deliberates. I was asked that.

There are three ways to choose a foreperson: One way, which is followed by Hiller Zobel in the state court, and other judges, is to let the jury elect the foreperson. Judge Keeton in the federal district court allows the jury to elect the foreperson. Second way: the person who sits in the foreperson's seat is the foreperson. That's the front row, first seat closest to the bench. That's the foreperson's seat. Judge Harrington in the federal district court chooses the person in the foreperson's seat. Third way: the judge selects the foreperson.

My view is I don't go for electing the foreperson. The jury may never get beyond that issue, and statistics show that there are more hung juries for judges who do that. You don't want a hung jury. I don't do that. For whomever sits in the foreperson's seat, I will not replace a minority with a nonminority. I will not replace a woman with a man. If a woman by chance sits in the foreperson's seat, I'll look over—this may be sexist, but I do it—I look over my array of women. I'll replace a woman with a woman, but I won't replace a woman with a man. I think it's wrong, because physically they have to change seats.

Other than that, I'm a judge who picks the foreperson. What am I looking for? Well, I look for a good discussion facilitator, someone who I think is good with people. This has nothing to do with education. It certainly has nothing to do with affluence. A receptionist, a shop foreman, a teacher and a housewife, if I think that she may have dealt with children, are all good discussion facilitators. That's what I want, a good discussion facilitator.

The Jury's Verdict

How do juries decide the verdict? Of course I don't know, but I'm a great fan of juries, and I've done a lot of reading on it, and I'll share with you my views. I think juries make up a story. I think juries try to harmonize the testimony into an understandable story. All the sociological studies show that. So I'm on fairly solid ground when I say that's what they try to do.

I know that the plaintiffs' trial bar says that you win your case or you lose your case on opening statement. The studies don't bear that out, but it certainly reinforces that you have to get your story before the jury early on so that they, of course, can test what they're hearing against the story that they've first been presented with.

I've been privileged to teach *Trial Practice* for a number of years, and I'll give you the basis for these next observations. Always in teaching *Trial Practice* we videotape the jury deliberations. The juries are not real juries. They come from retirement homes; they are the students' friends; they are not a fair cross section of the community. But I am struck with how diligent juries are after only a couple of hours at a mock trial. If the judge, if she plays it serious, gets into roles, and I'm talking fake cases, moot court cases, the juries go out, and they try to decide the cases, and here's what you learn from that:

First, juries may not think important what you think is important, and they may think other things are vitally important. For those of you who have taken Trial Practice or teach it, there's a case where the question is death by suicide or death by accident. It's the *Dixon v. Providential Life Insurance Company* case. Yeah, people smile. They've all done the *Dixon* case. I tried the *Dixon* case once with a student jury. And we had on our jury someone who had a close relative who committed suicide. That juror thought that she knew all about suicide because of that. The issues in *Dixon v. Providential* were whether there was a suicide note and should there be one and can there be a suicide without a suicide note? I don't know, but, you see, that woman was passionate about that.

Now, could you have discovered that in voir dire? Perhaps you should have, but in that jury room that juror played a very big role.

Now, what juries do, they try to make sense. They try to follow the judge's instructions, but they may not understand them. Typically, judge's instructions I think are poorly framed and poorly understood, though Massachusetts, again, I think is the leader in this area. But despite this, the jury will try desperately to do justice. They will try to follow the judge's instructions.

I'm going to tell you something about judges and juries. I think written evidence is more powerful than oral. If you have a contemporaneous written document, jurors look at that and so do judges. We like to see what was said at the time. Unless there's some question about whether it's authentic, that's what actually happened. Jurors look at that. Jurors tend not to compromise, though I won't deny that that happens.

After a lot of circling they then come down to answering the questions on the verdict slip, so those questions are crucial. Judges divide on those questions. Some judges favor general verdicts. That is, they'll only ask you do we find for the plaintiff, and, if so, how much, or do we find for the defendant? In criminal cases, except in racketeering cases, general verdicts are the requirement.

Other judges on civil cases, where they're not required to have general verdicts, go for detailed questions. State Judge Zobel is an example. Federal Judge Keeton is an example. And you get maybe page after page of questions to answer yes or no. If your answer is yes, go on to question such and such; if your answer is no, skip to question such and such.

But judges who favor that approach believe that that's just because it guides the jury to the proper questions to be decided. The judges who favor the other approach, the general verdict approach—I am one; Judge Mazzone is one; Judge Steadman on the state court is another—believe in that court of rough justice of letting the jury have all the issues before them and then come to the bottom line. For instance, on contributory negligence, are you going to tell the jury what the effect of contributory negligence is? I believe yes. Some judges believe no. The law itself is changed on that, but in a negligence case I just give them a bottom line: we find for the plaintiff and how much, or we find for the defendant. I tell them that if the defendant was more negligent than the plaintiff was, then their verdict is for the defendant; but if the defendant was 49 percent negligent and the plaintiff was 51, the verdict is 51 percent of what the total compensatory damages are. I think jurors can understand that, and so do the people who agree with me.

Other judges say no, no, no, let them find $100,000, and then you can figure it out. Let them find the percentage of negligence, and then of course you can calculate the appropriate damage, and that's more just.

The point I'm making in talking about how jurors deliberate is that the most important thing in the jury room is the verdict slip. That's where I want to end, on that. That verdict slip is the most important thing in the jury room. All too often lawyers don't pay enough attention to it. If you want to guide the pretrial conference in any case, as early as the pretrial conference say, "Your Honor, what will the verdict slip look like in this case?" Nothing so crystallizes the mind than to figure out what it is we're going to ask the jury.

Now, comments, before I get off juries and all of this stuff and other things you want to talk about.

AUDIENCE MEMBER: What do you do when you run into a judge like yourself who doesn't want to departmentalize the verdict slip?

JUDGE YOUNG: The best argument with those judges it seems to me is to argue legally why the issues should be broken out to have an adequate record on appeal. Again speaking personally, I think you should get an adequate record on appeal. I think that is an aspect of good judging, and, therefore, if you pitched an argument to a judge like this, "Judge, that prevents me from getting my rights as to the law. This is an interesting issue, a new issue, so at least break this out," I think you can sort of push a judge that way.

AUDIENCE MEMBER: I have observed a lot of mock trials, and it seems to me a common problem juries have is proximate cause. They seem to do well with negligence per se, and the other end of damages, but they have trouble with proximate cause. I think a lot has to do with the charge.

JUDGE YOUNG: I agree completely. I think the language that we use is poor. The language that I use is result within the foreseeable risk. I like to use names, so we'll say Smith is the plaintiff, Jones is the defendant. As I remember my charge on proximate cause, it goes something like this:

"Now, even if you find that Mr. Smith was negligent, then you have to ask whether that negligence was the proximate cause of the injury to Mr. Jones. Each time someone is negligent that creates a risk of something happening. And what you want to ask yourselves is whether what happened here was within the scope of the reasonably foreseeable risk caused by the act or the failure to act that you've already found was negligent. If that result was within the scope of the reasonably foreseeable risk, then you may say it was proximately caused by that negligence. But if it was not, even though there's negligence, there's no proximate cause, and you can stop your analysis at that point."

Maybe in an actual charge I would do slightly better. Maybe you don't like that. I think we do poorly on charges generally.

Some other things quickly just from that example. Notice I am standing. I was taught that as a superior court judge. Many of the judges stand. I think that's good. All too frequently judges will sit and they will read the charge. They're reading the charge like the Mass in Latin. They're reading the charge so they're sure they've got it right for the appellate court. They misconceive what their role is as judges, and let's get right to it.

JUDGES

The judge's role in society today is a teacher. That's what we all are. If we all understood it, we would do better. As judges, we are teachers of the law, not the facts.

The superior court has a magnificent tradition of standing up and charging. Some judges will come right down off the bench and stand before the jury. Some judges will draw on the blackboard to show the relationships, especially in damages. They will actually make their presentation down in the well of the court.

The spectrum then runs to the judge who sits there, looks down, makes no eye contact because it's not required and we'll never know on appeal, and reads to the jury about proximate cause and then reads about damages and the like.

We should be looking toward getting our judges to understand that charging the jury is teaching them on a vital point. Just to make a point, one of the things you can get through MCLE, and of course you should, is the ***Model Jury Instructions for Use in the District Court***. Now, those are the jury instructions the district court has adopted. If you practice in the state district court, you should get them. It's vital to you. You should know before trial.

The superior court has them too. They don't publish them. You ought to be breaking down their doors getting them to publish them. They've got them. They're all on disk. There's no reason why the public charges used by the public judges should not be public. And the same, of course, is true for the federal court. We don't even have a charge book.

I'm going off on charges. At least five, I think six, out of our judges have computer-assisted transcription, and some of them take the computer-assisted transcription and they have them in a database. If you want to know what the judge before whom you appear charges, what that judge thinks the law is, go to that judge's court reporter and find out. Get a charge like your case and find out what your judge thinks the law is.

To end up on this thought, because I was going to do this down the stream, judges enormously respect their colleagues, and this is true state and federal. We may differ on philosophy. We may differ on approaches to the law. But the judges who stand in the same shoes that we do, who put up with the same problems, who face the same type of litigants and docket, that's as persuasive as anything you can give us. And I say that with absolute sincerity.

One of the things that I think law school does not adequately prepare lawyers for is that all law is not equal. Law schools all run magnificent, and they are magnificent, moot court competitions to enable fledgling lawyers to argue the law. And the moot court competitions are all set in some mythical jurisdiction, like Ames or Grimes. That's the moot court. That's to make it even and so you can argue the policy; but it has an agenda, and the agenda is wrong. People come out of law school and they think all law is equal. Wrong.

A judge works for the courts in the hierarchy above that judge; that is, a state judge works for the Supreme Court of the United States, the Supreme Judicial Court, and the Appeals Court. A federal judge works for the Supreme Court of the United States and, in this circuit, the First Circuit; and if you've got an ***Erie*** question and state law supplies the rule of decision, the Supreme Judicial Court and the

Appeals Court. We know it, and we try to follow it, but it does not mean that your wonderful case on all fours with this case, the exact case out of the District Court of North Dakota, amounts to a hill of beans. I have heard a judge say, and he will be nameless, but I give it to you verbatim, "Ninth Circuit. Ha, ha, that's presumptively wrong." *(Laughter)*.

All law is not equal, and in talking about stare decisis now, I took an oath and my colleagues took oaths. We deeply try to follow our oaths. But I have just now named for you the courts for which I work. I don't work for the D.C. Circuit. I don't work for some other respected supreme court in some other state. Their law may be persuasive but it is not controlling.

I add to that this: Trial judges by their very nature work alone. We're out there all alone each day. We are truly fascinated and impressed by the work of our colleagues. That has nothing to do with seniority. I warmed to this when I was first on the bench. Now I'm an old guy, and I hope we're doing it with the people who come on board, but as soon as you are a judge, appointed by the governor, confirmed by the council, appointed by the president, or confirmed by the senate, you are a judge of that court equal with any other judge. And your sense of justice, your understanding of the commitment and the professionalism of the job, is equal to any judge no matter how old or how senior.

If state law supplies the rule of decision anywhere, we ll try to follow the state law. And I'll tell you—I'll make a little pitch for them—Massachusetts has the *Massachusetts Law Reporter* that reports the superior court cases now. You'd be wise to get it. You'd be wise to cite it. Other superior court judges and federal trial judges are going to be pretty impressed by it. Oh, I know in the federal court we're not bound by it. We're only bound by the state high court in an *Erie* problem, but we'll look at it because those judges walk in our shoes.

Every judge knows that it's at least a year and a half before something gets up on appeal—at least a year and a half. All the good questions are in the trial courts. They're out there now. And I want to know what my colleagues are doing. I want to know how they charge. I want to know how they rule on evidence. I want to know how they do the job that I do because nothing will impress me more, literally nothing, except of course, I guess, a case on all fours by a court that controls me. That controls me, and I know it, and I will follow it.

Before I generalize, though, one other thought on this. When I'm talking *stare decisis*, and it's something that you ought to keep in mind about appellate courts, I have a little line that I use frequently, and I'll use it now. There's something more profound behind it.

I heard a lawyer say this, and I've always remembered it: "We all know appellate courts. Them are the courts from down out the hills, when all the fightin's over, and all the dust drifted away, and then them appellate courts in the cool, clear reflective light of dawn, they shoot the wounded." *(Laughter)*.

Now, when I use that line in *Trial Practice*, that's to get your attention about how not to be wounded at the trial level. But, and let's be candid about it, there is a little bit of distance between us and an appellate court. I mean hierarchical distance. It's really a pyramidal structure. I have taken an oath to follow what they say.

I brought with me Frank Coffin's book, *The Ways of a Judge*, and he tells how as a judge of the First Circuit he decides cases and how that court decides cases. I want to cite that to you. It's worth your while. He's a magnificent appellate judge. (I also cite to you a book called *Judges Making Law*, which Chief Justice Hennessey wrote after he retired. That too is a magnificent book about how appellate courts decide.) One of the things Frank Coffin said was, "Of course time is different for an appellate court. An evidentiary ruling that took 10 seconds in the trial court takes two months in the appellate court while they wrestle out what they should do." Because of that we judges are bound to follow what appellate courts do; but let's be clear on this, the mystique among trial judges is the appellate judges don't have the particularly stressful burdens that we have. And that leads us sometimes to pay too short shrift to what an appellate court is doing.

If an appellate decision is on point and controls us, you want to be sure that you control us. And a couple words about how to do it: Quote them; don't just cite them; quote them. Make the quotes work for you; that is, change the names. Don't say "appellant" and "appellee." Follow proper *Bluebook* form. Say "Smith," in brackets, and "Jones," in brackets, so it applies to your case. Use ellipses—dot, dot, dot. I mean don't dot, dot, dot out the "not." We will never forget, and we will never forgive, and we will broadcast it to all our colleagues. We will talk about it over lunch. Don't ever do that.

But since you want to control us, you drop out a subjunctive phrase that has nothing to do with your case, and make it punchy. If you think this is the holding of the case, get that holding right out there.

One last thing, and I am now citing a case called *United States v. Houlihan*, 587 F. Supp. 352, 365 n.26 (1995), is what I call the fairness flaw. Just because you have an appellate decision where conduct that you want was upheld by an appellate court, don't think you're home free, because you're not. It inheres in the difference between appellate courts and trial courts.

Those of us who are privileged to sit as trial judges and justices are bound by our oath to be as fair and as just as is humanly possible. We fail, and it's inevitable in a system that reaches out for the impossible, but we each day go out onto the bench and try and reach out for the fairest possible result. George Hayer, my colleague on the superior court, used to say, "It's all fairness." And Hayer had a truly photographic memory. Hayer, to prepare himself to be a justice, read the *Massachusetts Reports*. This is true. But he says, "It's all fairness."

So when you come up to a trial judge with an appellate court decision that says this is perfectly appropriate, judge, you can let in this evidence. An appellate court has said it, and you've accurately cited it. The trial judge is going to look at the case and is going to say, "Remember, appellate judges have to ask themselves something that is less fun than what we do, and 'fun' is a good professional word. They must ask themselves, looking at a trial record: Is this good enough?" That's what they do. Is this good enough? Are we going to let this conviction, are we going to let this verdict stand? Remember that they don't try all the cases de novo. Whatever some trial judges may think, they don't try them de novo. They say, "Is this good enough? Will we let this stand?"

And the fact that they've let something stand doesn't mean that it's the way to go. It doesn't mean that it's the most just way to deal with the problem. So you've got a case, and it works perfectly. The judge has let in evidence X, and the appellate court opposed it. Look at the specific language of the case because the trial judge is going to be saying, "Are they telling me I have to do it?" If they're telling me I have to do it, I will do it, no questions asked. I am bound; indeed in a jurisprudential sense, I'm bound to get in their beds.

That was another great wake-up when I first went on the bench, in addition to figuring out whether someone's telling the truth or not. I read cases entirely differently, and many of my colleagues have told me the same thing. As a trial lawyer, I read the controlling law as, I dare say, most of you do. You keep up with the law. You keep up with your professional reading. You know that the Supreme Judicial Court, the First Circuit, or the Supreme Court has come down with this or that case in your area of the law. And you say, "This helps me," "This hurts me," "Gee, we're going to have to get around that this way."

The first or second day on the job a judge reads that same case and says to himself, "Mother of God, what did they mean? What am I supposed to tell a jury?" It enriches your approach to the law, and you should try to read cases the same way—not whether it helps or hurts your client, but look at what they are trying to teach. Think of them as teachers. What are they trying to teach? You get some plurality decision of the Supreme Court, and they're all over the lot. What do they have in mind here?

Now, let's talk about judges. I was asked during the break how they decide, so let me put that right up front. And in talking about judges let's consider, as we did with juries, who they are. I want to talk about judicial bias, and I want to be absolutely direct about it. Who are the judges you're going to be before?

Well, first of all, most of them are men. I have enormous respect for Governor Weld in the number of women he has appointed to the bench, but we'll deal with reality. Most of them are going to be men. Most of them are white. The vast majority of judges are white. To a certain extent it's a reflection of the bar because judges come from the rank of lawyers; we don't appoint nonlawyers to be judges. Most of them are middle-aged. For me it's interesting, middle age is creeping upwards, but the fact is that most of them are middle-aged.

And the critical legal scholars will generalize from that fact. They generalize that judges are going to react as middle-aged white men. I'm here to tell you that while I recognize that, I disagree entirely with the political underpinnings of the critical legal studies movement. I will tell you that we try desperately, whether we are men or women, black or white, Hispanic or Chinese American, to transcend whatever our backgrounds are to do evenhanded justice. But I would be a fool to stand before you to say that we are not products of our background, because we are. How could we be anything other?

So what you've got are people who have taken an oath to transcend their background, but they are part and parcel of their background. Your function is to deal with it. In the main, I will tell you that the judges that I have known by and large transcend it. Leave me out of this, but I'm here as a fan of judges. They transcend it magnificently.

They did a study of the superior court when I was a justice of the superior court, and apparently it was a valid study, statistically based. The study explored the fear that we were sending more black defendants, in Suffolk County, to the then Suffolk prison on Deer Island, than white. And they found that there was no statistical difference. And I submit to you that that's accurate. Judges try desperately to transcend their backgrounds.

One other thing, since in Massachusetts we actually gave the federal system its system. Our constitution of 1780 set up the appointment of judges for life—a good system. We gave it to the federal courts, and so the canard is, well, who is a judge? A judge is a lawyer who knew a governor.

I also would be a fool to stand in front of you and say that politics plays no role in those people who are fortunate or privileged enough to sit as judges in the vicinage where you will practice. I will say absolutely to you that politics plays no role or a very minimal role in the conduct of the judges. One, it plays less role than you would expect in the actual selection of judges, and, two, it plays utterly a minimal role once someone's gotten to be a judge because, of course, we're appointed for life.

And judges want to be good judges; many of us are not, but we want to. No one gets on the bench saying, "I'm going to be a bad judge" or, "Now I've retired." People don't do that.

I'm going to close with something from Judge Keeton where Keeton stresses profession and commitment, and those two words are important to judges. But judges do differ, I submit to you, in a very significant way, and how a judge falls on this spectrum is very important.

After 18 years of doing it I think there is a significant difference between the substance judge and the procedure judge. It has nothing to do with political philosophy. The words "conservative" and "liberal" don't make much difference to a judge, but there is a difference between substance judges and procedure judges. Though my descriptions by necessity are going to be caricatures, they color the rest of the morning because that's the spectrum.

So let me caricature a substance judge. A substance judge believes that he or she knows what is just in a specific case. He or she knows what is just in a specific case significantly because that's been the area of practice of that particular judge. That judge, having practiced in that area, has strong feelings about how justice works out in that area, and those feelings may be translated into how he or she presides.

Substance judges are more likely to be found in courts of limited jurisdiction, as opposed to courts of general jurisdiction, for the reason that the very qualities that befitted the person for appointment to the juvenile, probate, land or housing courts are the area of practice that the judge knows all about. This is what he's been doing. And he takes with him onto the bench a view about the justice of a particular cause.

At the other end of the spectrum are the procedure judges. The procedure judge is very diffident, completely unsure that he or she knows what's justice in a particular case. He is very hesitant about any confidence about justice, but believes that the procedure is just and the procedure gives rules. Therefore, if we only would follow the procedure, the result will, by definition, be just.

No judge of my acquaintance is wholly a substance judge or entirely a procedure judge, but that's the best way to characterize it. You can tell more about a judge along that spectrum than anything else.

Let me give you an example that we can talk about. How as judges will we resolve this problem? It's a simple criminal case: Young DA, absolutely. Give this young DA the case because it's a mugging and it's a straightforward case and it's easy to prove. And the DA puts in all the evidence except he fails to get the complaining witness to identify the defendant, and he rests.

Now, under this rubric the substance judge will either ask the question himself, remind the district attorney, or the like. And the procedure judge will say, "You've rested; directed verdict of not guilty because we have no evidence of identification here."

No judge will own up to doing one or the other of those. All judges worry about it. They worry about what they should do, and that's the way it is played out.

I'm going to try to identify judges here now, so you're going to get my bias. But I mean it with respect. I'm on the procedure end, which means that I think rules are pretty important, which of course translates into obeying the rules. Now, I'll bend the rules and the like because I'm not wholly a procedures judge, but I'm very diffident about knowing what justice is.

On the substance end, and he's absolutely a magnificent judge, I put my chief, Joe Tauro; he has strong views about the substance of specific cases and he is concerned about that. In state court, on the procedures end I'd put Judges Zobel, McHugh, Garsh and Sosman. They would tend toward the procedures end of a determination.

We will see how that works out in various guises, but I want to get to some discussion as to how judges actually decide. When judges come to decide a jury-waived case or a motion, how do they do it? I'm going to start with a case first. I'm going to generalize, but of course I've given you my bias.

About Judge Young as a Judge

But before I get to that I want to say something else about bias. I've told you, and I believe it, that judges try very hard to transcend their particular biases as human beings. But there are some built-in biases, if you will, that judges do not acknowledge as biases, but you must be very alert to them.

Here they are: On the criminal side it is the very glory of our system that the judge, especially the trial judge, stands between the government on the one hand and the individual on the other. By its very nature the judge rises to the understanding that her role in that system is to check overweening government power exercised against the citizen. That is expressed, of course, in all the criminal procedure and the like, and the judges who tend to be most skeptical of the government are those judges who were themselves district attorneys and assistant United States attorneys. And this has sort of been the historic course of how you get on the federal bench.

Unfortunately on the state level we don't have a good compendium of the non-judge backgrounds of our state judges, but it would be very valuable to have one. The federal system puts out ***The Federal Judges Almanac***, which sort of gives every federal judge's C.V., and then it gives little quotes, little things that are nice. They always put in some nice things, and they always put in some things that knock the judge. One that is said about me is, "Thinks he is Oliver Wendell Holmes, but he is not." ***(Laughter)***.

I don't think I'm Oliver Wendell Holmes, but I respect Oliver Wendell Holmes enormously. Another knock on me, just to converse about it, "Frequently in error, never in doubt." ***(Laughter)***.

And that observer is on to something about me. Of course I can be defensive now, and I have the floor, but there's a point to be made that transcends me. I am in error as often as I am in error. I try to follow the higher courts. I try to predict what they will do. I believe that we are teachers. I believe my duty is to teach what the members of the Supreme Court and the First Circuit and the SJC want me to teach in specific cases. But because I am a procedure-type judge, once I've gone through the process I believe it is equally my duty to decide, and I decide. And I try not to convey any doubt—sometimes in my opinions I say I'm in doubt about this, I'm going out on a limb on this, this is unclear, but I think thus and so; but I act, because I think judges should.

The judge who will not decide is not a good judge from my procedures point of view. Of course that translates in the eyes of the bar after someone has stood up and argued their heart out on a motion, and I say, "Denied" and go on. They can say that. I understand that. But that's why.

Now, if we talk about biases, I submit to you that an unstated bias, which nevertheless exists in the judiciary of the country, is the fact that judges, state judges especially, are truly ill-treated by the other two branches of government. And that ill treatment translates into a skepticism of their ability or willingness to legislate logically and appropriately for the people because around them the courthouses are falling down. There is a never-ending flow of litigants with inadequate resources.

It absolutely boggles my mind that a governor and legislature or president and congress of the same party who have a legislative agenda do not in effect make adequate provisions for the judges who have to teach it. Judges who follow the law, they know what the law is, but that skepticism is out there. I share it with you.

Now, beyond that, judges are individuals, of course, and they are very careful about what prejudices they may have. Again, I want to share with you three of mine simply to give you a norm.

Here are three things I've learned about myself, and they should be obvious, and I'll admit them and then cross you up when you come to court because I will try every case on its merits. It turns out that I am an enormous fan of the jury system, and I dare say most judges are, whether they agree with it or not. And so if I have any wiggle room, I'll try a case to a jury.

Second, I am rather surprised how far I've gone on the First Amendment. Not that we have lots of pornography and obscenity cases, but as I recognize that the First Amendment really seems to me to be pretty, pretty important.

And lastly, and now this does hit close to home, I'm pretty skeptical of insurance companies. I fight against that, but after 18 years of being a judge, I think that any enormous aggregation of economic power is suspect. Now, you see, I've said that to you here, and they're going to make a transcript, and I'm going to get the pamphlet as well as you are. Someone's going to quote that to me, and I'm going to say, "But not in your case." And then, as I am a human being, I'm going to try and fight against it, but I recognize it within myself, that's so.

AUDIENCE MEMBER: I vote in New York, and in New York you vote for the lower court judges—

JUDGE YOUNG: Correct. They're elected, right.

AUDIENCE MEMBER: For those judges who are elected or appointed at higher levels, to what extent is the electorate or the governor entitled to know substantive decision-making? In an electorate I have called, you know, to get a judge's opinions on certain substantive matters and basically been refused the information. At the U.S. Supreme Court level we do it in the grand hearing.

JUDGE YOUNG: You ask an excellent jurisprudential question, and I'll try to answer it directly. I think you're entitled. Of course in our system I've only been appointed twice. I was appointed once to the state bench, and I don't remember the questions the governor's council asked me. I think I'm the only judge in the United States who has commissions from Governor Dukakis and President Reagan. I do remember the questions that I was asked by the senate committee. I think they have every right to ask, and I tried to answer them.

But of course as—I'm not confusing myself with Oliver Wendell Holmes or any of his living descendents—how important that is differs. If you're going to be on the Supreme Court, which is the head of our whole judiciary, and you're going to make those decisions that bind the rest of us, the type of questions you're asked would vary, it would seem to me, from when you're a district judge. Even in the district court you are entitled to know. Again, and I've touched on this before, I am in favor of having recall—not recall of judges, but something more modest. I think that all of our opinions should be published. The state district court opinions aren't published, and you might want to know them.

We are on the verge, except we won't spring for it through taxes, of being able to have everything that goes on in the courts on the record. Here I have Ms. Emmel, a magnificent freelance stenographer, and I've got the best court reporter in the nation in Don Womack.

Don Womack has everything that we've said in open court for 10 years, and what's important to you is he can find it. So if I've called people by name, he could search for that name. Every time that term has been used, he can find it. You want any charge in my court, any evidentiary ruling, and he could find it.

It's not terribly important to you because we haven't networked it, but suppose you had all of us; that's what's important, and that's what I want to pick up on. The stuff is all public, and you should be able to find it. You should be able to find every state district court opinion.

Judge Kilmartin, what do you have, a tape recorder?

JUDGE KILMARTIN: Yes, a tape recorder, and anyone can order the tapes.

JUDGE YOUNG: Anyone can order the tapes. Ms. Emmel, if I gave her a chance to speak, would tell you how hard it is to prepare a transcript from it. It's a totally inadequate record, as far as I'm concerned, because you can't network across 10,000 tapes, and after two years they destroy them, or they have a rule that says they can destroy them or tape over them, or the like, because you don't need it. Yet you ought to be able to get the impanelment of any judge. You ought to be able to get any judge's charge, any judge's approach. We're on the verge of doing it. We ought to spend the money to do it. The advantage, of course, would be more even-handed justice because, as I'm saying, I am impressed by what my colleagues do.

JURY-WAIVED CASES

I want to get to actual decisions in a jury-waived case. Here's how I submit to you judges decide jury-waived matters. It's sort of the other shoe. How do you decide whether to believe the lady or not?

Most of us are real fans of the adversary process. We believe that we should not decide until all the evidence is in. We teach juries that, and we believe it. So the last witness truly is as important as the first, and we keep our minds suspended, a word that I try to use with jurors, but that's not to say we don't have a mindset about the case going in. We do.

There is the famous story told about Justice John Paul Sullivan of the superior court. He was hearing a motion, and he said, "My mind is tabula rasa on this subject." And the court reporter took down, "My mind is a table of raisins on this subject." *(Laughter)*.

While he's a good friend and I believe probably was tabula rasa on that particular subject, the more you're prepared, the more you have an idea. If you're intellectually engaged, you read the briefs. You also have had lots of cases. Even if you are just starting out, it's your first day in Room 227, you've been a lawyer, you've had cases something like this case, and you begin to judge right then what goes on. No one will tell you we don't. Honestly, we do. The point is we say we can't now make up our mind, so we won't; we'll keep our mind suspended; we'll wait.

But, remember, we're talking jury-waived now and state rules. Once the plaintiff's rested, if the judge is not arguably convinced by a fair preponderance of the evidence, it's over. The judge should have a directed finding, or whatever the language is.

In federal court we've gone one step further. In a jury-waived case, once all the plaintiff's evidence is in on an issue, if we don't buy that, you're out. Now we may want to hear more, or we want to hear what the defendant has to say about it, but it's over and it ends. That's a judicial efficiency rule, but it works. So when we come we know that that's our obligation.

So what guides us? Well, in any case we know that in order for the plaintiff to make out a prima facie case, these are the elements of the prima facie case—one, two, three—and we will try to orient ourselves on what the legal claims are. We'll try to figure out pretrial, civil or criminal, what the legal claims are. What are the elements of those claims?

Then we will concern ourselves with what is the standard of proof. And, from the highest to the lowest, we have proof beyond a reasonable doubt to proof by a fair preponderance. Proof by a fair preponderance is the only one that can be expressed mathematically, that's more than 50 percent. Various cases require clear and convincing evidence; administrative law cases require substantial evidence, which really means any evidence a reasonable mind can accept; and some pretrial motions to suppress require probable cause.

Then we're going to ask ourselves whether on each essential element of the case there is enough evidence, if it's jury-waived, that satisfies us. If it's a jury case and we're ruling on a motion for directed verdict, it's a different standard. There has to be enough evidence that a jury could be—not swayed by passion or prejudice—convinced.

So we're going to do something like a mechanical test. I've done this, and I call this vectoring evidence when I teach Evidence. What does that tell you about a specific case? In essence, judges will take that quasi-scientific or logical, and they'll say what does the side that has the burden of proof here, what does that side have to show? And then how much do they have to show on each of those elements? They'll try to think through what that is.

Now, some cases are done at that point, and that, of course, is the easiest way to decide. If you fail to carry your burden of proof on an essential element, the case is over. But in most cases, if they've been halfway well prepared and if they've gotten to trial, the proponent, the plaintiff or prosecution, will carry the burden of going forward, and there will be enough evidence before the judge. The lady testifies she didn't forge the deed; that's the issue. I've got to decide whether that's true or not.

Judicial Practices and Techniques in Jury-Waived Cases

What does the judge do then? Well, I submit to you some techniques, all of which have been mentioned to me by judges. They just don't come out of my head. First, and I think it is generally so, judges like contemporaneous writings. Contemporaneous writings have more power than oral testimony.

Judges also tend to place a fair amount of importance on the interest of the witness in the outcome of the litigation, which makes disinterested witnesses more persuasive, as a general matter, than plaintiffs or defendants, who are obviously witnesses who are interested in the outcome of the litigation.

Some judges, and I am one, believe that in a jury-waived case if I'm the factfinder I need to make up a chronology. So I literally try. I'll take all those written exhibits, and I'll try to put them in order in the order that chronologically they came into existence. I'll try to do the same thing with the testimony of the witnesses. That is to say, in a jury-waived case when I'm taking notes, dates make a difference. Dates are written down. When did this conversation take place? What did the person know at that time?

There is a construct, and again now I'm getting more personal, to the value of that chronology to me. I'll dip into history for a moment. One of the great biographies of all time—it won a Pulitzer prize—is Douglas Southall Freeman's biography of Lee. I'm a Civil War buff, so I've read it. The interesting thing about Freeman's biography of Lee is that he writes the whole history of Lee based upon what Lee knew at that time, and not what we know now. He reports that Stuart was lost and wouldn't arrive until the second day of Gettysburg, and so on and so forth, but he didn't know where

Stuart was. And at that time he didn't know, and, therefore, he didn't know what Meade was doing and the like.

That's an approach, not just mine, to try to get into the minds of the people. Now, what's after that? The same thing we tell juries. What makes sense? What is the logical course, the logical tendency of human beings? How are people expected to act?

But I share with you this and I'll ask Judge Kilmartin to dissent: Judges quickly learn that very few people lie. Lying is rare in court, at least in the courts where I sit where the stakes are high. Everyone remembers past events to their own advantage.

When I teach *Trial Practice* I try to get that out with a little trick with my students, and I'll try it on you just to bring home the truth of what I said. I want you, I seriously want you to think of the most embarrassing thing that ever happened to you. Then you sort of look them in the eye, and you see someone who's smiling, because you think you're going to call on them. Well, I'm not. But if you followed me and you thought of something truly embarrassing, you've resolved that in your own mind because you have a sense of your own self-worth. You remember that embarrassing event, I submit to you, in a way that makes you look good, as good as you can under the circumstances.

I'll go first. We're not going to do this, but I'll go first. In the 10 years that I was in practice before I was fortunate enough to be appointed as a judge, I was once complained of to the Board of Bar Overseers. And it still rankles me. I almost cannot tell you that without telling you that I was right. I did nothing wrong. That properly draws the laugh. I'm pretty defensive about that.

Most witnesses, most litigants are terribly embarrassed that they have to come to court. For us it's a job. For those of us who are trial lawyers it's the highest calling of our profession to be there. Nobody else wants to be there. They don't want to be there. It's all a big mistake. They wished they'd never merged a corporation, filled out the income tax form that way, or crossed the street when they did. For them it's filled with tragedy and revulsion, and, therefore, they remember it in the way that makes them whole. That's not lying, but judges are skeptical of that and try to translate it into what they think really happened.

Now, one other thing, and this is really personal. I think and was taught as a judge that it is bush league just to adopt one side's findings of fact. Because I almost recoil from doing that, because it seems like I won't do my job if I do that, I almost inevitably look at where the logic of that leads you. I'm being as candid as I know how. I'm going to change something. Does that mean I'm going to middle your case? I mean I shouldn't. That's not justice. That's what arbitrators do. I mean you're entitled to win if you're entitled to win.

But let's say you've got this magnificent case and you've got all your findings and rulings and everything. If I just have to say, you know, bang, that's allowed, I think I rolled over for them. But, you know, maybe I should. And so saying it, I should exorcise the evil. But it's out there. I tell you, I probably won't go with everything you say, but you want me to do something where on bottom line you'll win even if I don't buy it all. That's personal, because I want to have had some imprimatur on the case.

Having said all that, how do you decide? I think two things are essential, and judges don't have both. The thing that we don't have and we should have is time for reflection. We certainly don't have it in the state district courts or probate courts. We have very little in the superior court, and a bit more in the federal court. Somehow society thinks that we should have no quiet time, we should always be on the bench, we should always be trying cases, we should always be deciding them, and our decisions ought all be Solomonic. That's too bad.

The second thing is best expressed in Hennessey's book on *Judges Making Law.* He actually uses the word "hunch" and what seems reasonable to you, and then you just, as jurors do, you start to formulate an opinion.

Frequently you can tell in a jury-waived case what the judge's mindset is—that's a lot different than the final opinion—from the judge's questions during the trial, because, you see, I've told you the judge starts out the trial jury-waived thinking something about it. So the judge is going to want to test the veracity of the judge's view either by taking careful notes on the questions that you or your opponent asks on that point. If you don't ask those questions, the judge is going to ask them, because that's what the judge is concerned about. That's what the judge is troubled about.

It looks like there's no case here, or it looks like the plaintiff has a case here, but the plaintiff only has a case if he can prove thus and so. If you don't get to it and the judge asks about it, that's what the judge is concerned about. Now, those are jury-waived decisions.

There's one technique that's taught in the Federal Judicial Center that I think is very helpful and more judges should do it. I was taught and I now find the facts as soon as the trial is over. I do this right from the bench. That's when they're the freshest in your mind. That's when you're the most honest. That's when you haven't reflected on who's done the best findings and rulings and ruminated and, the truth to tell, forgotten the case and then remembered it from your notes. That's when everything is fresh in your mind.

You don't necessarily have to find the law then, but if you could press the judge to make the factual findings immediately when it's over, even if the judge is going to reserve on how the law applies to those factual findings, you get the best job. Comments or observations? Judge Kilmartin, anything to add to that?

JUDGE KILMARTIN: The only thing I would point out is that at the state court level we're often presented with trials where we don't go through the formal pretrial hearing process and pretrial conference process that you do at the federal level. It's extremely helpful and important from the lawyer's point of view, I think, to file requests for rulings or file some sort of report before the trial starts. The judge is going to go through the file and read the file, and even if they haven't formally sat down and spoken with the attorney, they're going to read whatever has been filed. I think the framework then is that you go onto the bench and that you're going to operate with them.

JUDGE YOUNG: Very true. I couldn't agree more.

MR. JAMES KRASNOO: The response I have, especially on the superior court level, is that I've gone in on a hundred civil pretrial conferences, and the very first question out of the judge most of the time when we were in chambers was, "What is this case about?"

It's lame to turn and say to the judge, "Well, judge, we filed our joint pretrial conference report setting out the facts." The judge will just respond, "So tell me what this case is about."

And I understand that the judge has read absolutely nothing, even though you've been required to file this document that's taken a lot of time to prepare. And one of my questions is: Why don't they read it, aside from the crunch of time? If they're going to be doing the pretrial conference in a case they're going to be trying, why shouldn't they have read it by that point?

JUDGE YOUNG: That's a very fair statement, and I will own up to it being accurate. I will say again personally that probably I do the weakest pretrial conferences of any federal judge. You put your finger right on it. I may not have read the joint pretrial memorandum until the morning before the pretrial conference. I was taught not to ask, "What is this case about?" because then you get lawyers just wandering around and making a jury argument, and that's not helpful.

I was taught on the superior court to ask, "What are the issues in this case?" Now, you want to know what the issues are because it starts framing this analysis here, and it starts in the final pretrial conference.

What Mr. Krasnoo says, and he's right, is that frequently judges haven't prepared themselves adequately in the superior court for the final pretrial conference. You've also given the answer, but there's another jurisprudential answer.

The first answer is time. There are 1,200 cases for a superior court judge. The second answer is, as a matter of appropriate administration, by making you file the document, there's a transaction cost that you have to invest in the case. I am being very candid here. Everyone hopes that you will go away, and that we will never have to have the conference because you will have settled the case. Even though the great glory and why we wanted to be judges and accepted appointments was to try cases, we now have various hurdles in front of trying cases that societally it's thought are appropriate.

My colleague, Chief Judge Tauro, says, and he does a very good pretrial, "Every time I try a case I believe that I have failed." Now, I cite him because, of course, by comparison I don't know what he's talking about. I thought that the whole goal of the system was to try those cases that couldn't be settled. So the point is to look at what use you make of the trial conference. He is right. In the superior court they want the conference because it helps them prepare for the trial—it helps me prepare for the trial—but they may not be crystal clear on the case at the time of the conference, which tells you what you want to do during the conference.

AUDIENCE MEMBER: One more question about findings of facts: What do you do about the practice of waiting for a transcript being prepared and having counsel prepare a request for findings of facts with citations in the transcript?

JUDGE YOUNG: Personally, I think it's dead wrong. It is a slow and improvident way to try cases, but we'll generalize from my approach to it. The better practice is to be ready to make a decision at the end of the case, which moves everything up because your decision will be better. Judges who are waiting for transcripts will wait for an undue amount of time and they'll up your transaction costs for having to buy the transcript from the court reporter. And they will, because we work hard, forget about the case. And it's just wrong. That's what I think.

Judge, want to comment on it?

JUDGE KILMARTIN: I would echo what you would say. I've said I'm not interested. I've taken notes through the trial personally. I've made perhaps subsidiary findings as I've gone along. And I would be inclined to follow the same procedure you've outlined. Make some general statement concerning the finding you're going to make, and you may make more specific findings in writing afterwards.

JUDGE YOUNG: That really is the best practice. Now, sure, all judges don't do it, but we should urge judges to do it. We ought to work toward that practice.

AUDIENCE MEMBER: On that point. Often by making those statements you help the parties settle the case also. The parties want to hear: What does the judge think?

JUDGE YOUNG: They really do. That's why they're there, of course. And that is what under our oath we're supposed to do.

MOTIONS

Motions. Preparation, hearing, decision of motions. First, preparation: The state system has evolved from a system where in the superior court there was no judicial preparation for the hearing of a motion. People who ask to go back to the motion session forget that in a busy county where 40 or 50 motions were heard between 10:00 and 1:00 and the lawyers got the chance to mark them up, no judge invested any time in preparing for the session. You didn't know what motions were to be heard.

With all the problems, and I admit there are problems, that Rule 9A has engendered on the state side in the superior court, you at least have a better chance that the judge is prepared for the hearing of your motion.

How can you tell if the judge is not prepared? The judge is utterly silent. There is no better way, no better tip-off that the judge doesn't know what's going on. He is doing his judge trick and knows that one side will argue and then the other side will argue and then he can say, "I will take it under advisement." You cannot go wrong with that approach as a judge, and then you can figure out what's going on.

If that's what is going on, you make the strongest presentation you can because it is not helpful to say, "Your Honor, do you have any question about this or that," because you don't want to put the judge on the spot and the judge doesn't know. A judge who is hot from the bench, though, does know and is prepared, and so let's deal with how you deal with that judge.

Let's take a step back. Judges have a lot to do. What the state court judges look at prior to the hearing of the motion are your papers. They'll look at your papers because in the Superior Court they have fewer law clerks than they have judges, and they pretty much do their work themselves. They'll look at your papers.

Your papers, of course, are only part of it. Think of what's behind your papers in a motion, all those affidavits that you've filed in a motion for summary judgment. And then of course the overarching law; will a judge have looked at that? Maybe, but don't count on it, state or federal. But you, by and large, go in with the idea that the judge would have looked at your papers.

In federal court each judge gets two law clerks; some have three; some have interns; and most, but not all, have their law clerks do bench memoranda about the motions. The judge will look at the bench memoranda. What will they look at beyond the bench memoranda?

Go in with the mindset that the judge has looked at your briefs and then, like a state judge, query whether the judge has looked at the affidavits or whether the judge has looked at the overarching law.

A trick that I learned from Judge Guy of the Fifth Circuit is that I always read the reply brief first but not for the reason that you hope. I read it because it tells me what you're worried about. That's why you filed it. That's where the other side has nicked you, and you want to be sure that I know that there's nothing to it.

Now, that's preparation. For the hearing, I've already talked about the judge who is silent. That judge more than likely is unprepared. What about the judge who is asking questions, especially on motions, as opposed to appellant arguments or trial? It's crucial.

By and large the judge is trying to have answered what troubles the judge about the specific case. So motion sessions tend to be much more free-form than appellant arguments because the judge may think the moving party is in pretty good shape but may want to know from the opposing party why, for example, summary judgment shouldn't be granted.

And we'll start with the opposing party. You may suddenly be put on the spot, though it really should be the moving party who argues first, to answer the judge's question about a specific point in the case.

How do you argue motions? You go with your strongest argument, and you go with the relief that you want. Never is it more important, as they teach you in appellate advocacy, to answer the judge's question and then try to segue into absolutely your best argument and what supports it. If you have case law to support your argument, mention the case law if it's cases from courts for which the judge works. Mention that the case of ***Abbott Laboratories*** requires whatever you think is this or that result. Whether or not the judge has read it, that's going to slow the judge down because the judge will be hesitant to ride right over you if there's a case that supports your position from the court for whom the judge works.

Both state and federal, have your cases, and have a copy for the other side. It's only courteous, and it's powerful if the case really says what you say. The judge may say, "Let me see that case." Don't think the judges will have the cases. They especially won't have the cases in state court. Don't think, state or federal, that the judges will have read the cases. If you're dependent on a case, have it. I've already mentioned citing it. If you cited a case, be aware it's not enough simply to cite the case. That may slow the judge down. You should be quoting from the case because it will slow the judge down from doing what you don't want the judge to do. So you make your best argument, supported by a case, and you should take the question as crucial because the question is what's troubling the judge.

One other thing on motions, especially if you're in a big firm. Whoever comes to argue the motion represents the client in that case. Judges will skitter off now, especially in the room lists in the superior court and in all the federal courts. Once they've decided the motions, they'll start managing the case. It absolutely will not help your cause if you say, "Well, your Honor, Mr. such and such will be actually handling this case. I just handle the motions to dismiss." The judge doesn't want to hear that. He wants to know when you'll be ready for trial, how many depositions are left, or whatever else the judge wants to talk about. Be ready for that.

If a preliminary injunction is going against you, always remember the amount of the bond; get in there what the bond requirement is going to be because the judge has that to consider and may then rethink the imposition of the preliminary injunction.

Let's talk about case management and a couple of things on evidence. In the state system we have the various tracking orders. In the federal system we have the Expense and Delay Reduction Plan. Judges' reactions to those rules, all of which we follow, will in significant measure be colored by whether we are substance judges or whether we are procedural judges.

With a substance judge, your best argument on any of those scheduling things is the practicality argument: that the other side is overreaching, that it is unfair, that a schedule should be extended or contracted, or the like, in order to do justice.

For procedural judges the best argument is the rules: the rules require A and B and C, and the other side didn't do it. You can't just be Scrooge-like; you have to say, and, therefore, that's unfair, because we will be surprised at trial, and this and that.

There are a variety of things to be alert to in getting ready for trial with respect to the judge. I want to talk about preliminary findings. I especially want to talk about them in the expert area. But I want to talk about the role of a judge in a jury case with respect to admitting evidence because there is an array of determinations that the judge must make with respect to admitting evidence that really is determined by the judge, and not by the jury.

EVIDENTIARY ISSUES

Relevance

And there are four things I want to talk about: Relevance, admitting something de bene, conspiracies and experts. First, relevance. Nowhere is it more apparent that the background of the judge is significant than in the judge's rulings on what is relevant. "Relevance" is defined as those things that make a fact of consequence to the outcome more likely or less likely than they would be without the receipt of that evidence. That's from 401 of the federal rules. The state rule is the same. That is not self-defining.

What things are logically relevant? There are those things that the judge thinks are relevant, and the judge thinks those things are relevant based upon his or her life experience for like cases. Judges by and large have not been numbers runners or dealt in drugs or the like. And, therefore, the manner in which that culture does its business will be completely foreign to the judge. It's like how a large building is built is foreign to a judge who has never represented a construction company. Judges don't just know this whole myriad of human experience. They don't know it, so you have got to get the judge into the picture, and you do it in two ways.

With your pretrial submissions you have got to in writing tell the judge what the case is about. There is nothing wrong with having a brief that exposes the relevance of a particular type or area.

I had a lawyer in a case that involved trade secrets, and the trade secrets were the infrared detectors in the nose cones of artillery shells. We had a physicist on the stand. This is jury-waived. I'm the judge. The physicist starts testifying, and he says, "Judge, this is really easy. This area, there's just one formula, and this is it: lambda nought microns is the disequivalent of one minus X to the tenth torr above the forbidden energy gap expressed in microhertz." And I take that all down.

Then he goes on. He testifies all afternoon. He testifies the whole next morning, and finally he's done. And I say, "You know, doctor, that's the first time I've ever had a witness testify a whole trial day in answer to a single question." He says, "Well, you know what they say, judge: You ask a physicist the question, and he tells you how to build a watch."

So I go to lunch. I'm in Middlesex. I was a state judge. There are 17 judges at lunch—district court judges, probate judges, superior court judges. I'm rather full of myself, and I tell this story. After all, I had high school chemistry, that's it, and I am jury-waived presiding over this case. I tell it to all my judicial colleagues just like I've told it to you. And then we get up to go back to our courtrooms. I'm sitting in Room 12-A.

Across the hall is the Honorable Robert Barton, who's sitting criminal in 12-B. So everyone is, as you are, taken by my story. And we go to walk out together, and Barton says to me, "Boy, Bill," he says, "you think you've got problems. I've got to go up there and tell the jury that a BJ is a blow job." ***(Laughter)***.

There's a moral to that story, and the simple moral is that the whole range of human experience is before the judges. It's in our courts, A to Z, abortion to zoning. It's all there. The judges themselves don't know.

Part of your job as a teacher is to get the judge in the picture. Get the judge in the picture factually because judges make their relevance determinations based on what they know.

Judges in this area will frequently say to you, "Counsel, have you got a case on this?" What they mean is not have you got a Supreme Judicial Court case talking about relevance. They know what the rule of relevance is. We've already mentioned it. They mean have you got a case factually like this case? And this is where computer searches help you.

What they're looking at is some reassurance that some other judge faced with this factual issue has admitted the evidence. Always take a judge up on that. If a judge says, "Have you got a case like this case?" say, "Judge, I don't have it on the tip of my tongue, but I'll have one for you tomorrow morning." Then you race to the computer. And, you know, the key numbers won't help you. That's law. You want to get into the computer and find a case that's factually like this case, where the judge admitted or excluded evidence arguably relevant in the same fashion.

Submitting Evidence de Bene

Second, de bene, we all know that we can't bring our witnesses in the order that we would like to, experts especially. "I can't have the doctor here until Thursday morning, Judge," and the like.

Here's another place that judges split. The substance judge is going to be more sympathetic to that. The procedure judge is going to want to see the foundation for that expert's testimony because that expert, if you're going to take the expert out of order, is going to be testifying as to a basis for the expert's opinion.

The procedure judge wants to be sure that the factual basis is already in the record lest the expert get a leg up before the jury. And the procedure judge can justify that. They can say, "Well, that's fair; otherwise we can't unring the bell." We can't have the jury not hear the expert's testimony. But you may be really in a jam then since the judge wants the case tried in a specific order.

Conspiracies

Civil or criminal, state or federal: if you have a conspiracy count in your case, it is the judge, and not the jury, that decides whether, as an initial matter, there was a conspiracy, because it's only if there was a conspiracy that the statements made by coconspirators in furtherance of the conspiracy are admitted.

Now, the state and federal evidentiary rules are different on this, but the point I want to make is be aware that that is a judicial finding. The judge isn't asking herself, "Could a reasonable jury find that there was a conspiracy?" That's what she'll ask herself on the directed verdict. Rather, she's asking herself: "Do I think there is a conspiracy?"

If she thinks there is, in the state system that's when you remove the limitations on evidence. In the federal system that's when you let it go to the jury without striking things out. But remember that's a finding.

Experts

That's the same thing we are taught to do under *Daubert v. Merrell Dow Pharmaceuticals, Inc.*, 113 S.Ct. 2786 (1993), the rule about being the gatekeepers on expert testimony, or its state counterpart, *Commonwealth v. Lanigan*, 419 Mass. 15 (1994). Because the practice is going to develop on this, it's worthwhile pausing on this for just a moment.

Lanigan just adopts *Daubert; Lanigan* is the state rule, but it adopts *Daubert*, so I can talk about the federal rule. *Daubert* teaches that the trial judge is the gatekeeper of scientific expert testimony. Now, expert testimony that we receive by way of opinion is of three sorts: scientific; technical, which tends to be the mechanical parts; and other specialized knowledge, which can be anything. It can be lobsterers or it can be auto mechanics.

Daubert is limited to scientific testimony. Be clear that it's so limited. And it's also limited to testimony that's on the fringes of science. Don't think that *Daubert* applies across the board. When you want to knock out an expert's testimony because you think that the science itself is junk science, you should make a motion. Judges will hear this motion, a motion for preliminary finding that the science is no good.

Now, *Daubert* teaches that we are interested in the theory of knowledge of the experts in the area. We're not interested in the particular opinion of this alleged scientist; rather, we want to know whether the science makes any sense or not. So what we are going to be concerned with is really a dictum, but this is the test:

We're going to be concerned with whether the science can be tested. How many false positives are there? How accurate is the science? Is it absolutely accurate, somewhat accurate and the like? We're going to be interested in whether there have been publications in magazines that are peer-reviewed within that scientific field. And we're going to be interested in whether that particular science has been generally accepted.

Now, if the answers to those questions are adequate, the judge should allow the scientific evidence. The reason you want to make a motion ahead of time and you want it for a preliminary finding is that it is a finding. If the judge makes findings against the expert, that will be reviewed under a deferential standard, a clearly erroneous standard.

While I'm talking about experts, this too is an area where there is vast difference in the views of judges. I can't think of any more descriptive terms—but I don't mean it in a political sense—there are liberal judges who are liberal on receiving experts, and conservative judges, who are skeptical, if you will, especially of hired gun experts.

Judges who are liberal on the receipt of evidence include: former Chief Judge Freedman, who sits in Springfield in the federal district court, and Judge Izzo in the superior court. Judges who are conservative on experts include: me; Judge Keeton; to a lesser extent Judge Woodlock; and on the state side, Judge Zobel.

Here are some of the ways that judges are conservative. Some judges want the expert to be qualified. The expert has to be qualified by experience, background, training and skill. The idea is that the expert is qualified and sought by society to give this opinion outside the judicial process. In other words, people voted this engineer to design these widgets, not because he's a forensic engineer and comes in to testify about widget design, but because he's designed a widget. Those of us who are strict on this are sensitive to the fact that if carried too far, that's a defendant's rule. Let's have no doubt about that, it's a defendant's rule, because then only the people who designed the widgets in the defendant's widget company would be prepared to testify. No one says that. That would be complete abuse.

On the other hand, the person, so say the conservatives, should have had something to do with design of this type. Let's say it's a heating element. The person should have experience in the design of heating elements in the industry or should have taught it in school or worked for OSHA on it. It shouldn't just be someone hired by one side to come in because he's a certified engineer and testify about that. Just be aware of the split.

SENTENCING

The federal courts have the Sentencing Guidelines, which are very complex. State courts are thinking of adopting them. State courts have a lot more discretion, but it is fair to say that most judges crowd toward the middle. They're just not clear on what the middle is, and there's a good reason for that.

Nothing is more problematic, and there is nothing for which a judge has less ability, than sentencing another human being. That in no way means that judges should be light on their sentences. Clearly, society is taking an increasingly harsh view, especially toward crimes of violence and crimes involving drugs. But judges, who have to live with their sentences, tend to crowd toward the middle, and that tells you a lot.

If you've got some idea of the range of sentences of other codefendants in a case or sentences for this type of crime, lots of us are very interested in hearing. There are only a few judges who will be comfortable being known as a light sentencer or, conversely, a heavy sentencer, but some of them do exist. Some of them have made the prudential decision that by and large, they believe that best justice is required to be light or to be heavy.

FINAL THOUGHTS

I want to share four things with you, and I can do it very briefly. Three are things that have helped me as a judge; one is a brief story.

When I was first sworn in as a judge on that February 23, they had two justices of the superior court stand up with me. I don't mean the swearing in at the State House; I mean the induction. They then tell you who had your seat before you, and the like. Well, one of them was Vincent Brogna, who was a great judge of the superior court.

When I got off the bench that first day, Judge Brogna said to me, "Bill, have the courage of your own error." Now, I think that's really profound, and some of the things I've said already bear that out.

I believe that judges are teachers, but judges should decide; and, therefore, they've got to have the guts, once they've done these things we've talked about, to make a decision.

Second, Justice Kaplan of the Supreme Judicial Court gave a really magnificent lecture, the Oliver Wendell Holmes lecture. Kaplan said this, and I've always believed it, and it's worthwhile in coming to understand judges. He said: "The judge has no problemsolver for every occasion, no normative rule to which he can refer the difficult decisions. And if he did have, he would think it was too self-regarding. We're not philosophers. We don't set ourselves up to be." That can be found at Benjamin Kaplan, "Encounters with O.W. Holmes, Jr.," 96 Harv.L.Rev. 1828, 1849.

I want to read you the beginning of Keeton's book before we end, and I want to get it on the transcript here, though I can cite it. This is my colleague, Bob Keeton:

> Judging is choice. Choice is power. Power is neither good nor evil except as it is allocated and used. Judging in a legal system is professional. Professionals, including judges, represent interests other than their own. One who accepts a professional role in a legal system accepts an obligation to confine the exercise of power within the limits of authority. For each professional role, the limits of authority are defined by law. One cannot fully understand the conduct of a professional without fully understanding the defined professional role. The quality of judging in a legal system depends on commitment. It depends first on commitment to the aim of justice; second, it depends on commitment to professionalism. The declared beliefs of all professionals in the system, including advocates, counselors, and the academic critics, as well as the judges, affect the quality of judging in the system.

Third, the quality of judging depends on commitment to method. Judicial choice at its best is reasoned choice candidly explained.

And now this story, a real story, told to me by John Ronan, Justice of the Superior Court, about Jim Roy, Justice of the Superior Court. Roy had a reputation, and Roy's reputation was that no one in the whole system—he sat criminal most of the time—would give you a fairer trial. He made the DAs jump over all the hoops. He turned every corner square. But when a guilty verdict came back, he smacked them in sentencing, and he made no bones about it.

So he's sitting in Middlesex. He's an interesting guy, Roy. He used to wear a homburg, and he'd wear a long topcoat with a velvet collar. This is just to give you some idea of Roy. He was a tall and imposing presence.

He was trying a biker for a sadistic assault upon someone else. And throughout the entire trial this whole row of bikers sat in the back row. The jury came back and convicted the defendant.

About this time of year it had gotten dark early. Roy, by the way, lived on Louisburg Square. Do you know where it is? The ritzy area. I don't know where his money came from, but he lived up there on Louisburg Square. A magnificent judge.

The jury comes back, "Guilty." And, as is the practice in the superior court, he dismisses the jury, and moves immediately to sentence the offender. Of course here's this whole row of bikers back there. Lots of court officers are now called into the courtroom because they got this jury verdict.

Roy smacks the guy. And the guy then is shocked by the sentence he had just received, and he goes:

"Well, well, - - - - you, judge."

And Roy goes, "Motion denied. Take him away." ***(Laughter)***.

And they grab the guy, you know, and they take him out. And there's sort of an uproar. And Roy says, "We'll recess," and he goes out.

So that's morning, you see. That afternoon, it's 4 o'clock and it's dark. Roy's going to leave at 5 o'clock. Of course, nothing is faster than courtroom gossip; you know everything that's going on. Everybody knows Roy's done this. And the gang members are not at all pleased. They preserve order in the courtroom.

So John Ronan, who lives up in Marblehead, comes by. And he says, "Jim, well, sort of a rough case."

"Oh, yes," says Roy, "but you know these cases, one case after another."

Ronan wants to give him a lift home, and he says, "Let me give you a lift home; it's snowing out."

And Roy says, "Don't be silly; don't be silly. That's ridiculous. You're headed north to Marblehead. You don't want to go across the bridge into Boston. You'll be forever getting out."

And so Ronan, not wanting to say, "I'd just as soon drive home with you, dangerous people are about," tries again.

Judge Ronan says, "No, no, it's okay. I really, you know, I don't have to get home for some time. It's cold out. Come and take a ride with me. I'll just drop you off, and then I can get north."

Roy again says, "Oh, no. Don't be silly. I won't do it."

Finally Ronan says—he told me the story himself—he said, "Jim, you know, you sentenced that one fellow, and from what I hear, there's a lot of people—he's got buddies in the courtroom. Really, I'd feel a lot better if you went home with me."

And Roy said, "Of course not. That's what it's all about," and put on his homburg and walked out into the snow.

Thank you all very, very much. ***(Applause)***.

". . . I want to keep emphasizing that the simple things are the things that actually work in court."

–Hon. William G. Young, December 7, 1996
From *Young on Evidence for the Trial Advocate*

CHAPTER 5

Judge Young on Evidence for the Trial Advocate

DECEMBER 7, 1996

I AM deeply and truly honored that you people would spend a Saturday talking over evidence with me. Let me sketch out what I have in mind here for today. In four hours, I want to do nothing more nor less than talk through essential rules of evidence, both state and federal, from start to finish. Now, that's a fairly tall order, and to do that I will have to move at flank speed—and I intend to do so. I truly want to be of service to you.

A word about the organization of today's talk. After some introductory remarks, the organization of the next four hours is going to follow the organizational format of the Federal Rules of Evidence.

It has always seemed to me that it was unfortunate—I mean no disrespect, and I can see why the Supreme Judicial Court of Massachusetts did this—but it remains unfortunate that the Supreme Judicial Court never adopted as rules of court the Proposed Massachusetts Rules of Evidence. You see, those proposed rules follow the format of the federal rules. Massachusetts, however, has never codified its rules of evidence. They are scattered throughout the common law and statutes. So when someone refers to Rule 803, that means something to people who practice in federal court, but it has no meaning in state court practice unless you find the specific case that either adopts or puts a gloss on Rule 803, which by the way is in the section dealing with hearsay.

So here is what John Pollets and Chris Poreda—a couple of Massachusetts attorneys who clerked for me during my superior court days—and I have done: Starting with the Proposed Massachusetts Rules of Evidence, we have created something we call the Massachusetts Evidentiary Standards. They should be out within a couple of weeks. These standards track the federal rules in state practice from start to finish. In other words, these standards tell you, much like the ***Restatement***, the black letter law of what the Massachusetts law is today. Where it comes from case law, the cases are cited. Where it comes from statutes, the statutes are quoted. But the organization is absolutely the same as the Federal Rules of Evidence. So when I refer to Rule 405, I am referring to Federal Rule 405 and its counterpart in the state common law Mass. Evidentiary Standard 405. So I'm using the Federal Rules of Evidence as the base, but I will bring out the differences between Massachusetts practice and federal court practice.

Now to give us a format, something to discuss, here is a case *(Commonwealth v. Marada*, Plymouth Superior Court 1981; Ford, J. presiding). What I tell you now is true. The only things that I have changed are the names that I do not remember.

In 1979, Mr. and Mrs. Southwick lived in Brockton, Massachusetts. Mrs. Southwick was having an affair with a fellow by the name of Marada. Mr. Southwick knew of his wife's infidelity, and, what's more, he knew the place of their next assignation: The Happy Haven Motel on Route 123, about four miles to the east of Brockton.

Mr. Southwick went to his friend Northrup, who had recently purchased one of those one-step cameras and said, "Northrup, how would you like to go field test your camera and create evidence that I can use in my expected divorce action against my wife?" Northrup readily agreed.

The two of them drove off to the Happy Haven Motel. Southwick, no fool, took a baseball bat just in case things got ugly. They go to see the manager. Discussion ensues. It turns out that no one registered there under either the name of Marada or the name of Southwick. Further discussion ensues, and the manager turns over to Mr. Southwick the pass key to Room 4A. The manager then realizes he has business elsewhere, so he departs.

The Happy Haven is a one-story motel; you know, one of those you drive in right in front. Southwick and Northrup walk along until they come to the door of Room 4A. Southwick takes the baseball bat in his right hand, holding it between his thumb and little finger so that he can still turn the knob. He puts the key in his left hand, the idea being to unlock the door rapidly and to throw it open. Northrup steps up to the square of the door; he tests the light meter on his camera. The stage is set.

When all is ready, Southwick inserts the key, unlocks the door, opens the door, steps inside and off to one side. Northrup steps up and raises the camera. Apparently, they have come at the right moment. Marada rolls over in bed, naked as a jay. In his hand is a .38 snub-nosed revolver. And as Northrup takes his picture, Marada shoots Southwick. Southwick, shot through the heart, is dead before he hits the floor.

This is absolutely true. I know that it is unbelievable, but truth is stranger than fiction.

Northrup drops the camera and departs. Marada gets up, dresses and departs. Mrs. Southwick gets up and commences to dress, when on the floor she sees the one-step camera. And just as you have seen in TV commercials, she bends down, presses the little button and out comes the blank, which by the magic of modern emulsifiers turns into a color photograph of her lover Marada shooting her husband Southwick. She files it away.

Marada, no fool, goes to consult his attorney. This is all real. His attorney is Jack Atwood, an eminent practitioner. Mr. Atwood tells Marada to turn himself in to the police, and he does. That is when Mrs. Southwick catches up with him at the police station, where she produces the photograph. Atwood believes that he is ethically bound to turn the photograph over to the prosecution, and he does so.

The prosecution loves it. They have never had a case in which they have a photograph in color of the murder in progress. And the very first thing they do is blow it up until it is 8 by 11. And I have that photo right here. Now, do you want to see it?

AUDIENCE: Yes.

JUDGE YOUNG: Okay. That's the hook by which I catch you. You've got to earn it. You've got to get through these rules and this lecture. But we'll use this. You'll see the photograph. I have it. It's real. I'll show you at the end—in about four hours.

We have a case now. This is the case. You have the facts in mind. Let's consider the system in which this case is going to be processed. We have to first step back and think about the institution.

Players in the Adversary System

Marada is charged with first-degree murder. He, we all know, will be tried in a system that we call the adversary system. It is very important as we start out to figure out the roles of the key players in the adversary system.

More than anything else, you need to know who you are as trial advocates in the adversary system. And who you are in this system depends significantly on the other two major players in the system: the jury and the judge. The first and most important role in that system is played by the jury. Now, very few cases are actually tried to juries. In all of your practice, most of you will most often appear before judges. However, the whole theory of the rules—the law of evidence—is what evidence will we present, what things will we show to juries.

Juries are nothing more nor less than direct democracy. What we judges say when we greet juries in the morning is literally true: the jury is an empowerment of the people; it is the people ruling. Now, because we can't get all the people in there every day, we do it in smaller groups, and we call them juries. Never forget that. That is not a platitude that the judge tells jurors so that they can be happy because the coffee is cold and they are kept in an underground dungeon until such time as we need them.

When it comes down to the wire, juries will come to understand that they have the say. In criminal cases, they decide whether the defendant is guilty or not guilty. In civil cases, they decide as between the parties who is going to get what.

Juries are an extraordinary empowerment of the people. If you doubt it, take a products liability case in which the issue is whether the product is defective in the eyes of the people, in the eyes of the jury.

So the jury is your ultimate and most important audience. The next player—and I do not mean to denigrate her by calling her a player—is the judge. Judges in our system are teachers of the law. In a very real way, that is what we are. That's why—and now a political statement—we should not elect them. We don't elect our teachers; we appoint them. Maybe we should review how good they are as teachers, but that is what we all are. Trial judges teach juries. Appellate judges are more scholarly in synthesizing things to teach us all.

And you people, less important than juries but far more important than judges, teach both the law and the facts. You teach the law to your clients—and you see many more clients in the course of your profession than I see litigants in the course of mine. Those of us who are trial advocates—I say "us," but I guess I never really was; I was just a minor litigator—those of you who are trial advocates, you teach the facts. You teach them through evidence, and you teach them to juries. That in essence is what it means to be a zealous advocate: to be a teacher of the evidence in light of the law as you know it to juries and, of course, to judges—to persuade judges as well.

THE LAW OF EVIDENCE

Now, if that's so, if that's right, what does it tell us about the law of evidence? The way evidentiary law works out, of course, it works out primarily at the trial level, and it works very fast. Judges have to make rulings on evidence really in split-second determinations. Note that evidentiary rulings are not appealable unless a substantial right of a party is affected, and an objection is made (except, of course, in criminal cases an appellate court may prevent a substantial risk of a miscarriage of justice even if no objection was made at trial). Mass. Evid. Stand. 103; *Commonwealth v. O'Connor*, 407 Mass. 63, 670, 555 N.E.2d 865, 867 (1990); *Abraham v. Woburn*, 383 Mass. 724, 726 n.1, 421 N.E.2d 1206 n.1.

And the first thing to understand about the law of evidence, the thing that makes it humane, the thing that should make you interested in mastering and working with the law of evidence and not frightened of it, is that the whole body of law, unlike any other area of law—and on which we are going to spend the next four hours—doesn't really exist, ladies and gentlemen, unless you want it. There are a few exceptions to that, and we'll touch upon them. But do you see that it's that fact that takes the 18 volumes of *Wigmore on Evidence* and collapses them into something that's humane and workable?

Unless you object, unless you ask for a ruling, these rules that I am going to talk about are of no use to you. Unless you object, blatant hearsay testimony will come before the jury and the jury will have every right to rely upon it. The same with privileges. We are never concerned about privileges unless someone invokes them. What about relevance? Relevance is an interesting issue, but who cares unless someone objects.

There really are only four areas where the judge on her own motion is supposed to intrude:

- The rape shield law–G.L. c. 221, § 21B; Mass. Evid. Stand. 412;
- The parole evidence rule in contract law–*See generally Cullinet Software, Inc. v. McCormack & Dodge Corp.*, 400 Mass. 775, 776, 511 N.E.2d 1101, 1102 (1987);
- Private communication between husband and wife–G.L. c. 233, § 20; Mass. Evid. Stand. 601(d); and
- The deference to legislative factfinding–Mass. Evid. Stand. 301(f); *See, e.g., Shell Oil Co. v. City of Revere*, 383 Mass. 682, 688–89, 421 N.E.2d 1181, 1185–86 (1981).

First, the rape shield law. You can't expect that a prosecutor is going to object to defend his complaining witness, because he'll be afraid that the jury will think he's hiding something. Therefore, the rape shield law is a witness protection law. The judge is supposed to deal with that directly. The judge should jump in.

Second, the parole evidence rule in contract law. The parole evidence rule, of course, is not so much a rule of evidence as a rule of commercial law to make sure that contracts in fact are enforced and writings are given some weight. Whether or not the parties invoke the parole evidence rule, the judge should.

In Massachusetts, although not in federal court, a third area in which the judge should step in regardless of whether a party has objected is the private communications between husband and wife. In Massachusetts, that's a rule of competency to testify.

Lastly, the judge intervenes to protect the deference to legislative factfinding (also known as the presumption of constitutionality). The courts, under the doctrine of separation of powers, defer to legislative factfinding, whether or not a party comes in to defend the constitutionality of a statute. As long as it is not one of those statutes that is subjected to strict scrutiny because it has an impact on race, gender or national origin, as long as it is just a standard statute construed on the basis of rationality, the parties do not have to defend it. The judge has the duty to defend it and to search for a reason why it is constitutional.

Now there are the four instances. Those are the only ones that I can think of where the judge gets herself involved and does not have to wait for an objection by a party. The rest of it, however, depends on you as lawyers. Remember, it will not happen unless you ask for it and raise the issue. That means that the law of evidence is a human process. It's a human process in which you are really concerned about the objections that the other side is going to raise against you and how you are going to deal with them. That is what we are talking about here today.

Remember, all breaks go to the judge. *(Laughter)*. No, no; that's a good rule. All breaks go to the judge unless the judge makes an error that affects substantial rights. Whether the judge is right or wrong, the judge is going to be sustained, affirmed on appeal.

These rules of evidence are mainly important in jury cases. They have less of an impact on jury-waived cases. Not that you shouldn't know them when arguing in front of a judge, or that you shouldn't be on top of them and urge them on the judge, or that the judge shouldn't conform her conduct to the rules, but it is important to realize that judges have a lot more flexibility when the case is jury-waived.

The last point to make on this overview is that the law of evidence that we are talking about only exists—to the extent that it does exist—in the adversary process where people come to court to have their disputes resolved. These rules have nothing to do with the Clarence Thomas hearings. They are absolutely immaterial to the Oliver North Irangate investigation. These rules and the concepts therein have nothing to do with legislative inquiries. They pertain only to the courts.

BURDENS OF PROOF

Let's think first in our criminal case *(Commonwealth v. Marada)* who has to prove what and what is it that they have to prove. The first thing you want to think about as you begin an evidentiary analysis regarding who has to prove what is what you have to do to bear what we call the burden of going forward or the burden of making out a prima facie case, i.e., a case that will get you to the jury. The burden of going forward really includes two concepts, which together I call "vectoring evidence."

These concepts are all simplistic. I don't apologize for giving you simplistic concepts. I confess to you that when I am sitting on the bench I am concentrating on the most simple things. Therefore, my advice: keep it simple.

Now, what does "beyond a reasonable doubt" mean? In state court, it roughly equates to proof to a moral certainty. As I recall the charge from my days on the superior court, it goes as follows:

> Not to an absolute or a mathematical certainty but proof to a moral certainty, a certainty that satisfied the judgements and consciences of the jury and leaves in their mind a firm and settled conviction of guilt.

Interestingly, to give that charge, which must be given in the state courts, is error in the federal courts. *Smith v. Butler,* 696 F. Supp. 748 (D. Mass. 1991) (Woodlock, J.). *See Oses v. Massachusetts,* 775 F. Supp. 443, 465–67 (D. Mass. 1991). But I am not here to teach consistency; I'm just here teaching law. So upsetting is that inconsistency to me that I have stopped defining the standard altogether. I simply say about 26 times in my usual charge "proof beyond a reasonable doubt," and I figure direct democracy can work that out. Jurors have seen enough TV; they'll understand what that means. And I am affirmed on that. ***United States v. Littlefield***, 840 F.2d 869, 871–72 (1st Cir.), ***cert. denied***, 109 S.Ct. 155 (1988) (holding that jury instructions defining reasonable doubt are not required but may be given "to the degree [that the judge is] so inclined").

In the First Circuit, a judge does not have to say anything more than "proof beyond a reasonable doubt," and so I don't. The important thing to understand is that legally the standard has nothing to do with math, because, you see, one of the other standards does have to do with math. Proof beyond a reasonable doubt, however it's defined in any of the circuits or states, is a concept that cannot be satisfied by math. It's not 99 percent or 90 percent or any percent. It's proof to some settled conviction that we should adjudicate a person guilty and, therefore, take the next steps of deciding about his liberty and, in many jurisdictions, his life.

Now, what about the other proof with which you are most familiar, that in a civil case: "by a fair preponderance of the evidence"? In a civil case that's math; that's anything over 50 percent. We don't say it, but that's true. The charge on this standard goes as follows:

> If, when all the evidence is before you, what it is that a party has to prove has not been proved, that something else is more likely to be true than not true, then he hasn't proved it. If all the evidence tends equally to two equal but opposite conclusions, he hasn't proved it. But as long as it is more likely to be true than not true, you may take it as proved by a fair preponderance of the evidence.

Most civil cases use the "fair preponderance" standard, but some require proof by clear and convincing evidence. A good example is a libel case. Because of First Amendment values, you have to have proof by clear and convincing evidence in order to prevail in a libel case. What does this standard mean? Nobody really knows. In an elegant Massachusetts decision written by Mr. Justice Quirico, he attacks this standard on the theory that we don't know what it means. ***Stone v. Essex County Newspapers***, 367 Mass. 849, 873–77 (Quirico, J. concurring and dissenting). And he's right; we don't know what it means. The best definition I found is in a federal case, which states: "Clear and convincing evidence is something more than a fair preponderance of the evidence, which means that it is a fair preponderance but we mean it." ***(Laughter)***.

When you go further down the burden-of-proof scale, you come to "probable cause." That's a concept you have to think about, but the words are pretty straightforward. There has to be probable cause to arrest. There has to be probable cause to indict. There are a legion of law review articles about whether those two types of probable cause are different, but the concept is fairly straightforward: Is there probable cause as reasonable men and women to take some governmental action that will affect the individual?

The lowest standard on the totem pole comes in administrative hearings: Is there substantial evidence to support the conclusion of the administrative agency? Well, of course that is the lowest because it doesn't really mean substantial at all. What it means is: Is there any evidence that a reasonable mind could accept to support the result that has been reached? *See* G.L. c. 30A, § 11(2). That standard has been adopted to keep judges away from the proper operation of the administrative agencies within the Executive Branch. It is a standard that is very easy for the executive to meet. It's not truth in advertising to call it substantial evidence because it is not substantial at all, but there it is.

At about the same level on the totem pole is the standard of "articulable suspicion." In order to make a *Terry* stop or to stop a person on the street or to interfere with a person's liberty and pat him down, the police have to have an articulable suspicion. *See Terry v. Ohio*, 392 U.S. 1 (1968). They can't go on a hunch; they need an articulable suspicion. That means that the arresting officer has to tell the reviewing officer, the clerk magistrate, the magistrate judge or the judge why it is that the person was stopped. As long as he can tell why, that's pretty much enough.

So, let's take our criminal case against Marada. The prosecution needs to produce evidence beyond a reasonable doubt as to many issues before the case can even go to the jury. Let's say that the prosecution does not introduce to prove the element of deliberate premeditation beyond a reasonable doubt. All they can get then to the jury in this case is second-degree murder and so on. In a civil case, the plaintiff need only introduce evidence by a fair preponderance of the evidence.

So we are concerned, just to get to the jury, with legally what types of things we have to introduce evidence on, and then we are concerned with what standard of proof we have to meet—depending on the type of case.

That only begins to explain it. There is another whole element of the burden of proof, not just the burden of going forward. I like to think of it as a river with pontoons trying to get across to the other side, which is where the jury sits. Now besides needing enough evidence that suggests to the judge that a jury could find our way, we have the burden of persuasion, that is to persuade the jury beyond a reasonable doubt.

The burden of going forward and the burden of persuasion—here is where the feds and the state differ. In a criminal case in Massachusetts there are matters of defense. In Marada's case, Jack Atwood argued self-defense on behalf of Marada. Atwood says that Marada shot Southwick in self-defense. Southwick had a baseball bat.

Under Massachusetts law, once the defendant raises an issues such as self-defense, licensure to carry a gun, possession of contraband or license to possess contraband, mental capacity, those things that are not the essential elements of the case but are affirmative defenses—like accord and satisfaction in a negligence case—the burden is on the Commonwealth to prove the opposite. Of course the defendant can't just raise the issue by saying, "Oh, by the way, I raise the issue of voluntariness of my statement." He must come forward with something, such as an affidavit expressing that he was not given his *Miranda* warnings or that they were given to him but he was so zonked out that his statement was not voluntary. So, when those things are properly raised, the burden is on the Commonwealth to prove that the statement was voluntary, that the person was not licensed to carry a handgun—and it has to prove those things beyond a reasonable doubt. Mass. Evid. Stand. 302(c); *Commonwealth v. Sires,* 405 Mass. 598, 600, 542 N.E.2d 580, 581 (1989); *Commonwealth v. Moreira,* 385 Mass. 792, 794 (1982). *Commonwealth v. Tavares,* 385 Mass. 140, 430 N.E.2d 1198 (1982), *cert. denied,* 457 U.S. 1137 (1982). That, however, is not required by the federal constitution.

In federal criminal cases, the burden of proving affirmative defenses may—and I say "may" because it depends on the case—rest with the defendant. For example, if the defendant raises incapacity as a defense to a criminal case, it is up to the defendant to prove it beyond a reasonable doubt. Otherwise, the defendant loses. *See Martin v. Ohio,* 480 U.S. 228 (1987), *rehearing denied,* 481 U.S. 1024 (1987).

In a civil case, however, those things that go beyond the essential elements of the case are the defendant's burden. For example, let's say that you can prove this contract, but the contract is a wagering contract, which is against public policy. Whereas the plaintiff brings the lawsuit to enforce the contract and has the burden of proving the existence of the contract, it is up to the defendant to prove that the contract is against public policy and therefore should be avoided.

Thus, in civil cases, the burdens of proof may be shared. Proof of contributory negligence, for instance, falls on the defendant. Proof of accord and satisfaction—a settlement—falls on the defendant. But in criminal cases in the state (in Massachusetts) all the defendant has to do with respect to affirmative defenses is raise them. Then the government (the prosecution) has to dispute them beyond a reasonable doubt.

How to Prove Things

How do we prove things? There are really two ways of proving things: proof by direct evidence and proof by circumstantial evidence. Proof by direct evidence is that evidence we think of as eyewitness evidence, i.e., evidence given by someone who actually saw what it is that is to be proved. Proof by circumstantial evidence is defined as a train of circumstances or incidents that tend to a conclusion that is sought to be reached by the factfinder. Judges will give charges that proof by direct evidence and proof by circumstantial evidence are of equal weight, and legally of course they are.

The best jury studies, however, indicate that we are extraordinarily enamored as a people with scientific evidence. Scientific evidence has great impact. I will tell you that in a case where a writing makes a difference (e.g., a contract case), a contemporaneous writing of what went on between the parties has great significance. As a factfinder, when I sit jury-waived, I am impressed by contemporaneous writings, and I think that most judges and juries are. But, legally, direct and circumstantial evidence have the same impact.

Mathematical Proof

A word about mathematical proof: mathematical proof, probabilistic proof, the math that goes into figuring out what the probability that an event occurred or that a situation is a certain way, is one of the hottest areas of theoretical evidence law. Evidence professors are really into this. You should read law reviews; I don't care what law review you read, it will broaden you. Reading law review articles will get you into stuff that you are not really thinking about. Try to find time to read them.

A conference was held on the subject of mathematical proof not too many years ago. Judge Hallisey and I were going, but I got sick and couldn't go. Hallisey went, and he told me this story. The conference was held at Boston University. He was sitting in the back of the room. The professor was talking and using the board. He was doing some type of math. The fellow next to Hallisey asked him who he was. Hallisey responded, "I am Bob Hallisey." The fellow continued, "And what do you do, Mr. Hallisey?"

Meanwhile the lecture is going on and these two are whispering in the back.

"Well what do you do? I haven't met you." Hallisey says, "Well, I'm a justice of the Massachusetts Superior Court."

The guy leaps up out of his seat. In the middle of the lecture, he signals the professor and yells, "Hold it! We've got a judge here. We have a live one who is actually listening to this."

Judges don't understand any of this stuff. I will tell you that right now. Here is what we know about mathematical proof. Mathematical proof is okay in civil cases. That is, if in the green buses versus yellow buses case you find someone who has bus tracks all over him and you know that 75 percent of the buses in town are green and 25 percent are yellow, then you probably have enough evidence to get the case to the jury against the green bus company. In a civil case in which the standard of proof is by a fair preponderance of the evidence, that may be enough. But as soon as the defense introduces evidence regarding bus routes and things like that, the proof tends to drop out.

It will not work in a criminal case. But in criminal cases you do see all sorts of things like blood typing and all sorts of mathematics that deal with existential reality—what I call first-order evidence. That stuff is admissible in a criminal case. Let's talk that through. We'll take something simple. Fingerprint evidence comes in, and if you press a fingerprint examiner, he will give you the math as to the millions of fingerprints on file and tell you that no one has ever found a match. No one has ever found two different people with the same fingerprints.

Also, you can get into how many people in the community have a blood type. Here's the crime. You have blood evidence. Is it the victim's blood? Is it the perpetrator's blood? Well, the lab tells you that it is not the victim's blood because she has type A blood and this blood is type O. You are entitled to introduce evidence regarding how many people in the community—how many people in society at large—have type O blood. Now of course scientists can analyze the enzymes in the blood, and it is perfectly all right to introduce evidence of how many people in the community have that sort of enzyme characteristic in their blood.

What you cannot do in a criminal case is use what I call second-order statistics. That is, you cannot take the evidence one step further than the existential reality and then say now in the city of such and such if so many people have type O blood, what's the chances that someone with type O blood lives in the community. You can't do that. The reason you can't do that is because proof beyond a reasonable doubt is not mathematical. To do it would be a violation of due process.

So, in a civil case, because of the standard of proof, you can introduce statistical evidence. You are entitled to introduce evidence of a statistical nature or, in other words, survey-type evidence. For example, in an obscenity case where the mores of the community (e.g., is this material patently offensive to you?) is something significant, you are entitled to introduce those types of things.

Now, before we go forward, let me say one other sort of hortatory thing. What we have been discussing is what the law says. If you stop there, if you stop with what the law permits you to introduce, then you have not begun to be a trial lawyer. It is all very well for me to tell you to go and read law review articles, but in order to deal with these concepts of what actually persuades jurors, what is relevant evidence, you really have to do more than that. You have to try to get your head inside the lives of other people.

It is probably the best and most interesting thing we do as lawyers. You should try to find time in your life to read good books, go to good plays and movies, understand the music of other generations so that you have some sense of how people tick. That is the gist of what you have to teach.

RELEVANCE

Let's turn our attention to relevance. Let's take a look at the rules of relevance that are in the federal rules. I'm not going to go through every rule, obviously, but I want to hit on the most important things with respect to relevance, and then we'll move on.

First, Federal Rules 401 and 402 (Massachusetts Evidentiary Standards 401 and 402, respectively). They, of course, are in Article IV. The definition of relevant evidence in the federal rules is probably the best definition going: evidence having any tendency to make the existence of any fact that is of consequence to the determination of the action more probable or less probable than it would be without that evidence.

Any fact of consequence to the action is the first aspect of the law of relevance. We no longer speak of materiality, but that is what is meant. Is it material to a determination of the action that we know this fact? Then you review the elements of the action or affirmative defenses. So those are the elements of the action. Does this piece of proffered evidence, this fact—this thing that is sought to be introduced—have legal consequence to the outcome of the action? That is the concept of materiality. If it does, then does the fact tend to make what is being sought to be proved (i.e., the elements of the action or the affirmative defense) more probable or less probable than it would be without putting that piece of evidence in?

In other words, is it dirt? Does it make a difference? Think of this for a minute: I'm on the superior court. I'm trying a case in Brockton. It's a backyard fence dispute. We are going question, answer, question, answer, question—

"Objection!"

"Overruled."

"Well, your Honor, may I be heard?"

Now, judicial temperament is very important, so I say, "Yes, you may; come to sidebar."

"Well, well, your Honor, I'm really unhappy. I'm unhappy that this matter has been raised and that it is being allowed."

And then I can't resist. It's all downhill from here. This is my best line as a judge. I look at the lawyer—I still have the transcript of this—and I say, "Yes, but your happiness is not the touchstone of admissibility. What is your objection?" *(Laughter)*.

The transcript of course doesn't show this, but there is a long pause. The objecting lawyer then says, "Nothing. I just wanted it on the record how unhappy I am." *(Laughter)*.

So the first aspect of relevance is materiality. The second is what we call "logical relevance." I know it's simplistic, but I want to keep emphasizing that the simple things are the things that actually work in court. Is it dirt? Does it make a difference? How do we know whether it makes a difference?

This is one of the most unsettling things about trial practice. The reason I start with relevance is because the relevance rules are the most important rules. Relevance is where all judges start. It is where all legal analysis about the law of evidence starts. If it's not relevant, it's not admitted. If it is relevant, it should be admitted unless it has some other problems, unless something else—some other rule—keeps it out.

Now, what's material. Well, the judge may know something about this because the judge knows what the elements of the case are and what has to be proved. Logical relevance is the judge's life experience. Judges have not dealt drugs. They may not even know what marijuana smells like. Judges by and large are not involved in sexual peccadilloes. I'm not citing morality here. *(Laughter)*.

I'm just trying to give you a picture of the group as a whole. I mean, you know, maybe they don't have much of a life experience at all; you know, they go around wearing a black robe. Your job, and this is key, is to make that judge understand why in the circumstances of this case this dirt is in fact dirt.

Let's think of some of the things that are really frontier things. The business about the language of the illegal numbers game—now the lottery has pretty much put those people out of business—and all the lingo about laying off bets and things like that, judges may not understand that. You may need to explain why that makes a difference. Judges may not understand the argot of the street. Likewise, they don't understand arbitrage or insider trading. There are a lot of things that we may not understand. It is your job to teach us.

Brief Briefs and Using Precedent

The way to teach us about something's relevance and really about all aspects of evidence is by submitting what I call a brief brief. You certainly don't learn the brief brief in law school. The brief brief is never more than three pages long and never more than three citations because trials are fast. The citations should come from the jurisdiction in which or for which the judge works. I work for the First Circuit. When I was a state judge, I worked for the SJC and the Appeals Court. So get something that controls the judge. Cite that thing and cite it properly. In the Massachusetts state courts be sure to cite to the *Mass. Reports* or the *Appeals Court Reports*. If you don't, the judge does not have the *Northeast Reporter* and will not be able to find the case. If they are lucky enough to sit in a courthouse that has a library, they will send the court officer to the library for the *Northeast 2nd* (you know, the N.E.2d) if that is what you cite, and the officer will come back with the *New England Law Review*. That just doesn't work. Therefore, cite to the *Mass. Reports* for SJC opinions and to the *Appeals Court Reports* for appeals court decisions. Then quote the case you are citing; make it work for you. In other words, do not use the names in the case you're quoting. Instead use the names in your case and apply the law of the case being cited to your case. Remember, however, to use *Bluebook* accuracy. Put brackets around it. Use ellipses—the dot, dot, dot. Don't use ellipses to drop out the word "not." That is wrong and misleading. *(Laughter)*.

Do you want to know something about the practice in Massachusetts, both state and federal? The practice in Massachusetts state and federal courts is of very high quality. When I said earlier that I am very honored to have you people spend a Saturday morning with me, I really am. I know most of you. And that is true about most judges. We talk about you. That is what we talk about—you.

Don't ever sell yourself short. Don't ever, ever, try to put something over on a judge. Even if you could, don't. If the judge is sliding into error and you need to correct the judge—even though correcting the judge may not help you or your case—say, "Judge, I really like that charge, but I think that it is a mistake." Tom Heffernan once did this when I was giving him a favorable charge. I have never forgotten that, and judges won't. We'll respect you for it.

On the other hand, if you tell us something that is not true, you might get it by us at the time, but we will never forget it. We will tell everyone we know, and they will never forget it.

In teaching you, the way I try to guard against that type of situation is to tell you to think of yourselves as teachers—not slick mouthpieces, you are teachers. You teach the law to the judge and the facts to the jury. Okay.

Now back to the brief brief. It cites the cases in the jurisdiction. The analysis is different than what you were taught in law school. In relevance matters, the judge is looking for a case factually like your case. That sounds pretty pedestrian, doesn't it? But I will tell you that that is how we work. We know what the doctrine of relevance is—logical relevance and materiality—but we are looking for a case like the one in front of us.

Let's take fresh complaint evidence in a rape case. I mean, what is fresh? And rape now of course encompasses child abuse where the child is in the home. We have come a long way as to that. Fresh does not mean just the next day. It does not mean when a kid goes to school. It could be the next summer when the kid's off at summer camp away from the abusive parents. Do you see?

How do judges figure those things out? We are looking for cases factually similar to the case that is before us. Those cases will give us guidance in defining what is fresh in the factual sense. Find us those cases; that's what helps.

Relevance, Rule by Rule

Rule 401 defines evidence. Rule 402 tells us that relevance is in and irrelevance is out.

Let's consider Rule 403, which is the federal rule and now the state rule as well. *United States v. Sutton*, 970 F.2d 1001, 1008 (1st Cir. 1995). Mass. Evid. Stand. 403; *Nally v. Volkswagen of America, Inc.*, 405 Mass. 191, 197, 539 N.E.2d 1017, 1021 (1989). Rule 403 is a trump card. If the prejudicial effect of evidence substantially outweighs its probative value, that evidence can be excluded. Understand that the balancing test is not scaled in equilibrium. The prejudicial effect has to *substantially* outweigh the probative value. Otherwise the evidence gets in.

Let's take a products liability case. A liquid sealant was exposed to a pilot light, blew up and hideously burned some poor guy. The warning on the bottle was tiny: "Don't expose to a heat source." The manufacturer later changed the warning and made it more pronounced. The new warning included a skull and crossbones and stated, "WARNING: DANGER TO FIRE." Of course, the plaintiff at trial has both of these and wants to show them to the jury. The defendant says, "Wait a minute." And you know what is coming. "This is subsequent repairs here. The second warning was placed on the bottle after the incident. That is not admissible under the subsequent repairs doctrine."

The plaintiff responds, "Oh. I am just showing it to demonstrate what was feasible and that the defendant could have printed skulls and crossbones on the first warning. The defendant could have put them on there back then. Because it was feasible—and this is a products liability case—I am entitled to admit this evidence."

I'm listening at sidebar and I say, "That sounds right to me." Defense counsel answers, "Your Honor, if you let that evidence in, it croaks me."

That is a 403 objection. See? That is what you keep in mind. If the evidence will croak you, then you want to raise a 403 objection. If you cannot think of anyway else to keep out such damaging evidence, think of Rule 403. That is what you want to raise with the judge. But remember, any prejudice must substantially outweigh the evidence's probative value. Prejudice by itself will not do it. In the actual case, I overruled the objection and admitted the second warning into evidence to show feasibility. Defense counsel was right. It did croak him. I was affirmed on appeal. Okay, there we are. ***(Laughter)***.

Next, let's discuss 404. This is where we begin to get technical. It is very, very important. Rule 404—and the state common law rule is very much the same as the federal—says that evidence of a person's character or trait of character is not admissible for proving action in conformity therewith. ***People v. Smith***, Florida Circuit Court (1991).

Let's look at the exceptions. Rule 405 tells us how to prove character, and Rule 608 is also relevant on this issue of how to prove character. Rule 405 says that you can prove character by reputation and then you can go into specific instances if character or trait of character is an essential element to the case. We are on very vague ground here. The people who want this type of mud in are keen on telling us that this case is one where character is an essential element.

Character is an essential element in the following types of cases:

- Discrimination cases of all sorts (racial, gender bias—character is essential to those cases). That's why, for example, in ***Brown v. Boston University*** you get in the remark made by the BU president about the English Department being a "damned matriarchy." 891 F.2d 337, 349 (1st Cir. 1989).
- Child custody cases and adoption suits. In those types of cases, character is an essential element of what the judge has to decide. So those statements, those specific incidents of conduct that bear on the character of the person to care for the kid are admissible.

Back to the exceptions to Rule 404. First, if the accused puts his own character into evidence, the government can rebut it. Second, if self-defense is raised as a defense—and here in the ***Marada*** case it is—then the victim's reputation for violence is admitted if the defendant first puts in evidence that he was reasonably in fear of the victim and that is why the defendant struck the first blow or went to the rendezvous armed. *See Commonwealth v. Edmonds*, 365 Mass. 496, 501–04, 313 N.E.2d 429, 432–34 (1974); *Commonwealth v. Rubin*, 318 Mass. 587, 588, 63 N.E.2d 344, 345 (1945). Then the third and most important—and most frequently used—exception states that once a witness has taken the stand, the witness's character is in play and subject to being examined.

There are cross-references in the rule to other rules, such as 607, 608 and 609. So let's quickly touch on those. Federal Rule 607 says that the reputation of any witness may be impeached by any party. So that means that you can put a witness on the stand and you can destroy that witness yourself. This strays from the common law notion that you vouched for your witnesses. In the past, if you put a witness on the stand yourself, you could not impeach that witness yourself.

In Massachusetts state court, you now can impeach a witness that you call if it is relevant for you to impeach, except that you cannot impeach by using a prior conviction. Mass.R.Civ.P. 43(b); Mass. Evid. Stand. 607. *See Walter v. Bonito*, 367 Mass. 117, 324 N.E.2d 625 (1975). If you call a witness to the stand, you cannot use the prior convictions against that witness. G.L. c. 233, § 23. However, in proper circumstances you can impeach your own witness if you are surprised—if the witness testifies in contrary to what you expected—and you justify it to the judge. Obviously, the other side can impeach any witness that is called.

The Seventh Circuit has said, and I agree, that you cannot call a witness to the stand just to impeach the witness. Let's say that you know the other side is going to call a witness. So, in the middle of your case, you call that witness.

"Hello. What is your name?"

"My name is William Witness."

"Mr. Witness, isn't it true that you were convicted of child molesting three years ago? Thank you very much. Step down."

Then you wait to see William Witness when the defense calls him. The Seventh Circuit says that you cannot do that. *United States v. Webster*, 734 F.2d 1191, 1192–93 (7th Cir. 1984) (Posner, J.). And I think that the Seventh Circuit's position is right. It's common sense. You have to have some good faith reason for calling the witness. Then, if the witness sabotages you, you can ask to lead the witness and you may impeach him.

It's Rule 608 that's tricky. I mean, how do we impeach witnesses? We impeach witnesses by suggesting that the witness has not been truthful on other occasions; she has lied. You are entitled to do that. You are entitled to go into the specific circumstances. This is true on both the state and federal level, in both civil and criminal cases. Once a witness takes the stand, on cross-examination you can bring out other instances when that witness has not been truthful, whether or not that instance has anything to do with this case. *Commonwealth v. Bohannon*, 376 Mass. 90, 378 N.E.2d 987 (1978). As always, of course, there are limitations on this. The judge may put limitations of time and cumulativeness, but you are entitled to do it absent any limitations.

Rule 608 states that you cannot do it by extrinsic evidence. Let me give you a case. It happens to be a rape case, and my ruling was in error—and I learned from it. I was sitting up in Newburyport, and a victim claimed to have been raped by members of a motorcycle gang. Among the defenses was that the victim was a prostitute and was upset because the defendants had not paid her. It was a tragic case. The victim was also involved in another rape case up in Essex. In the Essex case, the defendant claimed that he had had consensual sex with the victim and that he refused to pay her, and so she claimed rape.

Well, I had the biker case in Newburyport. Defense counsel in that case argued, "I want to put on the evidence of this other case in Essex. I want to call the defendant in that case. Here's his affidavit saying that none of this happened and that sex was consensual."

I said, "Wait a second. That has nothing to do with this case. That's another case. Besides, you can't get that in because of the rape shield law at G.L. c. 233, § 21B."

"Oh, Judge, we are not interested in violating the rape shield law. We are not interested in her character or anything like that. She lies. We are interested in showing that she lies. She is engaged in commerce, and then her way of enforcing her commercial contract is to say, 'If you don't pay, I'll cry rape.'"

I felt that the argument sounded pretty valid so I said, "Gee. I guess that's right."

First Assistant DA, Bob Winer, then went crazy. He went to Judge Braucher and claimed, "Young has lost his senses here. Mandamus him."

But Judge Braucher said that he wouldn't interfere. So in the middle of my biker case in comes Ben Businessman, the defendant in the Essex case, who gives us another entire story that has nothing to do with my case. It took about a day to examine and cross-examine him. I felt that I was right in my ruling. I guess I wasn't. You know why I wasn't right? Because the rule is that the defense had every right to cross-examine the victim about the other case when she was on the stand. They could have asked her:

"And isn't it true, madam, that this is not the first time that you have claimed you have been raped?"

"No, it's not the first time."

"And, in fact, isn't it true that on another occasion you have accused another man of rape because after prostituting yourself he wouldn't pay?"

And the victim witness would claim that it isn't true, or she could say whatever she wanted to. But the important part is that, even with the protection offered by the rape shield law, she is subject to cross-examination, to being hammered with those questions because, you see, that information goes to whether she is telling the truth.

The testimony of Ben Businessman was extrinsic evidence. He had nothing to do with the case in front of me. His was another case. You can't use him, but you can cross-examine her. Obviously, before you get into this other dirt, and it is dirt—I mean, "Where did you make this claim before? Were you involved with another man before in a similar situation?" You have to demonstrate to the court, especially in light of the rape shield law, a good faith basis for the questioning. In my biker case, good faith could have been demonstrated with an affidavit by Ben Businessman under oath in which he states that the woman tried to stick him up a certain way. Then you can try to impeach her through cross-examination. You can show her documents to impeach her, to get her to commit, but you cannot get the documents admitted into evidence. You cannot prove it except to the extent you can get her to admit to it on cross-examination.

Let's backtrack just a little. Rule 404(b) is probably the most glaring exception to the rule that character evidence cannot be introduced. There are examples that suggest that if the evidence of the other crimes, wrongs or acts is probative of a whole variety of things, such as intention, opportunity, etc., then such evidence can be introduced to prove those things. There is a significant gloss on this rule, and it is roughly the same in both federal and state court practice. Before you can get this 404(b) evidence admitted, you have to tell the judge and the other side before the trial begins so that they have some idea of what they have to meet. You are not supposed to spring evidence of other crimes, wrongs and acts in the middle of trial.

Let me just discuss some examples, and we'll move on. The prosecution in the Florida case tried to get in the statements of the other women, on the ground that it showed modus operandi. They're talking about the Florida Williams Rule. That comes from the Georgia case of the fellow they convicted in the case of all the young boys found dead in the Chattahoochee River—there were about 22 murders of these young men. *See Williams v. State*, 251 Ga. 749 (1983). Finally, they convicted a guy named Williams of one or two of the murders. They convicted him because someone had seen his car in the vicinity of the river at an odd time, and on a number of the victims, there were tiny microscopic hairs from a car mat that was from his type of car. Great forensic business by the FBI. But in the *Williams* case, the government, and the Georgia courts, allowed in evidence of nine other killings in addition to the two that Williams was being tried for to show modus operandi.

And here was the similarity: All nine of the bodies in the Chattahoochee River, had this fiber element. But I'm not sure of that fact. And then as to the two, it was something tying in this guy particularly. And they said that's enough; his thing was to pick up stray young fellows, to molest them, to strangle them—all nine had been strangled—and to throw their bodies in the Chattahoochee River, that's enough.

So on that theory, the government in this particular Florida case says picking up the women, being charming, so on and so forth, and then assaulting them is sufficiently similar. Judge Lupo says, no, it isn't.

Here are two other examples in other types of cases. In Massachusetts, I believe it's *Commonwealth v. Baker*, 356 Mass. 58 (1974), a fellow who was a bail bondsman was making off with the bail money. They had him for nine counts of larceny. They had the nine bail bonds and so on, then they put in 14 other bail bonds that he hadn't accounted for to show that that was the way that he did business—that he would take the bail from the person, then he would abscond with it.

In the *Clemente* case, the *Exam Scam* case, I permitted to be introduced evidence of sales to people other than the police chiefs who were on trial before me to show that Clemente and Doherty had the opportunity to steal the exams and were in an ongoing business of selling them. *United States v. Doherty*, 675 F.Supp. 726 (D.Mass. 1987), *aff'd*, 867 F.2d 47 (1st Cir.), *cert. denied*, 109 S.Ct. 3243 (1989). But that's heavy evidence, isn't it? Because some of these people who they gave immunity to came up and said, "Yeah, Doherty sold me an exam. Yeah, it was a sergeant's exam." They know nothing about the chief or the chief's exam. They never saw the chief. They don't know it was sold to the chief, but they're willing, because they've got immunity, to testify. And the government says this shows Clemente's and Doherty's operation. So you introduce it in the case as against Doherty but you keep it out as to the police chiefs because they were a coconspiracy.

Habit

Rule 406 is a rule inclusive of evidence. It's the rule that allows in habit and routine practice. Now, people think that you can get into evidence under this rule the fact that there were other accidents on the premises and that will show that the people were negligent. That's not what this rule means. Habit and routine practice has to be real habit.

For example, a fellow goes through a stop sign, and he gets into an accident. You ride to work with him, and you know that on another occasion he has gone through that stop sign. That's not admissible as habit or routine. Say you ride to work with him, and you ride to work with him because you went to college with him and have known him a long time. And you know that he would go through stop signs in the college town and in other places. This too is not admissible. Now say that you ride to work with him every day and he always goes through that same stop sign. That is admissible. That is sort of where the line is.

Habit and routine practice is terribly important in commercial cases where you are trying to show how a business operates. The foundation question is "What is the customary practice your company has for sending out these invoices and similar documents?" Rule 406 is the rule that lets that information into evidence.

Exclusionary Rules

Here is a litany of things, of rules that keep specific things out. I'll just tick them off very quickly. First, Rule 407 addresses subsequent remedial measures. If you repair the area afterwards, the plaintiff cannot get the fact that you made repairs into evidence to try to prove negligence. This rule is based on the social policy that we want people to make repairs. So, say you have a landlord/tenant case. The tenant falls down the stairs as a result of stepping on a loose board. The landlord then repairs the step. You cannot introduce into evidence the fact that the landlord subsequently repaired the step to prove negligence. Allowing such things into evidence may discourage landlords from fixing faulty conditions.

However, if the landlord is foolish enough to deny that he owns the house, then you can introduce the evidence that he repaired the step to show that he owns the house—because who would repair the step except the owner of the house? You can also get around this rule in a products liability case to show feasibility. In those cases, what is feasible is crucial. *See Schaeffer v. General Motors Corp.*, 372 Mass. 171, 175–77, 360 N.E.2d 1062, 1066 (1977). So if you could have designed the machine with a guard on it, the fact that later on you designed it with guards is admissible. What is not admissible is that you designed the machine with a guard later on to correct for the accident. But jurors are not fools. They know that the machine has a guard on it. So you can get it in in products liability cases.

Settlement offers are inadmissible pursuant to Rule 408. *See also* Mass. Evid. Stand. 408; *Murray v. Foster,* 343 Mass. 655, 659–60, 180 N.E.2d 311, 314 (1962). Although settlement offers may be relevant because the mere offer to settle may indicate that you think you are liable, that you have to pay something, they are inadmissible. Payment of medical expenses and similar expenses, if you try to resolve a matter, is not admissible.

Insurance is not admissible. *See* Mass. Evid. Stand. 411; *Goldstein v. Gontarz*, 364 Mass. 800, 807–14, 309 N.E.2d 311, 314 (1974).

In criminal cases, the offer of a plea is not admissible. Mass. Evid. Stand. 410. *See* Mass.R.Crim.P. 12(f).

Also, the rape shield law fits here too. G.L. c. 233, § 21B. Mass. Evid. Stand. 412. The prior sexual conduct of an alleged victim in a sexual abuse case is not admissible. There, however, are two exceptions in the rules. First, if the prior conduct reveals or is probative of some physical attribute, e.g., where the seminal fluid came from, then that type of evidence is admissible in the judge's discretion. Second, if the prior sexual conduct was with the alleged assailant, then that too may be admissible where a defense of consent is raised. That type of evidence is admissible on the theory that there may have been some relationship there. And, of course, as I mentioned before, you can try and get around the rape shield law in other ways if the evidence you want to introduce goes to truth telling.

Massachusetts state courts balance the probative value of the evidence against the injury to the witness. The feds balance the probative value of the evidence against the prejudicial effect to the trial in general. Compare G.L. c. 233, § 21B with Fed.R.Evid. 412.

Scope of Examining Witnesses

Let's describe the scope of examining witnesses, both in federal and state court. In the courts of the Commonwealth, there is what is called "wide-open cross." So regardless of the scope of direct examination, the cross can cover anything that is relevant. Mass. Evid. Stand. 611(b); *Davis v. Hotel Statler Co.*, 327 Mass. 98, 97 N.E.2d 187 (1951). Remember that relevance is the first and great rule of evidence. However, after your wide-open cross, the redirect must be within the scope of the cross and the recross must be within the scope of the redirect, and then eventually we can cut you off altogether. Mass. Evid. Stand. 611(c).

The federal rule is different—although in a moment I will explain why the practice is basically the same. In federal court, the rule is that the cross must be within the scope of the direct. However, the judge in her discretion may let you go outside the scope of the direct if you take the witness, when discussing those materials that are outside the scope of direct, as if you had the witness yourself on direct examination. Fed.R.Evid. 611(b). That is a long way of saying that, when discussing that other stuff that is outside the scope of direct, you cannot lead the witness. You see, in both state and federal court you cannot lead the witness on direct, but you should lead the witness on cross.

What do we mean by that? Let's review a little. This is sort of a trial practice thing. This is how you do direct examination to avoid leading. You take the same language that is given to the cub reporter: who, what, when, where, how, describe, explain, and if state of mind is an issue, why. Why did you do that? How did you feel?

So often you hear lawyers say, "Did you go to the store? Did you buy an orange? Did you put the orange in the bag?" All those questions are leading. Judges vary on how strict they are on leading, but none of those questions needs to be leading. Simply ask, "Where did you go? What did you do when you got there? Where did you put the orange that you just said that you purchased?"

Who, what, where, how, describe, explain. During direct examination, make your questions start with one of those words—and use proper grammar—and it will work because they will then be open-ended, nonleading questions.

Of course, on cross-examination, you want to lead. In federal court, if the judge allows you to go beyond the scope of direct, you will have to examine the witness as if the witness were on direct. The truth is that here in the District of Massachusetts we do not pay much attention to that. You get some mileage from that rule from Judge Keeton because he was a Texas practitioner and he really understands all this stuff. The rest of us were all Massachusetts practitioners and we are familiar with the Massachusetts rule. It works rather well. Because it is in our discretion anyway, you can't appeal it. Now, thereafter, the technical rules work the same. The scope of the redirect has to be within the scope of the cross, the scope of the recross has to be within the scope of the redirect and so on.

Moreover, at least two of our judges on the federal district court here in Massachusetts, Skinner and Zobel, have as a general rule that when you are done with recross, you are done. You only get two different rounds: direct, cross, redirect and recross. That is in their discretion. You may query whether they are absolutely rigid on that, but that at least is the way they do it.

Adverse Witnesses

What is an adverse witness? The adverse witness is the witness who is the other side or is so allied with the other side that he or she becomes the other side. In a criminal case, if you as defense counsel have to call a police officer, even though he's not in the prosecutor's office, he would be an adverse witness to your side.

The state and federal rules on adverse witnesses are roughly the same. The scope of the cross must be within the scope of the direct. If you were to let the scope of the cross go outside the scope of the direct on an adverse witness, you would be able to put your whole case in the middle of the other side's case, which would be unfair. Judges tend to follow that rule.

Let's say that in a case, I have to call the defendant's bookkeeper simply to identify the books and records of the corporation. Then, I'm going to croak them with those books and records with my accounting expert. It would be unfair to have the bookkeeper in the middle of my case tell all that he knows about this and that and the defenses and why there are two sets of books. I would ask my simple question: "Are these the books and records that were shown to the public?" If it's an adverse witness, I can lead the witness. But the cost is that the other side has to stay within the scope that I have set out, and now comes the dispute.

Can the other side lead? It's clear that I can lead on direct with an adverse witness, but when I have put an adverse witness on the stand, can the side whose witness it really is lead? The superior court is split pretty much 50/50 on that. About half the judges will say you can, and half the judges will make you take the witness on direct. That's true of the federal court, too. It sort of depends on your judge. For what it's worth, I will let you lead. Then, of course, the redirect, the recross has to be within the scope as it goes.

IMPEACHMENT

I want to go over the elements of impeachment. The only thing I'm going to deal with in any detail is Rule 613, concerning prior statements. Let's go over how you impeach a witness, looking at it in a trial practice sense.

Witnesses come up to build the case that the plaintiff has, whether civil or criminal. These witnesses are busily putting together a pontoon bridge to get to the jury. How are you going to deal with those witnesses if you're on the other side?

Probably the first thing you want to think of is the witness's faculties. Can the witness see and hear? Can the witness remember the things about which he or she testified? Cases take a long time to come to trial. People confabulate; they don't lie, but they tend to look at their earlier statements or someone else's statement and remember from the statement, rather than from what actually happened. You want to uncover logical inconsistencies in a witness's testimony, regardless of whether or not he or she had given a prior statement that's different. You've got some idea of how the witness says something happened, and it just doesn't ring true to you.

You read widely, and study the pertinent area of business or human behavior, but the witness's testimony doesn't ring true. Here's where cross-examination would be appropriate. How does the witness appear to you on direct examination? Where does the witness hesitate? Are there any verbal or body position clues as to where the witness may be weak?

You also can use prior inconsistent statements. We all ask interrogatories; we all take depositions in civil cases. We all are concerned with the statements the government has taken in criminal cases. We want to uncover all the things that may be different that the witness said to the government agents ahead of time, because we can use them to our advantage.

If a witness has a prior conviction, Rule 609 and the cognate Massachusetts statute (G.L. c. 23, § 21B) deal with that. The Massachusetts statute, which is also set out at Mass. Evidentiary Standard 609(b), by its terms doesn't give the judge any discretion, but by common law in Massachusetts, the judge has discretion not to admit the prior conviction. ***Commonwealth v. Feroli***, 407 Mass. 405, 408 (1990); ***Commonwealth v. Bembury***, 406 Mass. 552, 561 (1990).

These are the general rules with respect to prior convictions. The judge will not admit a prior conviction of rape in a rape case, because it is thought to be too prejudicial and goes directly to character. The only character that Rule 609 or the Massachusetts statute deals with is the character for truth telling. A prior conviction is supposed to show that a person is not a terribly truthful person. Obviously, the prior convictions you'd most like to admit are convictions for forgery or failing to pay your income tax—things that involve direct truth. Assault and battery, for instance, has nothing to do with truth telling. One that is perhaps on the cusp is drug dealing, on the theory that it involves surreptitiousness, being secret and falsification.

Another area to consider is bias. Does the witness favor one side or the other? In a criminal case the government may have cut a deal with the witness. Even if they didn't cut a deal, these people are hoping that the government won't prosecute them.

Cross-examination for bias is constitutionally based in a criminal case; it's part of the confrontation clause.

(15-minute recess taken)

To take a step back for a moment, I would like to address a question that was raised during the recent break, concerning what I mean when I say "burden of persuasion." That ties into another question: How does it work on a motion for directed verdict? I think I can answer the two of them together.

As a practical matter, the system is comprised both of the burden of going forward and the burden of persuasion. The burden of going forward refers to how much evidence there must be before a judge will allow a jury to decide a case. If the judge makes an error in calculating this, and the jury convicts or finds for the plaintiff, on appeal, the judge should be reversed because there is not sufficient evidence.

The burden of persuasion refers to convincing the jury. You must present relevant evidence that will make the jury believe you.

How does the judge do a motion for directed verdict? The judge simply asks herself: Is there enough that a reasonable jury could find for the plaintiff? The judge does not ask herself: Do I find for the plaintiff? That's absolutely wrong. In fact, I could tell you, again speaking personally, there are cases where I would go defendant but I give to the jury because there's enough that reasonable people could go to the plaintiff. That's the standard for directed verdict.

Prior Inconsistent Statements

All right. Prior inconsistent statements. Now, as a trial practice matter here's how you handle prior inconsistent statements. Think of the "Three Cs." In order to use a prior inconsistent statement most forcefully you want to ***confirm*** the witness's testimony on direct, if you're going to impeach it, you want to ***compare*** the testimony on direct with the veracity of what you're going to use to confront, and then you want to ***confront*** the witness with the prior inconsistent statement.

Confirm, compare, confront. And quick example, you've got a deposition that says that the traffic light was green; the witness has said the traffic light was red. Now, you shouldn't just go over the witness's direct so the witness gets a chance to say it twice. So we're on cross-examination; we've got a deposition that says the traffic light is green.

You do say, "Now, Mr. Witness, as I recall, you said something about the color of that traffic light."

"Yes."

"And you think you know the color that the traffic light was at the time?"

"Yes."

That's the confirm. Now the compare.

"This isn't the first time that you've spoken about this matter, is it?"

"No."

"In fact, you've given a deposition. Now, the deposition was much closer in time to the incident. It was under oath. You were trying to tell the truth then, correct?"

All the good things, or the statement to the police officer, the same type of thing, the compare. And only then, having done that, do you confront.

"I show you this. Look at the last page. That's your signature, isn't it?"

Never waive signatures on depositions because that is where you use them.

"That's your signature?"

"Yes, it is."

"Now, sir, I ask you, is it not true that I asked you this question?" Then you have the witness read the answer. This is how I think is a good way to do it, and get him to say it.

"No."

"That's what you said on the deposition, isn't it?"

"No."

And then of course you don't just want to impeach; you want to go to see if you can't get it as affirm evidence. You want the witness to agree to it.

Then you say, "And that's the truth, isn't it?"

There's a slight difference between state and federal practice. The state follows the rule in *Queen Charlotte's* case. 129 Eng. Rep. 976 (1820).

In the *Queen Charlotte* case, the wife of William IV was tried for adultery. Love letters were introduced with the queen on the stand. In the House of Lords, the rule is that you have to confront the witness with the inconsistent statement so he or she has a chance to explain. That's still the rule in Massachusetts. The rule is satisfied by simply getting the witness to authenticate what it is that you're ripping him or her with. *See* G.L. c. 233, § 23: Mass. Evid. Stand. 613(a).

For example, you would say, "That's your signature on that deposition, isn't it?"

The witness would answer, "Yes, it is."

You would say, "You said that, didn't you?"

You maintain complete control, and you don't give the witness a chance to elaborate. Leave that for redirect.

Under the federal rule, you can impeach the witness by introducing the inconsistent statement without the witness even on the stand, so long as the witness can be recalled to the stand to explain. *See* Fed.R.Evid. 613(a).

HEARSAY

Let's turn to the next concept—the law of hearsay. The diagram for hearsay that I prefer is that of Professor Michael Graham, the author of the Federal Rules of Evidence and various evidence texts.

A declarant, a person out of court, sees an event and says something about it that a witness hears. Then the witness is called at trial to testify. That's the setting.

HEARSAY

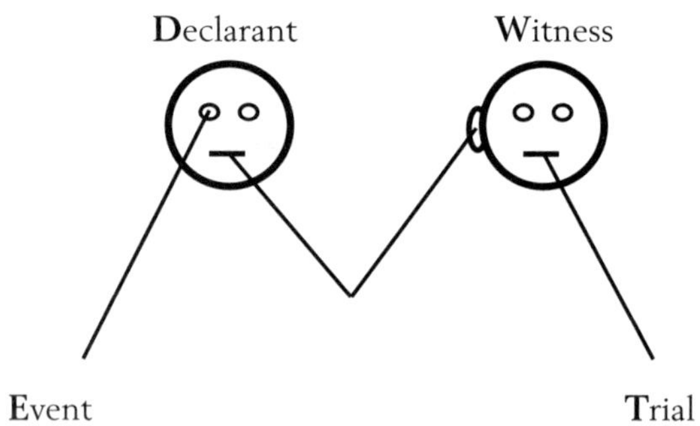

The rule against hearsay is that an out-of-court statement will not be admitted in court for the truth of the matter that the statement asserts. The rule against hearsay is the rule that most makes a trial in the United States different from any other proceeding, requires the best evidence and requires the expenditure of significant funds to get people to come in to testify. We follow the rule against hearsay in our courts so we have actual witnesses who have observed actual events. We also follow the exceptions.

I think of the rule against hearsay as the M rule. Here's what's the matter with hearsay: We haven't got the declarant, so we don't know how well the declarant could see, hear or observe whatever the declarant saw or heard.

Second, we don't know what's going on in the declarant's mind. The declarant may be very biased and may slant things when he or she speaks. Likewise, we've got a witness. It's sort of like the game of telephone: Did the witness hear it right or is the witness biased, and is the witness telling it correctly?

With the witness, there is a guarantee of reliability, because we're going to cross-examine the witness on his or her ability to testify truthfully or his or her willingness to testify truthfully. We're also going to cross-examine the witness on the witness's ability to hear what the witness says he or she heard. Simply put, we are unable to know whether the declarant actually saw anything properly, and what's going on in the declarant's mind that the declarant speaks about.

With that in mind, the search is to find something that satisfies at least one of these other two prongs. Most of the exceptions can be grouped under things we either think under the circumstances that the witness would not have testified, or the Rule 803 grouping of exceptions, where we think that the witness would not have said the things that he or she said unless he or she was talking reliably.

An example of one of these exceptions is the excited utterance. An example of an excited utterance is when someone speaks right out, saying something like, "Oh, my God, look at this." Even though the declarant's not there, we'll accept the excited utterance if it's really excited. The common law theory is that people who are excited tell the truth. Whether it accords with reality is not important. With respect to the witness who heard the excited utterance, the witness who didn't see anything, we can cross-examine that witness on what he or she heard and what his or her bias is.

But suppose the declarant and the witness are the same person? An out-of-court statement offered in court for the truth of the matter asserted is hearsay; that obtains whether the declarant is someone other than the witness or whether the declarant and the witness are the same. So the M Theory doesn't work when the declarant and the witness are the same. And, in fact, there are two whole bodies of exceptions to the hearsay rule that operate when the declarant and the witness are one person.

Remember that you want to be concerned with whether the statement is offered for the truth of the matter asserted. If the statement is independently relevant, there is no hearsay problem.

Here's an example. In a contract action, if I say, "I offer to sell you this blue pen for 25 cents," and you say, "I accept," I haven't transferred it. There's some question as to my title to the pen for full disclosure, but what we've said is what's relevant under the law. I don't have to give the pen to you. If it's a general offer, and I say, "I offer," and the person says, "I accept," that's what's significant. That's what the law will enforce. If I'm lying at the time I make the offer, it's a Chapter 93A violation so the other person would get $25.00 plus attorney fees. *See* G.L. c. 93A, §§ 2, 9, 11.

When you get a hearsay objection, the first thing you want to think of is, "Is there a reason why the statement should be admitted?" If there is, and you've got a witness who heard it, you don't have a hearsay problem at all. If what is relevant is that this was said, then you've got a witness who can testify, because the witness is competent on personal knowledge. They heard it, they're competent to testify, and you can cross-examine on both sides of their observation. That's how you want to analyze it.

If something's hearsay, you've got a fallback position. When you hit a hearsay objection, ask yourself: Is the statement itself relevant? If the statement itself is relevant, you don't have a hearsay problem.

In negligent cases, for instance, you frequently get the situation where the statement puts the tortfeasor on notice. An example of this type of statement is, "You'd better clean up the floor in front of the cabbages; it's all slippery from cabbages having fallen on the floor." If you're trying to introduce that statement to prove that the floor is slippery, and that cabbages fell on the floor, none of that is admissible. If you're trying to introduce that statement to show that the store owner had the opportunity to rectify the condition because he was on notice of it, you're going to need some independent evidence that the condition actually obtained. However, it's admissible for the fact of notice, because the witness who heard the statement can testify that the store owner was present and heard it.

Exceptions to the Hearsay Rule

There are four major exceptions to the hearsay rule. The first exception deals with situations where the declarant and the witness are the same. In the Federal Rules of Evidence, those situations are simply declared not to be hearsay (*See* Fed.R.Evid. 801(d)), but I treat them as exceptions because it's easier for me to understand.

The first major exception deals with prior statements of the witness. The second major exception is where the declarant, or the declarant's agent or the like, is a party. The excited utterance example above falls into the third major grouping of exceptions. Rule 803 spells this out, where by life experience, we think that the statements are reliable. The fourth group of exceptions are based on necessity. It's just straining and an act to say we think they're reliable.

Now, let's go over each of them quickly. What statements are admissible where a declarant is the witness? In federal court, any prior statement of a witness given under the pains and penalties of perjury is substantively admissible under Rule 801(d)(1)(A). So in federal courts, the prior deposition testimony is admissible in evidence for the truth of what it asserts, even though it was given out of court, because the witness is on the stand and has given the prior statement under oath.

In state court, you can use the prior statements to impeach, but they are not substantively admissible standing alone where it's a witness (as opposed to a party). *See* Mass. Evid. Stand. 801(d)(1)(B)(i); *Commonwealth v. Balukonis*, 357 Mass. 721, 726–27 (1970). Likewise, where a prior inconsistent statement is offered in those circumstances so that you now want to introduce a prior consistent statement to rebut the inference of recent fabrication, then the prior consistent statement is admissible to corroborate the witness's testimony but not as substantive evidence. This is true in both state and federal courts. The prior consistent statement doesn't have to be under oath. *See* Mass. Evid. Stand. 801(d)(1)(B)(ii); *Commonwealth v. Zukowski*, 370 Mass. 23, 26 (1976).

The third situation is fresh complaint in a sexual assault case. In a sexual assault case, it comes in only as corroborative evidence, and the alleged victim has to testify first. Then, simply to corroborate the victim's testimony, another witness to whom the victim complained can testify. *See* Mass. Evid. Stand. 801(d)(1)(B)(iii); *Commonwealth v. Connor*, 407 Mass. 663, 669–70 (1990); *Commonwealth v. Blow*, 370 Mass. 401, 406 (1976); *Commonwealth v. Hanger*, 357 Mass. 464, 466 (1970).

There are two circumstances where prior statements of a witness, even in Massachusetts, do come in substantively. If a witness has given inconsistent grand jury testimony, once the witness testifies, that inconsistent grand jury testimony is admissible substantively. Mass. Evid. Stand. 801(d)(2)(B)(ii); ***Commonwealth v. Daye***, 393 Mass. 55, 66–75 (1984). Also, a prior identification by a witness of someone who the witness recognizes is substantively admissible if the witness testifies. *See* Mass. Evid. Stand. 801(d)(2)(B)(ii).

The second major exception deals with the situation where the declarant is a party, and that's the whole area of admissions. I treat admissions as exceptions to the hearsay rule. Federal Rule 801(d)(2) doesn't call them exceptions. The test for determining whether a party's admission becomes substantive evidence is the following: Is the party against whom the evidence is offered on the opposite side of the versus from your client, as in ***Smith v. Jones***? That's a simple way of looking at it. If it's on the opposite side of the versus from your client and it's relevant, in it comes.

Admissions are not the same things as confessions. A confession would be something like, "I did it. I'm liable," whereas an admission might be, "Yes, I knew him." Anything that's relevant that the other side has said is admissible. And the theory behind that, is that if the other side said it and the other side is a litigant, if it's not true, he or she can get on the stand and deny it. And because he or she can deny it, it's okay to hear what your side says he or she said. There is not a hearsay problem.

Here's what's admissible: Any statement by the party, any statement that's ratified by the party or that the party has adopted and any statement that deals with admissions by silence. For example, say you're standing around, and a house is burning down, and someone in the crowd says, "Gee, I know you. I saw you running out of that house with gasoline trailing behind you." And you don't say anything. If you don't say anything where it's thought that a reasonable person would deny it, that then is admissible against you. It's like an adoptive admission that you are the person.

The law for statements by a party's agency has changed. ***Ruszcyk v. Secretary of Public Safety***, 401 Mass. 418 (1988). Under both state and federal law, ***Ruszcyk*** says that a statement by an agency or agent must pertain to the scope of what the agent's employment is. For those of you who are somewhat older, like I am, who remember the old Massachusetts rule where the agent had to be authorized to speak, that's now gone. The standard is simply this: Is the agent talking about something that's within the scope of their responsibility? If they are, then they're authorized to speak about it. And what they say about it binds the corporation, or the entity, or the employer, or the superior, so long as it specifically has to do with the agency.

There are limits to this where the agent is talking and he or she is away from the place of employment and in some other circumstance, but so long as the agent is the one that you would speak to about a particular function, then that's what governs; that is an admission by the outfit.

Statements by coconspirators—both civil and criminal, state and federal—are admitted on a partnership theory. Fed.R.Evid. 801(d)(2)(E); Mass. Evid. Stand.

801(d)(3)(E). *Greenwald v. United States,* 353 U.S. 391, 404 (1957). *See, e.g., United States v. Twitty,* C.A. No. 95-1056 (1st Cir. 1995) (Boudin, J.). If there is a conspiracy, then the conspirators are partners. If there is a partnership, and there may be some litigation out of the demise of the partnership, then the statements of each of the partners bind the other partners, or at least their admissions to the other partners. One is the litigant or the defendant, and the statements of any of the coconspirators are admitted.

The state and federal rules with respect to making the determination of whether there's a coconspiracy are different. How are you going to know whether to admit the statement of a coconspirator unless you have a conspiracy?

Here's the Massachusetts rule. You have to have sufficient independent evidence of a conspiracy before you can admit the statements of the coconspirators against each other. *See Commonwealth v. Stasium,* 349 Mass. 38, 50–53 (1965). Who decides that in the first instance? It's a preliminary finding. The judge decides it. *See* Mass. Evid. Stand. 104(a). It has the unfortunate result of forcing your testimony to go in. Some testimony is limited to this coconspirator because it's an admission of this coconspirator if he's the one who said it. Somewhere along the line, the judge decides there's enough independent evidence as to each one of these folks that they were in a conspiracy that the judge thinks by a fair preponderance of the evidence that it was a conspiracy. The judge then removes those limitations. *See Bourjaily v. United States,* 483 U.S. 171 (1987). That's sort of a subtle croak rule, because when those limitations are removed, if they've been placed on the evidence, the jury sees the case in a different light.

The federal rule starts out differently and more smoothly and, if the government makes its case, is probably a better rule. The federal rule in the First Circuit starts out like this: If the government says there's a conspiracy, we'll assume that there is and we won't need any sort of independent evidence. We'll listen to what the coconspirators have to say, without saying it's limited or admissible, and then we'll decide if there's a conspiracy by a fair preponderance of the evidence. If we decide that there is, we make a finding out of the hearing of the jury, and that's all that's ever done. In the federal courts, that's called the *Petrozziello,* and the *Ciampaglia* rules. *See United States v. Petrozziello,* 548 F.2d 20 (1st Cir. 1977); *United States v. Ciampaglia,* 628 F.2d 632 (1st Cir. 1980).

What happens if we decide that there isn't a conspiracy? I had a case like that. I didn't believe the people who turned state's evidence, I didn't believe them worth a darn. I said to myself, "I don't believe there was any conspiracy between the defendant and these two guys. I think this is ridiculous, but, you know, there's enough independent evidence that this could go to the jury. It happens I don't believe it, but there's enough that a jury could believe it." So I struck it all out. I said, "You remember what he said and what he said? Strike all that, pay no attention to that, that has nothing to do with this. Strike all that from your minds." *See United States v. Pitocchelli,* 830 F.2d 401 (1st Cir. 1987).

The defense counsel apparently thought that that was such a forceful and good instruction that even though I was letting it go to the jury, he thought that was it. The jury convicted, ostensibly on the independent evidence. I gave him 12 years. He appealed. You might think this should have been a mistrial—the judge himself didn't believe it. That's not the way it works. All I was deciding was whether there was preliminary evidence of a conspiracy. There wasn't. The independent evidence was sufficient. I happened not to believe it, but the jury did.

If you get a case where you actually get a judge to find that there isn't a conspiracy, you've got to think very carefully about whether the trial can possibly go on fairly or whether the judge has to give a mistrial.

There is a third way to do this, but no one does it. The third way to decide whether a coconspirator's evidence is admissible is to have a pretrial hearing that goes for days and days. You hear all the evidence, and then you make the decision. If it is admissible, it is, and if it isn't, it isn't. Then you start the trial, and you have the guidelines clear. We don't follow that in the First Circuit nor in Massachusetts because it takes too much time.

AUDIENCE MEMBER: Do you have an opinion on the value of defense request in a federal conspiracy case asking the court for limiting instructions during the course of the government's case?

JUDGE YOUNG: His question is asking for limiting instructions in a conspiracy criminal case, federal. It's not valuable because under *Petrozziello* we're not supposed to give them, we're not supposed to limit things at all, so long as there's some good faith here, until we've heard what the government's case is. So we won't give you those instructions. We'll just let it go, and then we'll unwind it afterwards, because that's what the rule says.

If you think you need a remedy, your remedy is to ask for a mistrial then. That's what maybe I should have done. Your remedy is not to ask for limiting instructions. We don't do that in federal court. In state court they do. So that's a significant difference.

There are two other areas of Massachusetts practice on preliminary findings by the judge, and they're both in criminal practice. The judge independently has to be satisfied beyond a reasonable doubt that a confession is voluntary before a jury will ever hear it in Massachusetts. Mass. Evid. Stand. 104(b)(1). *See, e.g., Commonwealth v. Day*, 387 Mass. 915, 921 (1983). That's not the federal standard. The federal standard is by a fair preponderance of the evidence; and then the jury independently has to be satisfied—and the judge will so charge—beyond a reasonable doubt before they're told they should utilize the confession. *See Lego v. Twomey*, 404 U.S. 477, 489 (1972).

And, by the way, Massachusetts and New Jersey are the only states in the nation that make you go over both hurdles beyond a reasonable doubt, the states most hostile to confessions.

The other one, which is lesser known, is dying declarations. The judge first has to decide that a dying declaration is in fact a dying declaration and that it fits all the criteria. Homicide cases are the only cases where there are dying declarations. An example would be "X killed me." Second, the judge has to tell the jury that the jury has to make an independent determination about whether the dying declaration is really a dying declaration before it can be admitted.

Those are the first two exceptions. The first is where the declarant and the witness are one. The second is admissions. The third are all the exceptions in Rule 803, and all of those are ones that we think or that the law thinks are sufficiently reliable as not to be hearsay.

The Massachusetts rules are somewhat different than the federal rules. As an example, we'll discuss business records, so you can see as an evidentiary matter how to lay the foundation to get a business record in.

The federal rule pertaining to business records is Rule 803(6). For the Massachusetts rule, see G.L. c. 233, § 78 and Mass. Evidentiary Standard 803(6). The federal and the state rules are virtually identical. Actually, the federal rule is a little less strict. Let's say I have a witness on the stand. I'll make my witness Clarence Custodian. Because a business record is not self-authenticating, I'll need a witness. The custodian can be anyone who has a business duty for the regularity of the record-keeping. So I have to find that out. And that can be all the way up and down the corporate ladder. It can be the file room clerk, the manager of the file room, the secretary, the adjustor, the person who works with the file, the office manager, the division head, the corporate president or the chairman of the board, so long as among their duties is the keeping of the records in a regular fashion.

Here's what you ask the custodian; here's how you do Rule 803(6). We'll make the records manufacturer records. It's a products liability case. The defense wants the manufacturer records of the stress tests on an elevator. So I've got the custodian. He is the custodian of the Widget Elevator Company.

"Mr. Custodian, I show you what's been marked for identification as Exhibit B. Do you recognize it?"

"Yes."

"What is it?"

"It is the stress tests on the M101A elevator for the months of May through June 1979."

"Is it the usual business practice of the Widget Elevator Company to maintain records such as this?" That's the Rule 406 question, the habit and routine practice question. It's leading, but that's okay with foundations.

The answer is "Yes."

In my hypothetical, you might want to object to that question, because the custodian hasn't worked there since 1979. Does he know? But when I play all the roles it can come out the way I want it, so no one objects, and so he answers yes. Now you need a second question.

The first two questions on authentication or on laying foundations are always the same:

"I show you what has been marked X." "Do you recognize it?"

The third question is, "What is it?"

The fourth question is, "Is it habit and routine practice to keep this record?"

"Is this record, Exhibit B for Identification, kept in the course of ordinary business practice?"

Answer: "Yes."

You need at least the first two questions in Massachusetts; then it gets in if the judge can infer that the record was kept in a routine manner and it was kept in good faith.

Under Federal Rule 803(6), you need a little more. You need to know that the record was made contemporaneously with the events it records, and you need to know that the record was made by someone with personal knowledge, not the custodian, because that would defeat the whole purpose of the objection. The custodian could testify to what he saw if he made the record. He could describe how he did the test. So I ask one more question:

"How is this record prepared?"

And he testifies: "It's prepared by the safety engineers, who write down their findings as soon as they read the galvanometers. Then it's typed up the next day and bound in this book."

"I offer it."

That's the foundation. You can take any of those exceptions—excited utterance, statements for the purpose of medical diagnosis and treatment—you can go through each one of the exceptions found either in the federal or in the state rules and lay a foundation.

The last exception to the rule against hearsay depends on the declarant being missing. If the declarant is there, none of this works on the fourth major type of exception. *See* Fed.R.Evid. 804; Mass. Evid. Stand. 804.

An excited utterance gets in evidence even if the declarant is sitting in the front row. You don't need the declarant on the Rule 803 exception, on the theory that it's reliable. If we don't think he's a very good witness, we may want to put it on through the person who heard it, who's a much better witness. For purposes of the fourth major exception, you've got to prove that the declarant is not there, because if they're there, and available, the exception doesn't work.

A declarant is unavailable if he or she is not there, but a declarant is also unavailable if he or she has a valid privilege against testifying, such as the Fifth Amendment. If you refuse to testify and they've got you in the can for contempt but they've got some earlier statement; if you don't remember, you're unavailable. If you're sick or dead—if you're dead you're clearly unavailable—if you're sick and you can't come to court, you're unavailable. If you're alive and well but somewhere in the United States where we can't reach you, you're unavailable. All this can be found under Rule 804(a).

Here's what gets in: former testimony; former testimony under oath in a hearing; in a homicide case, testimony under the belief of impending death (a dying declaration under Fed.R.Evid. 804(b)(2) and G.L. c. 233, § 64); a statement against interest, including pecuniary interest—that is, the statement in a civil case, "You know, I'm liable to repay this note" and in a criminal case, "Yeah, I did it," (under the limitations). I must caution that on the criminal case, you have to have independent guarantees of trustworthiness of such a statement. Think about it for a minute. You say, "Oh, I've got a witness—in a murder case—who said he did this. Well, he's unavailable, but I heard him say it, so I'll get on the stand and say, 'Yeah, I've got a witness.'"

"And what is your name?"

"My name is Professional Witness."

"And what did you hear, Mr. Professional Witness?"

"Oh, I heard Vicious Killer say, 'I did this crime,' not Donald Defendant."

"Thank you very much."

We won't allow that. But if there are independent guarantees of the trustworthiness of the statement, and the declarant is missing, such a witness can testify, but you have to prove the unavailability. *See Commonwealth v. Gagnon*, 408 Mass. 185, 194 (1990).

And in Massachusetts, baptismal records come in that way, but also the declaration of a decedent comes in that way. We are virtually alone in the United States—everyone talks about the Dead Person's Rule. In the United States, the Dead Person's Rule keeps out testimony. In Massachusetts, it embraces it. We allow dead people to testify. *See* G.L. c. 233, § 65; Mass. Evid. Stand. 804(b)(5). There are some limitations in the statute, but by and large, we allow them to testify. And make no doubt about it, that's terribly important.

There are three places in the Federal Rules of Evidence where if you have a diversity case, the state rules govern. In a diversity case, the state rules as to presumptions govern, Rule 301; the state rules as to privileges govern, Rule 501; and the state rules as to who is competent to be a witness govern, Rule 601. You might think that competence is just personal knowledge. And it is, under Rule 601, except the Massachusetts dead person's statute is framed in terms of competence. It makes private interspousal communications incompetent evidence, but it makes dead person's communications competent evidence. *See* G.L. c. 233, § 65. So if you've got a diversity case in the federal court, you can get the testimony of dead people so long as it was on good faith and it was prior to the litigation.

Now, one other thing: In the federal rules, there is what's called an innominate exception. It means if none of these other exceptions work, you can argue for an exception. I would have said we're very hostile to that. It appears that the First Circuit is less hostile to the use of the innominate exception—the "nothing-else-works-so-I'm-going-to-try-this" exception. In the federal rules, it's Rules 803(24) and 804(5). It just says if nothing else works, and if it looks reliable to the court and looks just, you can let it in. Federal courts have been very hostile to that, but now against drug defendants, they're letting in a variety of things.

The state rule has no counterpart rule; you either fit in with one of the common law or statutory exceptions or the rule against hearsay keeps it out. The rule against hearsay is: An out-of-court declaration offered in court for the truth of the matter asserted is hearsay and not admissible unless it fits within one of the exceptions.

The Confrontation Clause

A concept not yet discussed but of vital importance in criminal cases is the confrontation clause. The confrontation clause, Article VI of the U.S. Constitution, was taken from one of the Declaration of Rights of Massachusetts, so we have indeed a more forceful confrontation clause in Massachusetts than they have in the federal courts. *See* Article XII of the Massachusetts Constitution. The confrontation clause in criminal cases has four major strains.

The idea is that a defendant in a criminal case is entitled to be confronted with the witnesses against him or her. The constitutional confrontation clause essentially is a guarantee of the right to cross-examine the witnesses against a person.

How does it work? If you have the constitutional right to cross-examine the witnesses against you, that may well trump the hearsay exceptions, especially the Rule 803 hearsay exceptions, which don't turn on the unavailability of the declarant. Are there any hearsay exceptions that work under the confrontation clause?

In fact, most of them work, but we're not exactly clear how many because of a case called *Ohio v. Roberts*, a 1980 Supreme Court case that can be found at 448 U.S. 56. Most of the law on the confrontation clause is straight out of the Supreme Court. In carrying out this right to cross-examine a witness in *Ohio v. Roberts*, the Court said that the proponent of evidence in a criminal case, usually the prosecution, has to show that the witness is unavailable or that there is an indicia of reliability surrounding the out-of-court declaration. The indicia of reliability surrounding the out-of-court declaration can be secured in two major ways: an opportunity to cross-examine at some other time out of court, a preliminary hearing and the like (*California v. Green*, 399 U.S. 149, 157 (1970)) or a traditional hearsay exception. We've been waiting for cases to tell us what are the traditional, or long-standing, hearsay exceptions. *See Lee v. Illinois*, 476 U.S. 530, 551–52 (1986).

The Supreme Court cases, *United States v. Inadi* (475 U.S. 387 (1986)) and *Bourjaily v. United States* (483 U.S. 171 (1987)), are right on point in admitting the coconspirator statement. Excited utterances, statements from a medical diagnosis and business records are the standard hearsay exceptions, and even in a criminal case, they will work. Query whether some of the more esoteric ones—some of the newer ones in the Federal Rules of Evidence—work in a confrontation clause situation.

The second point about the confrontation clause is in multidefendant cases. The admission of one defendant that inculpates another defendant runs afoul of a case called ***Bruton v. The United States***, 389 U.S. 818 (1968). In other words, if A confesses and says, "Yeah, B and I rob gas stations," and you put A and B to trial, the confession of A, we clearly know, is an admission by A and, if voluntary, it comes in as evidence as against A. But that hurts B, because the confession is, "Yes, B and I rob gas stations." B is sitting right there, but you can't cross-examine the confession. The result under ***Bruton*** is that you either have to sever the trial, drop the confession altogether or redact the confession. The Court is split on that. Suppose the confession says, "Yes, a fellow by the name of X and I rob gas stations," and B is sitting right there. Query whether that's enough of a redaction. That's fairness in the eyes of the Court. Courts vary.

Suppose the confessions interlock. A confesses and says, "B and I rob gas stations," and B confesses and says, "A and I rob gas stations," There is recent Supreme Court case law saying that makes no difference, indeed that's the paradigm case. A has to have his separate trial with his separate confession and B gets his separate trial, because they'll both croak each other with their interlocking confessions. *See* ***Cruz v. New York***, 481 U.S. 186 (1987).

The third element of the confrontation clause is that it trumps state privileges. The major case is ***Davis v. Alaska***, 415 U.S. 308, 318 (1974). It's carried out in the Commonwealth with a case called ***Commonwealth v. Ferrara***, 386 Mass. 182, 188–90 (1975). For instance, generally in Massachusetts, juvenile proceedings are confidential. A government witness in a criminal case was a juvenile, and he was under a period of probation. The government could lean on him; they could revoke his probation. The defense didn't know about it because the juvenile proceedings were confidential, which of course is to protect the kid so the kid can be rehabilitated. The defendant said, "Remove the confidentiality." To show the kid's bias, the defense needed to know that the kid was going to testify for the government because the kid was afraid that if he didn't testify, they were going to revoke his probation and put him back into Youth Services. The government said, "Wait a second; we've got a good law, designed to protect kids; that wins." The defendant said, "You're trying to take away my liberty, maybe my life. That trumps it all under the constitution. I get to know." The defendant is right, according to the confrontation clause.

Here's one that hasn't been tried in Massachusetts. The Commonwealth is hurting for money, so they've got a whole bunch of laws that say they don't need to send experts into court; they'll send in a certificate. They send in certificates for fires or drugs. *See, e.g.*, G.L. c. 147, § 4D. The statutes all say these are to be admitted in evidence, and of course they routinely are admitted in evidence.

Nearly one out of five, 18 percent, of the tests that they use to show drugs are overinclusive, so that something that's not a drug is going to show up as a drug. Do you have a right to see the person who did the test and gave the certificate testify? Yes, you do. If you bring the person in, and he croaks you, that is tactically not efficient. However, if you've got some way to put the government to the proof, you can put them to the proof. As another example, the government might say that something is a handgun and submit a certificate from a state trooper who is a ballistics expert. You have a right to see him, according to the confrontation clause.

Chambers v. Mississippi says that the defense has a right to put on a defense. If the rules of evidence in effect croak the defense and tie his or her hands, the defense has some latitude to confront the government's case and to confront the witness against him. The confrontation clause we're concerned about is only in criminal cases.

THE LAW OF EXPERTS

One of the hottest areas of the law is the law as it relates to experts. When you have an expert, you want an opinion from the expert, which is the capstone of two building blocks. (This is spelled out in Article VII of the rules of evidence.) The first of the building blocks has nothing to do with the case—it's noncase-specific, or general. The second building block is case-specific, that is, you've got the greatest hand surgeon at Mass. General Hospital. That's still not good enough. What does he know about this case? What does he know about this person's hand? Does he know anything that helps us? We need case-specific information. There are four ways to get it.

First of all, the expert can be the examining physician. It doesn't have to be in terms of physicians, because, of course, anyone can be expert; a mechanic can be an expert.

By examining physician, I mean the person who actually did the work, who fixed the car, graded the road, set the bone or constructed the building. In other words, the expert can be a percipient witness because he or she did the hands-on thing that we're concerned about, and he or she happens to be an expert in the field.

Another way that the expert can get case-specific data is to sit through the entire trial. Then the expert knows about the case, because the expert has seen and heard what the jury has seen and heard. You can say to the expert, "What do you think about it?" because you're an expert. Once you qualify the expert with the general data, "What do you know about this? Do you work in this area (headaches, broken hands, grading roads)? Do you know about it?"

"Yes, I do; I've been to school."

"And have you listened to what the jury's listened to?"

"Yes, I have."

"What do you think about it?" And then the expert can testify.

We rarely do that these days because experts are so expensive. The one place that they do it is in land taking cases. Appraisers somehow have convinced us all that they can't give their testimony unless they listen to all the other appraisers. So they sit there throughout the whole trial, you pay them this fancy fee, then they testify, and then they come on as rebuttal.

The hypothetical question is tricky. You can see the need for the hypothetical question once you understand the building blocks. If you've got an expert who has general noncase-specific knowledge about the event or the area of knowledge, how can you get them to know about the event quickly and efficiently? You say to the expert, "Madam Expert, I ask you to assume," and then you ask the expert to assume all those things you have already proved to the jury.

We take experts out of order and there are trial practice problems, but the theory of the hypothetical question makes excellent sense. You ask the expert to assume that they have knowledge that is specific to the case. Then you would ask, for example, "Do you have an opinion to a reasonable medical certainty as to the cause of these seizures?"

"Yes, I do."

"What is your opinion? What is the basis of your opinion?" That's the classic way to get it out. The reason that a hypothetical question is tricky is that if you mistake something or the judge doesn't think you have proved this before the jury, or at least put on evidence before the jury, the hypothetical question is flawed. And unless you can convince the judge you're going to come up with the proof of the matter, you don't get to put it in.

That was the state of the law in Massachusetts at the time the federal rules were adopted. The federal rules added a significant additional way to get case-specific data, and in essence the expert can be told about the case out of court.

I'm talking about blatant hearsay. In other words, the expert can read hospital records or look at drawings of a building; he or she can be told about the case. And it can be hearsay. It can be hearsay out of the case, but under Federal Rule 703, it's got to be the type of data that the expert is accustomed to rely upon objectively in that area of knowledge. The "objectively" is crucial. It's got to be the type of data that the judge is convinced that experts in this field of endeavor rely on. But if it is, it makes no difference that it's hearsay. The theory is that if the doctor would amputate the arm after looking at the X-rays, if you give him the X-rays and the hospital records and say to him, "Doctor, should you cut off the arm?," you ought to be able to have him rely on this type of hearsay—if relying on the X-rays, he were to cut off the arm in real practice. It makes perfect sense.

The problem is that it's very elastic, and creative counsel have done a great deal with this hearsay. The fact that the expert can base his or her opinion on what the expert was told does not mean that the hearsay itself is admissible. When the expert is asked, "And what is the basis of your opinion, doctor?" he or she should be limited to saying, "I looked at these X-rays that were provided to me; I looked at the hospital records, and, based upon that data, I believe thus and so."

What in fact happens, is that the expert says, "I looked at the hospital records where the hospital records say this and that and the other thing, and when it was noted that her blood pressure was thus and so." You've got to get all those things in evidence. We are too sloppy on that as judges. We've let that get away from us; let's be clear on that. But the theory of the rule is only that the person who based their testimony on hearsay would tell us the types of data that they based it on. They would tell us "Yes, in our area of expertise, we base our data on this," and it comes in.

In Massachusetts, the stuff that the expert is entitled to base his or her opinion on must be independently admissible. It doesn't have to have been admitted, but it must be independently admissible. My example, I think, is a good one. Hospital records in Massachusetts are admissible. However, under ***Bouchie v. Murray***, 376 Mass. 524 (1978), hearsay within the hospital records not for the purpose of diagnosis and treatment, or challenged opinions, may not be admissible. But if the hospital records are admissible, then the doctor can give his or her opinion if his or her opinion is based on hospital records. How do we know whether they would be admissible? It's not as sweeping as the federal rule, where the judge just makes a choice on whether these would be admissible, but in Massachusetts it's nevertheless admissible.

Commonwealth v. Lanigan, 419 Mass. 15, 24–26, 641 N.E.2d 1342, 1348–49 (1994). In this case, the Supreme Judicial Court adopts, as the Massachusetts evidentiary rule governing admission of expert scientific testimony, the general proposition expressed in ***Daubert v. Merrill Dow Pharmaceuticals, Inc.***, 509 U.S. 579, 113 S.Ct. 2786, 125 L.Ed.2d 469 (1993). Under ***Daubert*** (and now ***Lanigan***), the overarching issue is the scientific validity of the principles that undergird the opinion. In determining such validity, the trial judge first, and ultimately the factfinder, may consider the following nonexhaustive list of factors, no one of which is determinative.

a. The general acceptance of theory or technique in the scientific community. In determining whether a scientific method has been generally accepted, a court may look beyond the evidence of record to the reasoning and conclusion of other courts and the writings of experts. *Commonwealth v. Curnin*, 409 Mass. 218, 223, 565 N.E.2d 440, 443 (1991). *Commonwealth v. Mendes*, 406 Mass. 201, 205, 547 N.E.2d 35, 37 (1989).

b. Whether the technique can be or has been tested.

c. Peer review and publication of the theory or process.

For further discussion of the federal rule, see § 325 of the Supplement to *Mass. Evidence* Vol. 19. See also Linda Sandstrom Simard & William G. Young, *Daubert's Gatekeeper: The Role of the District Judge in Admitting Expert Testimony*, 68 Tu.L.Rev. 1457 (1994); Paul Nemser, *Foundation and Sufficiency of Expert*

Testimony: Recent Massachusetts Authority, 77 Mass.L.Rev. 113 (Sept. 1992); David R. Geiger, Paul R. Rocklin, and Stephen D. Sowle, *The Judicial Gatekeeper: Should Massachusetts Apply Daubert to Screen Expert Testimony*, 79 Mass.L.Rev. 94 (1994).

Applying these principles, admission of DNA statistical evidence is upheld where the "ceiling frequency" protocol is strictly followed. *Commonwealth v. Lanigan,* 419 Mass. 15, 20–23, 27, 641 N.E.2d 1342, 1346–48 (1994). This ruling was presaged in *Commonwealth v. Teixeira,* Bristol Superior Court No. 26551-63 (12/7/92), where the superior court accepted a DNA test where the "ceiling principle" statistical procedure used along with the "floating bin" analysis, both procedures being more conservative than those used in the original *Lanigan* case, *Commonwealth v. Lanigan,* 413 Mass. 154, 159–63, 596 N.E.2d 311, 314–16 (1992), rejecting DNA match without appropriate statistical support. *Commonwealth v. Dube,* 413 Mass. 570, 572–75, 601 N.E.2d 467, 468–69 (1992) (evidence of blood alcohol test performed on defendant involved in a motor vehicle accident is admissible over defendant's objection where the test was done as a routine medical procedure).

Commercial Union Ins. Co. v. Boston Edison Co., 412 Mass. 545, 549, 551, 591 N.E.2d 165, 168 (1992). Computer-generated models or simulations are treated like other scientific tests. Their admissibility is conditioned on a sufficient showing that: (1) the computer is functioning property; (2) the input and underlying equations are sufficiently complete and accurate (and disclosed to the opposing parties so that they may challenge them); and (3) the program is generally accepted by the appropriate community of scientists.

Commonwealth v. LeFave, 407 Mass. 927, 934 n.9, 556 N.E.2d 83, 88 n.9 (1990). In *LeFave,* a United States postal inspector specializing in the investigation of child pornography was permitted to testify as an expert, giving his opinion concerning the nature of the photographs in underground circulation as child pornography. The Supreme Judicial Court considered that such testimony would assist the jury in evaluating the motive of the defendant charged with child abuse. The precedential value of this decision is much diminished by the well-reasoned dissent of Chief Justice Liacos. 1995 Massachusetts Evidentiary Standards (West Pub. Co. 1995).

Where do most government experts come from in criminal cases? They're FBI guys.

Now, I have no problem with FBI guys who are fingerprint experts or what I call "shoemen" in a case. They can say this shoe came from this lot and this footprint in the snow—these guys are absolutely mesmerizing. And I go back to *Williams*: We find these little microscopic things on the victim and it's found in this type of old Chevrolet. That stuff wows me; I make no bones about it.

But how about the guy, who, when you ask who is he is, says, "I work on the Mafia desk of the FBI."

"All right. What do you do with the Mafia?"

"I track 'em."

"Okay. Well, what do you know about the Mafia?"

"I know the Mafia is organized like this: They've got a godfather, and then they've got a consigliatore, and they've got these underheads, and they've got these..."

"And what did you do to prepare for this case?"

"Oh, I read a lot of FBI reports."

"What do you think about this case?"

"I think he's the godfather. I think he's the consigliatore."

Do these guys come here and make this stuff up? Take a look at *United States v. Zannino*, 895 F.2d 1 (1st Cir.), *cert. denied*, 494 U.S. 1082 (1990). An FBI guy got on the stand and said exactly that.

But suppose you have people like clinical ecologists, who are in new areas? If you're in a new area, it seems to me that it ought not be enough, as the supposed Benedictine doctors, which has been rejected, said, "Oh, I've done clinical studies."

"Who did you do clinical studies on?"

"I did clinical studies on 26 people."

"Who are they?"

"They're the plaintiffs in the 26 cases around the country."

"And who are you?"

"I'm a medical doctor."

"You're employed by these men?"

"Yes, I am, but I've done these studies, and I think these studies are valid. And I, as a medical doctor, think that A causes B."

The courts are against that, and the tide is running very much against it. But suppose you get something that's new like that? It seems to me that if it's a doctor, it ought to meet the standards that doctors meet.

If it's toxicology, it ought to meet those standards. And if it's a new standard, then the protocol for ascertaining the truth should be explained either on voir dire or in court at the judge's option. That will keep out the dowsing rod people or the astrologers, because they can't explain it.

But you've got to ask yourself when you come to an opinion in court where the standard of proof is by a fair preponderance of the evidence, what is the level of the opinion that the expert is offering? Is it only that there is some relationship? And if it is, respectfully, that's not good enough. That's why the classic way to ask the question of a doctor is, "Do you have an opinion to a reasonable medical certainty," which is under your standards as a doctor sort of the equivalent of by a fair preponderance of the evidence.

A big exception to that is in FELA cases and in admiralty cases, which are like FELA cases, where to protect the worker, any relationship, no matter how slight, will be enough to get you to the jury on causation. But the general rule is by a fair preponderance of the evidence, and so the opinion should meet that standard. The expert believes under the protocols of her profession that it meets the standard. Be aware that there have been big changes with respect to experts.

PRIVILEGES AND CONFIDENTIAL DATA

With respect to privileges, Article V of the Federal Rules of Evidence (and the Massachusetts Evidentiary Standards), the doctrine is easy to state. This is also a very hot area. If we look at the statutes that have been passed in recent times, the legislature in Massachusetts is passing all sorts of privileges. I am going to give you a catalogue of them, and again I cite you to the Massachusetts Evidentiary Standards where they are all set out.

The theory of privilege is in essence this: there are a variety of relationships in society that are so valuable that despite our need for the truth in the courts we are going to protect those relationships because we believe that the disclosure of what goes on in them will do damage to the relationship, so much so that the relationship is more valuable than truth in court. In the federal courts, where we have the death penalty for over 50 crimes, you can see that the stakes are fairly high there, but that's the theory. Privileges tend to be personal in the sense that, unlike a competency issue where you just can't have the evidence even if you want it, privileges can be waived. They can be given up by the person who possesses the privilege. Generally, the person who possesses the privilege is the person who is seeking the help or the advice of the professional. That's the person who possesses the privilege. If the person who possesses the privilege waives it, then it is gone. Mass. Evid. Stand. 518(a). *Compare Montgomery v. Pickering,* 116 Mass. 227, 231 (1874) *with Woburn v. Henshaw,* 101 Mass. 193, 200 (1869).

Note that a privilege is not the same thing as confidential data. We have a whole lot of data in the Commonwealth (all sorts of personnel data, all sorts of medical data, all sorts of data regarding people on Welfare)—again, mostly by statute—that for perfectly good reasons are confidential. However, confidentiality can be beaten by a court order. Once you are in court, the need to resolve a case overcomes the social policy behind the protection of such data. Mass. Evid. Stand. 520.

Privileges, on the other hand, trump everything. No court order can overcome a privilege. If the judge says that a privilege does not apply, the judge can require the information and can put people in jail if they do not comply. But the theory is that if you have a valid privilege, the court should know not to try to take it away from you. It is yours; it's the individual's.

One of the most important privileges is the attorney-client privilege. Mass. Evid. Stand. 503. *Flynn v. Kasnet,* Norfolk Superior Ct. No. 92-0287-B (August 10, 1993). The privilege belongs to your clients but you have to know about it to adequately represent your clients. It works like any other privilege. The social policy behind it is that every person, every company, every party, every litigant should have someone in their corner devoted only to them. Those things that pass in confidence in the attorney-client relationship should always remain confidential.

For the best formulation of the common law privilege—and that is the privilege as it stands in Massachusetts—I refer you to Judge Wyzanski's decision in *United*

States. v. United Shoe Machinery Corp., 89 F.Supp. 357, 358–59 (D.Mass. 1950), which provides the touchstone with respect to all privileges.

The person who claims the privilege is or has sought to become a client. The person to whom or from whom the communication was made is a member of the bar, that is, a real lawyer, or the lawyer's subordinate, someone working for the lawyer. The lawyer must be acting in the scope of rendering legal services and must be acting in connection with the communication as a lawyer. The communication cannot just be cocktail party conversation unless you are asked for your advice at a cocktail party and you are invoked as a lawyer. The communication has to relate to a fact about which the attorney was informed by the client in the absence of strangers, that is, in circumstances of confidence. It must be made for the purpose of either obtaining an opinion of law (legal services) or in the context of some legal proceeding and not for the purpose of committing some future crime or tort. The privilege has to be claimed and not waived.

There are three aspects of the attorney-client privilege in Massachusetts. First, there are some indications at the superior court level regarding the scope of the privilege as it pertains to communications in a corporate context. In this context, there are two standards: the duties-of-employment standard and the control group standard. The duties-of-employment standard covers anyone who makes a communication as part of the duties of his or her employment. Such communications are privileged. In other words, if you represent the company and go to the stock boy in the A&P after a lady has fallen and ask him what happened, it is part of the kid's duty to talk to the company lawyer. Whatever he tells you is privileged.

The other standard is much more narrow. It only applies to those communications made to and from the control group, that is, the people who run the lawsuit. They are the people who are truly the client, the ones who can act on the legal advice you furnish. That does not mean that they have to be high up in the corporation. The adjuster, the person who has the judgment call about a case, is the person I'm talking about. That's the client.

Massachusetts is not clear on this point. The federal courts follow the common law as stated in *Upjohn Co. v. United States*, 449 U.S. 383 (1981), which middles the two standards and says that the standard to follow pretty much depends on the circumstances of the particular case. It is sort of a duties-of-employment test plus. It has to be something more than just that the kid had the duties of employment. It has to be something more with respect to the facilitation of legal services. The federal courts take it case-by-case.

The second aspect of the attorney-client privilege—and this applies in both federal and Massachusetts state courts—deals with inadvertent disclosure. It used to be that an inadvertent disclosure operated as a waiver of the privilege. Also, if an eavesdropper heard something, then the privilege was waived. That's gone now. If you make a mistake in your production of documents and you disclose an attorney-client communication, the other side can't use it if the disclosure was inadvertent.

The third aspect is sort of unique to Massachusetts and holds true only for the attorney-client privilege and not the other privileges I am going to list later. The claim of attorney-client privilege in a trial or at a deposition leading up to a trial can, by itself, give rise to an adverse inference that you are trying to hide something. Mass. Evid. Stand. 519(a). The other side can argue to the jury, "Did you hear when Mr. Smith said, 'Oh, don't answer that question,' and then William Witness refused to answer that question? What do you think they are hiding? We know very well that they knew exactly what was going on, don't we?" In Massachusetts, you can do this. When I point that out to lawyers, they invariably waive the privilege.

Now for the list of privileges. I think that you will be very interested to see how long it is. You are probably familiar with most of them. There is of course the privilege against self-incrimination, the Fifth Amendment privilege. United States Constitution, Amendment V; Massachusetts Constitution, Article XII, Declaration of Rights; Mass. Evid. Stand. 502.

I have already mentioned the lawyer-client privilege. Mass. Evid. Stand. 503.

There is a husband-wife testimonial privilege. G.L. c. 233, § 20. Mass. Evid. Stand. 504. In federal court, this privilege is possessed by the witness. *Trammel v. United States,* 455 U.S. 40 (1980). In state courts, the litigant possesses it. It is up to the litigant to claim the privilege.

Communications with members of the clergy are privileged. G.L. c. 233, § 20A. Mass. Evid. Stand. 505.

Your political vote is privileged. Mass. Evid. Stand. 506. *See McRobbie v. Registrars of Voters of Ipswich,* 322 Mass. 530, 533–34, 78 N.E.2d 498, 500–01 (1948). Trade secrets are privileged. Mass.R.Civ.P. 26(c)(7). Mass. Evid. Stand. 507.

In federal courts—but not in state courts—there is a governmental privilege, or what is called a deliberative privilege. *See* Mass. Evid. Stand. 508(a), (b). That privilege deals with how government policy is worked out. Although the federal government has to disclose the policy, it does not have to disclose how they made the policy or how it was worked out. The idea is to have full and frank discussion of the adoption of regulations and the making of government policy. There is no such state governmental privilege.

The identity of an informer is privileged. Mass. Evid. Stand. 509. *Roviaro v. United States,* 353 U.S. 53, 59 (1957). *Worthington v. Scibner,* 109 Mass. 487, 488 (1872).

There is also a government state secret privilege. M. Graham, *Handbook of Federal Evidence* (3rd ed.), 358–61. It works like this: simply by claiming it, the government is entitled to refuse to disclose its secrets of national defense. But the government can use it only as a shield, not as a sword. If it claims the privilege, it cannot prosecute; it cannot hide behind the privilege. Once claimed, the government has to drop the prosecution or the tort case, or whatever it is. Otherwise, they have to disclose the information. If you sue them, however, they can refuse to disclose on the basis of state secrets.

In Massachusetts, there is a social worker-client privilege. G.L. c. 112, §§ 135, 135A, 135B. Mass. Evid. Stand. 510.

There is a patient-psychotherapist privilege. G.L. c. 233, § 20B. Mass. Evid. Stand. 511.

There is a rape counselor privilege. G.L. c. 233, § 20J. Mass. Evid. Stand. 512.

There is a domestic violence privilege. G.L. c. 233, § 20K. Mass. Evid. Stand. 513.

There is also a privilege dealing with surveillance locations. Mass. Evid. Stand. 514. *See Commonwealth v. Lugo*, 406 Mass. 565, 574, 548 N.E.2d 1263, 1268 (1990).

Now, here are some confidential data—as opposed to privilege—protections, which of course can be trumped by a court order: reports of rape and attempted sexual assault (G.L. c. 41, § 98. Mass. Evid. Stand. 521); personal data held by the Commonwealth (G.L. c. 66A, § 1. Mass. Evid. Stand. 522); hospital records (G.L. c. 111B, § 11. Mass. Evid. Stand. 523); medical records (243 C.M.R. § 2.07(13)(b) (1985). Mass. Evid. Stand. 524); records concerning physically and emotionally injured children (G.L. c. 119, §§ 51D, 51E, 51F. Mass. Evid. Stand. 525); records of examinations and commitments to mental institutions (G.L. c. 123, § 36A. Mass. Evid. Stand. 526); records of decisions of the parole board (G.L. c. 127, § 130. Mass. Evid. Stand. 527); and fire insurance information (G.L. c. 148, § 132. Mass. Evid. Stand. 528).

Admitting Evidence

I want to take just a few minutes to tell you how to put stuff into evidence. Then we'll put the photograph of Marada shooting Southwick in evidence. Then we'll call it a day.

I have one more chart, one more acronym: ARBPHU. It's really a checklist. With respect to every bit of evidence you want to put in, you want to think of ARBPHU. Is it authentic (i.e., is it the real one, is it the genuine one rather than an example)? Is it relevant? If it is both authentic and relevant, it gets into evidence unless its not the best evidence, it's privileged, it's hearsay, or it's unduly prejudicial. There you have it: ARBPHU. Don't go whimpering and whining up to the judge and say, "Judge, I object. That's prejudicial." There still are some snide judges who will look down at you and respond, "Counsel, it's intended to be prejudicial; it's evidence against your client." That's another definition of relevance, dirt. You have to persuade the judge that the information sought to be introduced is unduly or unfairly prejudicial. Fed.R.Evid. 403; Mass. Evid. Stand. 403.

Now, you all know Fort Ticonderoga. You went there when you were kids. *(Judge Young gestures to the chart)*.

Here is a cross section. Ticonderoga is built like Marshall Vaban Fort. Here is the glacis. Here's the start. There's a first step, but it doesn't fit in theory so I cut it out. See. This is if you are outside and trying to get into the fort. The French were very smart. Even though you get over the wall, you have to crawl over these fire pits *(Judge Young points to the BPHU)* to get your information into evidence.

EVIDENTIARY FOUNDATION

Authenticity
Relevance

Best evidence
Privileged
Hearsay
Unduly prejudicial

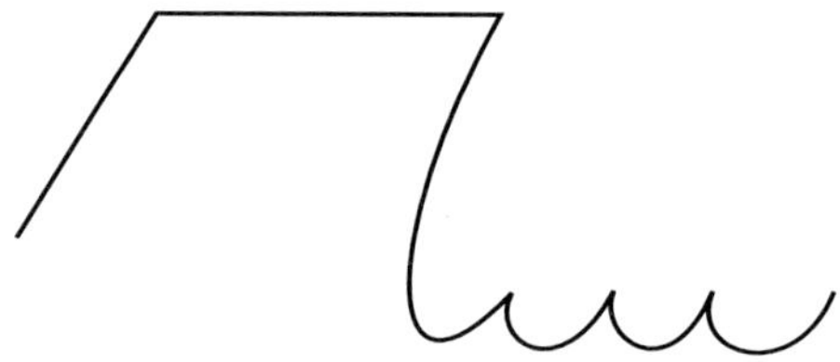

So think of it like this: If it's authentic (A), you are climbing the glacis. If it's both authentic and relevant (R), the evidence is admitted, unless horror of horrors, it's not the best evidence (B), it's privileged (P), it's hearsay (H), or it's unduly prejudicial (U).

A brief comment on Best Evidence. The best evidence rule applies to writings (Fed.R.Evid. 1001(1); Mass. Evid. Stand. 1001(1)), it applies to photographs (Fed.R.Evid. 1001(2); Mass. Evid. Stand. 1001(2)), it applies to movies in obscenity prosecutions. The best evidence rule simply means that you have to have the actual thing to put in evidence—the actual contract, the real writing—or you have to explain its absence (Fed.R.Evid. 1002; Mass. Evid. Stand. 1002). We rarely see this rule. Therefore, not much of an explanation is required. If you think that the other side has it, the original thing, prepare a request for production. If they don't produce it, you have explained its absence and you can go forward with a copy. We tend to go with copies anyway, but sometimes it comes up.

There, however, is a significant best evidence objection that is often overlooked. How often do you hear counsel say:

"And, well, did you get a letter back?"

"Yes, I did."

"And what did it say?"

That's objectionable. The best evidence of a writing—remember I said that best evidence applies to writing, photographs and movies—is the writing itself. Therefore, you should object and say, "I object, your Honor. The document speaks for itself." That will force the other side to produce the document or at least explain its absence. The federal rules are more liberal. They allow for duplicate originals, but the idea is essentially the same. Fed.R.Evid. 1003. Compare Mass. Evid. Stand. 1003, which limits the use of duplicate originals to the extent permitted by the statute. *See*

G.L. c. 233, §§ 76A, 77, 78, 79A, 79E. You still either have to have the document or explain why you don't have it. It is the document that should speak. You really want to do that rather than have the witness characterize the document.

So we've got ARBPHU: Is it authentic? Is it relevant? Then it has to go through the fire pits of best evidence, privilege, hearsay and unduly prejudicial.

Now, in the very few minutes remaining let me put the photograph into evidence. We'll take it step by step. The photograph is not self-authenticating. Some things are self-authenticating, for instance, birth records, municipal records, vital statistics. They're self-authenticating. I mean, so long as you get a certified copy of the record, you just pick that up and show the judge you have a certified copy. You don't need a witness. Fed.R.Evid. 1005. Mass. Evid. Stand. 1005. *See* G.L. c. 233, §§ 76–76B.

So, in our actual case, because this is not a record that is self-authenticating, we need a witness. All of this is now review. Who do we have? Well, we don't have Southwick; he's dead. We're the prosecution now. We don't have Marada; he has a Fifth Amendment privilege against testifying, so we can't call him to the stand. We have Mrs. Southwick, and this is terribly important. She could testify, though her view of the scene was different from Northup's, but she was there, and she can testify if she can answer these questions. But in the actual case at the time of the trial she had married Marada and Marada said he didn't want her to testify—No, no, no. They've since divorced. ***(Laughter)***.

But at the time of the trial, they were married, and Marada said that he didn't want her to testify, and that's it. And so we're left with Northrup. No, I love the story, but it's a bad teaching tool in this respect because of course Northrup is the photographer, and you don't need the photographer. That's why I emphasized to you Mrs. Southwick could do it for you. You don't need the photographer, but you do need someone who could answer these questions. I'm going to go through it step by step, and then we'll see the photo.

First, you put Northrup on the stand. Obviously he's sworn in. I'm just doing the evidentiary foundation now so you get the steps all correct. You obviously put him at the scene as you would as a skilled trial advocate.

Now we're ready to use the photo. Let's say the jury sits over there (indicating). You pick the photo up, and the very first thing I think you should do is show it to the other side. Now, you don't have to do that under the law, but I recommend it, as a trial matter. Show it to the other side.

Now, if it's premarked—and we all have these complex orders in big cases—if it's premarked maybe you don't have to do it. If it's not premarked, you show it to the other side. And if you're the showee, you look at it because, for instance, if you know the photograph is going to get in but on the back if it it says, "Marada Murdering Southwick, Brockton Police Department," that's hearsay, isn't it? That's an out-of-court statement, and you better get that taken off. Let me tell you there are all sorts of tags and stuff with assertive language on them in these types of cases. So look them over.

The reason that you show it first is suppose I get up here and I'm working with Northrup and opposing counsel says, "Your Honor, could I see that? I'm not sure I've seen that." I look like a jerk. I mean, I look like I've tried to pull a fast one. You're bona fide in front of the jury. You're teachers. One, you don't pull fast ones, and, two, you never want to be caught short like that, so you show it to the other side first. You don't have to ask permission to show it to him. "Let the record show that I'm now showing it to him." You just get up and you go over and you quietly show it to him, and he looks.

And the next step, if you haven't done it already, is to mark it for identification. Now, if it's not marked already, now's the time to mark it. In Massachusetts it's usually the clerks that mark things, and that's also true in the federal courts. In some states it's the court reporters that mark them.

So the first step is to show it. The second step is to get it marked for identification, unless it's already been done.

And now we're going to deal with the witness. The test here is not how many questions you can ask, but how few, and the reason is juries know that when you're doing evidentiary foundations you're sort of off track, you're not teaching them the story. You're doing something elitist with the judge. So you want to keep the questions just as few as possible.

Now let's do the questions for a photograph. Notice that the first two questions are exactly the same, and here they are:

"Mr. Northrup, I show you what has been marked as Exhibit A for Identification. Do you recognize it?"

Now, the reason you ask it that way is that's the best way I know how to ask it, because I haven't characterized it. I'm not saying I'm showing you the picture of the murder. I'm not even calling it a photograph. "I show you what's been marked as Exhibit A for Identification." I'm saying that on the record so now the Appeals Court is going to know exactly what I'm doing. The cold record will show what I've done.

"Do you recognize it?"

Answer: "Yes."

Next question?

AUDIENCE: "What is it?"

JUDGE YOUNG: Exactly. You're all thinking what is it. Ask "What is it?" The question may be objectionable with the photograph because, you see, the photograph speaks for itself. And if you've got a garrulous witness who's going to tell you in glowing detail what it is, competent defense counsel may object. If they object, back off and say, "Just identify it generally." But even though the second question is risky, I always go for asking it because that's what the jury is thinking, and the more you're a surrogate for the jury, the better you are. The jury's thinking, "What is it?" So you ask, "What is it?" And he says, "It's a photograph of Room 4A."

Now look, we now have an authentic and—if we look at it, we will see the shooting—we have a relevant photograph, so it should come into evidence. But despite everything I've said, there's one other question you must ask with respect to a photograph. "Is it a fair and accurate representation of what you saw?"

The way I learned in law school was a fair photographic representation, but either one will work. "Is this a fair and accurate representation of what you saw?"

The reason for that is, it goes back to ***Wigmore on Evidence***, photographs, when Wigmore wrote, were thought to corroborate the testimony of witnesses. But Northrup's got to say that this is something he, Northrup, saw.

Three questions. I offer it. Now, the offer, that's the time, if you haven't shown it to opposing counsel before, that you have to show it to him. That's the time you argue at the sidebar with the judge. That's the time for a brief brief, folks. You know what evidence you want to get in. You can plan for that. So if you have evidence that's questionable or something that is flawed technically, and you really want to put it to the judge, that's the time for a brief brief. And you walk right up there with your brief, give a copy to the other side, give a copy to the judge and say, "This evidence should come in."

The judge rules, and then the evidence goes into the custody of the clerk. But of course if you stop there you fail entirely, because with respect to every exhibit, it should be shown to the jury.

Now, I'll show you the photographs. ***(Judge Young displays the photo to the audience.)*** You see that I have oversold this only a fraction. In the center of the photograph there is Marada sitting up in bed. You can see the pistol. He's holding it in the approved Miami Vice position. ***(Laughter)***.

That's really the photograph. That's the exhibit in the trial. He's about to extend his arms and kill Southwick with one shot. You see Southwick to the right. You can see his shoulder. You can see the top of his head. You see his ear there.

Marada took the stand in this case. Atwood put him on, and his defense, as I indicated when we started, was self-defense. He said that he shot in self-defense. You see, there was this flash, and the flash went off a millisecond before he shot Southwick. And he said when the door burst open a guy came into the room. Now, Southwick was not advancing on the bed; he stepped off to one side, and that wasn't disputed. And Northrup stepped up to the door, and there was a flash from the camera. Marada fired immediately because he thought they were shooting at him.

Cross-examination, of course, was vigorous. Why was he armed? What was that .38 snub-nosed doing there in bed?

And Marada answered, "You always go armed when you are philandering; only a fool would not." ***(Laughter)***.

The case was tried in the spring of 1980 before the Honorable Joseph Ford, who gave me this photograph. The verdict was not guilty.

Thank you very much. ***(Applause)***.

Doorway into the Suffolk County Courthouse in Boston, Massachusetts, where Judge Young began his judicial career as a Justice of the Massachusetts Superior Court.

The John W. McCormack Building, which until August 1998 housed the United States Courthouse in Post Office Square, Boston, Massachusetts.

The new United States Courthouse at One Courthouse Way on the Fan Pier in Boston, Massachusetts, which opened in August 1998.

CHAPTER 6

A Case Study of a Session in the U.S. District Court

DECEMBER 6, 1997

MY voice isn't that good, and I appreciate this. I've had bronchitis. So the voice is only half here, and I leave it to you whether the mind is entirely here. You can critique that when it's over.

I was appointed a Justice of the Superior Court on November 27, 1977. I was confirmed in early January. I first sat on February 24th, 1978. And they induct you before you sit. You get sworn in. I was sworn in at the statehouse, and it was very nice, and people spoke, and lots of people came. But let's talk about the judge's work. I'm inducted, so I go to one of the old courtrooms in the so-called new courthouse. It might have been on the 10th floor. I'm not sure. It's a very nice ceremony. Two judges sit on the bench with you, and the Chief Justice reads your commission and pronounces "You are now confirmed as an Associate Justice of the Superior Court." Then you're a judge.

So I remember that the judges who stood up with me were Justice Vallely and Justice Brogna, who were very distinguished judges of the superior court. We go through the ceremony. And I get off the bench, and I'm going to be assigned to room 227. I'm ready to start my judicial career, and Judge Brogna says to me, "Now, remember, have the courage of your own error."

So here I go, and I report to the courtroom where I am first to preside. I've got a clerk—someone in the Suffolk Clerk's Office. I've got a court officer, Eddie Kelly. I've got a wonderful court reporter. And what am I going to do? Here I am. So I send over to the Suffolk motion session. Back in those days they had motion sessions. I asked, "Do you have any extra motions?" Well, the judge over there—I think it was Judge Mitchell—said, "Yes, we do." He sent me over some motions. And the lawyers trail over to my courtroom, not too happy to come to this greenhorn. And I go out on the bench.

So, I have these motions. And I haven't read them, of course, but back in those days you had 40 or 50 motions in a day. So I take the motions, and I ask myself, "How do judges behave?" I mean they imitate judges that they've seen. I've never been one, so now I am one. And I hope I'm not too puffed up myself. I want to be a good one, but I'm imitating what I think judges do. So I say, "Yes," "Now," and "What do *you* say?" And I listen to the argument, and I take notes. The Court gives you a black notebook. It says Justice Young on it. I still have mine on the federal court. It's like a security blanket. And I listen, and I take some notes on this motion for summary judgment. Then I say, "Yes," and I turn to the other counsel and ask "What do *you* say?" And I'm thinking to myself: This is not too hard; it's like I used to do when I was on the other side of the bench; these people are making sense to me. And then, "All right," "Thank you," "I'll take it under advisement."

The other court sent me only about five motions, so that takes us about half an hour, 45 minutes. And I go back and I start going through the papers and reviewing my notes. The principles are either there or I think I know what I'm doing. I decide the motions, my first judicial orders. I write in the margin "Allowed," "Denied," or something else.

All right. Second day—don't worry, we're not going to go day by day here, but I want to start out by giving you an idea of the day in the life of a judge. So, we're on the second day—you see, they don't start new judges with jury trials. They start you jury-waived. So now that I'm on the job, I have a trial, my first trial presiding as a Justice of the superior court. The case is jury-waived, and the factual issue is: Did the wife forge her husband's signature on the deed?

I come out on the bench. "All rise," blah, blah, blah, blah. We start. I sit down. And we're sitting. In the days when I was in Room 227 they had a very long bench. I guess they could get three or four, maybe even five of the justices of the Supreme Judicial Court if they wanted to sit there. The chair was placed right in the center of the bench. And I go there and sit there. And there are books behind me. It's very impressive. Counsel give their openings in this jury-waived case. And I perceive the issue. And then they call the wife. They call her as an adverse witness. That's sort of a dramatic opening. I know enough about trial practice to understand what's going on. And it suddenly comes home to me that I have to decide whether that woman is telling the truth. Nothing in my ten years of practice has prepared me for this, nothing, because, of course, I've been a lawyer; I've been on one side or the other. And now it falls to me to decide whether that lady is truthful. And I have whatever life experience I have, but I don't know how to do that. There's been no course; there's no school. And I think to myself: How do I do this? This is not law. I'd better watch her very closely. ***(Laughter)***. I'm not making any of this up. This is what's going through my mind. And I think to myself, "You know, I can't really see her very well." She's over there at the side of the bench, and I'm in the center of this awesome bench, so I'd better get over there, get the chair over there and look down at her because she may wring her hands—literally I'm thinking she may wring her hands. I'll look at her and maybe she won't meet my eyes, or maybe she'll perspire. And I say to myself, "okay, well, that's the plan, that's what I'll do."

But I'm a little afraid to stand up, to drag the chair over there, because I had stood up on my first day on the bench. I had been hearing those motions and I thought that I could use one of the *Mass. Reports* that were on the bookshelves behind the bench. So I stood up to get one. I figured that it would be nice from time to time to see what the law actually is. So, I was going to get a book to check the law on a particular issue, a particular case. When I stood up, Eddie Kelly, the court officer, was right on the ball. He thought as a new judge I wanted a recess. So when I stood up he yelled, "All rise." Gee, I thought that a judge had come into the courtroom, so I sort of snapped to attention. *(Laughter)*. And we had to kind of sort that out.

So, anyway—back to my story about moving the chair over to get a better view of the witness—I didn't want to disturb Eddie. He was fine over there. But I wanted to get over there to view the witness, and I thought what I'll do is I'll just take the throne—it's on a swivel chair—and I'll slowly slide it on over there. This would have been a minor advancement in my judicial development except for the fact that the chair was on one of those plastic mats. When I slid it to the edge of the mat, it stops and I go headlong behind the bench. *(Laughter)*. This is absolutely true. I go "splat" behind the bench. And I think, "That's it. It's all over; what a buffoon. How could I have ever been appointed?" I get up, and my face is crimson and I am so embarrassed. So I get up. And, you know, nobody is laughing. And I think to myself, "Why aren't they laughing? I've never seen a judge do something as stupid as I have just done, but nobody is laughing."

Then it comes to me—another great truth—they're not laughing because, my God, I'm the judge who's presiding in this session. I take that chair, and I yank it over to the side of the bench, and I put it down, and I sit in it, and for about 20 minutes I sulk. Whether I'm paying attention to the lady or not will now never be known. I just sit there and relive what a fool I am. After about 20 minutes I figure maybe I have a job to do, so I pay attention to whatever they're doing during the cross-examination of the lady, and life goes on.

Okay. I tell that story because to me the story has a couple of things that I want to emphasize today. First, I don't want there to be any distance between us. I'm going to speak in a moment about asking questions. This is a perfect size group to do what I have in mind to do this morning. And I most sincerely want your questions. Make this work for you. I know what I want to do. In fact, I have an agenda here. There are some things that I want to get out or get across, but make this work for you. So please give me your questions.

Second, I want to start in a very human way. And that story actually happened. It happened just the way I said. Judges are all human. I am a fountain of judge stories. One other comes to mind of a judge behind the bench. He is Sammy Flaxman. Justice Flaxman was not too tall. He was sitting over in Middlesex in one of those round courtrooms where they're arched in the center. And, you know, the books are behind the bench in that courtroom too. There weren't many people in the courtroom. It was Earle Cooley and one other attorney in some jury-waived case in the middle of the afternoon. Cooley was arguing for the plaintiff. So the defense closed first. That's the order in state court, the defense closes and then the plaintiff closes.

Earle Cooley, whom I revere as one of our finest trial lawyers, is a heavy set fellow, and he was much heavier set in those days than he is now. The defendant had argued. And now Earle got up to argue, and he pulled himself up off his chair, and he stepped to the well of the courtroom, and he looked at the bench. Flaxman wasn't there. I mean he wasn't there. That was pretty discourteous, don't you think? The trial wasn't over. The plaintiff hadn't made his closing argument. And you looked, and you saw a bench. And the clerk was there, and there was his bench. There were books behind the bench, but no Flaxman. So he turns to defense counsel, and sotto voce he says—except it's all picked up because he's in the very center of those courtrooms, and with the arched ceilings you'd better watch out what you say because your whisper will be picked up—"What happened to the little bastard?" *(Laughter)*. Whereupon Flaxman, who has reached down for a book, comes up, just like someone in a shooting gallery, and says, "Here I am. Go on with your argument." *(Laughter)*.

STRUCTURE OF LECTURE

All right. I want us to talk about trial practice, about judging. I want your questions. Here's what I have in mind to do: I named this *A Case Study of a Session of the United States District Court in the District of Massachusetts;* not anybody's session, the session in which I'm privileged to serve, my session. For a long time I've thought that it would be worthwhile to have a substantive discussion of all the things that happen in a session of the United States District Court. And I intend to provide such a substantive discussion this morning. That is, I'm going to talk through who all the people are, what resources they have, and what we all do in every case, every type of case—civil and criminal.

In short, my goal this morning is to give you in as much detail as I can all the boilerplate that makes our session work. Everything that's routine; everything that you could find out if you went to Bonnie Smith, my courtroom deputy clerk, or Don Womack, my court reporter, I will tell you. In fact, I want you to ask questions about it. There is no such thing in this group this morning as an impertinent or an unethical question. If you wonder why a judge does anything, ask it.

Well, let me pause here. Why is it important to you that I want to tell you everything about *my* session in the United States District Court? You may ask, "Who cares?" If I thought that the course was only for people who were going to practice in a session over which I preside, I am not so self-regarding that I think that's terribly worthwhile or worthwhile to spend four hours in a morning. Those of you who do practice in the sessions where I preside may get something out of it, but that doesn't justify the course. Here's why I think it's important. I may be wrong. I'm interested in your critique. By going over in detail everything that I do and my people do and precisely how we do it, I hope to give you a baseline for approaching every other session of any court, federal or state. Courts are not that different. So if I am honest—and I will be honest, as honest as I know how—about how I do everything, you'll have a compendium by which you can approach any court and see what variations there are. Also, you might learn how to deal with the judges and deal with the trials in those courts.

I welcome your questions of all sorts. I'll answer as follows: If I have thought of the issue that you raise in your question and I have a routine for dealing with it, I will of course share it with you; nothing at all will be held back. If I know how other judges deal with it, I will tell you, and I will name names and give you my best impression as to how others judges do it—and we do vary. If, however, you ask a question which maybe theoretically I could answer but I've never really thought it through and I'd have to sort of analyze the specific case, I won't answer it. Doesn't mean it's a wrong question. Please don't be put off, but I won't answer it because that's not my goal here. My goal is standard boilerplate regarding what judges routinely do so that you will be better off dealing with judges.

So I did the first two days of my practice as a judge. Now we fast forward to today. I'm a judge in the United States District Court for the District of Massachusetts. I've been one for 13 years. I hope that I will remain one for the rest of my professional life.

My approach is going to be as follows, just structurally: A session of the court is people. That's true if you are in the juvenile court. It's true if you are in the Supreme Court of the United States. I want to introduce you to the people, the real people in our session, including myself. Once we've done the people, then we will talk about the resources of the session, the actual equipment, the books upon which I rely, the things that are at my hands to assist me in doing the judicial job. When we've got those structural elements in place, I want to tell you what I think the job is and how I propose to work with the people and the resources that I have to reach out for justice.

When we've got those three pieces in place, we're simply going to go through trials, civil and criminal, from the moment the complaint or indictment is filed through post-trial procedure. And we'll do every routine. Every time I stand up in front of a jury and say routine things or start a motion session or impose a sentence, I will declaim it for you this morning.

Remember that this morning is for me pretty intensely personal. I don't need many notes for this. This is what I do. I don't think what I do is necessarily right. I very much want to show you the weaknesses in what I do, but I persist in doing it because I think that the benefits outweigh the weaknesses; but there are always benefits and burdens to proceeding in a certain fashion. Compare what you hear today about what I do with how other judges do it.

So this is the idea: If you're coming in to practice in my session, here are some things you should know. Let's start.

THE PEOPLE WHO MAKE UP A SESSION OF THE U.S. DISTRICT COURT

I first will discuss the people that make up my session, because people are most important. A session of the United States District Court in the District of Massachusetts is authorized, all of us are all authorized, the following resources in terms of personnel: Each judge has a courtroom deputy clerk with whom we work routinely. We have a court reporter with whom we work routinely. We have a docket clerk with whom we may or may not—judges vary—work routinely. Those first three people are what are called in the federal system "the clerk staff." That is, they are employed by the Clerk of Court. While they are detailed to me, they work for the clerk. He is their executive head.

Then a judge in the United States District Court is authorized three chamber staff. He has hiring and firing authority with respect to chamber staff. And they work just for the judge: a secretary, or administrative assistant, and two law clerks. There's a hierarchy with respect to law clerks. A magistrate judge and a bankruptcy judge each get one; a district judge gets two; the Chief Judge of the district court gets three; every circuit judge gets three; justices of the Supreme Court of the United States get four. That's how it works with respect to law clerks. So that's the organization.

Courtroom Deputy Clerk

Now, I will tell you a little about the people in my session. My courtroom deputy clerk is Ms. Elizabeth Smith, Bonnie Smith. Before she worked for the court she was a teacher. She's married to a Coast Guardsman who is now retired. He is a superintendent of buildings at Boston University. Bonnie has done a number of jobs in the courts. She was the MBD clerk, that is, the clerk for the emergency judge who handles emergency motions routinely. The way our court works, one of us is the emergency judge, so you can always get a judge. She was that judge's clerk. The judges varied. That's where search warrants are approved, wiretaps are approved. If there is a fight during a deposition and for some reason you need a judge from the District of Massachusetts, that's the emergency judge. Bonnie did that work. She was docket clerk in my session. She was the person who made all the docket entries and worked with the courtroom deputy clerk. Now she is the courtroom deputy clerk.

The courtroom deputy clerk is the person with whom the judge works most closely, the person who pretty much runs the session. And we'll talk about the principles on which she runs it in a moment. I see Bonnie every day without fail. We talk about the case on trial. We talk about the cases coming up. We talk about the cases that I thought were resolved but are not resolved. She is a magnificent representor of the bar. If you call Ms. Smith and say, "Tell the judge this," she always will tell me, and she'll tell me that day. You can get your concerns through her to me constantly.

I am surprised, I will tell you, by how frequently the clerk is given a bad time by lawyers. The clerk doesn't have the power. The judge has the power, and the clerk is speaking for the judge. So when the judge says, "We're going to hear this motion at such and such a time," and then you come in, and the clerk let's you know what the judge said, the clerk is saying what the judge has ordered. Ms. Smith is authorized to speak for me in a variety of ways. She may come to me and ask, "Judge, what do you want me to do with this? I know you're strict on continuances, but here's the problem. I told these people this; is that all right?" She and I discuss that type of thing daily. I work with Ms. Smith. I think she's great. I want her to stay until she retires. She takes an active role in settlement. She'll tell you when you're talking with her, "You really ought to settle this case." She's really quite experienced; not a lawyer. And, of course, I back her up on that. She's welcome to say this kind of stuff. She's always letting me know what she's telling people. She will not discuss with me on the criminal side the substance of plea negotiations if she knows what they are, and she may know. What she will say is, "Judge, it looks like this one is going to plead; let's have a back-up," because we want to keep rolling.

So that's the courtroom deputy clerk. She's the one who sits in front of the bench, swears the witnesses, handles the juries. That's really not the heavy lifting part of her job. Her job is to manage the entire session, the part of the session that deals with you, that deals with the trial of cases. She manages it in accordance with the broad outlines that I give her, and we're going to go over what those are. She is your prime person to interact with when you're dealing with our session. Her number is (617) 223-9156. She is the person with whom to speak.

AUDIENCE MEMBER: Judge Young, do you have a sense that the other judges of the federal district court use their courtroom deputy clerks the same way?

JUDGE YOUNG: Good point, and that's just the type of question I want. Yes, in large measure, yes. All of the judges are closer to their courtroom deputy clerks than any other nonjudicial person. Now, I started with the courtroom deputy, not law clerks. I love my law clerks. We'll talk about law clerks. But it's the courtroom deputy that is the top professional. Now, in any human system, some are closer to their clerks than others, and the difference is how much they delegate to them. I'm on the end of the spectrum of broad delegation. Ms. Smith has a great deal of power in our session with respect to case scheduling. Now, I have every sense that she uses that power appropriately. She doesn't play favorites. Cases can't jump one

> over another. Power like that can be abused. But I make no bones. We have a little saying in our session, "We all work for Bonnie." Well, there's a lot of truth to that because, you see, I want Bonnie to keep things rolling.

Now, Chief Justice Tauro has a clerk, Chickie, and he has the same confidence in her. They've been working together for a long time. On the other end of the spectrum are judges who have more control or want to take more control over scheduling themselves. And if they schedule themselves more, then that means that while the clerk is their spokesperson, the clerk has less—and so you have less—ability to predict what's going to happen.

If you talk to Bonnie and she says, "Next Monday X is going to happen," it's only if we've slipped a stitch that next Monday and I'm giving a speech somewhere, and, shame on me, she has to change everything around. But save for my fault, she's right; on Monday X will happen. If I'm healthy, I'll be there.

That's the spectrum. But all of the judges in the Federal District Court are closer to their courtroom deputies than they are to anyone else. Counsel, don't give courtroom deputies a hard time. Who do they talk to? They talk to the judges. And they talk good and bad. They'll say, "You won't believe it; I just got off the phone with such and such; what a horse's ass; he says..." Now, we know that. And then what could be more craven when the alleged horse's ass comes in and could not be more obsequious to the judge, "Oh, your Honor, Oh, your Honor, Oh, yes, Oh, your Honor." I mean that is absolutely "B.S." If you have some beef with the judge, you've got to have the guts to put your beef on the record with the judge and say, "Respectfully, your Honor, it is just a violation to force me to trial on such short notice; I cannot properly represent my client; it's unfair." Whatever you want to say to the judge, put it in writing, get it on the record. Of course raise it anyway you can, but don't scream or hector at the clerk. She's doing what the judge told her.

Court Reporter

Next, the court reporter. I have the finest court reporter in the United States. Donald Womack is a realtime court reporter who at his own investment has given me a computer-integrated courtroom, for a long time the only one in New England. Now that's not really so. They have another one in New Hampshire.

What do I mean by a realtime computer-integrated courtroom? We have a variety of the court reporters now who can take realtime. Realtime means that as the court reporter is taking words down, what's being said scrolls on a screen in English. Now, some court reporters, both state and federal, are capable of doing that. In the federal courts we have about four or five of them that are capable of doing that.

Don has bought the computers to put on my bench and on the counsels' tables at no cost to you so you can see the transcript as he's taking it down. That's a computer-integrated courtroom. What can you do with this? This is the wave of the future. This is coming. We'll expand on this. There's a great interest in realtime court reporting among all the judges in the United States District Court. We have a Windows application, so if you have your litigation support, your depositions, if you've optically scanned your documents, you can close down the window or foreshorten the window that has the transcript and bring up the deposition of that witness on the other side of the screen. You can go back, juxtapose the two, and cross-examine from them. And lawyers have done that.

Now, of course, it's up to you to have the appropriate computer equipment to tie into Don's equipment to get this facility, but because of his investment, not a penny from the government, that's all there.

That only begins to scratch the surface of what Don Womack can do for you. He is, in Massachusetts, the leading expert on electronic databases. He's the one who is putting together our web site, for instance, so that all this data that we're talking about this morning will be there. He's putting it together. He's working with a computer professor at Providence College. The man is an expert on computer databases.

Why is that important? Three reasons, three examples: Don Womack has been with me for as long as I've been a federal judge. He was a Superior Court court reporter down in Brockton. I hired him when I became a federal judge. I'm in my 13th year. He's been here 13 years, working primarily for me. Now, they're in a pool. When I don't sit, he works for other judges; but every time I sit, he works for me. He has a database for everything that has gone on in our courtroom, and he can find it. You see, that's the key: He can find it. So if you were going to practice in our session of the court and you wondered how I charged in a products liability case, civil rights case, contract case, any kind of case—if I've ever had that type of case before and it's gone to the jury—Don can find it. We had a copyright case recently, and one lawyer had the wit to go to Don—this is what I'm telling you to do—and get a charge I had used in an earlier case. Therefore, this lawyer got my charge in the earlier case. He cited the charge as law because that's what it is, you see. In my charge, I was explaining to the jury what I thought the law was. Now it's being cited back to me as law. There's nothing in F. Supp. here on this, but the words I used—the way I had explained it to the jury—were being cited back to me as law. I actually made a few changes to it the next time around. I thought I could do a little better, but I praised the lawyer for doing that. That was real power in that case because, you see, he was able to find it.

Now, let's say, not to be too self-regarding, you have a case in the United States District Court and you wanted to know how I charge on products liability or civil rights or something that comes up frequently. You can get it from Don. I mean you can buy it from Don. He's entitled to sell those charges at the transcript rate.

Maybe you have a case in the superior court. It has nothing to do with our court, but it's the type of case over which we have concurrent jurisdiction—we hear those type of cases. Products liability is a good example. And you simply would like an example of a charge. If you think my charges are any good, buy one from Don and cite it to the superior court justice. And that's true, of course, of drug cases and the like where we have concurrent jurisdiction. He has every charge we've ever had.

How about this? Wouldn't you like to know if the expert that you have to cross-examine has ever been in court before and how that expert was cross-examined before; or if you have hired an expert and your expert is going to testify, don't you want to see what problems that expert may have? If that expert has ever, ever in 13 years testified in our session, you can buy it from Don. He's got it because it's transcript. It's there.

Now, how valuable is this? Not too valuable, because I'm only one judge—and not a particularly special judge at that—and, although I try cases frequently, the chances of us having every expert that testifies are remote. What is important here is that this is the direction that we're going in. You don't even need to have realtime. As long as you have computer-aided transcription, as long as the way the stenographic court reporter takes down the record is tied into a computer and if the reporter knows how to maintain a database with a search engine, you can get that stuff. That is a resource of an incalculable value to you.

A couple of more things while we are on this subject. The first one is known as seeding the database. I try to plant seeds in the database during side bar conferences. The federal rules are all numbered. I teach evidence, and, although I may be too self-regarding on this, I think I know a little about evidence, and that makes me dangerous. Anyway, at the side bar I will try to mention the number of the evidence rule that I think we are talking about. I may say something like, "Well, under 403, how can you say that the prejudice unduly or substantially outweighs the probative value?" By mentioning "403" it helps when we search. You can get all the 403 rulings by using that number in your search.

Now, there are limits to this. I was told of a judge in the Northern District of Alabama who routinely made his rulings as follows: "Sustained, 701." "Overruled, 615." "Sustained, 1131." There is no 1131. This judge was just making up numbers. Apparently he went for months with great success before the bar caught on that the numbers bore no relationship at all to the rulings. ***(Laughter)***. He was confident, but he had no idea what the actual numbers were. I leave the accuracy to you. But at least in the database if you want all of our 403 rulings or 612 rulings, whatever, you ought to be able to find them.

On the criminal side, we have sentencing guidelines. Sentencing guidelines were designed to create a common law of sentencing so that you could go from case to case, judge to judge and really learn what those variables were in a human sense that affected the sentences that were being given to people. The federal sentencing guidelines are a failure. I'm a supporter of the state sentencing guidelines, but the federal sentencing guidelines are a complete and utter failure; they're morally bankrupt. My colleague Judge Woodlock calls them "a massive exercise in hypocrisy." But I'll get back to that later in the morning, except to tell you now that when I sentence, there's a transcript. I look at those transcripts. When I say Don can get it, I go back to see other defendants in like situations and read about what I said about them and why I came to the sentence that I did.

Now, if I'm doing it and if it's informing my further sentences, counsel should be doing it. They should be going to those transcripts. Because one of the things about sentencing is you want to be equitable defendant-to-defendant—and I feel terribly keenly about this—one way to find out is to look at the transcripts. I urge you to do that. I call Don the long-range historian of our session. It's all there. He will sell it to you at the page rate that is authorized. He is certainly someone to talk to and is an absolute mainstay of our session. For instance, he keeps my charge bank. When I want to do a charge, I don't go to a file; I go to Don and I say, "What have we got on this area of the law?" And he has software called "Build-a-Charge," where he will change the names. I like to use the actual names of parties instead of "plaintiff" and "defendant." He'll change the names. He'll change from singular to plural if we go from a one-defendant to a multi-defendant case. He'll take parts of one charge, willful blindness, say, and put it in another charge. He'll put the proper caption on it, and then he will transfer it to my secretary's computer. He'll give it to me in hard copy because I can only work in hard copy. That's my starter for the charge. And we'll talk about that later when we come to the charges.

So that's Don Womack, world's best court reporter.

AUDIENCE MEMBER: How widespread is this with other judges?

JUDGE YOUNG: How many other judges have this type of resource? On our court we have, I believe, five who have realtime technology. Of the 13 judges, about nine use computer-assisted transcripts, but they don't keep the databases. The best one in this area is Judge Keeton—he's much more facile than I am. He has a really extensive computer database on which he and his secretary work, and he's very good.

The most computer-facile judge on our court is Judge Gertner, junior in seniority but, perhaps because she's junior, far better on the computer than I am.

Judge Woodlock, he's quite facile on the computer. Actually, it's an age thing; the younger you are, the better you are on the computer. Keeton, though he's an older judge, is just brilliant. And he really has a computer database. I hope that answers your question?

AUDIENCE MEMBER: What's the best way to make a request of Mr. Womack? In writing or on the phone?

JUDGE YOUNG: His phone number is 367-2029. I mean, in a way he's in business. He's a government official, but he's allowed to sell his transcripts, so call him up and find out, depending upon what your need is. He's the person to call if you want to import your own computer stuff into the courtroom. Even if you have nothing to do with our session but you'd like what you think is a good charge, or you've heard that we had expert X, or you're off there in the Berkshire Superior Court but you've got this protean expert who testifies everywhere and you're hoping he may have testified before us. Just give Don a call, and he'll tell you.

AUDIENCE MEMBER: Speaking of computers, do you allow laptops in your session?

JUDGE YOUNG: I do.

AUDIENCE MEMBER: How do I get them through Security?

JUDGE YOUNG: You call Bonnie, and if that won't do it, you draft a letter for me to sign enough time in advance, and I sign it. I allow laptops. I have one caveat, and it is this: your laptop must have a silent keyboard. "Silent" means "cannot hear it." If I hear it, I don't want you to use it because I think it distracts the jury. I don't want to turn a courtroom into a city news room. The courtroom is a courtroom. It should be quiet. Now, in fact, we have various keyboards, whether you bring one or not. We have the court reporter's keyboard, and they tend to be silent. Bonnie has a computer on her desk that ties in to all the docketing. It's a government computer. She can bring up all the dockets in every case. And she works there while the trial is going on. It's a fairly silent keyboard. Sometimes I can hear it. I have a keyboard on the computer that Don has given me, which is showing the transcript. And though I am virtually illiterate on the computer, I know how to take notes, and I know how to go back and see other parts of the transcript. Therefore, during a specific trial I can go back to an earlier day, earlier hour, and find my notes on something. It's very valuable on deciding whether there's sufficiency of the evidence.

Docket Clerk

Next, my docket clerk. The docket clerk in my session is Ms. Dianne Smith. She was a clerk, not necessarily a docket clerk, for the Bankruptcy Court before she came over to us. She's a dedicated and consummate professional. The docket clerk does all the data entry in the clerk's office, and she makes the docket. The docket is available to you, you realize, on our PACER system. You can get the dockets in any pending federal court case. You don't have to come to court. You can get them through PACER over the phone. You may have to make advance arrangements. You may have to pay for that. It's some modest thing. In any event, they're available. If you come to court by use of the computer, you can get the dockets all through PACER.

Now, Ms. Smith, Ms. Dianne Smith—not to be confused with Bonnie Smith (no relation)—makes all those entries, but that only begins to describe her work. If you think of a docket clerk as a data entry person, at least in our session, you are making a big mistake. What she does is handle all the discovery motions. She batches them up. When you file a discovery motion she keeps it; she doesn't file it away; she keeps it until the opposition comes in. Then she brings it to me herself, or really brings it to chambers, and then I rule on it, and I give it back to her. She does all the tickling on that.

Once you've filed a complaint, she's the one who is seeing whether you made service within 120 days, because if you haven't, you're out or you need to get an extension. She's following that. She does all those procedural things that inure to efficiency with respect to our cases.

If you file an emergency motion, if it has the word "emergency" on it, she will stop everything and bring it to me. As soon as she sees a motion that has the word "emergency" on it, she will physically bring it to the courtroom. And that's terribly important to you because one of the big raps on federal district courts nationwide is that they're so removed from the bar that you can't grab their attention. You may have some crucial thing, but the judges are busy, and because they have real staff, it's hard to get through the staff. You put the term "emergency" on it, it goes into Ms. Dianne Smith's hands, and I will see it as fast as she can get it to me. However, if you file an emergency motion, ask to have Dianne Smith come to the intake, come to the desk, because that's not a strong part of our office. It may get filed and put into a box with the little "WGY" that indicates that it's my case, but it doesn't get forwarded to Dianne until later in the day or sometimes not until the next day. The foreclosure may have taken place by the next day. You get it into Dianne Smith's hands that day.

AUDIENCE MEMBER: What do you regard as an emergency motion?

JUDGE YOUNG: Well, I think that emergency motions are overused. People will call a motion an emergency motion if they've run out of time on discovery or they don't know whether to produce the person for a deposition or not because of the way things have worked out and so they want an emergency ruling. Now, I give all credit to Dianne. I will see it. I won't do anything with it. I mean I'll just hold it and let you sort of work it out yourselves. A real emergency motion is there's going to be a foreclosure or, in a huge case, the parade permit has been denied and the parade is Saturday and it's Friday, those things—like a TRO, genuine emergencies. I don't really fault you if you call something an emergency and it's not. I'm not hostile to that, but I just pay no attention to it. If it's not really an emergency, I just wait for the opposition to come in. I really believe in the adversary process. I think people can pretty much work it out themselves.

Also Dianne, because she is fully integrated in our session, is a person I don't see so often. Obviously I see Bonnie Smith, courtroom deputy clerk, and Don Womack. I see them every day. If I go to court, I see them. Dianne I don't see every day. I know she's there because I'm seeing her work and I'm giving it back to her, but I don't see her every day; however, she's fully integrated in the session in the way that Bonnie is. She knows a great deal about practice and procedure. She knows a great deal about the stuff that we're going over this morning. She speaks for me. She and Bonnie speak for me. If they say, "he won't hear evidence on this" or "he will do that," by and large they are right. Otherwise, I should change my routine because those are my spokespersons.

She'll be the one who may answer when you call. You won't get Bonnie. Bonnie will be in court with me. You'll get Dianne. She knows everything about our cases. What she says about them is accurate and to the point.

Let me pause. Sadly, there is an issue whether we will continue to have individual docket clerks. I am strongly in favor of continuing the practice. I have an argument that it is the best service to the public. It is argued that really they are only data entry people and fewer data entry people can service more of the court and, therefore, we ought to surrender our docket clerks to just a pool. They'll just do docketing. And then what we'll have is more automation people. And automation is the world of the future. Well, to that I say, "hah!" You can see just the way I describe it that I'm hostile to it. I'm not only hostile to it, it will be over my dead body because I think that the docket clerk is so vital to the system. That's a voice, not one of these electronic things at the end of the phone. That's someone you can tell a story to and she will get it heard. If our focus is on the trial and you're not on trial, how do we deal with you? How do you break into that orbit? You need a human being who will break into that orbit so we can at least pay attention to your case. That's the docket clerk. Whatever her title, she is a deputy clerk. The way we use her is very vital. Now, some of you have asked a good question. And on this there's a split. Not everyone uses them the way I do. Some of the judges don't know who their docket clerks are. Some don't care. If in the name of, quote, "efficiency sake" we lose the docket clerk, it is my opinion that we lose a valuable resource. I'm trying to hang on to the docket clerk.

Chamber Staff

Now, let's discuss the chamber staff. Judges have a great deal of discretion. I don't have to have a secretary. I could have a third law clerk if I didn't have a secretary. And while none of the judges in Massachusetts have done this, in other districts they have. I don't have to have a secretary. In some districts it is the secretary who manages the cases. That's not the tradition here in Massachusetts. The secretaries deal with the noncourtroom work of the judge. And in our session and in most sessions that's the dichotomy.

The ethics in the District of Massachusetts suggest that you call the courtroom deputy or the docket clerk; they speak for the judge. Of course you can talk to the court reporter. They deal with the public. But don't call my secretary or my law clerks about a pending case. It's not hideously forbidden, but it's just not the way we do it, and the secretary will refer you back to Bonnie, the courtroom deputy. The one judge who is a little more liberal on that is Judge Gertner because she had a nationwide practice before she became a judge and, for instance, in the Southern District of New York you call the clerks and say, "When are we going to get that opinion?" Don't do that in the District of Massachusetts. We all think that's improper. To us, such tactics suggest that you are leaning on the clerk. The clerks are my little law office.

My secretary/administrative assistant is Sharon Atkins. She has been with me 13 years. Before that she worked in the Office of the District Attorney for Middlesex. Before that she worked with Charles Nesson, professor at Harvard (you know, Green and Nesson, "On Evidence"). She was his secretary. Before that she was secretary to the Honorable Franklin Flaschner, first Chief Justice of the district court system here in Massachusetts. She is a wonderful secretary, wonderful person, and has the best telephone personality of anyone I've ever met. Judges from around the country who have business with me will call Sharon, joke with Sharon, and leave messages for me. They have never met Sharon, but she just is very good. And if you have anything, any bar association thing, anything about this course, anything like that, Sharon is the person to call. She handles all my teaching obligations. She handles my calendar other than my court calendar, and she pretty much runs the 19th floor, which is where my chambers are located.

I have two law clerks. Over the 13 years that I have been a federal judge, my law clerks have primarily been from schools around here. They don't have to be. I've had clerks from Fordham, Washington University in St. Louis; but primarily they've been from Harvard, BU, BC, Northeastern. My two clerks this year are from Harvard. I don't have any specific preference for Harvard, though I went there.

The clerks do a year clerkship. One starts in September; one starts in November, so they can teach each other. So, for instance, my November clerk will stay on and orient the new clerk coming in September, and the like.

Primarily the law clerks are my lawyers, and primarily their work is the written research work of the session. They do the first drafts of most opinions. We'll refer to that. That's important. They'll do bench memoranda on motions. They will sit with me as a clerk when I'm sitting jury-waived. In the days when we really had 500 cases, they handled what were known as summary jury trials. I'll get back to that later. But today their primary work is research and drafting. And I use them all the time for that. I rely on them, and we will talk about how I rely on them.

Our session is, again, not unique. Judge Saris uses interns, and I always use interns from law schools. I pay an enormous debt to Northeastern. I always have a Northeastern co-op law student; though self-selected, I never have less than one. If I have only one intern, it's a Northeastern intern. I never have more than three because it becomes too unwieldy—they get in each other's way, candidly. It's a small law office. I have had interns from Harvard, Suffolk, and New England School of Law, BU, BC. Never had anyone from Western New England, though I know that Judge Ponsor out there has had an intern from Western New England Law School.

How do I use the interns? Just like law clerks. They get their work from the law clerks, but they do their work for me. They do the work that law clerks do. They do research. They do drafting. They do the first drafts of opinions. And then we have sort of an internal check, and I'll go over how we do that at the appropriate time. That's the work of the law clerks.

The Judge

And, lastly, there's me, the judge. We'll devote a little more time to me. I want to now tell you things that you could find out about any judge. Then I want in sort of a personal way to tell you what difference these things make or don't make. And then, having done that, we can talk a little bit about resources.

You see me. I'm a middle-aged white guy. I'm a product of public schools on Long Island. I was a scout. I was an Eagle Scout. I went to Harvard. My major was History, and got a Bachelor of Arts. I was in the military for two years, in peacetime. Very important that you understand it was peacetime. Served in Korea, but it was in peacetime. I was an artillery man. I'm very proud of that. Came back from my stint in the military service and went to Harvard Law School. My record was undistinguished. I was not on Law Review or the Board of Student Advisors. I didn't dislike it. I liked law school. By a fluke really, because I am interested in Civil War history, I got to be a clerk to Raymond Sanger Wilkins, father of the present Chief Justice of the Massachusetts Supreme Judicial Court. I was the clerk to Herbert Wilkins' father. That's how I started out. That was my entree to practice in Massachusetts.

I became an associate with the law firm of Bingham, Dana & Gould. They just went modern and became Bingham Dana LLP, but I liked it in the old days, when they were Bingham, Dana & Gould. Al Gould was a famous sailor. I don't know what's happened to him now. He's in lawyers' limbo. In that firm I was a litigator. I wasn't much of a trial lawyer. I hope I was competent. I wanted to be a trial lawyer. I left there to serve for two and a half years as counsel to Governor Sargent, the last Republican governor before Governor Weld. I went back to the firm when Sargent was defeated by Governor Dukakis. They were nice to make me a partner. After being back at the firm for about two and a half years, Governor Dukakis appointed me associate justice of the superior court, where I served for eight years. President Reagan appointed me to be judge of the United States District Court. Though I'm going to tell you I don't think it's significant, I am registered as a Republican.

Now, you can find all that stuff from my resume. How does that stuff—and I'm going to try to be honest here—how does that stuff affect me?

Oh, one personal thing: I married when I got out of law school. I have three children, all grown now, all boys. One is a lawyer and a partner in Peabody & Arnold. One is in corporate communications in a corporate communications firm north of Boston. One is a musician and music teacher.

With that background, how has that translated at all into my legal practice? I guess I should say at Bingham Dana I represented plaintiffs and defendants, more or less equally, but the plaintiffs I represented were business plaintiffs. In tort cases I represented insurance companies, tort defendants. But in commercial litigation I represented plaintiffs and defendants about equally. I have had no criminal experience at all. I was a special assistant attorney general on a long criminal case, but I was one of three handling the appeal for the government.

So I become a judge. Here are the things I think that have carried on. I don't think judges, if they were plaintiffs' lawyers or defendants' lawyers, become plaintiffs' judges or defendants' judges. I don't think they carry that further. My view of other people is, if anything, the ones who are hardest on the government in criminal cases tend to be those who have been assistant DAs or assistant U.S. attorneys. They know the games that are played, and we all know that we have to be evenhanded as judges, so we are careful not to slide into the point of view of the area of the bar that we perhaps represented in our practice before we became judges.

Now, you can say I'm biased on that because I am one, but I really believe that the great majority of judges are and try desperately hard to be completely neutral, completely fair to the litigants who come before them.

Again in an attempt to be honest, in an attempt to tell you what you would want to know about how you could find out about a judge, let me touch on these things: I suppose I do have an interest in the outdoors. Does that translate into an interest in the environment? I don't know, but that's why I mentioned my scouting experience.

My service as counsel to Governor Sargent taught me a little bit about state government and taught me how intractable the problems of government are and convinced me that government lawyers are as good as any lawyers. At Bingham Dana perhaps there was a little sense that you look down at government lawyers; they work 9:00 to 5:00 in government jobs. Very wrong, very wrong. It was very helpful to me to have served a while in state government, and my experience has been that the federal government is not much different than the state.

I did have a good experience in peacetime in the military and thought that these were splendid young people who were off in Korea in the days of the Cold War. That experience has translated into an enormous respect for our armed services. One way that that has, I think, still carried on is I have been known to depart downward for those who have a distinguished combat record in the service of the nation, though that is a discouraged departure under the federal sentencing guidelines.

I don't think I came on the bench with any particular preconceptions, even preconceptions to fight against. I didn't think I was plaintiff; didn't think I was defendant. I've been trying to think of how to say this, I don't mean it to be mawkish: If you're looking at values, and of course all judges should have a very high value of integrity—and I'm not here to judge my own integrity; we'll leave the record to do that—I think that I am enough of an authoritarian type to believe in the Westpoint theme that such words as duty, honor, and country mean something. Those words resonate with me.

At the same time, and I guess I'll give Harvard the credit for this, more important to me than even those words is to believe in the truth. Now, I'm here to say many times I'm not clear at all as to what the truth is; but much more important than those other values (duty, honor, country) is to believe the truth, even if the truth is completely contrary to what your mindset was or what your life experience had been.

And then from my parents and my family, I really believe that love is the transcendent human value, more important than any of the others. Now, that construct may be too simple—and it is too simple—nevertheless, those words are very important to me: Duty, honor, country; they're trumped by this need to believe the truth, whatever the truth is, which is trumped by love. But I'm not really here to express that except to say it, because I think that's fairly said.

Resources of the Court

So there we are. Now fast forward to today. You've met the people. We're in court today. What resources do I have? What resources does the session have? I think it's important that you know this because it shows you where the judge is looking. What am I reading? What am I thinking about? What's going into the mix of my knowledge about deciding cases?

And let's start in a physical sense right in the courtroom. We've talked about the transcript, which scrolls up. I have only to whisper to Bonnie—it's not hooked to my computer, but she can tell me any docket data in any case. I say, "Did they file the answer to summary judgment in this case?" And she will click it and whisper back to me on the bench, because she has that docket computer; I have my transcript computer. You can see how we could do it better, but that's where we are now.

Behind the bench I have the following aids: I have that West book on civil procedure and rules. It has all the civil rules; it includes the Rules of Evidence; it's got most of the statutes. I have *Criminal Rules and Procedures.* The West book has all the criminal rules of criminal procedure. It's got all the criminal statutes right there at hand. I have the United States Sentencing Guidelines because I have to use them all the time. I have the following books on evidence: Michael Graham, *Handbook of Federal Evidence.* It's just the best organized book on that subject that I know. I have a book called Cotchett and Elkind, *Federal Evidence.* It's nice because it's loose-leaf and you can thumb through it quickly. I have my book on *Massachusetts Evidentiary*

Standards. Now, this was an attempt to take the Massachusetts common law of evidence and codify it like the federal rules. Well, of course, I'm on the federal court. I don't need the Massachusetts common law, but because I wrote it together with two other folks, it tells me pretty quickly, though it cites Massachusetts cases, what I think about all the hot issues of evidence. Because I'm the author of it, I can find stuff quickly in it, and I use it. So it sits there behind the bench. I have a loose-leaf notebook which has the proposed criminal charges. There is now a guideline of criminal charges in the First Circuit. Rock Hornby (phonetic) and a group in Maine put it together. I have it right there, so I can thumb through it. I've got a couple other charges that I need, the Allen or Rodriguez charge, the dynamite charge, if I ever needed that with a jury. I have it right there. I xeroxed from the *Mass. Practice Series* those pages that Kent Smith authored on how to take a plea , and I still use it in the federal courts. That's my guide for doing it. When I take a plea I open up and take the plea that way.

That's pretty much it. A couple of other books, but nothing stands out. The books behind the bench, though it looks nice in the courtroom, are all F. Supps. They're not *Supreme Court Reports.* The *Federal Supplement*, of course, is where the decisions of the federal district judges can be found. I've heard Judge Irenas from the District of New Jersey say, "Yeah, it's the Vanity Press for district judges." There's some truth to that because, you know, you don't get your stuff published there unless you want it. Somehow when I was a lawyer I thought everything was in there. Wrong. Only the stuff the judges want to put in there is in there. You can go Westlaw and find virtually everything, but the stuff that judges want to put in there is there. The reason I have the most recent ones—and as you can see they fill the box—is because my stuff is there. And it's not that my stuff is so impressive, but in the one drawer that I have in my desk I have a listing of all my decisions from the time I got on the bench, and I can find my stuff. And frequently I look at it, and I look at it because, just as I am sure you like to keep copies of the briefs you file—and you should; you've sweated over those briefs—that's what I think the law is. Now, two years later you know you ought to take that with a grain of salt because the law may have changed, but the fastest way into the law for me is to go to my opinion in a certain case. It shows me what I thought about this subject three years ago, and it cites all the relevant cases. I think I've got good law clerks. It's all there, and then I can go from there, so that's why the F. Supps are there.

Back in the lobby I have some loose-leaf notebooks of other charges and similar things, but nothing else that I need terribly frequently. Up in chambers we have at our work stations both Westlaw and LEXIS, and we have NEXIS, so we can get newspaper articles and the like. We frequently do searches of the popular press to look for things. We have the *United States Reports*, the *Federal Reporter, F. Supp.*, the *Massachusetts Reports*, and the *Appeals Court Reports.*

Remember, I was a justice of the Superior Court for eight years. That is where I learned how to be a judge. I have enormous regard for the men and women who are justices of the Massachusetts superior court. Their stuff now is on-line. *The Massachusetts Law Reporter* is not on-line yet, but you can get that too. We always look at it. I tell my law clerks to look at it out of respect for the superior court. And when I've got a diversity case, I know I'm not bound by a superior court opinion under *Erie*—it's has to be a high court opinion—but my druthers are to look favorably on the decisions of the superior court. I'm for those people. I was one, and I was proud to be one. So I look at that stuff too.

What does that tell you? To me, anyway, you want to cite that stuff, and not only to me. The tobacco litigation about the ingredients was started, of course, in the superior court . Immediately the tobacco folks removed it to the federal court. Some supposed pundit from the tobacco industry said, "Go to federal court where everything is fairer. Who would want to go before the state superior court?" Well, that sort of rankled me a little bit, though I would never let it be known. Who did they draw? The Honorable George O'Toole, former justice, Massachusetts Superior Court. That's stupid talk. *(Laughter)*. I mean I know that Judge O'Toole did everything absolutely correctly and equally. I've not talked to him one word about the case, but, you know, these people come from somewhere. If I was making a book on Judge O'Toole, I would have found out that he was a justice of the superior court and before that he was a justice of the Boston Municipal Court and before that he was at Hale and Dorr. Those things mean something. Not that the judge is biased, but they mean something. That was a stupid tongue.

All right. So we have those resources. We have those books, but we have a lot of periodicals too. Let me share them with you because I read—or at least thumb through—these for ideas. I am always looking for how the law develops. And these provide some guidance.

I'm allowed to buy *Massachusetts Lawyers Weekly*, and I buy it, and I read it faithfully, and I use it. I'm not shilling for them or for Don or any of these for-profit operations, but I'm trying to tell you what I look at. I read it every week, and I look at the recent cases, and I don't just look at the federal ones. I look at the state ones because I'm writing on evidence, and that's how I try to stay on top of what goes on in the state courts. I'm looking for the state evidentiary decisions, things like that.

I'm authorized to have in my own chambers library two law reviews. And I have the *Harvard Law Review* and the *Boston University Law Review*. I thumb through them when they come. I am authorized and I buy *Litigation Magazine* from the ABA and I thumb through that. I get the *Massachusetts Law Review* courtesy of the Massachusetts Bar Association. I used to get the *Boston Bar Journal*, but I think I do not because they don't send it to me free, and I won't get it unless they send it free. If I get it, I look at it. Of course, I can get it out of the library, but these are the things that I look at.

Interestingly, various institutions will send you their magazines for free because they want you to look at them. Here is a list of some that I get: I get *Trial Magazine* from ATLA, the plaintiffs' trial bar organization. I thumb through that. I get something called *The Champion* from the National Defense Lawyers, the criminal defense lawyers. I look through that. Various right wing institutions, like The Manhattan Institute, send me position papers about things. They come. I look at them. They're there. I'm not saying I'm swayed by it, but I have access to it. The various periodicals I've mentioned, the books and the like, I save. We don't save the *Massachusetts Lawyers Weekly* more than about three months. I'm also given the house organ of the judiciary, something called *The Third Branch*. It's on-line. It's really very bland. It just deals with judicial administration.

THE GOVERNING PRINCIPLES

Okay. Those are the resources. Now let's get to it. We've got the people. We've got the resources. What are we going to do with them? What are the unifying principles, if you will, that govern the operation of the session where I preside?

Judges Should Try Cases

The major principle is this: I believe that the core function of an Article III judge is to try cases. I believe that that is the most important thing that a trial judge can do, is simply put on the robe, go out on the bench, and try cases. And so we have organized our session to do that every single day.

We do it like this: First of all, if you're going to try cases every single day, you have to have some system of lining them up. We know that in both state and federal systems—but I'm talking about this federal session that I'm in now—the criminal cases come first. They must be tried first because of the speedy trial requirement. So criminal cases get a specific Monday. We only impanel juries on a Monday, so they get a specific Monday, a specific trial date to start.

Civil cases have to take second place to criminal cases. And I run what is known as a running or a trailing trial docket; that is, I line the cases up and I give them a month and a year when they are to be ready for trial. When I get to that month and year, we try the cases for that month. I never advance a case. I would think that that would be really unfair if I've told you a month and a year. But also note that I'm death on continuances. We'll talk about that later. In other words, you don't get a specific trial date from me; instead, you go on a calendar, you go on a calendar in order. I do the order faithfully. I don't jump cases over other cases to grind people down, with the possible exception that I use jury-waived cases to fill in. I want to be busy. I want to be on the bench every single day trying cases.

When I joined the superior court the senior justice of the superior court was Jack Meagher. We used to call him "King in Worcester" because he sat in Worcester all the time. He's from Worcester, the Honorable John Meagher, and was a very respected judge. And he told me, "This is a trial court"—he was talking about the superior court—"this is a trial court. The trial judge should go on the bench every day and try cases." And I believe that, and I believe that passionately. That is not generally shared. There's a real spectrum among the judges about whether that is the core value. As a matter of fact, there's a real issue among federal judges whether that's the core value. And this effort, this interest in having judges manage things tends to count against that. I've heard a judge say, "I believe that if a case goes to trial I've failed." Well, of course that's anathema to me. I'm all for you going to trial. Oh, yes, you can settle. Oh, yes, that's fine, go ahead. I'll try to encourage settlement. But the idea, the ultimate thing, is to have cheap, efficient, speedy, and just resolution of cases. And the way to resolve cases is to try them. I believe in you people. I believe that you know how to mediate, how to negotiate, how to settle the cases. And I'm here to give you trials if they cannot be resolved otherwise.

Judges Should Have a Routine

Before we go through the day of trial, let me say one of the things I've learned over the last 21 years is that the judge should have a routine. You only get one judge in a session, and everybody else, the docket clerk, the law clerks, you, litigants, the lawyers, has to play off the routine of that judge. Therefore, the judge ought to have a routine and you ought to know the routine. Every day should not be a new adventure. If every day is a new adventure, no one knows when to talk to the judge or what to do. We believe that the trial is the new adventure. But every day is the same.

Here's a day in our session: I'm usually at my desk between 8:00 and 8:30, sometimes a little before 8:00. I don't particularly want to be bothered during that time. Trials begin at 9:00 a.m. I want Bonnie to have us a trial. I don't want everything—something ought to back up something else. If we've run out of cases, we ought to go to other sessions to get trials. We should be trying cases.

9 o'clock, the doors open. Bonnie goes and gets the jury. The judge gets on the bench. Five minutes after 9:00 a.m. witnesses should be on the stand and we should be taking evidence. This routine should happen every single day. I go for an hour and 45 minutes and then take a break. I take a half an hour break. That's a big break. I justify that. I think the jurors are paying close attention. I always get them snacks during the break. Regardless if its a short case or a long case, we always get snacks for the jurors.

At 11:15, we promptly start up again. We run until 1 o'clock. At 1 o'clock we stop. The jury goes home unless it's going to deliberate. If the jury is deliberating, it deliberates all day. The lunch hour is from 1:00 to 2:00. That's the traditional lunch hour, state and federal. That's when the judges tend to go to lunch. In federal court the judges all have lunch together on Mondays. I have lunch with my staff on Fridays, but that is the hour I usually take for lunch. If I'm not having lunch with someone, I go back and sit at my desk.

At 2 o'clock, the afternoon begins. Now, the afternoon varies. It can be filled with motions, sentencings, status conferences, and the like. That's the day. And every day is the same.

Judge as Law Teacher

So if I think that that's the unifying principle, that it is incumbent upon judges to try cases, let me give you the biases, if you will, or the things that I want to mention to you now after 21 years of being a judge. This is how I look at things.

First of all, after 21 years I've come to believe that the major role of a United States District Court judge is to try cases because that's what we do as an Article III judge. What are judges in our society? Judges are nothing more nor less than law teachers. That's what we are. That's why we have lifetime appointments—you know, other people set the curriculum. The legislature sets the curriculum or the curriculum has been set for us in the Constitution.

Judges are law teachers. And everything we do revolves around that role. When we are interacting with the lawyers, when we are interacting with the jury, what we are doing is teaching law. That's it.

Now, if that's what we do, just a word about how I think it's done. If we are law teachers, that means that my job as a trial judge is to figure out in the most accurate—and I emphasize the word "accurate"—fashion possible what the law is, the law in sort of the "One L" sense, and then to apply it in the specific case.

When I became a superior court justice I knew that I wasn't being appointed to the Supreme Court of the United States. I thought I would go and look the law up and then teach it to juries and write it out in opinions and that was it.

And I remember, when the opportunity to become a judge came up, my wife and I talked about it, because it was a cut in pay and the like, and she said, "You know, you're not going to like being a judge, and the reason you're not going to like it is because it is too passive. You're now a partner. You've got these cases. You're charging around the country. You're not going to like just going to the same place every day and sitting there." And I said, "No. I think I'm going to like it." And on that discussion anyway I'm right. I love it. But I love it in the sense that—and this has come as a dividend that I was not prepared for—at least once a month in our session there's a case of first impression. Now, I set the threshold for first impression pretty low; that is, the First Circuit hasn't spoken on this specific issue; other circuits may have, but it's the first impression in the First Circuit. And ultimately, I have to figure out what law it is that I'm going to teach, what will be the law as it's applied to this specific case.

Now, let's for the moment put constitutional law to one side; let's take statutory law or common law application. How do I learn the law and learn what to teach?

I try as hard as I know how to figure out what my bosses—and I think of it in that sense, my bosses either in the higher courts or in the legislatures; if it's diversity, it's the Massachusetts general court or the Massachusetts legislature—I try to figure out in the most human possible way what they want, what do they really want.

For instance, when I am trying to divine what the high courts of Massachusetts or the First Circuit want, I get all their opinions, and I at least look through them before filing them away. I won't say I read them all, but among the things I get are the advance sheets of the Massachusetts Appeals Court and the SJC and the advance sheets of the First Circuit. I look all through that.

I also get the advance sheets of the U.S. Supreme Court. Candidly, that's a little distant. If there's some real hot thing that I'm interested in, I'll read that, but I tend to wait until I've got a case. I also get the advance sheets of the Massachusetts legislature and the Congress of the United States. I throw them away. I wait for cases to come up before I try to master new legislation because I just don't have a knack for reading legislation. It's dull anyway. But court opinions I at least will thumb through for interesting things.

When I find an opinion that governs, an opinion interpreting a statute or not, I try to figure out what those judges want me to do as honestly as I know how. I work for them. And I try and figure out what they want me to do, what, in a predictive sense, is the idea here.

Now, with the Constitution of the United States or with other problems which are interstitial, that is, you don't have a case on point, you have cases in other jurisdictions. They, however, don't govern you. Then again I try to do this predictive thing. I haven't got any case above me or statute that tells me what to do, but I've got stuff that is close, and I have opinions of other high courts telling me things. Then I try to figure out what the people for whom I work, i.e., the First Circuit, want. Is this going to be a judicial interpretation?

Then I try to figure out what they would do if they had this case, not because I worry about them or worry about being reversed, but because that's my job. It's not for me to make it up. It's my job.

Now, what do I do in those cases where I don't have that guidance, and nothing is that close? I've got a pure question of the reach of the Fourth Amendment (search and seizure) and every so often you have a question like that. Then I try—though this becomes, not sophistry, but it's much more difficult—I try to figure out what the people for whom I work, ultimately the founders if it's the Constitution, would have done if they had this case.

Now, how much of that is honestly trying to figure out what they would have done and how much of it is me? I am one of those judges who feel that all I am doing is teaching what others higher, those who came earlier or were elected, want me to teach. And I take comfort in that. I don't think I'm making it up. I don't think we're getting Bill Young on the common law. It doesn't amount to anything.

The opinion is what I'm trying to express, what I think captures the views of the legislature, the views of the founders, the views of the higher courts. Now, that's how I interpret the law.

I didn't say anything about your briefs. We're going to get to them. And of course I read them; of course I look at them; of course I pay attention to your arguments; but when I come to decide, that's how I'm trying to teach the law.

Judge Young's Biases in Favor of Juries and Fairness

So after 21 years, do I now have biases? Do I now have ways that I'm going to come on the bench and I'm going to see certain things? In some respects, yes. And one of them is that I have come to believe that we trial judges, state and federal, are the guardians of the American jury system, and I am in love with the American jury system. I think that is the the best, most just way to decide any dispute.

And so that has a couple of impacts practically. If I can try a case to a jury—naturally I'm following the law now, I'm not making it up—if I had my druthers, if a case can be tried to a jury, even an advisory jury, I'll put it to a jury. I try 93A cases to juries all the time. You're authorized to do it. I do it. I think that's the way it should be done. Everything I do is done to empower the jury. I think the jury is the direct democracy, the expression of direct democracy that lends its moral force or is the moral force, the moral engine behind the whole third branch. So I'm for juries.

What other practical effect does that have when you're dealing with me? Frequently now we will see that very special interests, not being able to control 50 state legislatures, are seeking or supporting legislation in Washington. One of the hot issues in most federal cases today is pre-emption. You have some federal law, and then does that take away the remedies that the people had under state law? Frequently, when you look at those issues, the federal law gives you much less of a right to a jury of the people than the state laws do.

Again, no one is going to get me recused on a case. I am not saying I am biased. I am not saying that. I am trying to be honest. To the extent that the law gives me leave, I am trying to preserve that right to trial by jury, which tends to make me narrow in my interpretation, to the extent I can be, of the sweep of pre-emption and pre-empting people's rights in federal court.

Also, I really think that judges do exist to introduce an element of fairness in cases. In criminal cases, I think that judges introduce rather an unshakable element of fairness as between the government with its great powers and the individual. In civil cases, its an element of fairness as between those institutions usually with great economic power and the individual.

I really think it's important that judges not let class differences dictate the outcomes in lawsuits. Again to bring it back to the practical, how does that translate into what we do? Well, it translates into rulings on discovery and on what's burdensome and what can be done, and the like. And it tells the lawyers, especially those that are representing a large company or a corporation, that they should always appear to the judge to be reasonable. You should have an explanation for why you want discovery, don't want discovery, and the like.

It is the weakest of arguments simply to point to the rule. The rule let's me have this, and I want it. Because, with me anyway, if I think that you are using the rule for what I think is an improper purpose, I've been around long enough that I can figure out some way to even things up.

INSTITUTIONAL LITIGATION

I have a view about institutional litigation. It's a hot topic, at least with Congress. Institutional litigation is that litigation dealing with prisons, mental institutions and the like. People argue that the federal courts are running the prisons, federal courts are running the mental institutions, and the like. I've had little institutional litigation in my 21 years, but I do have a view about it. I do have an approach to it, and so I'll share that here.

Where the institutional litigation arises out of a challenge to the liberty interests of an individual, it does seem to me that the way that the three branches of government work best is if the judiciary does not intrude on the other branches but simply extinguishes the impairment on the liberty of the individual.

Let me give you three examples of outstanding institutional litigation by my colleagues right here on the federal bench. The first example deals with Chief Judge Tauro and his reform of the mental institutions in Massachusetts. Chief Judge Tauro is justly famous for reforming the tragic and notorious neglect of the Commonwealth of Massachusetts regarding its mental patients in various mental institutions, Belchertown and the like. One of his most famous causes was to reform that with a very detailed consent decree.

I respect that enormously, but I have to say I think my first approach would have been to be as careful as I know Judge Tauro was in finding the facts and then to say, "Well, the conditions you have these people in are unconstitutional. Either remedy it up to constitutional norms or close them." You have a year to close them, put those people out on the street, and then I expect that the legislature would get hopping. The legislature would raise the taxes or do what has to be done.

A second example deals with the double-bunking, or the alleged double-bunking, of prisoners. Judge Keeton undertook a remarkable and careful review of the Suffolk County House of Correction. Indeed, he caused a whole new correction facility to be built over the time he was overseeing it. I think my approach would have been as follows: If it is unconstitutional, I would encourage the legislature to correct it somehow. "You're the state legislature, you correct it or in a year's time shut this facility, and let those people out. You just cannot constitutionally keep them behind bars."

And lastly, my third example in the area of institutional litigation deals with Judge Mazzone and the harbor cleanup. What a wonderful job he has done, and at no insignificant expense. Again, these are examples of outstanding institutional litigation.

I had a cleanup in Gloucester, and for starters I said, "If we find that the state agencies are violating the Clean Waters Act and are discharging pollutants off Cape Ann—we haven't found it yet, but just so you understand—if we find it, we're just stopping the sewer hookups. That's it, no more sewer hookups. All development will cease, there will be economic chaos, and everything will come to a halt because you're violating the law. So let's get together and see how we can resolve it." And they're still cleaning it up. They have come to a resolution.

Here is an obvious limit to that: This fall I drew *Wessman v. School Committee of the City of Boston*, the affirmative action case about whether Ms. Wessman should now be admitted to the Latin School. I will say nothing about that case. It is a major institutional civil rights case. I have recused myself from that case, but for a time I was the judge charged with that case and it became immediately clear to me that what I've just been saying doesn't work in that type of litigation at all because what we have is competition for a scarce state-provided resource (schooling), not the imposition by the state of some unconstitutional or illegal conduct. Nothing I've said applies to that type of case. You don't close the schools because you found someone was discriminating. That's the most difficult of these types of cases.

And again completely disparate, but just to give you another example that I've come up with—I haven't had a case in which I can use this—what about the First Amendment, particularly the obscenity issue? It does seem to me that the only things that can be obscene and subject to the reach of state interest in this area can only be visual obscenity, in the form of photographs and videotapes and movies and artwork—if you can call it that—which requires the participation of actual people because it's that degrading of the human individual that the obscenity laws properly can prevent, just as the laws against prostitution are perfectly valid and constitutional.

My view is, however, that—oh, yes, I know Chief Justice Burger's decision in the appropriate cases—if all it is is words, so long as the words are not inciting people to break the law (and I think that's a different standard), or even if it's a drawing, so long as the drawing does not have models who are actual individuals, then those are ideas and the First Amendment cannot make war on an idea.

So no matter how disgusting an idea is, it is protected by the First Amendment. Let me address something horrific just so you have the understanding. I don't know if any of this is true, but it has been reported that the people who are alleged to have murdered Jeffrey Curley had in their possession, or one of them had in his possession, tracks of some group, Man/Boy Love Group, or something like that. I'm here to say that, in my opinion, if that material is just writing, then no child obscenity. If it's just writing, it is protected by the First Amendment as just an idea or ideas. To me it's a horrible idea, but ideas are protected by the First Amendment. It's inciting, of course, to violate the law. That isn't protected. Admittedly, its a fine line; the line is not clear.

So after 21 years those are the things I guess that I've learned. I love the jury system. I like people to be even before the court. And I have these odd ideas about institutional litigation and the First Amendment. Any questions?

AUDIENCE MEMBER: Judge Young, with regard to the jury issue, particularly if it's chemical or biotechnical patent litigation and the case is beyond the jury's capacity to evaluate, what resources are available to you as a judge in your library, et cetera? What have you seen to be the most effective approaches in making the extremely complex available to the jury intellectually? What types of visual media, et cetera?

JUDGE YOUNG: My whole goal as a judge is to make that chemical, biological, whatever, understandable to a jury. You are teachers as much as I am. There are a variety of techniques to get to that. I'm going to talk about how we do Markman hearings. A jury, direct democracy of the people, is what brings these elite down to deal with the actual reality, and that's how I propose to do it. There are a variety of approaches. First of all, there are all sorts of things that the judge can do, and here are the things that the judge can and should do and things I do: You can't keep jurors there forever, so the trial cannot last more than a month. We have time limits. And what we do is polyfurcation. We'll just break down the issues. And so different juries will deal with different issues. The jurors should take notes. The jurors should ask questions. I do that in every case but especially in this type of case.

In addition, I am in favor of all sorts of demonstrative aids. I encourage them. I'll work them out with the lawyers ahead of time. As I mentioned before, one of the trial practice things that I teach and encourage is to look for materials in the popular press about your subject. They may not be entirely accurate in the scientific sense, but they will give you an idea about the area and maybe help you convey your complex ideas more simply. By the popular press I mean the news media, the good news media, the *New York Times*, the *Boston Globe* and similar outlets, such as *Scientific American*, that type of thing. They try to explain very complex things to the general populace. You want those articles.

I had a friend at Bingham Dana who did computer litigation. There was an article in *National Geographic* about computers. The article is pretty good and had good visuals. He carried it around with him everywhere—it became very dog-eared—not because he was going to use that with the jury—you can't do that—but because that gave him the language to convey to the jury.

I on a much more pedestrian level carried around an article from *Cosmopolitan* on low back pain because I had some cases in that area and the article was well written. The science wasn't wrong, and at least it was a start because the journalist wrote it, and journalists are used to simplifying concepts so that readers can understand the issues.

Your question really is an excellent one. What resources do I have? Not much. The Federal Judicial Center, after *Daubert v. Merrell Dow Pharmaceuticals, Inc.*, 509 U.S. 579, 113 S.Ct. 2786 (1993), put out a book on the protocols to use for qualifying experts. And, as I should have mentioned before, that book is also right there behind my bench. I have yet to use it. I've thumbed through it a little bit, but I have yet to use it. That's in part I think because the attorneys don't press as much in that area.

Another technique of which I am aware but I've never used it is to give the jury an orientation course without regard to the case. The court appoints an expert, or the litigants agree upon an expert, who will not be the forensic expert who will be pressing one side or the other. And then that court-appointed expert teaches the jury the fundamentals of the area in which the jury is going to have to operate.

I know of a judge in the Ninth Circuit who did that when she was a district court judge in California. She used that technique in a computer case, and for a week the jurors just played with computers and they learned about them.

I'm sure there are other techniques. For example, I'd support the CD-ROM presentation of things visually, if it was fair to both parties. But, again, I have little science background myself. If we are going to use me as a baseline, I was a History major. I was one of these guys who took History of Science in college to satisfy my science requirement. All I have is high school physics and high school chemistry, and yet here I am arrogantly saying, "We'll try anything, anything, just give it to us, we'll try it."

But of course, you see, behind that is a jurisprudential rule. I think that's what you're entitled to under a justice system, the justice of the people. And I fear getting things too elite, too removed from the people.

So I welcome your full question. Yes, it's your job to be teachers. You're much more important than I am. I want to work with you believing that the jury will come to a just verdict. Of course I'll do everything to see if we can help it be a just verdict. But when you say or suggest that the jury can't handle the case, I'll never go for that, in part because I know I can't do it and I think jurors are better than I am.

AUDIENCE MEMBER: In certain situations, such as an appeal from, for example, the U.S. Bankruptcy Court to you or an appeal of one of your decisions to the Court of Appeals, is there any formal communication between the judges? In other words, are there any discussions between the reviewing court and the trial court as to "What were you thinking here?"

JUDGE YOUNG: No, never, there is no discussion between us about pending cases. I consider that unethical. In fact, that's a very strong sentiment among judges, both state and federal. We all know each other. I mean I know all the circuit judges, and I see them frequently. I know the bankruptcy judges, and they see me. And there just is no mention at all of any pending case.

In the trial bar I come and teach and answer questions. I'm in a law club, a luncheon club. There are lawyers in that club. They don't come when they are trying a case before me, but I see lawyers who have cases under advisement before me. And the ethics in this region is just enormously high, and we always want to preserve it. I have no problem being seen in the presence of a lawyer who has a case that's under advisement because I believe the bar will understand that that lawyer will never by any stretch of the imagination say one word about the pending case and nor will I—not even a tangential mention.

AUDIENCE MEMBER: That goes for between just the two judges or the judges in general?

JUDGE YOUNG: Well, the bankruptcy judge won't talk to me, and I won't talk to the bankruptcy judge. None of the appellate panel will talk to me nor I to them.

Now, on a lateral level, we talk: I told you that I have lunch with all my colleagues every Monday. At lunch people frequently bring their problems, such as, "I've got a case and it has this issue, did you ever have that?" And everyone will talk. Everyone will say what they think.

For instance, Judge Keeton was my first law professor, my first law professor. I get to sit on a court where he sits as an active judge. I can call up Bob Keeton. He'll stop the presses. He'll say, "Well, did you see the law review article on that issue?" I'll respond, "No, no, I didn't." Then he'll send you stuff out of his database. We all try to be like that. I'll give him the credit for being the quintessential mentor.

But always among judges people will ask about sentencing or something like that and say, "I've got this difficult thing, now, what do you think about this and that?" People will say very candidly, "I think you should do it" or "I think you shouldn't." They'll say, "I don't think you can do that; isn't there a case on it?" et cetera. They will give you their opinion or thoughts. But everyone will always say, because it is important, trial judges work alone. I don't think it's lonely, but it's an individual responsibility.

Stated or unstated, there is always the belief among my colleagues, and this was true on the superior court too, that X is the judge on a case and that whatever he or she does will be right. And we don't go around criticizing any of our colleagues for a decision. Never at lunch have I heard someone say, "Boy, you really blew that one." We don't do that to each other, whatever our personal views. That's not institution building.

But yes, we do talk about your cases, and yes, we talk about you laterally. Don't get a bad reputation. It will come up at lunch. We do talk about you. And I have no ethical problem with that, but never, never in the hierarchical sense. In the hierarchical sense there is just no communication at all that I've ever seen, and I would take it as an ethical violation.

AUDIENCE MEMBER: Are we committed to having both the Federal Rules of Evidence and the state rules, or is there any move afoot that eventually states will adopt the Federal Rules of Evidence?

JUDGE YOUNG: I think that under our federal system it is unlikely that the Federal Rules of Evidence will ever be adopted nationwide. They have had quite an effect on state rules of evidence but not as pervasive as the Federal Rules of Civil Procedure. The Federal Rules of Civil Procedure were intellectually more acceptable to the states and really reformed state practice.

There are efforts within Massachusetts to codify the Massachusetts rules, though the Supreme Judicial Court rejected that once. But when you see the differences between state and federal, especially now that Congress has started making up rules of evidence without regard to the Rules Enabling Act—for example, Rules 413, 414, and 415 that make prior sexual activity probative for character evidence are so contrary to all theories of evidence that most lawyers know—you will understand why I don't believe that the states are going to go for that.

So the short answer is no. They'll be similar but only insofar as the federal rules intellectually get the adherence of the states.

AUDIENCE MEMBER: Summary judgment is a way of taking away somebody's right to a jury. What is your view?

JUDGE YOUNG: You just want to pick your shots. Don't take my love for the jury system to mean that I bend the rules. Let me talk a little bit theoretically, and then we'll talk practically about summary judgment. Theoretically, if there is not a genuine issue of material fact, granting summary judgment is merciful; you might as well kill a case rather than just go on through a jury trial, because that's how it has to come out. I'm not doing violence to the jury system. I guess I'm pretty careful. If I think a jury could possibly go that way, then there's no summary judgment.

In the state court, where the judges move around and where the burdens are so enormous on the judges, if you make a motion for summary judgment and it's not the judge before whom the case ultimately will be tried, or at least we're not clear who the judge will be because that's downstream, there may be a greater chance that you will not succeed on your motion. I know that as a superior court justice if I don't really have a firm hand on the case or the relevant issues and I deny the motion, nothing can ever go wrong. I can't be reversed for denying it. The case simply goes forward.

As a United States District judge, if I deny it, I have to try it. It's not going away. I deny it, and you're still there. So maybe there's a little more inclination to get rid of you when I should get rid of you.

Likewise, while I think the rules are evenhanded in their application, the First Circuit is much more supportive of the district courts than the appeals courts are of the superior court. To be candid, Superior court judges believe that they are frequently reversed at the appeals court level. District judges are reversed too, but we are perhaps more confident in the Court of Appeals. And so we may be more likely to grant summary judgment.

Again now talking personally, a rule that I follow is this: If I see my way clear to giving summary judgment, I give it. I think I should. Now, say you move for summary judgment but opposing counsel

> doesn't. Instead, she just opposes your motion. If, when I look at the case, I think that summary judgment should go to her, I grant her summary judgment. I think the federal rules will allow summary judgment to be used that way. The federal rules are not clear on that point though. Likewise, because we have more resources on the federal courts, I will give partial summary judgment to narrow the issues.
>
> Also, if you make your motion for summary judgment late in the game—I hate to call it a game, let's call it procedure—and you're crowding up against the trial date, then I will treat that motion as a motion under Rule 16 to narrow the issues, and in the final pretrial conference I'll take your motion with all its affidavits. I won't make her respond to it because it's the eve of trial. That wouldn't be fair; we're going to trial the next month and she's probably getting her witnesses. However, I will ask her, "How do you oppose this?" And I'll be specific. I'll say, "Who is going to testify? Are they going to say that?" And then maybe her responses will suggest that there really isn't a case there and I can use that for settlement and the like.
>
> Lastly, if I don't understand your motion, I can always deny it. It's not the height of intellectual honesty, but I am quick to say if I cannot understand this, I cannot grant summary judgment.
>
> I can recall a motion where one law clerk worked on it and said, "Judge, I'm awfully sorry, I'm terribly chagrined, I don't understand this at all." So I said, "Well, ask Helaine. It's okay. Work on it together." They came back and they said, "Judge, we don't understand." I responded, "Oh, all right." So I just wrote "Denied, William G. Young, District Judge." I didn't have a clue what they were talking about. I just figured that was in the interest of justice. The case went to trial. It tried for five weeks. It had to do with computer modeling. It tried for five weeks, to a jury by the way, who gave the plaintiff $549,000. No one appealed, so I guess justice was done.

Pretrial Matters

We've done all the theory we're going to do. Now we're going to try cases. I am going to go civil and then criminal in each element so I get to the things that I want to cover. We'll start civil.

So you filed your complaint. It's drawn to me. As soon as one defendant has been served and has responded, Dianne, who knows that from the docket, tells Bonnie and

Bonnie schedules the case for a 16(b) conference or a 16.1 conference, an initial case management scheduling conference.

That's the first time that you see me. And I do it differently than almost any other judge because I have a cattle call. I do about half a dozen to a dozen in an afternoon. Everyone pretty much knows under our plan how you get ready for those, or at least that's my experience. What you and opposing counsel have to do is you have to work out a joint proposed case management schedule.

I will approve anything that you agree on. If you agree on it, I will approve it. However, a couple of things that you should know: We are so much on top of our schedule now that I allow only a year from the initial case management scheduling conference until the trial. The fact you want 18 months makes no difference. You get one year from the initial case management scheduling conference.

The other thing I find that people really could do better on is the briefing schedule. They plan their own briefing schedule. Because I've agreed on everything else, why don't I agree on their briefing schedule? What do I mean by that? The briefing schedules will read "motions for summary judgment due April 1, 1998; opposition due May 1, 1998; reply briefs due May 15, 1998." I'll cross that out. The reason is that as soon as the motion for summary judgment is filed, we have a procedure to get that motion on for hearing and I don't want to wait a month for the opposition. The local rules say 14 days. I expect you to have it in in 14 days.

But you do have a way around it. Let me share that with you. As long as you're all cooperating—and this is one of the things you should negotiate—follow the Rule 9A practice in the superior court. Don't file the motion at all until the opposition and everything is together and you simply say we agree that motions for summary judgment, opposing papers, and the like will be filed on X date. I'll go for that.

My reason for not going to these long schedules is I want the law clerks to get busy. If you give me a packet and that gives everything for the law clerks to work on, I'll go for it, so negotiate it with the other side.

The Initial Case Management Scheduling Conference

So you file the the motion. You arrive the afternoon of the hearing. The stage is set. Now let's start the boilerplate. I'm just going to play my role now. You come into the courtroom. Bonnie is there. You see there is no court reporter. Now here is the 16.1 conference:

> Ladies and gentlemen, good afternoon. Thank you for attending the initial case management scheduling conferences for these various cases. We have a number of people here, and you notice I have not called the court reporter out here. I want to explain to you how things work in this session. When that's done we will have the call of the 16.1 list.

The reason I don't have the court reporter out here is that there is really very little that I want to know from you. I want to know when you want to try your case. I want to know whether you are willing to have your case tried by a magistrate judge. I want to know if you have filed the proposed joint case management schedule. And I want you to take a copy of our alternative dispute resolution plan here in the district court.

That's all I want to know, but I want to take a moment to explain to you directly how we work things in this session. And I do this so that in a year's time—and that's all we're going to take, a year's time; that's when I'll want these cases to come on for trial on the outside—you'll know this is in fact how we're going to handle things.

So let me explain the general provisions for practice in this session. First, I will not give you a fixed trial date. I really can't. I have criminal cases to try, and so I put you on what's known as a running or a trailing trial list. If you want a fixed trial date, you can agree to go to Magistrate Judge Cohen. I am paired with Magistrate Judge Cohen and I will be until the end of next year. Then we re-pair with different magistrates.

Magistrate Judge Cohen is our senior magistrate judge. He is an excellent judge, equally as good or probably better than I am. And you don't give up a jury by going to Magistrate Judge Cohen. But it's only a carrot; it is not a stick. I'm not asking you or requiring that you go to Judge Cohen, but, unlike me, he will give you a fixed trial date, and he will give you, if it suits him—I'm not telling him to do this—more than a year to prepare. I will not, and I won't give you a fixed trial date.

So the first question we'll be asking each one of you when we call the list is: Do you want to go to Magistrate Judge Cohen and have him be the judicial officer? You do not give up your right to trial by jury. It will be the same jury, although he'd preside instead of me. And you go after trial from there, if there are further proceedings, directly to the Court of Appeals—the same as if you appealed the case from my court. But you have to consent to a trial in front of him. I'm not asking you to consent. I'm just telling you how it works.

Now, as I say, we run a running or a trailing trial list, and I'm going to ask you what month and year you want the case on for trial, your pick.

I expect you'll be able to agree here. One restriction, today is December 1997, the latest trial date we are going to accept is January 1999. So that's the time your case will go to trial.

Here's what that means: That means that on the first Monday of that month (January 1999) you have to be ready to go to trial. It does not mean I'll call you on that date. You've got to be ready to go to trial. And then you just stand in order until we reach you. We'll give you such notice as we can, recognizing that we'll start every jury trial on a Monday. Maybe we'll impanel two or three on a Monday, but we'll get them lined up to go to trial on a Monday. Here are the grounds for continuance: If you, when we reach you, are on trial in any other jurisdiction or location or any other court—and I mean on trial, not before Endispute, not taking a deposition in Kenosha, Wisconsin—I will respect it and we will wait until you're done. Likewise, if you are representing an individual client and that client dies, you've got 30 days to get someone substituted so you have a client, and then we'll get the case to trial.

That's it. There are no other grounds of continuance. I don't care where your witnesses are. I don't care what problems you have with experts. When I want you on the month and year that you now agree, that's when you will be ready for trial. If that's hard on you, you may want to go to the magistrate judge who can give you a fixed date.

Now, if I don't reach you in that month—and I will tell you we seem to be on top of our dockets; for the past nine months I've been trying every case within the month assigned—but if I don't reach you in that month, then I will respect your vacations. In other words, let's say it's September 1998 and I don't reach you in September—that's a busy month because people come back from vacation and they're all ready to go to trial and they keep me busy so that I cannot get to your case—and one of the lawyers—I do not honor the parties' vacations—has a vacation in October, just drop us a line. We'll wait until you're back from vacation before we go ahead. These are the grounds for continuance.

Now, if that's the trial date, subject of course to the cases that are on that month and what criminal cases are ahead of you, you must file within the first Monday of the month before that your final pretrial memorandum. I'm not going to enter any separate ruling or make any separate order. I'm telling you now. The first Monday of the month preceding the month for trial you must file that final pretrial memorandum. The rules don't make this clear, but I want to make it clear now, that final pretrial memorandum must be a joint memorandum. That's the expensive one, the one that lists all the witnesses and all the exhibits. That's the one that you file then, the month before. During that month preceding the month of trial we'll have a final pretrial conference and get ready for trial.

Now, let's work back from that fixed trial date or from the month and year that you picked, because that's the one thing I won't move. Anything else I'll move so long as you agree, but I'm not moving that trial date for any reason. You're picking that this afternoon.

Many people let summary judgment get too close to that date. You should understand I need about three months between the date of the filing of the motion for summary judgment and the date of the trial, and here's why: I give you an oral hearing on those motions, so we have to get the motion filed, we have to get the oppositions in, and I want advice from my law clerks with respect to it. I'll give you an oral hearing, and I have to decide the motion, and then we have to figure out whether we're going to trial and, if so, on what. Don't let your motions for summary judgment crowd up against the trial date.

Another matter of practice, experts. The federal rules now are very detailed with respect to testifying experts. You must file a report of a testifying expert. That report must list the payment arrangements with the expert and must also list all the times the expert has testified in the past four years prior to this trial.

Now, I take those reports very seriously, ladies and gentlemen. Let me tell you, no one will testify in this session of the court unless I have such a report timely filed, and it must be to the level of exquisite detail of a patent claim. No expert will say anything that is not in that report. Let me make that clear. It is totally unacceptable to file a report which says, 'Doctor Larson will testify as to the defect in the machine and how that defect injured the defendant and will explain the basis for his opinions.' That is not enough. In fact that is nothing. I will not let such an expert testify or, at most, I will let him testify that he thinks there's a defect in the machine and that the defect caused the injury. That's it, because that's all that's in the report. I'm not kidding on this. Understand I'm serious.

At the same time, I want you to understand that there are the rules—I don't want anyone blindsided. I've told you now what my requirements on reports are, and I want those reports, but if there's some technical defect in the report, for example, you don't have all the times that the person has testified, or something like that, that information must be brought out at the time of the final pretrial conference or forever hold your peace. I don't want someone at the time of trial arguing that the expert must be precluded from testifying because of some technical defect in the report. Experts are so often outcome-determinative that I want that all squared away at the time of the final pretrial conference.

One last thing you should understand regarding your joint proposed case management schedule is that I'll go along with anything you agree to. If you want more depositions than the rules apply or require, you may have them. If you agree to less, that's fine, whatever you agree to.

And as lawyers have gotten better on this they have gotten quicker, and I get these short one-pagers, and they tell me how many depositions, they tell me when discovery is over, they tell me when they're going to file their motions for summary judgment. That's fine so long as you know your opposite number and so long as you're comfortable with that and that will govern.

But if you have filed a one-page report like that, don't think then that you can get into big discovery disputes over what the protective order will be or where the deposition will be held or things like that. The whole idea of our Expense and Delay Reduction Plan is to get those things fleshed out now, not later.

If you haven't done it and I think you should have done it, because it's something you could have known now when we first meet, then I'm simply not helping you. I'm not entering any orders, I'm not entering any protective orders; no state action will be available to you.

So I don't want people blindsided. You get ten days from today's date to file a supplemental proposed case management schedule. And let me tell you that if you disagree—no one says you have to agree—if you

> disagree, this is how you do it: You set forth your position; the other side sets forth its position. I will treat these as if I were a baseball arbitrator. That is, I will take the most reasonable position. So if one of you says two depositions and the other says fifty, it's either going to be two or fifty. It's not going to be ten or seventeen. I'm taking what is the most reasonable given the positions that you've given me.
>
> Now, why do I do it that way? It's simple. That's an incentive to be reasonable. Usually people can work it out, and I expect it to be worked out.
>
> Lastly, we have an outstanding alternative dispute resolution mechanism in this court chaired by Judges Mazzone and Skinner. They are excellent mediators. We favor every type of voluntary alternative dispute resolution. I will participate in any way. I will aid you in any way as long as you agree and as long as it will not postpone the trial date. It's voluntary. The trial date that you fix will be the established trial date."

I think that's about everything. I'm sort of done with the thing. Then I'd sit down and take the 16(b). Now I'll take questions if you have any.

AUDIENCE MEMBER: Regarding the 26(a)(b) expert reports, if you have a situation where discovery is ongoing, more information comes in, so the expert has additional information on which to base his opinion, how do we handle that based upon your warning at the beginning of the case management scheduling conference?

JUDGE YOUNG: Well, you simply supplement and you keep supplementing. The problem is people don't prepare their cases until the month before and I'm holding the pretrial conference the month before. If you've got your case in the can before you file that final pretrial memo, which will be a month before, you'll have no problem; but you'd better have it in the can. It's when it's in the last month and you're back and forth that you've got problems.

AUDIENCE MEMBER: Two questions on the expert report. I was not clear on the date that it's due and, more importantly, when it's submitted.

JUDGE YOUNG: The date that it's due is negotiated among the parties and is something that they can work out; but, if it is not worked out, the last date would have to be that final pretrial conference.

AUDIENCE MEMBER: Is it then submitted into evidence, is the report then in evidence?

JUDGE YOUNG: Oh, no. It's not in evidence, nor is it a chalk, but I want a copy. I sit there on the bench with it and I read it as the person testifies. I am death on these because I think they're fair. I think that's how they should be. That is, at least if you're taking me as a baseline, a reason for coming, you won't be blindsided. Don't give me some piece of trash on the theory that the other side has given a piece of trash and everything is just going to go along like it usually does. No. The rules now say reports. I want them. I do no more than the rules require.

AUDIENCE MEMBER: Assuming it's a bench trial. What is that report in terms of the record?

JUDGE YOUNG: It's nothing. Even if it's a bench trial, it's nothing. It's nothing unless you make it something.

Okay. Back to trying a case. So I'm now done giving my spiel. I sit down. Bonnie calls the list. These are the questions that are put to counsel:

"Do you want to go before Magistrate Judge Cohen?"

"Not at this time, Judge."

"Well, not at this time. All right."

"When do you want to go to trial?"

"October '98."

"October '98 it is. Have you filed a joint proposed memorandum?"

"Yes, we have, your Honor."

"Take those pamphlets on the court's ADR program, give them to your client, and goodbye."

That's it, and we get them out.

So that's how cases get underway. That joint proposed case management schedule is the schedule. One thing that should be in my spiel—sometimes it is, but I left it out this time—is don't be afraid in my session to file motions to compel. Of course you have to file them. If the other side is not coming forward with the discovery, file your motions to compel.

Handling Discovery Motions

We'll quickly go through how discovery motions are handled. Then we'll do dispositive motions, motions to dismiss and the like, and then we'll get to trial.

First discovery motions. You file your discovery motion. Dianne, the docket clerk, sees that it's a discovery motion and sets it in a pile. She waits 14 days. That's the deadline for the opposition, ten plus the time for mailing. On that date, unless the opposition is there—she doesn't wait any longer than that—she'll put a yellow post-it sticker on it saying "No Opposition," and she will carry it up to chambers. Dianne is the mistress of yellow post-it stickers.

If there is an opposition, she will take the motion and the opposition but nothing else in my session. So think about that. She won't get the case file. She'll just take the motion and opposition. I, remember, can get the docket. That's easy. I'm computer literate enough that I can look at the docket on my computer screen. And she then gives me the motions that are pending or are in my "In Box."

I take them, and I work on them. This is the type of stuff that I work on on the bench during other trials, the type of stuff I take home at night. I usually do not consult law clerks about these at all because usually they're the stuff that now I've been doing for over 30 years. I've got ways to do them, and I'll tell you what my ways are.

First of all, on motions for further answers to interrogatories, I read those over, and I sort of do it depending upon what I think is logical in the case. I am not a great fan of contention interrogatories. We all know what contention interrogatories are: State every fact upon which you rely in order to support your claim that my client was negligent. The rules permit it, I think, and so I allow those, but I may put my own date and say these have to be answered but they only have to be answered at the end of discovery, or I can quickly check and see what the case management schedule is so I'll know when the end of discovery is. And I may set those off until then.

Requests for productions of documents, there's law out there—I've contributed to some of it—that says that if you use the words "everything relating to"or "relates to" or "relate to," that's vague, unduly vague because it doesn't tell the other side what they have to do because all life relates to all the rest of life.

Let's say for some reason it's relevant that I spoke here this morning, and MCLE is handed a request for everything that relates to my speaking here this morning. Well, I guess MCLE has a schedule of the hall. It would have to produce that. And I guess MCLE would have to produce your attendance forms. My notes such as they are probably have to be produced. My schedule from work, produce that. How about if I bought gas for my car and I drove in here, do I produce that? You just can go on forever. I'd cross those all out ruthlessly. "Relates to" is a kick in the head. I've been teaching it this way for years. Learn it.

Now, people have other things. They say, "everything concerning," or they have other circumlocutions. I really like "evidencing." Any document which is evidence of my being here, that would be the things that talk about my being here or directly evidence the schedule at MCLE, which evidences that I'm here this morning. Otherwise, I cross it out.

There are stays for discovery, and a lot of people favor these stays. "Stays of discovery, Judge, until the motion to dismiss is heard." It depends. To me it depends on how rapidly I'm going to hear that motion to dismiss. The kick of death is when lawyers request to stay the discovery so they can file their motions to dismiss. If I don't have your motion before me, I'll never stay discovery for that.

Now, the new securities litigation law has passed, of course, to favor the securities industry. It really does. It's against plaintiffs, and it says what it says, and of course I follow it. It's the law. But unless I have law on it, I won't stay discovery for that.

I'll stay discovery if you've got a medical malpractice case in our courts and we need a medical malpractice tribunal, though I have to send it over to superior court—but not forever. I'll stay it for a set period of time, and if I haven't received the report of the medical malpractice tribunal by then, then discovery may commence. What period of time? Tell you the truth, I'm not sure. Sixty, ninety days, something like that.

The ones that give me more trouble, and sometimes I do refer to the law clerks, are the ones where the attorney-client privilege is asserted. That's a little more technical. I'm inclined where the attorney-client privilege is asserted to require that there be a privilege log. And if I call for a privilege log, I want every document, document-by-document, set out, and I want at least a generic description of the document, from whom it was sent, to whom it was sent, and the basis for the privilege. In other words, I want to put the burden, I want to put an expense burden—let me be very clear—I want to put an expense burden on the side that is claiming the privilege. And if they really want the privilege, then let them detail it document-by-document.

But if they fake me, if they say, "And all documents in the file entitled this and that are privileged," I'll order the production of the file because you haven't given it to me document-by-document. I do not want to see the stuff in camera. It's a terrible waste of time, boring, and besides, I'm no longer a trial lawyer. I'm a judge. It's hard for me to know what's relevant. You're the lawyers. I want to follow the law.

Remember that statements of witnesses are work product except there is a way to get around that. The way that I honor is if one side has been quick off the dime, either a plaintiff or the insurance company has been very quick off the dime, and has taken statements of witnesses within 45 days of the accident, I think that those have to be produced because the witnesses' memories are fresh then and I think when you go from short-term memory to long-term memory it may not be the same. They may confabulate by other people they've talked to.

So if one side has in their file a witness statement that the other side has no chance of getting the equivalent because while they can take the deposition, they're taking the deposition a year or a year and a half later, I'll require the witness statement to be produced.

Now, requests for admission: In huge cases I do have a very nasty pretrial order that I use. The cost of complying with it is, for starters, a million dollars at base and then up from there. So it would be an abuse to use it in anything but the most monster case. But if I get a case that is absolutely a monster, all over the lot, and I need to define what the universe of facts in dispute are—in my harbor cleanup case in New

Bedford I did this, and in one case between Honeywell and Arthur D. Little in the superior court I did this because I just could not get a handle on the facts and there were explosive discovery disputes all over the place—I turn to the plaintiffs and say, "All right. Request the other side to admit every fact that you want established, every fact, to the level of detail of a patent claim. I don't care how many requests for admissions there are, there can be 200,000 requests, but I want every fact to the level of detail of a patent claim. Then those they admit are out of the case. Those that they dispute are in the case." I then turn to the defendants and tell them to request everything they want the plaintiffs to admit. If they have any affirmative defenses to establish, it all has to be there to the level of detail of a patent claim. This approach works, but it's an enormous burden to the litigants and is justified only in the most extraordinary case.

How about sanctions? I'm not a sanctioning judge, but when I am I hit very hard. I think that discovery disputes are virtually inevitable. I am turned off by these discovery motions that say, "...and costs and everything," et cetera. I'm so hostile to them that I was once reversed when I should have granted the motion. The case was *Metrocorps*, a First Circuit case. So now when I get those motions and I think there's been an abuse, I allow them, but I make the payment of the sanction wait until the outcome of the case because usually I don't have to do anything, the case will settle or it will go away or something like that.

Now, suppose you mess me up, that is, you have allowed yourself to be defaulted through your own negligence but now you want to get back in the case, or I call you for trial and you don't come. Then my sanctions are based upon the actual cost to the justice system. Justice system costs for a district court session run the taxpayer $17,500 a day. Then I figure I work a ten-hour day—I don't, but it's generous to the person I'm sanctioning—and I figure how much of my day you've wasted? That's what you have to pay to get back into court. It's all detailed in a case called *In Re: Prevett.*

I love this *Prevett* case. Prevett didn't come. I sanctioned him $5,250 when I defaulted him, but then he wanted back into court. I said, "You can get back into court if you pay $5,250." He pays it. Then he wins the case. He nets eight grand after he has paid the $5,250. Then he appeals the sanctions.

The Court of Appeals says, in an unpublished decision—now I'm going to tell you what it says so you can't cite it—"While the judge has every right to sanction him, we don't understand how he got to $5,250." Oh, I warm my hands with glee, and I write a *Harlan* opinion. *In Re: Prevett* tells you how I figure this.

The judges on the Court of Appeals says, "These figures are questionable." I don't know how they think that. I'm on the Budget Committee of the courts. The figures are accurate; but they say they're questionable, a thousand dollars is good enough.

Well, stand me up for a morning, a thousand dollars, what am I going to do in the next case? I don't know because I have to follow the Court of Appeals. It's an unpublished decision, but the reasoning is all there, in ***In Re: Prevett.*** That's my view on sanctions.

Don't cross me once I've entered an order. In other words, if they haven't made discovery, move to compel. There will just be a little motion, "Motion Allowed." Then, discovery must be made in 30 days. If they fail to make it in 30 days, then that's time to throw them out of court or have them pay money, or something. That's when my sanctions kick in. It's not that you get one free bite, it's just that I think there are bound to be those things.

Any questions before we move on to dispositive motions?

AUDIENCE MEMBER: I have one question. Can you give us a sense of how other judges handle the motion or opposition? Would they request a file or only consider the papers that you do?

JUDGE YOUNG: Most judges request the file. Some judges do it different ways. Some judges won't look at it at all until their law clerks have reviewed it. That's very slow. With respect to the procedure I've given you, of course, I don't even talk to my law clerks because this is scut work, and I'll do the scut work. It's no heavy lifting. It's the stuff I've been doing all my practice now, over 30 years, so I do it myself. Also, it familiarizes me with the case.

Other judges are more standoffish and let their law clerks work on it. I think it's a terrible waste of time of law clerks because what do they know about further answers to interrogatories? That stuff's hard unless you've actually practiced. And law clerks haven't been in private practice; they've been law clerks. I save them for the heavy stuff, these other motions we are about to discuss.

Most judges do ask for the whole file. Our file room, though much better than the state, is really in a disarray now, and so you get motions; you don't get the whole file. I'll ask for the whole file if I can't figure the case out from the motion and the opposition. But most of the time I'll do it from the motion and opposition. Most of them want more. You can criticize me for that. I'm faster, more efficient, but maybe more sloppy because all I'm looking at is the motion and the opposition.

And sometimes we'll find, for instance, that Intake has not given the opposition to Dianne. The opposition is date stamped on the 14th day, but she doesn't get it until the 16th. I've already allowed the motion. I've got to go back, that type of thing. That's a weakness in our procedure.

AUDIENCE MEMBER: Assuming, your Honor, someone brings a motion to compel and then you're running up against your 14-day requirement deadline and you negotiate with the other side an extension of a week so that Dianne gets you only the motion that has been filed. Should we drop a note to Dianne?

JUDGE YOUNG: No. File an assented-to motion to extend the time. And then that goes on the docket. I'll agree to anything that doesn't move the trial date. That will be automatically granted—as a matter of fact, she's authorized to allow that herself. It will be allowed, but it will just be Dianne Smith, Deputy Clerk, as long as it's assented to.

AUDIENCE MEMBER: Judge, can you talk a little bit about the mandatory discovery procedures under the federal rules because there's nothing in the state system?

JUDGE YOUNG: No, there aren't similar rules in the state system. We have opted for mandatory discovery, which, simply put, is that with respect to facts pleaded with specificity in the complaint, all relevant evidence supporting or opposing those facts is to be disclosed even without motion and it's to be disclosed right up front. It's to be disclosed mandatorily. *See* Local Rule 26.2 and Rule 2.02 of the Expense and Delay Reduction Plan.

I, candidly, pay little attention to that one way or another. I think it's working by and large. I'm eager to get the case on a trial track. Chief Judge Tauro, for instance, won't even hold his initial case management conference until he's satisfied that mandatory disclosure has been made, and there are time limits for making it.

When I go to these various conferences of lawyers I hear lawyers talk about the disputes that they run into with respect to mandatory disclosure. For whatever reason, I see little of that. I don't know. Do I have a reputation of being stern on sanctioning or something? I don't know. I see little of that. I have not bestirred myself to write great opinions on discovery matters. If we look at the body of my opinions over the 13 years I've been on the federal court, I have nothing really significant on discovery. Judge Ponsor, who was a magistrate judge in Springfield, is one of the most thoughtful judges on discovery and has written the best opinions that we have in this district on mandatory disclosure. That's sort of an answer. And that's my practice.

Dispositive Motions

Okay. Now, if that's discovery, let's discuss dispositive motions. I'll give you an oral hearing on motions to dismiss, motions for summary judgment, motions for preliminary injunction, and motions for class certification.

Let's take motions to dismiss and for summary judgment. You file your motion. As soon as a motion to dismiss is filed, it comes to Dianne's attention. She flags it for Bonnie. Bonnie then sets it for a hearing. We have a hearing about once a month, and we try and gather those types of motions for that hearing. Bonnie puts it in her book. The law clerks check her book. The law clerks go and get the file sometimes before the opposition is even received, but as we're going along there the opposition is received.

The law clerks take all the files and deliver them to me for initial screening. I look at the files to see whether I want law clerk help. In most circumstances I do, but sometimes I've been over and over the case, I know the case, I think I know it better than anyone else. I don't ask the law clerks for help. I just take it.

Of the ones I want law clerk help on, the law clerks prepare bench memoranda. The bench memoranda analyze the issues and advise me what to do. It's not just to analyze the issues. The law clerks gives me their advice as to the outcome.

I get the file and the bench memo not too many days before the actual hearing and, candidly, sometimes not until the morning of the actual hearing, a morning, of course, where I'm trying some other case. So I take the whole thing out on the bench, and I'll tell you how I look at it. Sometimes we do better than that, but rarely do I see the file again more than a week before the hearing, and usually it's two or three days before the hearing that I'll get the file. So I've got the whole file. I've got the bench memo, and I'm supposed to be ready for the hearing.

First I read the bench memo. That's my lawyer. You may not like that because you've poured your heart into the briefs, but I'm reading what some other person says about your case. I read it with care. I then read your briefs, I really do.

I look through what briefs I have, and I look to see if there's a reply brief, and I start there. This is a trick taught me by Judge Gunn of the Fifth Circuit. I start there not because your reply briefs are so swell and punch out the other side but because I start there with the idea that this is what they're worried about or they wouldn't have filed a reply; this is what really worries them, this argument. So I read the reply brief, and then I go back into the other briefs. Believe me, I will have read the briefs before the hearing.

Now, "read" is not skim, but "read" means read. I just look at them. I may very well not have read the affidavits. I do not promise that I've read the affidavits. I may not have looked up the law or the controlling cases. Sometimes I'll think I know them. Sometimes I'll be in an area that I won't know.

Frequently the law clerks will append the controlling cases to their bench memos so I've got them. Sometimes I read them; sometimes I don't. But I promise that I have read at least that bench memo and your briefs.

Now, the actual conduct of motion sessions. Here's how I do it. The stage is set for a motion session.

> Ladies and gentlemen, good afternoon. Thank you for attending the Court's motion session. We have a number of motions here this afternoon, six to nine, and we'll proceed in the usual order, and the usual order is as follows: We'll have three calls of the list. First call of the list I simply want to know how long in the aggregate the argument on your motion will take. If in the aggregate, both sides, the argument on your motion will take ten minutes or less, you'll be on second call. If it will take slightly more than ten minutes, you'll be on third call. Once we've lined the motions up, then we'll go through second and third call, calling the motions.
>
> When your motion is called I ask you to come up to counsel table, introduce yourself and who you represent so that I may have a complete and accurate record. Now, first call of the list.

Ms. Smith then calls the case. People stand up in the back of the room and they say, "Slightly more than ten minutes, Judge." I then respond ominously, "Third call." And so on. And we get them all lined up, and then we're ready.

Let's do a motion to dismiss first. Actually, motions to dismiss and motions for summary judgment can be taken together. I try to be a hot bench. I come out on the bench in a motion session knowing what I'm going to do. Hold on, I stated that too strongly. Let me back off. I come out on the bench with a tentative idea of what I'm going to do. The weakness in the way I conduct motion sessions is that you may think I'm too brusque and you may think the oral argument is just a go-through or that my mind had already been made up to do X or Y, and that I just toyed with you a little and then made my ruling. I hope not. I hope not, one, because I truly value courtesy as a judge, and, two, I can tell you my mind is not made up, despite that Freudian slip. All it is is that I have some idea. I'm ready to engage intellectually. I think I know the way things ought to go here.

How do you deal with a judge like that, like me? We'll use me as the baseline. In almost every motion to dismiss or for summary judgment I go where I think the weakness is, and that's not plaintiff/defendant or the moving party or not. It's the argument that I think won't make it. And I ask the party that's making that argument, "What about this?" And so it's almost a tip-off with me. When I ask, "What about this?" you're in trouble because I'm not buying that; I'm thinking of doing something else.

Now, what will stop me is if you can cite specific cases or if as we talk it's clear that I've misread the facts—that happens, again, because some other judges are far more prepared than I am, so if I haven't gotten the case in focus, you have to jerk me right back into focus and say, "Judge, I don't represent Smith here. You called on me. I represent Jones. Smith bears the burden of proof." Then I'll say, "Oh, oh. Well, what about that?" I've gotten it completely backwards, but if I am generally oriented, you have to say, "The First Circuit has held X, Judge." That slows me down. I work for the First Circuit, and that case had better be in the bench memo as well as how we've distinguished it, in which case I'll try it out on you and say, "Ah, but in that case," thus and so.

Well, if that's wrong, remember, I may not have read the case. I've got the bench memo here and I have read the briefs. Maybe I've read the case, so maybe you want the case. Maybe you want to pass it up. Maybe I have it.

If I can make a ruling from the bench, I will, because life should go on. If you slowed me down, I'll take it under advisement. If I think it warrants an opinion—and really most of the opinions that I am most proud of come from motion sessions—then I'll take it under advisement.

A way to slow me down, but it may slow down your case too, is to say, "Your Honor, this is a matter of first impression; this is the first case to raise this issue." I love that stuff, see. I say, "Oh, first impressions. We're going to write an opinion on that." Bonnie sits there shaking her head, and afterwards she says, "Don't let it disappear into the black hole," because I then think I'm going to write some opinion on this case of first impression.

Six months go by. Now, we're pretty good. We don't have anything older than six months now. We have to report everything that's six months old. But you may just have gotten yourself six months. Maybe you don't want six months. Maybe you want it decided right there and then.

I do believe it is the job of the judge to decide. Let's go back a little bit to what Judge Brogna said when I first became a judge. It was very profound. We're doing the nuts and bolts now, but when he said, "Have the courage of your own error," he was right. A trial judge must decide. The hallmark of a trial judge is to decide something, decide the evidence, decide the motions, get on with the trial. Sure, to decide it right is very important, but our whole role in the process of shaping it is to get a decision so we can play off that decision and ultimately have an appellate court speak to it.

I feel very keenly it is my duty to decide, not to flip a coin and decide, but to decide, and to decide perhaps without every available case. But when you say "a case of first impression," well, then I want to really decide. It may slow things down.

I have no particular idiosyncrasies on motions to dismiss or those for summary judgment. We are required to cut pro se litigants some slack, and I try to, but I try not to become their advocates.

We talked a little bit about summary judgments. I do believe in partial summary judgment in the event I don't give complete summary judgment.

The motion for preliminary injunction: In my session that's nuclear war because that gets you a trial instantly. We have so few cases now that as soon as we get a motion for preliminary injunction, my eyes light up and we set a hearing. This is how that hearing goes:

"Thank you, counsel. All right. Do you want a jury on this?" I'm not pressing it one way or another, but it's not clear, or you've claimed a jury. "Do you really want a jury or do you want it jury-waived?"

Counsel responds, "Why do you ask, Judge" or "Of course we want a jury."

"Well, because my intention is to collapse the hearing on the motion for preliminary injunction with trial on the merits and to commence. And the question is: When can we commence? Will it be next Monday or will it be this afternoon?"

"Oh, your Honor, we've had no discovery, and we have a constitutional right to discovery," et cetera.

I'm not kidding with you now; this is how I do it. This is our session. The rules permit it. It's just I want to get going. We're waiting there, so don't make a motion for preliminary injunction unless you're ready to go.

I'll say to the defendants, "I'll protect you. All this discovery stuff, look at the Rand study; most of that's a waste of time. I'll let you subpoena your witnesses in here. Don't worry. It's Monday. We've got the weekend, you know. Let's get a jury." It's part of my faith in the jury system.

If it's a patent case and you want to enjoin the other side, let's go to trial. It's just wonderful. Most people settle, of course. Private ordering is a good thing, but I'm not doing it just to settle. And I'm not kidding. And I do it all the time.

Therefore, if today you are seeking a preliminary injunction, what you'll get is trial on the merits. Now, in the old days when I had 500 cases that was not so, but today I think that's the best justice. I'm doing that all the time now. You better have a good reason not to be ready to go forward if you ask for a preliminary injunction because the most you can work out will be a week, while I get a jury panel in if I'm really pinned down.

Now, class certification. I think the class action rules are overused, and I've come to believe that I'm not going to rule on that motion for class certification until I've had some sort of motion for summary judgment. And I'll press the defense. I'll say, "Well, don't you want to make a motion for summary judgment or even partial summary judgment?"

And maybe they say no. They're just whining. They say, "This is a strike suit, Judge. Deny this class." And I say, "You know, I really can't tell." But if I have to deal with a defendant's motion for summary judgment, you see, the defendant may lose it, but I will see then how many factual differences there are between class members. That may tell me that there shouldn't be a class action. Of course, conversely, I may see that they're all the same and then croak the defendant on summary judgment. Then you'd better settle because then we'll just have all those plaintiffs, class members, hopping in to take offensive collateral estoppel from the decision on the summary judgment.

I tend really to like to know something about summary judgment before I rule on class certification, but you get an oral hearing. I'll give oral hearings on all those things.

While I've done the standard types of motions, there are a variety of motions upon which I haven't touched. I haven't touched on criminal at all yet. Let's just take a moment on criminal cases.

In criminal cases, its the magistrate judge who handles the arraignment and the bail hearing so I usually don't see you, the lawyers, until the appeal of the bail hearing. And I tend to look at the record that was before the magistrate judge. I don't want to have an entirely new hearing, and the law doesn't require me to.

Then there are types of what I call evidentiary hearings, and now is the time to mention it. Obviously a motion to suppress on the criminal side is an evidentiary-type hearing, a jury-waived hearing. But also you want to make *Daubert* motions now, and in state court it comes under *Commonwealth v. Lanigan*, 419 Mass. 15 (1994), which has the same rule. If you think that the science that's being used by the other side is junk science, make a motion that the scientist not be permitted to testify under *Daubert*.

I'm not seeing this in my practice, but I know, because I teach Evidence and because I'm going down Monday to a bar association meeting of defense lawyers on medical device and pharmaceutical litigation, that many lawyers think that they can get *Daubert* hearings by snapping their fingers. And they're attacking not only the science but the scientist.

For instance, let's say epidemiology. That's accepted under *Daubert*. That's one of the things we've had around for a long time. They say, okay, epidemiology requires the following protocol. They look at this FJC (Federal Judicial Center) book that I mentioned before. They say, "This scientist may be a qualified epidemiologist, but he didn't follow the protocol."

Now, what do we do under *Daubert*? I've never done it. I've never yet had a *Daubert* hearing, but I have a view on it and I have a protocol already, and I'll share it with you—although you may push me off it if I ever get to do it. I think those hearings come up under 104(a) of the Federal Rules of Evidence—the state's roughly the same—in which I'm making a preliminary finding. That's why I mentioned motions to suppress. That's what I'm doing in a motion to suppress, I'm making a preliminary finding about how the constitution has worked, but it's a finding. It's not a ruling. It's not like summary judgment where the Court of Appeals reviews me de novo. It's a finding where I myself decide whether the criteria of *Daubert* has been met or not met.

So I'm prepared at this hearing to hear testimony from both sides and make that finding that then will govern the trial. I expect, though—this is a matter now before the Supreme Court—to be given deference from the Court of Appeals because it's a finding.

Now, I repeat that I've never had one. Few judges, state or federal, in Massachusetts have. Judge Stearns has. Justice Kottmyer has, and probably you people know more than I what others do.

AUDIENCE MEMBER: When do you want the *Daubert* motion to be filed?

JUDGE YOUNG: I really don't care except it better be no later than the final pretrial conference because I don't want to move the trial, and I really should get this evidentiary hearing squared away in that afternoon the month before. If you want the *Daubert* hearing on the eve of trial, on the morning I'm impaneling the jury, then I'm really likely to say, "Let the jury sort all that out because I'm ready for a trial with the pièce de résistance there, which is the jury."

So while I'm open to them, and I'm pretty strict on experts, you want to get it in and, in fairness, you want to get it in as soon as you know what expert they're using that you think is no good.

There are *Markman* hearings now for those in the patent bar. Very briefly, I've never done one, but I'm being required to do one. I'll do one before Christmas. In patent law of course you've got a patent. That's what the case is about; it's about the patent. And patents are very complex. And the Supreme Court has decided that it is a function of the judge to determine claim construction under the patent, in other words, to determine what's the law.

And, loving juries as I do, the way I conceptualize what they mean by that is that this is like interpreting a contract, and judges all have the final words on interpreting the contract. And so the way I'm doing *Markman* hearings is this: I'm going to start out looking at the claims, just the claims. And I'll hear argument from the lawyers. I won't take any evidence, but I'll hear arguments from the lawyers.

If I can figure it out, that's it. If I can't figure it out from the claims, every patent has a file history. It's before the Patent Office. I analogize it to the legislative history of a statute. If I can't figure it out from the claims themselves, I'm going to look at the file history. Again, I don't want evidence. I don't want affidavits. I'll take briefs. I'll have people tell me what they think it all means. I want to look at the file wrapper. If I can't figure it out from that, then I'll take affidavits.

And the reason I'll take affidavits is I don't want to make it evidentiary. I don't want to look at the person as I looked at my witness here to see whether she sweats, because I don't think I'm deciding believability. They can just file these long affidavits, which read, "I'm Sam Scientist, and I'm brilliant, and I know all this stuff, and, Judge, let me tell you what this is." I don't need to see Sam because I'm not making findings.

The problem is if I can't figure it out on that third level, then *Markman* still says it's my job. And I sort of then slide over by *Daubert*. I've got to then—I'll want to then see the affiants, to see who I believe. If affiant A says black and affiant B says white, and that really is the determination and it's which one I believe, then at least I'll make a record and we'll see what the Federal Circuit thinks about it. I think I'm following the Federal Circuit on it. But for those of you who do patent practice, that's the way I think that should be done.

AUDIENCE MEMBER: A brief follow-up question, your Honor. You mentioned earlier the restricted or limited resources that you have available to you for scientific research.

JUDGE YOUNG: I guess that should be a reflection on me. I told you what was in my chambers and that I'm really not a scientist. We're pretty good if I go looking. If I go looking, I can find pretty much anything. I mean here we are in Boston with all the magnificent research libraries. And I have wonderful clerks who understand both the Internet and understand all the resources. We go looking.

But on the other hand, this sort of initiative of my going looking and searching is not necessarily a great idea. When we get into fact stuff I have a problem. I rather want the adversaries to serve it up because they can control it more and they know what the other side is doing. I'm a little hesitant to embark on my own self-taught human genome project. It's not something I'm likely to do. I believe in the adversary system. Let them teach me. I'm not a Luddite. I'm not putting my head in the sand with respect to science, but I want the adversary system to work.

On these other things, the reason I listed all these periodicals and stuff, I think that's the law broadly conceived. I want to see the trends in the law, that type of stuff. That I do try to read broadly.

AUDIENCE MEMBER: Is that position shared by your fellow judges, to your knowledge, letting the adversary system teach you technology?

JUDGE YOUNG: As a practical matter, I think yes, because at least among my colleagues none of us are scientifically trained to any great degree. Clearly the intellectual leader of the court, Judge Keeton, is such a marvelous intellect, and his approach to litigation is more cerebral and intellectual, and I could conceive of him training himself in ways that most of the rest of us would eschew, saying, let them tell us how it works.

On the Federal Circuit there are judges who are distinguished scientists in their own right. That's not true in the District of Massachusetts. I'm not putting us down, but none of us shows any particular science banner.

Judge Woodlock, of course, who built the new courthouse, is in my opinion as good an architect as there is, if that's science; but you're talking about more pure science, and none of us are particularly strong on that.

The Final Pretrial Conference

So we get to the final pretrial conference. We're not to trial yet. We've had the discovery. We come in, sit down. I will offer you my execrable tea. I drink Lapsang Souchong tea. Some people want to curry my favor, and they say they will drink it. Then it always amuses me. They hate it, but they pretend to drink it. But some people like the stuff. But I want to be casual in the lobby, and so we sit around a table, and here's how the final pretrial conference works in our session.

How have I prepared? Not much. Another perhaps weakness in our session, I'll be candid.

You will have filed by then your joint pretrial memorandum. It is required to be very detailed. I may or may not have read it. I do not warrant that I've even read it. The case file is there because Bonnie brings it, and we have this, and she'll put on the top outside the joint pretrial memorandum, and I glance at it, or I've read it earlier.

And I inevitably will start talking settlement, so let's talk settlement here. If it's a jury case, I expect to know the figures, and I expect the plaintiff to have a figure, and I expect the plaintiff to state the figure.

Now, I don't usually have litigants in the lobby or require litigants to be present for the final pretrial conference. I want the people (the lawyers) who are going to try the case, but I will accept people other than the people who will try the case. Note, however, that I advise them—so you're at your own peril if you don't come to the final pretrial conference—that I want the people there to have authority to settle.

So I'll press for settlement. I want to know what the plaintiff wants, and I'll want to know what the defendant offers. I will engage in discussion. I am not much different than other judges. I will try to think of arguments why the plaintiff should reduce its demand and why the defendant should increase its offer. That's my institutional role.

I will explain those arguments. I will never fake it. I believe the arguments that I am stating. Some of them are stronger than others. They are biased or make-weights only in the sense that I want to have something to say to both sides, but I believe it.

If I get any movement, any interest in settlement, I will suspend the conference and let people call their clients. I will go do something else and have you talk in the hall. If I get any interest in settlement, I will ask how I can be of service.

I'm perfectly willing to be a mediator; that is, I will talk to one side without the presence of the other side so long as everyone agrees. We have to get it on the record how we're going to do it, but I am willing to do anything that you jointly want to do.

I try to be innovative. I try to understand settlement. I am not a screamer on this. I do not demand settlement or demand that people move. I've been known to be forceful, to say that I think your position is way out of line, and I expect you to tell your client that, but that's about as strong as I am on settlement.

If the case is not going to settle, I say, "How long will this case take to try?" You're required to state it in the joint memorandum, and so that is recalled to me. I usually say, "That is fine."

Bonnie then is choreographed to interject—I never meet with you alone; I have my clerk there, and almost always it's Bonnie as the key person for running the trial—"He means it. Judge, explain to them your time limits."

I always try civil cases with time limits. We agree upon the time limits ahead of time. They make cases much better to try, much more just. My general rules are as follows:

You pretty much can have what you want so long as it's reasonable. You know what my trial day is; it's three and a half hours of trial time, from 9:00 to 10:45, a half an hour break, and then 11:15 to 1:00. That gives you three and a half hours of trial time. And I want real trials. I don't want lawyer talky-talk. We can do that stuff in the afternoon.

We agree upon the aggregate amount of time. Usually I split it 50/50, but we don't have to if that's not fair. And we talk about that, and generally I will give you what you want.

There are some restraints on giving you what you want, however. I cannot conceive of a civil case taking more than a month to try, 20 days. And if it takes more than a month to try, we'll go to bifurcation, beginning with liability and then going to damages. If that isn't enough, 20 days for liability, we'll go to polyfurcation. I've never had to do that, but this is my plan, so you know. We'll try out one element of the case first.

For example, in a huge antitrust case, that first month we will try the issue of whether there is monopoly power. If the answer to that is yes, then during the second month we try whether the power was misused. If the answer to that is yes, then we spend the third month, the third part of the trial, on damages. Maybe there'll have to be a fourth month. What is the market? We'll work it out.

So those time limits that we have agreed upon are all for real. If you're on your feet, the time counts against you. So figure it right to the hour. I keep the time. I keep the time to five-minute increments. I can't be more accurate than that. There is no appeal. Well, there is an appeal to the Court of Appeals, but you don't want that while the case is going on. I don't argue about it. I tell you what it is at the end of each trial day. I will tell you how much time you have left.

And then when you are almost done with your time, I will let you know where you stand. For example, if you are on your last witness, I'll say, "If you want a half an hour for closing, you have about ten more minutes for this witness."

When you are done, you should just end and sit down. It's over. I have one case in which one side now claims that they were shortchanged and will take it up. I had Joan Lukey from Hale and Dorr take me up once, but she never pressed it as an appeal point, but I wrote a decision, which discusses how time limits work. That's how I do time limits.

After we discuss time limits, I then want to know what the issues are in the case. I want to know what the major evidentiary issues are. My rule is one expert per discipline. I don't go for having a host of experts on the same issue.

Then, I'll ask if you have premarked your documents. If you haven't, I want them premarked, and I have a protocol for that. Documents that are going to be admitted in evidence get numbers, and the numbers go from 1 to infinity, without distinction between plaintiff and defendant, government or defense. They just are in evidence. That's a fair way to do it.

If documents are marked for identification, and I'm not forcing you to agree on documents, if they're marked for identification, I expect you to mark them with letters to the base 26, A to Z, and then AA, AB, AC, AD, not AA, BB, CC, because when you get involved in a big case, and we do frequently, you get QQQQQQ and you'll be all messed up.

There is a limitation on my theory. This actually happened. I will read from an actual transcript. In ***United States v. Owens,*** Allison Burroughs, Assistant United States Attorney, for the Government:

"Your Honor, we offer as the next document–"

"No. It's excluded. Give it the next letters for identification. What are the next letters, Ms. Burroughs?"

"FU, Judge."

"What?" ***(Laughter)***.

"FU, your Honor," she says. And then we both smile at each other. Yeah. Okay.

That's true. It was so intense that neither she nor I realized what we were saying. But those really were the next letters in the sequence. So there's the limitation, but that's the way I expect it to be done. Generally, it goes very smoothly.

Now, here's one practical thing: I'm assuming, and I operate on this assumption, that documents are authentic, that they are all authentic. My assumption on that is so strong, as it is with most judges, that if you argue that a document is not authentic, you'd better come up with something to suggest why you think that the document is not authentic, because having to go into the issue of authenticity is just a terrible waste of time. It is not enough just to be a dog in a manger and say, "Well, Judge, I insist upon its authenticity being shown. The rules entitle me to that."

I say, "It looks authentic to me. What's the matter with it?" And if you do not give me a reasonable argument, we're going to take that document as authentic. So be ready to deal with authenticity.

Trial of a Case

Impanelment

Final pretrial conference is over. We now come to the actual trial of the case. Let's do impanelment, and we'll go step by step.

We'll do a civil case here, and I want you to get the steps very clear. We bring in at the far back of the courtroom about 35 people to choose 12. I always impanel 12, even in a civil case. I believe strongly that 12 is the number. The rule says I can't have less than six. I always impanel 12. All of them deliberate, no alternates.

If I'm going to impanel 12, that gives you six peremptory. I introduce myself. I talk to the jury—all 35 or so of them. I try to build the jury up. I tell them about direct democracy and the like. Then Ms. Smith swears them.

I'm not so interested in having you ask the jury any questions; as a matter of fact, I am very much against that practice. I ask them the stock questions. If you want to get me to ask more questions, make a motion. I'll look at it, and I may do it or not. You will only know whether I've done it or not when I ask the questions. And if you think you want another question, ask to approach the bench.

If anyone answers "yes" to any of my questions, I don't deal with them right away, I wait until I've asked all the questions, and we see who else answers "yes." After I have asked all the questions, I have those who answered "yes" come one by one up to the side bar. I ask each one, "Please state your full name." The juror states his or her full name. I then say, "Now, you answered 'yes' to a question," and I then ask some other questions to see if I think that the witness is impartial.

I then rule. You're standing there, but I haven't consulted you. I then rule. I either say, "Thank you, ma'am. We'll ask you to stay," which means I am not discharging the juror, or, "Well, all right. We'll let you go back to the jury lounge."

And Bonnie has the juror number, and the juror sets off.

If you challenge my ruling for cause, or if you think that the juror is prejudiced and you therefore don't want that particular juror, or if you think the juror was fine and I shouldn't have let him go, after the juror steps away—Don, my court reporter is standing right here, of course—just get my attention by saying, "Your Honor." I will ask the juror to stop. I'll say, "Hold it a second." Then I'll hear you. Then I'll rule. And sometimes I'll reverse myself and ask the juror to stay, but usually not.

So it then continues, and then I say, "I find this panel indifferent." Then once we have the panel indifferent, Ms. Smith fills the box with the 12 jurors.

Now, we have gone more like the state system. The jury list that you get is already randomized, which means that Ms. Smith will call the names in the order that they appear on the list, less those who have been excused. That's important to you because if you like a juror who is almost there but not in the box and you like that juror more than someone who is in the box, exercise the challenge because the next juror to be called is that juror who is next on the list.

Once I've got the jurors in the box, I ask each juror to tell us where he or she works and what he or she does and, if married, what the spouse does and where the spouse works. I like that because it gives you a chance to hear them speak.

Then once we've heard that, I invite you to the side bar. I invite you immediately. I don't give you much time to think about it. If you don't come up right away, I will wait, but after a while I will say, "Counsel," because I want to keep going. So you had better be ready on these jurors. Then what I do is I look at either the plaintiff or the government and I ask, "Any peremptory challenges?" And that side gives me its challenges. Then without filling the box I look at the other side and I ask, "Who don't you like?" Then that side gives me its challenges.

There are no back-strikes. The ones who survive that stage are going to sit on the jury. Then we leave side bar and go back. At that time, Ms. Smith, without of course acknowledging who has challenged which jurors, excuses those jurors who are going to be peremptorily challenged. They go, and then we refill the box. We replace those excused jurors.

One thing to note is that, for some reason, we do not get many minorities. Overall, we do pretty well in picking diverse juries. In fact, we do better than any district in the United States in our way of getting diverse juries. We follow the state system. We take names directly from the census list, like the state does, right from the city list. In fact, we have a deal with the state. They give us its jury list, and that's how we pick our juries.

Every district court in the nation but ours picks from the voter list. We pick from everyone who is resident within the district, regardless if they are registered to vote. It's fair. It's better. We still, however, do not get enough minorities on our juries. In fact, if you challenge a minority and he or she is the only one in the panel, I'm not waiting for any more of a pattern than that. You'd better have a good reason for your challenge because I'll ask.

This story actually happened. I said, "Counsel, that's the only black person in the venire. You've challenged him. Do you mind telling me why?" He replied, "What? Is he black? I didn't—I didn't—oh, Judge, is he really—I didn't see that, no. That's not the reason I challenged him. No, Judge. This is a sexual harassment case. I challenged him because he's a man." I said, "That's not a ground for challenge. He's seated, and that's that." And that man was seated. By the way, that side who had challenged him lost the case. So, as you can see, I don't wait for a pattern in your challenges before I ask for your reasoning.

Then in the next round—as we attempt to replace all the excused jurors and fill the jury box—it's the defense who goes first, and so on. So that's fair, until all the peremptories are exhausted or we have our jury.

We then swear the jury. I do a pretrial charge, and I explain to the jury the elements that the plaintiff will have to prove. And I demonstrate those elements, usually by a fair preponderance of the evidence, by waving my arms like this (Judge Young gestures). If you want any say into that pretrial charge, you must talk about that at the final pretrial conference.

I let jurors ask questions. I let jurors take notes. And I explain all that to the jury, and that's in every case.

Motion for Directed Verdict at the End of Plaintiff's Case

Once the plaintiff has put in the plaintiff's case, that's the time you—defense counsel—should make your motion for directed verdict. That's really the time you've got your best likelihood of winning it because if you wait and move for a directed verdict at the close of all the evidence, I'll wait and see what the jury does. So you really should make it at the close of all the evidence because if you don't, you're not in a position to make a motion for judgment notwithstanding the verdict—a JNOV. You must move for directed verdict to preserve your right to later move for a JNOV if you don't like the jury's verdict. You've got to make the motion, and I'll rule on it. I'll say, "I can unwind this after the jury verdict is returned." Then we'll just go right ahead because I'm hoping the jury will save me and that I don't have to deal with some delicate legal issue. I am hoping that, if the plaintiff has a very thin case, the jury will in fact do whatever it has to do and decide in favor of the defendant, or whatever.

Jury Charge

Now, I give the jurors the charge. Charlie Hely in the superior court writes out his own charges on the computer. He makes copies, gives each of the jurors a copy so that they can follow his charge. I don't do it that way. I first declare the charge to them. Then, because I have a copy and I have realtime, we give the jury the actual charge that I have already declared so that they can see it in writing.

I am a fan of sometimes drawing things for the jury. In a case of a prior injury, I will draw a line and say:

> Now, pay no attention to the angles here, but this is, let us say, an average person's level of health. In this case, however, there is some evidence that Ms. Jones' health was less than the average. If you believe that evidence, that her health was less than the average before the incident, and the incident occurred here, then she is entitled to recover for however long, for whatever injury drove her down from the level of health that she had prior to the incident. She's not entitled to recover back to perfect health if you believe she was of less health prior to the injury. She is only entitled to recover for the difference between her health before the incident and her health after the incident.

Also, in cases dealing with contributory negligence I explain to the jury:

> Now, ladies and gentlemen, there is some evidence—or at least the defense, the Widget Company, has stated—that Mr. Jones did not act in due care. They have to prove that. Now, suppose that you think that the Widget Company was negligent and its negligence was a proximate cause of Mr. Jones' injury, but you also think that Mr. Jones, himself, was negligent. What you do is you consider the negligence of the two of them and then determine what Mr. Jones can recover, if anything. Let me give you some examples now. I don't suggest anything by way of recovery here, but if you get to that stage, here's how it works:
>
> Suppose you find that the Widget Company was a hundred percent negligent and that Mr. Jones wasn't negligent at all. Your damages then, and I'm just making these figures up, would be a dollar or a hundred million dollars, whatever.
>
> Ah, but suppose you think that Mr. Jones was 10 percent negligent himself. Then the damages are 90 cents or $90 million, or whatever. 25 percent negligent? The damages are 75 cents or $75 million. Mr. Jones was as negligent as the Widget Company, 50/50? The damages are 50 cents or $50 million.
>
> Now, even though you think that the Widget Company was negligent, if you find that that Mr. Jones was more negligent than the Widget Company, then your verdict must be for the Widget Company. You must come back with a verdict for the Widget Company. Mr. Jones does not recover.

This is how I finish with the jury, in every charge, civil or criminal:

> Now, ladies and gentlemen, just a few words about your deliberations. Madam Forelady, as forelady it doesn't mean that you do all the talking; it doesn't mean you keep your mouth shut either. What it means is that you set things up there in the jury room so that each and every one of the jurors can fully and fairly express his or her opinion in circumstances where all the other jurors can listen to the opinion that has been expressed and discuss it. You should all discuss the matter together.
>
> It's perfectly all right for you to take breaks. Some of you smoke. If you want to smoke, take a break, and you can go out in the hall. A court security officer will be there, and you can have your smoke. But dur-

ing the break don't discuss the case. Jury deliberations are all of you together, all 12 of you.

Now, it's probably not a good idea to take a straw vote at the outset of your deliberations lest you think that under your oath you are bound to adhere to the position that you originally announced.

If you have a strong view of any aspect of this case, by all means adhere to it. There is no pressure on you to return a verdict or any sort of verdict. But jury deliberations are just that, deliberations. And you are entitled to be persuaded by your fellow jurors who, after all, have seen the same evidence as you and heard the same witnesses as you have heard. So you could listen to your fellow jurors to see whether you are persuaded. But each of you must agree upon the verdict. Your verdict must be unanimous. It cannot be ten of you and the other two just going along. A unanimous verdict is what the law requires. You'll have your notes in the jury room. You may use your notes, but don't pass them around to your fellow jurors. The notes aren't evidence. The notes are to be used only to jog your recollection.

If you have any questions about the law as I've explained it to you, write your question out and give it to the court security officer. We will bring you back in here, into this courtroom, and I will answer your question further because, since you must follow the law, naturally you're entitled to know what it is. If you have any questions about the law as it applies to this case, it's my job to teach it to you.

Now, once we excuse you, we'll knock on the door to bring in the written copy of my charge. Ms. Smith will be talking with the lawyers, and then she will bring in all the exhibits that we agree that you may have. Then the door will shut, and we'll leave you alone.

We've made arrangements to take you to lunch. If no verdict is returned by 5:00 this afternoon, I will stop you for the day. There's no pressure on you to return a verdict. As I promised you, I'm going to let you go home, and you can come back tomorrow and continue your deliberations.

Now, when you have returned a verdict, knock on the door and tell the court security officer. Don't give him the verdict. Just tell him that you have a verdict. And he'll set things up in the courtroom. Then we will

> all return here. This will prove to you that in fact we worked this afternoon. When we're all ready we'll have you come in. You will come in to the jury box.
>
> Ms. Smith will say to you, 'Ladies and gentlemen of the jury, have you agreed upon a unanimous verdict?' If that's why you're back here, the forelady will say, 'Yes,' and Ms. Smith will ask, 'Would you pass the verdict slip?' And then you pass the verdict slip. Don't bring all exhibits, just the verdict slip, to Ms. Smith.
>
> Ms. Smith will give the verdict slip to me. I am the first one to look at it. I look at it for one single reason: I look at it simply to see that it's logical, that you've checked one or the other box here and that you have signed and dated it.
>
> If the verdict is logical, I will give it to Ms. Smith and say, 'The verdict is in order. It may be recorded.' At that time she will ask you all to stand. You stand then, and you're the only ones that stand. The rest of us sit here. You stand up out of an acknowledgment of the duty that's imposed on you. And if each of you is satisfied with the consciousness of your duty faithfully performed, you will have done what's required of you as jurors in this case.
>
> The word 'verdict' come from two Latin words: verus dictum. They mean 'to speak the truth.' And that is what is asked of you at this time, to speak the truth. Now we'll recess to await the verdict of the jury.

All right. That's how I end with the jury, and that's how I am ending with you today. Thank you all very much. I really appreciate your taking the morning to be here with me. We stand adjourned. ***(Applause)***.

"What are judges in our society? Judges are nothing more nor less than teachers."

—Hon. William G. Young, December 6, 1997
From *A Case Study of a Session in the U.S. District Court*

CHAPTER 7

Judge Young on Experts, GHOST and *Daubert*

APRIL 28, 1998

CONCURRING in *General Electric v. Joiner,* 118 S.Ct. 512 (1997), Mr. Justice Breyer said that the bench and the scientists have to work closely together, and that there must be ways that we can mesh our two disciplines. He followed that up with a speech that I think is very significant with the American Association of the Advancement of Science, and this type of gathering is to me enormously significant. Understand though the method in our madness. Distinguished scientists–physicians–who devote their lives to this have explained it to us, and now I'm going to tell you the law.

But understand that my framework is different. I'm going to go like the wind to make up some time, but part of the message here is how different the framework is. If you've been following the scientific method and the reasoned disagreements, now try to fit this into the legal framework. We'll try to do this very quickly. And much of what I'll say is review.

Understand that I have never had an MCS (multiple chemical sensitivity) case. I have been on a program where we talked about MCS. These issues are of interest to me. But I've never had an MCS case. I have no idea what I'd do if I did get one, but here's the law as I understand it.

Now, what we're talking about here is the use of experts. Are we going to let so-called–and I mean no disrespect to anyone–so-called experts testify about something? So here's the law in a nutshell, the evidentiary law on experts.

GHOST

Expert testimony can be thought of as two building blocks that lead to an opinion. You need both of them. What I'm telling you is true both under the Federal Rules of Evidence and under the Massachusetts common law. The expert building blocks are of two types. One is noncase specific. It doesn't have anything to do with the specific case. Logically, then, it is general. The expert has to be possessed of some general body of knowledge—we'll come back to the word "knowledge"—that average lay jurors or judges don't have. Because if the jurors and judges know the stuff, we don't need the experts.

It's not enough that the expert has noncase-specific knowledge, the expert has to know something about the case. This is the second type of building block. This is not something that we're going to spend much time on today, but it's important that you get the whole framework. Under our law, there are four ways that the expert can get his or her case-specific knowledge—four ways that are accepted:

- Counsel can give the expert a hypothetical question from the evidence that already has been put before the factfinder.
- An expert can be an observant or a percipient witness—like in the case where counsel hires a consultant expert. The hired expert can take the measurements, and therefore can obviously testify to the measurements he or she has taken. Also, a treating physician is a percipient witness.
- In patent and in land taking cases, probably not the type of cases that we're talking about here, counsel can have the expert sit in the courtroom and listen to the other experts or listen to the evidence that's before the factfinder. That is a rare situation.
- Finally, counsel can tell the expert about the case. In other words, an expert can base her opinion on hearsay. It has to be a special type of hearsay. In federal courts, it's the hearsay upon which experts in this field of human endeavor are accustomed to rely outside the courts. In the state courts, it's hearsay that if you brought it into court, it would be admissible—like hospital records.

So there you are. The whole evidentiary law of experts can be expressed in the word GHOST. *(Laughter)*. Hey listen! When you stand on your feet, leap to your feet, to make an objection, the adrenaline rush is there—you laugh now, but you won't when you're in court. You can remember this stuff. GHOST is the law of experts. G for general (noncase-specific knowledge); H for hypothetical question; O for the expert that is an observant witness; S for those experts who sit in the courtroom and listen to the evidence; and T for when counsel tells the expert about the case.

GHOST: THE LAW OF EXPERTS

G	H	O	S	T
General knowledge	Hypothetical question	Observant/ percipient witness	Sit and listen to evidence	Tell expert
Not case specific	Case specific			

Today our focus is only on the general "G," which comes out of the *Daubert* analysis, from the landmark case of *Daubert v. Merrell Dow Pharmaceuticals, Inc.*, 509 U.S. 579, 113 S.Ct. 2786 (1993). Is there this body of knowledge that an expert can master and therefore we will allow the expert to express before the factfinder, whether the factfinder be a judge or jury? We will start with the federal, but then discuss the state standard. While the federal and state principles are generally the same, there are some significant differences.

DAUBERT

Daubert, of course, is the Supreme Court decision that was supposed to rein in and regulate junk science. Remember that *Daubert* depends on the Federal Rules of Evidence, and the old federal standard under the *Frye* test was that the science be generally accepted. *Frye v. United States*, 293 F. 1013 (D.C. Cir. 1923). But there's nothing in Federal Rule of Evidence 702 that says anything about general acceptance, and so there was a concern over what the standard was—the old *Frye* standard. Judge Kozinski of the Ninth Circuit wrote the decision dealing with the birth defect cases and the use of the drug Bendectin. In his decision, he said, in essence, that general acceptance is right in the rule. In *Daubert*, the Supreme Court tipped that Ninth Circuit decision, which is not surprising—of the last 29 cases that went up from the Ninth Circuit, 28 were reversed. But in any event, the Supreme Court tipped the Ninth Circuit and said a couple of very significant things.

Everyone, when they saw the *Daubert* case, thought it was a win/win case. The plaintiffs' bar thought, "Heh, heh, this is wonderful. We win." And the defense bar said, "This is terrific for us." The truth is it's a defense case. Let's face it, it's a defense case.

First, under *Daubert*, the judge—who by definition doesn't know the science anyway, because if he knew the science he wouldn't need the expert—is the gatekeeper. Second, only reliable science, which we don't understand to begin with, will be admitted. Now, as soon as you tell that to judges, that's a defense step, whether it's perceived by the "Supremes" or not. If you tell a judge they have a gate, they think they got to swing it. They have to close it in some cases. It's inevitable. I'm telling you the truth here. Okay? So we are the gatekeepers. Then, Chief Justice Rehnquist said, essentially, "Don't tell them how to do it. Stop there. Let them figure it out themselves." In one of the last opinions he wrote, however, Justice Blackmun went ahead and told us how to do it—how to be the gatekeepers.

While the *Daubert* analysis consists of a four-part test, which I will discuss later, it is important to look first at whether the body of data that we're talking about is "knowledge." Knowledge, that is, in a scientific sense. Is this body of data scientific knowledge? Now we're not really clear what we mean about that. In the materials that accompany this program, we have included an article by Professor Linda Simard and me; you'll find it starting on page 33. I'll summarize it. In essence we say the knowledge requirement is satisfied by an analysis of the epistemology, that is the theory of knowledge of the people in the field. You start out asking yourself, "Why do these people think whatever it is that they think?" And, "Is that just sort of basically reasonable? Does it make sense?" This scientific knowledge requirement, you see, is what wipes out those folks that can't explain how they do something—they have no theory of how something works, or at least none that commends itself to judges, and so we don't let them in.

Then, the *Daubert* test is a four-part test:

1. Can you test the theory?
2. How good are the tests? Are there false positives? What is the error rate?
3. Does the theory appear in peer review journals? Interestingly, the Supreme Court is not so hot on clinicians—I say this with all respect—it likes more of the research science. That's what they go to in *Daubert*.
4. Then, the old test: Is the theory generally accepted?

In *Commonwealth v. Lanigan*, 419 Mass. 15 (1994)—*Lanigan II*—Massachusetts supposedly adopted the *Daubert* test. Or did it? It does sort of. Massachusetts reverses it, or rather relies more heavily on the last part of *Daubert's* four-part test—not so much in *Lanigan II*, but in the cases that follow it. Remember the federal courts have Rule 702, and the state courts have the common law. So the common law test in Massachusetts in the cases following *Lanigan II* seems to be this: If it's generally accepted, it's in. If it's not generally accepted, then you look to: can you test the theory? How good are the tests? Has the theory been published and subjected to peer review?

The standard of review by the higher courts is different under the two systems. Federal first: The federal standard of review is an abuse of discretion. We trial judges love that. In other words, it's pretty much—and that's the whole teaching of *General Electric v. Joiner*—if we say it's in, it's in unless we abuse our discretion. If we say it's out, it's out, unless we abuse our discretion. This I think is a real retreat from *Daubert*. It's what the judge thinks it is.

Well, the state doesn't go for that. They sort of divide it up. They say that on the question of general acceptance, the review at the appellate level is de novo (not abuse of discretion). When you try to work it out, that's a conservative test. You see, the trial judges in the superior courts and the various other courts are looking to cases to see whether the scientific theory at issue has been generally accepted. But who decides that? The high courts decide that. So that's going to slow down the receptivity to the "new" science. I suppose it will cut out "junk" science, but the beauty of science is significantly in the eye of the beholder. On the issues of whether you can test the scientific theory, how well you can test it, and is it in peer review journals, deference is given to the trial court and its findings on those issues.

Knowing the Legal Framework

Okay, now if that's the law, it's terribly important that you understand that law in the context of the legal framework. We'll take the big ticket item, something that perhaps you came to hear: Toxic torts. That's where you win the money if you do. You don't win the money, and I say this with all respect, in workers' compensation cases. You can make a good living on that, but there's not big money there or in Social Security Disability determinations and the like. So let's take as our paradigm toxic torts. What do you have to prove? The prima facie case. Well do this quickly.

In a negligence case you have to prove duty, negligence, causation and damages. If you want to make it a products liability case, you have to prove duty, defect (the strict liability), proximate causation and damages. How much do you have to prove? What is the burden of proof? Beyond a reasonable doubt? No, most of these are civil cases. That's reserved for criminal. Clear and convincing evidence? No, that's for libel. Fair preponderance of the evidence? Yes, that's what we're talking about. Fair preponderance of the evidence is mathematical, i.e., "more likely to be true than not true."

BURDENS OF PROOF

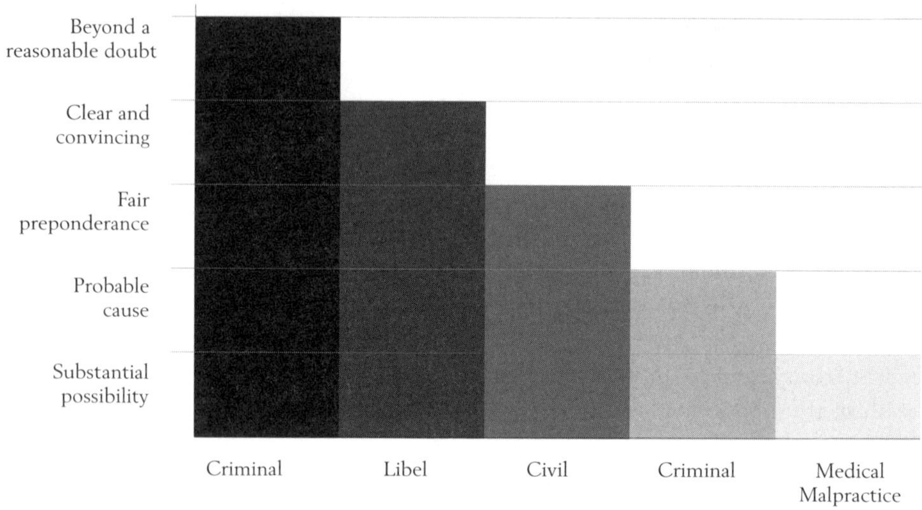

There are a couple of standards less than this. Probable cause—that too is reserved for criminal cases. We're not interested in that. New Jersey and Oklahoma have a standard for loss-of-chance cases in medical malpractice actions called substantial possibility. So don't just assume that the legal framework, the legal terrain, is always what we have. Cases may change it. But let's take the legal terrain we're used to, a civil case. The burden of proof in toxic tort cases is "proof by a fair preponderance of the evidence."

Now, where are we going to use these experts? If they are experts, on what aspect are we going to use them? Not on the duty, that's a legal thing. Yes, they'll help us on the aspect of damages; and, yes, they may be key on whether there's a defect. But really they are key on the issue of causation: i.e., that exposure A or incident A or insult A produces (or causes) result B. How strong do they have to be on that? They have to be more likely to be true than not true—that is, more than 50 percent. They're put on their oath as they are experts to make that connection more than 50 percent. The clinicians may say, "Hey, someone's sick here. She's really sick here. No one says that she is not sick. And we suspect it's this, we're testing for this; it may well be that." But if they cannot, in a standard civil case, say more likely than not that cause A gives you result B, then we shouldn't admit it. Forget ***Daubert;*** we just shouldn't admit it. That's the standard. Okay, now not all cases are like this. Let's focus on different types of cases and then we'll come to some specifics.

There are situations in the law—these are not the big money situations, but after all we represent all people—situations where the major concern of the law is not what caused the effect (i.e., the clear sickness of the person) but the fact that the person is sick. Social Security Disability is such a thing. We are more interested in how disabled the person is than in what specifically caused the disability. ***(Judge Young holds up and points to an MCLE book)***. And these books are great. You learn all sorts of things about people in these books. And then I go back and I proselytize my colleagues. I say, "Look at you, you're in an MCLE book and it said…" We don't get our cases around enough. But again I wander. Did you know that the Social Security Administration (SSA)—I'm on page 305 of the course materials—has stipulated that it recognizes multiple chemical sensitivity as a medically determinable impairment? The SSA did that before Magistrate Judge Neiman in *Creamer v. Callahan*. I'm not ever going to let them take that back. They stipulated, and there they are.

Interpreting the Americans with Disabilities Act (ADA), where we're more concerned with whether we are going to accommodate the disability than what the disability is, my colleague Judge Woodlock, in *Jones v. Metrowest Medical Center,* has decided that MCS is not a disability within the purview of the Americans with Disabilities Act. *Transcript of Hearing on Motion for Preliminary Injunction*, C.A. No. 96-10860-WD (May 10, 1996), pp. 34–36. Now I know that people will tell me what is going on in "other jurisdictions" and the like, and that "it's been accepted there." I'm telling you how judges really work. This is Massachusetts—we don't work for the Ninth Circuit! I've heard a First Circuit judge say, "Heh, heh, Ninth Circuit? Presumptively wrong!" ***(Laughter)***. Ah, but when Judge Woodlock does it here in the District of Massachusetts, he's my buddy. He's right down the hall, right? Or when the Social Security Administration stipulates something before Magistrate Judge Neiman out in the federal district court in Springfield—that's Massachusetts—we pay attention to that.

Also, lawyers say that there are no reported decisions in Massachusetts examining the admissibility of expert testimony on MCS, and they cite to an opinion by Justice Houston in the Massachusetts Superior Court. That case is *Rhilinger v. Contract Cleaning Collaborative,* Norfolk Superior Court, Civil Action No. 93-2223 *(Memorandum of Decision and Order on Defendant's Motion Under Daubert,* at p. 4) (January 6, 1998).

So basically we have the Social Security Administration stipulating to the validity of MCS, Judge Woodlock rejecting the validity of MCS under the ADA and no reported Massachusetts decisions from the Supreme Judicial Court on the admissibility of MCS. Now, if that's the state of the law, understand the legal requirements. Depending on the type of case, the burden of proof varies and does not necessarily have to be by a fair preponderance of the evidence. There are types of cases where it works out differently. Let me touch on three: an admiralty case, a case under the Federal Employer's Liability Act (FELA) and a workers' compensation case.

My friend David Kaplan is here. This story goes back to the days when we actually tried cases against each other. In an admiralty case, or an FELA case, once you have shown the unseaworthiness as the defect, the proof of causation is marginal—all you need is a scintilla of evidence. So David gets a case in which a guy gets bonked on the head and he tells me that the guy has Guillaume-Barré syndrome. That, I will tell you, is a crock! But if he's trying to prove a negative, all he has to prove is that it's just some cause. He doesn't have to get his expert on and have his expert leap up to the level of a fair preponderance. It's a different standard. You see, the law protected longshoremen in those days. And in those days, it protected them and FELA workers. That takes a lesser degree of causation. So if you have a case in which a lesser degree of causation is needed, you may find yourself more receptive to these theories.

Lastly, I will say a word about workers' compensation. We have Judge Lamothe here, a distinguished judge of the Industrial Accident Board. I simply just want to tell you about the standard in workers' compensation cases. Remember, workers' compensation is insurance, a public insurance. It doesn't have the same burden of proof seen in the private adjudicatory system before a jury. Candidly, in order to save money and make cases move along, what the workers' compensation system has done is establish a panel of impartial medical examiners. Again, the beauty of the science is in the eye of the beholder. What the impartial medical examiner says in a workers' compensation case is prima facie evidence. That means: Even though you can introduce evidence to the contrary, the effect of the neutral medical examiner's report doesn't disappear like a presumption. It remains. Although other evidence can be introduced, the presiding judge at the Industrial Accident Board has to say that he will only take additional evidence if he finds that such testimony is required due to the complexity of the medical issues involved or the inadequacy of the report submitted by the impartial medical examiner.

Now let's say you get an examiner who just doesn't believe in MCS—just doesn't believe in it. You've got a long road to hoe. Let's say you have a medical examiner who believes in MCS. Unless the judge wants to stand up against that medical examiner, the medical examiner's opinion is going to carry the day. My citations by the way are to General Laws Chapter 152, Section 11A—that's the one for the impartial medical examiner. And we have here today people who are very experienced in workers' compensation litigation. But don't think that acceptance before the Industrial Accident Board in that statutory framework means acceptance in the superior court in the common law framework. It doesn't. Where it would have an effect, and we'll hear what the judges and the practitioners have to say, is where the impartial medical examiner says, "MCS. Never heard of it," or "I don't believe in it," and the judge nevertheless, based upon other evidence, goes ahead and finds it and adopts it. That would be a case to conjure.

Thank you very much.